POLITICS, POWER AND AUTHORITY

John D. Molloy
Michigan State University

PREFACE

The new edition of this book focuses on problems of political power and authority in American society, as did its predecessors. Although many new issues confront the Obama Administration and the 111th Congress, others are as old as the Republic itself. Some scholars would even argue that they are rooted in human nature.

As we enter the second decade of the 21st Century, we face many problems, some national, others global in their scope.

The nation, however, has always been concerned about how leaders exercise political power and authority as they attempt to meet the challenges of their times. Our concern with abuse of power by the British monarchy and Parliament in the 18th Century led to the American Revolution.

Throughout U.S history, Federalists and anti-Federalists, Jeffersonians and Jacksonians, Whigs, Republicans and Democrats, have argued over the "proper" role of government in exercising its power and authority. Political leaders have not always been consistent in their positions on the issues. From the era of George Washington to the time of Barack Obama, history has taught that there is an enormous difference between holding abstract political positions and having the responsibility for making governmental decision. Obama is neither the first President, nor will he be the last, to be criticized for switching positions taken during a partisan campaign to deal with problems as Chief Executive.

Since the age of Franklin D. Roosevelt, scholars have focused on the inevitable conflict between President and Congress. In the post-World War II period, the U.S. entered the age of political television, where "image" has become vital in the quest for votes.

Media are now an important part of the power equation. Although Jefferson and other Presidents have praised the virtues of a free press and the First Amendment, other Chief Executives have waged "war" with modern print and electronic media. "Who elected you?" has become a common question raised by politicians whose conduct and policies have been placed under the media microscope.

Intended to be a watchdog, "barking" to alert the public about the conduct and policies of the nation's leaders, the media must also be held accountable for its use, or abuse, of power. This volume is an attempt to explore some of these historic and current dilemmas of power and authority.

Chapter 1 focuses on basic concepts, such as how political systems are organized. Attention is given to democracy, its values and its future. Basic definitions are explored. What is politics? What are some of the meanings of power and authority? What are the tests of a democracy, and what is the democratic prospect in the 21st Century?

The second chapter deals with the origins and development of the U.S. Constitution. Particular attention is given to the Framers' distribution of power and authority among the three branches of government. Students should note that in a democracy, the Constitution not only confers power, but also limits it. One of the major questions raised is: "Can a Constitution, written in the late 18th Century, serve the needs of the American people in the 21st Century?"

Chapter 3 analyzes the American Federal system, particularly the "power-authority" relationship between nation and states. We also consider the relationships of the states to one another and the history of the Federal union. The "pros" and "cons" of Federalism and alternative systems of political organization also are explored.

The fourth chapter deals with the American Presidency. We survey the roles played by the President and historic arguments about presidential power and authority. Selected problems are considered, such as presidential tenure, disability and succession. In the TV age, one also must consider presidential character and "style." The historic House impeachments and Senate trials of Andrew Johnson and Bill Clinton are discussed, as is the George W. Bush Administration's response to the terrorists' attacks on the U.S. on September 11, 2001.

Attention is devoted to the landmark election of 2008, featuring the most diverse field of presidential candidates in American history, and the election of the first African-American to the nation's highest office.

Chapter 5 focuses on the constitutional and political roles of Congress. Although Congress does not receive the amount of media coverage the President does, it is a coequal branch of government.

The chapter considers the bicameral system and its consequences, congressional leadership, relationships between President and the Congress, the Supreme Court and Congress. Although it may be the most criticized branch of government, we explore the question of what the Framers intended Congress to be, as well as what it has become.

This edition of the book covers the impact of the last two congressional elections of 2006 and 2008 and the political consequences of a switch in party control of the national legislature. Senate controversy over the use of the filibuster to block presidential appointments also is considered.

Chapter 6 considers the judicial branch of government. We survey the American legal system, the constitutional power and authority of courts, as well as structure and jurisdiction. Also considered is the role played by judges in exercising their power of judicial review. Attention is given to the classic question: "Should judges exercise self-restraint, or be judicial activists?" We analyze the politics of judicial selection, particularly the process of choosing Federal judges. A description of how the U.S. Supreme Court operates follows. The case of *Bush v. Gore* is considered because of its importance in determining the outcome of the presidential election of 2000.

The nomination by President George W. Bush and Senate confirmation of two new Supreme Court justices, Chief Justice John Roberts and Samuel Alito, is considered. So is the historic nomination by President Obama of Federal Appeals Court Judge Sonia Sotomayor to become the first Hispanic ever to sit on the nation's highest tribunal.

Chapter 7 deals with political parties and pressure groups. Although neither is mentioned in the Constitution, their existence makes the system very different from that devised by the Framers.

We look at the nature of parties and interest groups and their respective roles. We briefly examine the evolution of the American party system and its contemporary organization. We consider the two-party system, as well as its alternatives. Considerable attention is given to the change from the "old politics" (pre-television) to the "new politics." The latter is characterized by candidate merchandising, sound bites, negative political ads and "spin doctors." Consideration is given to the question, "What did the elections of 2000, 2004 and 2008 really decide?" Finally, we explore the media's enlarged role in the selection of the President.

Brief consideration is given to Barack Obama's sophisticated use of e-mail, You Tube and other aspects of "new media" in his historic presidential campaign.

The eighth and final chapter focuses on the nature of public opinion. We consider its characteristics and measurement. We also explore the role of politicians who must decide whether to try to lead, or simply follow, opinion. Considerable attention is given to the media and their history. Are the media "biased?" That and related questions also are explored.

ACKNOWLEDGEMENTS

I acknowledge the encouragement and help of several Michigan State University colleagues in producing this text. Among them are Thomas Summerhill, Associate Dean of the College of Social Science and Center for Integrative Studies Director. I also am indebted to former CIS Directors Phil Smith and Assefa Mehretu

My late publisher Paul Tavenner and his wife Clarice encouraged the original and later editions of the book, and Publisher Cindy McDonald assisted with the development of the 2010 edition.

Jean Robinson, formerly of CIS and now on the Psychology Department staff, was helpful with computer production and reading of several drafts of the manuscript.

Last, but certainly not least, I thank my wife Carol for her help and encouragement during the period of research and writing.

John Molloy
June, 2009

TABLE OF CONTENTS

I. INTRODUCTION: WHO SHOULD RULE?

A. TYPES OF POLITICAL SYSTEMS

All societies have five major social institutions. They are the family, religion, education, the economy and government. Governments come in a wide variety of forms, but all of them have formalized institutional structures, such as legislative, executive and judicial branches. These "organs" of government develop and translate public policies into law. They normally operate under a constitution, either written or unwritten.

The term **"government"** also is sometimes used to refer to those who control the decision-making machinery of the state. In the United Kingdom, for example, leaders of the majority (Labour) party in Parliament, led by Prime Minister Gordon Brown, are referred to collectively as "the Government."

Laws enacted by governments are binding on all of us, whether we think they are wise or unwise, moral or immoral. They may indeed be obsolete, the product of an earlier age and an earlier technology. How else can one explain county government in America? Political scientists have called it the "dark continent of American politics." Newspapers sometimes run stories about obscure laws that still are on the books but are not enforced. Times and conditions of life change, but law does not always keep up with the changes.

If duly-elected democratic governments enact laws, the people tend to regard them as **"legitimate"** because they are the product of "legitimate authority."

Before the age of the great democratic revolutions, it did not particularly matter what the people thought. Absolute rulers, such as monarchs, or small groups of people (oligarchies) were free to make law by decree. Modern 20th Century totalitarian systems, however, were more sophisticated and used controlled media to develop mass support for their regimes.

It matters little how government is organized when we define it. It is clearly the most powerful **instrument of social control** yet devised.

1. Three Views of Government

Basically there are three views of government: it is a positive good, it is a necessary evil and it is an unnecessary evil.

Most people probably would agree that government is essential in modern society. Whether one views it as a **positive good** or a necessary evil depends upon one's philosophical predisposition. Liberals are inclined to say, "Look at what government can do for you." Oliver Wendell Holmes, a noted Supreme Court justice, once remarked that he liked to pay taxes because "taxes are the price of civilization."

Conservatives are more likely to say, "Look at what government can do to you." It has enormous power, and it must constantly be watched. In short, many Conservatives view government as a **necessary evil**.

Government can conscript youth, send it to war in far-off lands and demand the ultimate sacrifice, one's life. It can impose burdensome taxes. It can and does redistribute income through the tax system. In short, government has profound power and influence over the lives of all people.

Have you ever considered how many times during the course of an ordinary day your life is touched by government or its agents?

When did you get up today? Consider that in most states alarm clocks are set to take advantage of "daylight savings time." A governmental decision that this is a good public policy influences when your day begins and ends.

On your way to work or school, you may drive your car. If you are a licensed driver, it is expected that you will not exceed posted speed limits, will stop for red lights and stop signs, stay in your traffic lane and generally observe the rules of the road. Failure to do so may bring you into contact with police and the courts.

During the day, you may lose your temper. But you had best not lose control of your emotions to the point of committing an anti-social act, assault. Not only police and courts may become involved. So could prison administrators.

If you are under the age of 21, you had better not get caught driving with alcohol in your bloodstream. Zero tolerance laws bring sad awakenings to many young motorists who should not have been behind the wheel.

Government, of course, does protect the law-abiding citizen from social predators. Police officers do more than stop motorists and issue tickets. They sometimes put their lives on the line in life and death situations.

When a sociology professor complained several years ago about police, one of his colleagues interrupted and said, "What would you do if you were threatened by a deranged individual with a gun? Call a sociologist?"

Governments provide many social services. A good society requires education, medical care, help for the aged, disabled, and the physically and mentally handicapped. We also need a good modern infrastructure, modern highways, bridges and public buildings.

Without government, we would live in a state of **anarchy**. Anarchists believe that government is an **unnecessary evil,** responsible for everything wrong in society. They look forward to the day when all governments will be abolished.

Although anarchism never has been a successful political ideology, its advocates have terrorized European royal families and political leaders in both the 19th and 20th centuries by use of violence, particularly political assassinations. While standing in line, shaking hands with well-wishers at the Pan-American Exposition in Buffalo, N.Y., President William McKinley was shot and killed by an anarchist. Leon F. Czolgosz said that he shot McKinley on September 6, 1901, because he wanted to "kill a ruler." Czolgosz was tried, convicted of murder and executed in New York's electric chair.[1]

We must admit that governments not only can establish justice and rule of law. They also can establish injustice and make aggressive war. They can violate human rights, as well as protect them. But most Americans are pragmatists. They want results from their government and they appear to agree that government is necessary.

But is government a positive good, or a necessary evil? This question evokes very different responses from Liberals and Conservatives. Prior to the Great Depression, many Americans assumed that their national government had little or no responsibility for employment, public relief, education, health or security for the aged. The Age of Franklin D. Roosevelt changed all that.

Roosevelt and his successor, President Harry S. Truman, responding to a changing public opinion and emerging new popular consensus, worked with Congress to bring about fundamental change in American life. Under FDR, there were programs to develop public works jobs for the unemployed, "relief" for those who could not find work and food stamp programs.

The United States, in 1935, became the last of the world's major industrial nations to create a Social Security system for the elderly, the disabled and others. The Truman Administration produced the Employment Act of 1946. Almost a generation later, during the presidency of Lyndon B. Johnson, the government adopted Medicare and Medicaid programs. Federal aid to education, virtually non-existent until the Eisenhower years, received a major boost in the 1960s. In short, a change in popular consensus brought about major liberal changes in public policies.

The classic question, "What should government do?" will bring different answers at different eras in a nation's history. What was considered good and wise in the realm of public policy in the era of Roosevelt, Truman, Eisenhower, Kennedy and Johnson (1933-1968) may not be considered as favorably by citizens of the 1980s, 1990s and those of the early 21st Century.

When Ronald Reagan was elected as the nation's Chief Executive in the 1980s, his view was that government was too big. It was the problem, rather than the solution, to the nation's social, economic and political woes. One of Reagan's favorite 1980 campaign slogans was, "Let's get government off the backs of the American people." This viewpoint marked a sharp and clear departure from the policy preferences of Jimmy Carter, his Democratic Party predecessor, as well as Republicans Richard Nixon and Gerald Ford.

Although the first President Bush (1989-93) did not deviate much from Reagan's program, his successor, Bill Clinton, did. Clinton, however, had to deal with a Republican Congress in his last six years in office. Much of the debate between Texas Gov. George W. Bush and Vice President Al Gore in 2000, President Bush and Senator John Kerry during the 2004 presidential campaign and between Senators Barack Obama and John McCain in 2008 focused on these questions.

2. Autocracy, Oligarchy and Democracy

Governments must make decisions. They can be made by one person, in which case we call the system an **autocracy**. Some students are familiar with the autocrats of the past, such as absolute monarchs. We think of Russian czars Ivan the Terrible and Catherine the Great or of British kings like Henry VIII. Modern dictators like Hitler, Mussolini, Franco, Peron and Stalin are other examples of autocrats. In brief, autocracy is a form of absolutism, involving unrestrained exercise of power by government. The autocrat has unlimited authority over others.

It is the opposite of **constitutionalism** or limited government. The American Constitution, for example, not only is a blueprint, establishing an organizational structure for government and stipulating its powers. It also sets limits to those powers, as we will detail in succeeding chapters.

The most common form of government in today's world is **oligarchy**, or rule by a small group which dominates a particular nation. These elites may consist of oil sheiks, clergy of the dominant religious faith, a military junta or some other faction. The main point is that a handful of individuals dominate and control public policy decisions.

Democracy is a form of government in which the majority rules. The term is taken from the Greek words "demos" (the people) and "kratos" (authority). Americans long have assumed that the only "legitimate" form of government is one in which ultimate political authority resides in the people. But we sometimes need to reflect on the past.

Prior to the great democratic revolutions in England (1688), the U.S. (1776) and in France (1789), few thought that **popular sovereignty** was either legitimate or possible. Indeed, even a tyrant should be obeyed, medieval theologians taught, because he ruled by **"Divine Right of Kings."** Any challenge to royal authority or any attempt to revolt against it was regarded as sinful, as well as treasonable. Absolutism was supported not only by theologians, but also by leading political theorists who believed that it was legitimate authority, received from God.

This theory was practiced throughout the Western world from the 15th through the 18th centuries. It was maintained by hereditary succession to the throne and intermarriage of ruling families. Eventually the divine right of kings was overcome by the new theory of a "Social Contract," which held that a ruler's power was granted by the sovereign people.[2]

B. DEMOCRATIC VALUES

Governments and political systems have been "invented" by human beings. Because they are human inventions, they are naturally imperfect. The ideals of democracy, described below, may be achieved only to limited degrees. Democracy recognizes that there can be no perfection in human nature. Its basic purpose is to provide popular control of government rather than to impose "infallible" political truths.

All forms of government and conceptions of the state are rooted in the dominant values of a society. These values may be widely accepted by free choice, or they may be imposed from above by an elite. Perhaps it is not the "soundness" of a society's views, so much as the fact that they believe certain things that determines their institutions.

What are the major values of democracy?

1. Relative Optimism About Human Nature

No democratic system, most political scientists agree, can function effectively if there is widespread pessimism about human nature. If people think that human beings are brute animals, dominated primarily by emotion rather than reason, it is a short step to the conclusion that they are incapable of self-rule.

To deny the human ability to reason leads one to conclude that some form of absolutism is better than democracy.

For democracy to succeed, there must be a consensus that human intelligence is sufficient to select competent leaders and to evaluate their actions to decide which set of public officials are deserving of continuation in office and which ones should be removed from power. Without such a conviction, democratic government is difficult, if not impossible. Optimists believe that individuals are rational animals, capable of self-government. This was the assumption of the Enlightenment philosophers, and American democracy is largely the result of the "Age of Reason."[3]

Democrats also are skeptical of those who claim to know all the answers. They believe devoutly in human rationality and consider today's truth no more than a probability. One can and should change one's mind if new facts are developed. In his *Philosophy and Politics,* Lord Bertrand Russell said that the genuine Liberal does not say "This is true." Rather he says " I am inclined to think that under present circumstances, this opinion is probably the best."[4]

Such British civility may be lacking in the contemporary world of "in your face" American politics, but at least in theory most Americans agree that free expression of ideas is the best way to approximate the truth. True democrats do not believe that they are infallible and have all the answers.

They recognize the value of free-wheeling political debate.

Since no one has absolute truth, both sides to an argument have something to contribute to the best possible answer. The only way to get the answer is to listen to all the available evidence.

John Stuart Mill, in his classic essay, *On Liberty*, wrote: "If all mankind, minus one, were of one opinion, and only one person were of the contrary opinion, mankind would be no more justified in silencing that one person, than he, if he had the power, would be justified in silencing mankind. Were an opinion a personal possession of no value except to the owner, if to be obstructed in the enjoyment of it were simply a private injury, it would make some difference whether the injury was inflicted only on a few persons or on many. But the peculiar evil of silencing the expression of an opinion is that it is robbing the human race, posterity, as well as the existing generation, those who dissent from the opinion, still more than those who hold it. If the opinion is right, they are deprived of the opportunity of exchanging error for truth; if wrong, they lose what is almost as great a benefit, the clearer perception and livelier impression of truth, produced by its collision with error..."[5]

2. State Means, Not End, in Itself

Democracy assumes that the state and its primary agent, the government, are means, rather than ends, in themselves. No democracy can exist where society and the state are considered to be identical, and the promotion of the state becomes the major objective of political life. The state, in democratic theory, must be viewed as merely an instrument by which individual citizens pursue their political interests.

Democratic theory assumes that the state never can be viewed as dominant and the people as subordinate. Democracy depends upon a belief that the state is a means of promoting the well-being of both the individual and the society. The state itself is not something whose glory the nation must constantly seek to promote.

From a religious (Judeo-Christian) viewpoint, the instrumentalist theory of the state holds that the highest values in a person's life relate to God. No earthly law can claim to supersede Divine Law.

The state must maintain law and order so that people can devote themselves to higher purposes.

From a secular (rationalist-humanist) viewpoint, it is vital for individuals to use their reasoning power to discover what is right and wrong. This is the ultimate test for political authority. The state cannot turn good into evil or right into wrong simply because it has the coercive ability to do so.

3. Individualism

Modern democracy rests to a large extent on the concept of individualism. The duty of the state, democrats argue, is to promote the individual's development and well-being.

The roots of this concept lie in the ancient stoic faith in the universal rationality of people, as well as the religious emphasis on the human moral personality. Individuals are considered divinely created. The Jewish concept of one God leads to the notion that all humans are children of God and brothers and sisters to each other. The Christian doctrine of the indestructibility of the human soul holds that whatever social differences may exist, all people possess a spiritual equality and uniqueness that no earthly power can override. All people are created by God in His own image and each soul is equally precious.

Contemporary advocates of democracy insist that individuals are both the source and the object of political power and authority. They believe that the state should not exist to glorify itself, but should stress the value of the individual. As American democracy has evolved, individualism has come to mean protection of the basic rights of personality. These include freedom of expression, of conscience and of association. Democratic theory holds that governments must enable individuals to develop their abilities in accord with their capabilities.

Democracy assumes that those in power must be responsible to the electorate. Perhaps above all, democracy assures intellectual freedom, the right to think for ourselves and then to unburden ourselves of our ideas.

4. Equality

The paramount importance of the individual is enhanced by the democratic value of equality. Nearly every American schoolchild is taught that "…all men are created equal, that they are endowed by their Creator with certain unalienable rights, that among these are life, liberty and the pursuit of happiness…"

But what do we mean by equality? Early democrats in America believed in equality before the law. An individual should not be judged on the basis of his or her social position, economic class, sex, race or religion. They also believed in political equality, equal access to political influence. Over time, however, the notion of equality has taken on new meanings which go far beyond legal and political affairs. Equality has come to embrace equal educational opportunity, equal access to job opportunity, equal housing opportunity and equal access to public accommodations.

Traditional American concepts of democracy did not include equality of condition or social outcome. Do we want equality of results? Thomas Jefferson recognized a "natural aristocracy" of talent and ambition. Individual merit and hard work are not equally distributed in the population.

The Founding Fathers did not approve of "leveling," and it clearly is not a part of American democratic ideology. Some contemporary Americans believe that all that is required is that everyone should have a fair chance at "the starting line." But should the race always go to the swiftest, the most talented, the most intelligent, the strongest? Or should American democracy guarantee a basic minimum standard of life for those who fail, through their own fault or through no fault of their own, in the "race?"

5. Freedom

Nearly all Americans cherish freedom. Some of them love liberty above all other democratic values. It was to "secure the Blessings of Liberty" that the Constitution was drafted and ratified. The basis of liberty is that individuals are free not only from government restraints, but also have liberty to pursue their individual goals.

The Constitution probably would not have been ratified had the Federalists not made a promise to correct its most obvious deficiency, the absence of a Bill of Rights. Those first 10 amendments, effective in 1791, have been the backbone of American democracy.

We speak often of the "First Freedoms." That is because those liberties contained in the First Amendment are so vital to the success of the U.S. "experiment in democracy."

Freedom to express oneself is basic to democracy. We need the free exchange of ideas in our pursuit to the best solutions to our problems. We need free media to speak or print the news. An informed citizenry is essential to the nation's well-being. We need the freedom to criticize the government and its politics. If the government controls the media, there can be no real democracy. Indeed, one of the characteristics of totalitarian regimes is a controlled communications system.

Opposition parties must be able to express their ideas about public officials and public policies. Voters must be able to "turn the rascals out" in free and frequent elections. Without free expression, elections cannot be truly democratic.

Many persons came to America to escape religious persecution in the Old World. The Constitution guarantees one the **liberty to practice his or her faith**, or to practice no religion at all. There is **no established church** in the U.S., as there was in nine of the 13 colonies and states before the First Amendment was adopted. Religious toleration was not found, and orthodoxy of belief in the established faith was required.

The First Amendment also gives us the right to peaceful free assembly. But, like all rights, it is not absolute and does not include a "right" to incite a riot or disrupt traffic during rush hours.

Liberty of association and peaceful protest is also a democratic value. We have the right to join with others of like mind to promote our ideas, to "petition the government for redress of grievances," if we feel aggrieved. Citizens must be free to join voluntary political associations. One may elect to join the Republican Party, the Democratic Party, the Libertarian Party, the Socialist Party or any other group that he or she pleases.

Americans constitute a nation of joiners. Many of them belong to several interest groups, some of which have contradictory values. We join churches, labor unions, business and professional associations, racial and ethnic groups. Farmers join agricultural interest groups. Even state and local public officials organize, seeking to influence Washington policymakers. Many large universities maintain full-time lobbyists there to ensure that they will get their share of Federal tax dollars.

Pressure groups sometimes are accused of being selfish, but they have a fundamental First Amendment right to try to convince citizens of the wisdom of their values.

6. The Right to Revolt

The fundamental belief in the right of revolution is at the core of any democratic value system. It is the ultimate threat against the forces of absolutism, should they become dominant. Revolution is not something to be treated lightly, however. Change can occur without violence as long as enough individuals want such change.

However, democratic ideology does maintain that acceptance of an absolutism that is imposed on the community is wrong. Resistance is viewed not only as a right, but also a duty. That was the view of many colonists during the American Revolution. It was the view of the French underground which resisted the Nazi occupation of their country during World War II.

This concept of the right to revolt has pervaded modern democracy from the English Revolution against royal absolutism in the 17th Century, through the American and French revolutions, as well as those of other democratic nations. Without this revolutionary value of democratic ideology, the three major democratic states might never have been established. Their examples have been responsible for the rise of almost all of their imitators.

From the totalitarian viewpoint, the state is the master and the individual the servant. One of the most horrid statements ever made—from the democratic point of view—was that of German philosopher George Hegel, an intellectual ancestor of Hitler's fascist regime. In his *Philosophy of Law,* written in 1821, Hegel argued that the individual finds liberty in obeying the state, and the fullest realization of liberty in dying for the state. Only when an individual dies for the state does he lose the last trace of any personal whimsicality and uniqueness and become completely a part of the state.[6]

For a sharply contrasting point of view, students should examine the writings of the great English philosopher John Locke. Locke saw the essence of humans in resisting the authoritarian state, rather than obeying it. The liberal principles of life, liberty and property are the opposite of the authoritarian values of duty, discipline and death for the state. Locke's justification of the Glorious Revolution in England (1688) later supplied the intellectual weaponry for Thomas Jefferson, who adapted it slightly in the form that we know as the Declaration of Independence.[7]

Jefferson lived a long life and wrote much, so much that he sometimes is quoted on both sides of an issue. One of his most famous remarks about the right to revolt was penned in a letter to Colonel William Smith in 1787: "The tree of liberty must be refreshed from time to time with the blood of patriots and tyrants."

In a perfect world, democratic values would not conflict. But on this imperfect planet, they do. Individualism can be carried too far and when it is, we have selfishness. The common good suffers as a result. Unbridled selfishness could lead to anarchy. Equality can sometimes come into conflict with freedom. When it does, what choices should be made?

How much leveling should occur in the name of equality? How much redistribution of market-determined incomes should be done by the tax laws? These are policy choices—and they are made through the political system and elections.

Much of the debate between Senators Barack Obama and John McCain during the 2008 presidential campaign focused on these questions. The debate intensified early in the first 100 Days of the Obama Administration.

Much of contemporary American politics is a struggle to strike a balance between liberty and equality.

The Progress of Democracy

Despite the growing cynicism of Americans early in the 21st Century, a careful study of American history may well lead one to conclude that our society today is more democratic than it ever has been.

If one studies the expansion of the suffrage, for example, one will note a constant move in the direction of more popular participation. The property-holding and taxpaying qualifications, common requirements for voting early in our history, disappeared with the advent of Jacksonian democracy. The Congress intended to enfranchise the Black male with the 15th Amendment. Women were given the right to vote in all states by the Susan B. Anthony (19th) Amendment.

During the Civil Rights Revolution of the 1960s, the 23rd Amendment extended the right to vote in presidential elections to the District of Columbia. In 1964, the 24th

Amendment banned the poll tax in Federal elections. Later, the Supreme Court banned it in all elections.

The Voting Rights Act of 1965 revolutionized southern politics by putting teeth in the 15th Amendment and making Black political participation a reality. Blacks began to elect their own sheriffs, mayors, state legislators, members of Congress and other public officials in areas where they were in the majority.

The 26th Amendment enfranchised young people between 18-21 in all states in time for the 1972 presidential election.

Democracy also has been made "more direct" by a number of reforms, associated with the Progressive Movement of the late 19th and early 20th centuries. Most notable have been the popular initiative, the referendum and the recall.

The Progressives proposed what were then considered some radical solutions to the problem of the declining prestige of governing bodies in the last half of the 19th Century.

The popular **initiative** rests on the assumption that the people are sovereign. If the legislature fails to enact needed legislation, then they can do it themselves. The procedure calls for a small, legally-defined percentage of the electorate to sign petitions which, after verification, will require officials to put the measure before the voters. Proposed changes can be suggested in constitutions, charters, laws or ordinances. Voters decide without recourse to the legislative body.

The **referendum** differs from the initiative in that it follows action by the legislature, whereas the initiative takes place independently of it. The referendum is a procedure in which the people may require a measure passed by the legislature to be submitted for their approval. A small percentage of voters may delay legislation from going into effect until they approve it. Or, in many instances, the intention is to kill the measure entirely by persuading the electorate to reject it.

Today it is common to hold referenda on a wide variety of issues. Only rarely do state elections occur without ballot proposals being submitted to the people.

Some political scientists argue that the initiative and referendum have not worked as well as its proponents had hoped. At the time of their adoption, there was a great demand for "more democracy," so that people could govern themselves more effectively. Opponents said that these two devices of direct democracy were unnecessary.

It was further argued that the initiative and referendum confused legislative responsibility and created a bad psychological effect on governing bodies. They also were criticized on grounds that they encouraged radicalism, fostered disrespect for property rights and were opposed to the principles of representative government.

Finally, it was argued that individual voters do not always make informed ballot decisions. We do not normally expect them to make policy choices directly, but to elect representatives to do this for them. The initiative and referendum demand more of the voter in regard to the ability to make decisions on public policy questions that often are complex and highly technical.

The **recall** is a measure in which voters may remove a public official before expiration of his or her term. Reformers argued that citizens should not have to endure a faithless or incompetent public official for the entire term. A small percentage of voters may force a ballot on the question, "Shall Sen. Jane Roe Continue in Office?" If the answer is no, she is recalled, and in most states may not be a candidate in the next election for her vacated job. A new election is held and the voters choose a replacement.

The main argument for the recall was that it ensured continuous responsibility. With a sword hanging over one's head at all times, the public official needs to be alert to the needs and wishes of constituents.

One should remember that the Framers of the Constitution were skeptical about "democracy," a word which, at the time, was equated with mob rule. They carefully described the new American Constitution as one creating a republic or representative democracy. Whether these devices of direct democracy have been successful is debatable.

Elections exist, many political scientists argue, to give us policy and candidate options. If a candidate is elected to public office, why not give him a chance to do the job? Particularly, if a term is short, why go through the expensive procedure of a recall election? A recall election is not really an attempt to prove charges against a public official. Rather, it is merely an attempt to get rid of an incumbent.

If there really is improper conduct on the part of a public official, a recall election may be unnecessary. Virtually every state provides that improper conduct is grounds for removal by executive, legislative or judicial action. Voters, however, sometimes want to vent their anger, particularly when it involves taxes. The recall sometimes may be a viable option.

During the administration of Gov. James Blanchard, the Michigan legislature increased the state income tax. For a time it was at a level of 6.1%, giving the state the dubious distinction of having the highest flat-rate state income tax in the nation. Angry voters in two Senate districts near metropolitan Detroit forced recall elections, and the two area Democratic senators who had supported the higher taxes were recalled.

They were Sen. David Serotkin of Mt. Clemens and Sen. Philip O. Mastin of Pontiac, first lawmakers in Michigan history to be removed from office.

Two Republicans replaced them, removing Democrats from control of the state Senate. Suddenly, John Engler was no longer the minority leader. He became the majority leader, and from this position launched his successful bid to replace Governor Blanchard in 1990. Senators in both parties got the message. They have been slow to increase taxes ever since. Some legislators remembered that the recall was originally described as "the gun behind the door."[8]

Others lamented the action of the two Michigan Senate districts. The recall, they argued, can serve as a tool of well-organized groups with partisan objectives. It can be used to nullify the results of the last election. If a few well-organized, well financed groups insist on intimidating public officials, who will want to run for public office?

C. WILL DEMOCRACY SUCCEED OR FAIL?

Years ago, a professor who taught comparative political systems liked to give his students a tough problem. Here, he said, is a nation state. This is its size and territorial extent. This is the kind of climate, natural resources, population and culture that it has. Your task is to draw up a constitution to fit. When one student responded that all one needed to do was to imitate the American system of democracy, he got an F for his answer. Why?

Democracy may not succeed, in fact it probably won't, if certain conditions are not present before it is introduced. What are these pre-requisites for democracy's success?[9]

1. Education

We start with the assumption that there are no guarantees in life or in politics. Although an educated and literate population generally are considered essential to democracy, their presence is no guarantee that democracy will work. Certainly, it's tough to expect a nation of illiterate peasants to succeed in their democratic experiment. Some nations, like India, struggle to make it work. Most of the world's nations are not democracies, although many of them use terms like "People's Republic" to try to convince us otherwise.

If one assumes, as most Americans do, that to have a democracy, you must at least have opposing political parties, free and frequent elections and basic civil liberties, few of the members of the "Third World" nations in the United Nations are democracies.

But a study of 20th Century history shows clearly that one of the most highly educated and literate people on earth (the Germans) voted Hitler into office and then watched as he destroyed the infant Weimar Republic. Hitler turned his nation into a totalitarian state, dedicated it to world conquest, liquidation of "inferior races" (Jews and Slavs), and the creation of a new order, The Third Reich, which would last, he boasted, for 1000 years.

By itself, therefore, education and literacy are no guarantees that democracy will work.

It is reasonable, however, to assume that democracy demands an electorate with at least moderately high standards of literacy and education. We face, in the 21st Century, complex problems in a complex society.

Voters today have abundant opportunities in the "information society" to use information made available to them by media. They have not only newspapers, magazines and books, but also radio, television and the internet. If they cannot read well, are computer illiterate, or watch only "trash television," they likely will have opinions. But those opinions likely will be held as prejudices, rather than be formed by information and the process of reason.

Americans and citizens of many other democracies today have the chance to learn a great deal about government and politics from the media. These tools of public opinion formation can help citizens to make intelligent political choices in a free society. American media are, perhaps, the freest in the world. Indeed, the question here is not freedom from government control, but rather how much criticism of government is appropriate.

It often is said of media in our democracy that they have a legitimate role to play as "watchdogs." But no one loves a watchdog that is always barking, particularly when there is no reason to do so.

Political scientists have conducted many studies on the relationship between economic and social conditions and democracy and have found that democracy thrives best when certain educational, economic and social conditions are present.

2. A Democratic Tradition

The German case is often cited, not to prove that literacy is no guarantee, but to prove that a nation without a history of democracy will have trouble in establishing one. It is beyond our purpose to dwell on the history of Germany. Suffice it to say that it had an authoritarian tradition. Germany was united relatively late in history after Chancellor Bismarck fought three wars to unite it under Prussian leadership. Not until Kaiser

Wilhelm was forced to abdicate at the end of World War I, did Germany ever have a democracy.

Unfortunately, it did not last very long. The Weimar Republic was blamed for the disastrous (from the German perspective) Treaty of Versailles, which was extremely punitive in its provisions on detachment of territory and reparations. The infant democracy also was blamed for disastrous hyper-inflation and the massive unemployment that resulted from the world-wide depression. Out of such chaos came Adolf Hitler, a fiery orator, World War I wounded veteran and street brawler. Hitler originally was Party Member #7 in the fledging Nazi Party. His rise to power has been documented in a number of excellent biographies.[10]

The absence of a democratic tradition is a particularly important point today when so many nations, including the former Soviet Union, are struggling to establish "democratic" systems. Russia also was noted for its long tradition of absolutism under the Czars. As a result of World War I, centuries of authoritarianism came to an end in the first of Russia's two revolutions in 1917. The Kerensky Republic was created as a result of the "March Revolution," but was overthrown by Lenin and his Bolshevik colleagues in November, 1917. Russian democracy is almost an oxymoron when one looks at the history of that nation.

Another major question faced by the world today is, "Can democracy succeed in the Middle East and in post-Saddam Hussein Iraq?"

3. Social Consensus

It is difficult for democracy to work unless there is an agreement that it is a desirable form of government. Clearly, it is a peaceful way of settling an argument, preferable to the violence and bloodshed which mark political change in many other societies. Americans generally agree that when a party in control loses an election, the new majority should take over control of the government. The defeated administration, while perhaps lamenting the voters' bad judgment, yields the reigns of power. It will have its chance in the next election.

Some historians say that the "finest moment" for American democracy came after the election of 1800, when the Federalists and President John Adams peacefully yielded the reigns of power to Thomas Jefferson and his followers, whom they hated and feared.[11]

Democrats, Republicans and most minor American parties agree on political fundamentals. The election can and should be hotly contested. There will be free expression of political ideas. It is basic to democracy that the party out of power will have the right to criticize the government and to offer alternative programs and policies to the electorate. The government will defend itself and criticize the ideas of the opposition. In a democracy, we assume that the best way to arrive at political truth is through competition in the free marketplace of ideas. Democracy is a peaceful method of settling a political argument. The answer to political problems, democrats agree, is resort to the ballot, not the bullet.

4. A Strong Middle Class

Comparative government scholars have long suggested that there is a clear-cut correlation between social class and democracy. Democracy seems most likely to work where there is a strong middle class and an equitable distribution of wealth. If one looks at nations where there is great poverty, one also may find great wealth. The problem is that the economic "pie" is not shared.

Under such conditions, where social class feelings are deep and where class consciousness is very real, democracy may not work. Class antagonism and hatred has led to movements like Communism and fascism. Hitler's ability to exploit economic misery in post-World War I Germany led to the extremist ideology of German National Socialism (Nazism).

Americans have never been very class conscious. Countless surveys of "class identification" have asked citizens to locate themselves on a scale as "upper class," "middle class," or "lower class." Historically more than 90% of Americans view themselves as middle class. This is, of course, statistical nonsense, but the most important thing is how people view themselves, not what is objectively true.

As a nation, the American people never experienced feudalism. "Equality of opportunity," so much a part of the American dream, has fueled a burning ambition in many people to succeed in the "New World." Here the accident of birth was not to determine one's entire life, as it commonly has in other lands with rigid systems of social stratification.

Hereditary occupations, although a minor factor in American economic life, are not deeply ingrained in our culture. Certainly, they are not required by it. The hope of many immigrants to the U.S. was that their children would have a better life and greater opportunities than they did. In many nations of the world, that is an impossible dream.

One American President who thought that democracy was the only "legitimate" form of government was Woodrow Wilson. Known as the "scholar-president" because he held a Ph.D. in political science from Johns Hopkins, Wilson greatly admired the British parliamentary system. He detested autocracy, which he was personally convinced was the cause of war.

Wilson led the U.S. through World War I. He was convinced that only the end of autocracy would ensure world peace. He was hopeful when the Russian Czar was overthrown, the dual monarchy collapsed in Austria-Hungary and Kaiser Wilhelm was forced to abdicate in Germany. He looked forward to a peaceful world with the birth of his dream: a League of Nations.

Unfortunately, Wilson's dream was never realized. The Senate rejected the Treaty of Versailles and the League of Nations. Even worse, revolution and bloodshed marred the democratic dream in Russia and in Mexico, where new regimes won power by bayonet and bullet, not by the ballot. Wilson flatly refused to grant them diplomatic recognition.

President Wilson and his Republican successors of the 1920s, Harding, Coolidge and Hoover, all refused to recognize the Soviet Union. Not until 1933 did Stalin's regime win recognition from President Franklin D. Roosevelt.

Wilson departed from traditional international law in insisting that a regime must be "democratic" to be recognized. Usually, only three things are required for recognition: people, territory and a government which controls them. Some criticized the Wilsonian view as unnecessarily idealistic. Others thought it entirely appropriate for the U.S. to indicate its extreme displeasure with autocracy, revolution and bloodshed as substitutes for democracy.

D. WHAT IS POLITICS?

Every social group decides "who gets what" through an activity we call "politics." Who pays the cost of these benefits and who receives them are always major questions of public policy. Politics always is associated with power, and power struggles are natural in political systems.

Ordinarily, politics is carried on through the instruments of government that provide for the authoritative or legitimate exercise of power. In the U.S., this means essentially that political parties, pressure groups and the media constantly struggle to gain their ends with executive, legislative and judicial branches of government. We will explore this theme more fully in the chapters dealing with these particular institutions.

Politics refers to the techniques by which individuals or groups seek to win or maintain political power. It also can be used to refer to the means by which decisions are made and executed within a society. Through political activity, pressure groups contest for benefits. "Politics" decides not only "who gets what" but also "who pays" for those benefits. Politics is closely associated with political influence and the interest group struggle for power that is inherent in any political system.

Political scientists have defined politics in a variety of ways. The late Professor Harold Lasswell said that "the study of politics is the study of influence and the influential. The influential are those who get the most of what there is to get."[12]

Politics also has been called "the art of the possible" and "the competition among individuals over the allocation of values or rewards."

Politics is not confined to government, although we may be inclined to think of President, Congress or some interest group first when we hear the word politics or politician. In a broad sense, politics goes on in the family, in the church, our schools, particularly colleges and universities, and a wide variety of other non-governmental institutions.

Politics, most social scientists would agree, is an inevitable human activity, if disorder and anarchy are to be avoided. Above all, it is a way of settling an argument. In the democratic system, we settle arguments by means of campaigns and elections. The rule is that the majority wins. This may not be an infallible system, or it may not even be a good system. But it is, as Churchill observed "better than all the alternatives."[13]

E. THE MEANING OF POWER

Power is one of those often-used words whose meaning people seldom stop to consider. It has a large variety of meanings, however, depending upon the context in which it is used.

Religious people attend church or synagogue on Saturday or Sunday, for example, and hear their rabbi, minister or priest talk about the power of God Almighty, the omnipotent being. Wow! That's ultimate power. The Scriptures are filled with stories of miracles and many other illustrations of Divine Power.

On a much less elevated level, baseball fans discuss the power-hitters on their favorite team. One baseball broadcaster in a major league city once was embarrassed when he asked the manager of the local team, "What's the difference between singles hitters and power hitters?" The manager replied: "Well, singles hitters ride in Fords and home run hitters ride in Cadillacs." The broadcaster was embarrassed because his pre-game program was sponsored by Ford.

We also hear a great deal about the power of the media, the power of the President, the enormous power of Federal judges, the power of Congress, the power of corporations and unions. We hear also of the power of giant universities and their influence on young minds because they can disseminate ideas, which have great power. It often is said that "there is nothing more powerful than an idea whose time has come."

As a people, Americans appear to be somewhat ambivalent about power. We admire strength, one aspect of power, particularly when it is used properly. We are very skeptical about the power of such institutions as President, Congress, the Supreme Court and the media. Perhaps we are most skeptical about the misuse or abuse of political and economic power. Money can mean power. Wisely used, it can do great good. But nearly all students recall that old phrase, "the love of money is the root of all evil." Money itself is not evil, but those whose values are entirely economic may not be the most pleasant people we know.

In the world of international politics, we speak of the bipolarization of power in the post-World War II era, where only the U.S. and the Soviet Union emerged from the ravages of the global conflict as major world powers. They clearly had the greatest military power and the largest arsenal of nuclear weapons. We hear today that the U.S. is the only remaining superpower in the world. Professors in International Relations and Foreign Policy courses often give lectures early in the semester on "The Elements of National Power."

Germany's Max Weber, one of the most famous social scientists in history, once said that "power is the possibility of imposing one's will upon the behavior of other persons." That idea, of course, is a common understanding of power. The greater the ability of individuals, institutions and nations to impose their will on others, the greater their power. Weber suggested that power is intimately related to legitimacy and authority. To be legitimate, power must be exercised "properly," by authority that people perceive to be rightful and just. Weber suggested three general sources of legitimacy. These are tradition, charisma and legality.[14]

Under **tradition,** legitimate exercise of power is based on established beliefs in the sanctity of authority and the moral need to obey leaders. Historically, kings ruled because "it always has been this way." The age of the democratic revolutions changed that, but today we have democratic rule because of the democratic tradition which holds that the people legitimately should rule.

Charisma refers to the personal qualities of a particular leader. Few leaders have had charismatic personalities. Those who did either achieved great things or brought great suffering to humanity. In 20th Century America, three Presidents, Franklin D. Roosevelt, John F. Kennedy and Ronald Reagan had charisma. The most outstanding negative charismatic personality, one who produced great horrors, was Adolf Hitler.

Legality is based on a commitment to rules that binds leaders and their people. Weber called this rational-legal authority. Rulers exercise power and authority because of the office they hold, not because of tradition or personal charisma.

The late John Kenneth Galbraith, a noted professor of economics at Harvard, suggests that an interesting question is how the will of individual, institution or nation is imposed and how the acquiescence of others is achieved. The key to understanding power, Galbraith suggests, lies in the concepts of physical punishment, the promise of economic reward or the ability to persuade one to do "the right thing."

Galbraith classifies power as falling into three categories: condign, compensatory and conditioned.

"Condign power is the ability to impose an alternative to the preferences of the individual or group that is sufficiently unpleasant or painful, so that these preferences are abandoned. There is an overtone of punishment in the term…condign power wins submission by inflicting or threatening appropriately adverse consequences." [15]

Compensatory power, Galbraith says: "…wins submission by the offer of affirmative reward—by the giving of something of value to the individual so submitting…praise is a form of compensatory power…in the modern economy, the most important expression of compensatory power is, of course, pecuniary reward—the payment of money for services rendered." [16]

In the cases of both condign and compensatory power, the individual or group is aware of the submission to the will of another, in one case because of compulsion and in the other case because of reward. It is a case of the proverbial "carrot or the stick."

Conditioned power is exercised, Galbraith contends, by changing an individual or group's belief(s). He writes: "…persuasion, education, or the social commitment to what seems natural, proper, or right causes the individual to submit to the will of another or of others. The submission reflects the preferred course: the fact of submission is not recognized. Conditioned power, more than condign or compensatory power, is central…to the functioning of the modern economy and polity, and in capitalist and socialist countries alike." [17]

Social scientist Thomas R. Dye, in his book *Power & Society*, defines power as "the capacity to affect the conduct of others through the real or threatened use of rewards and punishments." Dye appears to agree with Professor Galbraith's essential notions, but does devote more attention to the problem of power as it is exercised in large institutions. [18]

Not only governments and churches exercise power. So do corporations, colleges and universities, the military, print and broadcast media, and major law firms, among others. Dye, like most other social scientists who consider the issue of power, addresses the issue of elite and pluralist theories of power.

The **elite,** Dye says, are the few who have power. It is to be contrasted to the masses who do not. The masses' lives are shaped by their leaders and their institutions. Dye follows in the footsteps of C. Wright Mills, a left of center sociologist, who published a book, *The Power Elite,* which has had a profound impact on several generations of sociologists. Tying together the relationship between power and institutions, Mills wrote: "If we took the 100 most powerful men in America, the 100 wealthiest, and the 100 most celebrated away from the institutional positions they now occupy, away from their resources of men and women and money, away from the media of mass communication that are now focused upon them—then they would be powerless and poor and uncelebrated. For power is not of a man. Wealth does not center in the person of the wealthy….To have power requires access to major institutions, for the institutional positions men occupy determine in large part their chances to have and to hold these valued experiences." [19]

Mills is considered by some to be the father of "elite" theory. In politics, this view holds that a small minority of wealthy, well-connected leaders makes the most important political and economic decisions. According to those who subscribe to elite theory, the U.S. is not a democracy. It is an oligarchy. Although it may appear that voters control the government through a system of elections, those who have power define the issues and limit the possible outcomes of policy debates to protect their own interests. This is not the view of democracy presented in most high school textbooks!

Elitists insist that it does not matter whether Democrats or Republicans win the presidential election. Clinton, they note, did not have any trouble getting along with Republican holdover Alan Greenspan, who chaired the Federal Reserve Board of Governors. The "Fed" controls the nation's supply of money and interest rates. Indeed, some media described Greenspan as the most powerful unelected official in the nation. Many of Clinton's key advisers, according to elite theorists, were simply "cut from Republican cloth."

Although political scientists have conducted several studies designed to test elite theory, they have developed no consensus to support it. The theory is loved by radical critics of the American system.

Other political scientists, who call themselves **"pluralists,"** have a rather different view of American democracy. They basically approve of the "system," and stress the fact that it gives virtually all groups access to it. Groups can press their views in the media. They can seek to testify before committees of legislatures. They can organize to support or oppose candidates who are either friends or foes. Pluralists conclude that as long as groups have the chance to participate in the decision-making process, it is democratic.

Another key question is, "Why do individuals, groups and nations seek power?" Although we may think that we know the answer to that question in some cases, we probably do not speak or write about it very much.

Individuals and groups, as well as nations, seek to advance their own political, economic, social, religious, and other values. Corporate America wants workers to submit to its economic purposes in order to make money. Religious leaders attempt to persuade their congregations to follow their views in order to be saved (ultimate case of compensatory power) by reaching eternal joy in Heaven. Or, should the unrepentant sinner not follow the path of righteousness, he or she may suffer the eternal pains of Hell (ultimate case of condign power).

Most Americans understand that our political system is one in which competing political, economic, social, religious and other values compete in a highly diverse society in the free marketplace of ideas. These values and ideals, embraced in particular by public policy stands by thousands of interest groups, occupy a great deal of media time and attention.

More important, in the case of the American political and economic systems, their competition for favors from government and society results in heated debate. Are interest groups inherently selfish? Or do they pursue policies that clearly serve the public interest? We shall examine this question in much greater detail in Chapter 7.

F. AUTHORITY AND LEGITIMACY

The word **"authority"** has a variety of meanings. It may mean a citation to be used in defense of one's argument, such as a book. Some religious persons constantly quote the Bible as the ultimate authority, the inspired Word of God.

Authority may also refer to an individual who has a reputation as an expert. It also means the power to influence or command thought or behavior. Still another widely-understood meaning is a "person in command." Government officials and agencies are thought of as authorities. Clearly, authority is intimately related to the concepts of power and influence.

Political authority is usually considered **legitimate** power, the right to impose rules that people have an obligation to obey. A government can no more function without authority than it can maintain order without effective means of coercion. In general, the more people believe in the legitimacy of their government, the less they will need to be forced to obey it. Conversely, the lower the level of legitimacy, the greater likelihood that government must use coercive means to obtain obedience.

But is it realistic to suppose that people will obey laws simply because government can appeal to their reason and sense of self-interest? Long ago, British philosopher Edmund Burke rejected that notion, commenting: "On the scheme of this barbarous philosophy…laws are to be supported only by their own terrors and by the concern which each individual may find in them from his own private speculations or can spare to them from his own private interests. In the groves of their academy, at the end of every vista, you see nothing but the gallows. Nothing is left which engages the affections on the part of the commonwealth."[20]

Authoritarianism, a related term, has negative connotations to most Americans. It refers to a political system characterized by concentration of power and favoring a blind submission to an authoritarian leader.

Some of the classic questions of political theory revolve around the question of the legitimacy of authority. Nations must decide "who should rule?" By what right does one rule? The answers to these questions have varied throughout history. One person should rule because he or she is "chosen" as an instrument of God to do so (Divine Right of Kings theory). The people should rule because they are the legitimate source and object of power and authority (Theory of Popular Sovereignty).

The French monarchy, which Burke defended, was one of the last significant Western examples of an ancient type of political authority, divine right absolutism. Rulers typically claimed that they were descended from divine ancestors whose authority on Earth is embodied in the living ruler. In ancient Egypt, religious leaders taught that the Pharaoh (king) was the divine protector of cosmic and earthly order.

Divine right monarchy never took extreme form in medieval Europe, mainly because of the competing authority of the church. The beginning of the end of this type of legitimacy was symbolized in the trial and execution of two reigning kings, Charles I of England in 1649 and Louis XVI of France in 1793.

G. TESTS OF A DEMOCRACY

"Beauty," an old saying has it, "is in the eye of the beholder." But concepts of beauty are strongly related to a nation's culture. Americans are obsessed with beauty: witness the billions spent each year by consumers trying to improve on what Mother Nature has given them. American culture prefers the young, the thin, the fair of complexion, the active and energetic, those with a toothy smile. Other cultures venerate wisdom of the elderly, admire heavy-set people and the contemplative lifestyle.

So it is with political systems. As the world nears the second decade of the 21st Century, nearly all nations call themselves democracies or republics. But what are the standards of measurement? If one looks at the 192 members of the United Nations, he would be hard-pressed to count more than two dozen democracies by Western standards. But what are these standards, and are they "fair?"[21]

1. **Most adults can participate in elections**. Democracy is based on the idea of free and relatively frequent elections. Citizens exercise their right to evaluate the performance of their public officials. They then "stamp the report card" pass or fail. Without free elections, officials cannot be held accountable.

2. **Citizens enjoy the right to the secret ballot and are not coerced at the polls**. One does not wish to vote with government or party officials looking over one's shoulder. The secret ballot and the absence of coercion at the polls have marked significant signposts of progress on the road to democracy.

3. **Leaders are chosen in free elections, contested by at least two viable political parties**. It is vital to democracy that a minimum of two political parties exists. They must have a genuine chance of victory at the polls, giving the electorate a choice between candidates, parties and public polices. Without political competition, there can be no democracy.

4. **The government bases its legitimacy on representing the will of the people**. In politics, there are winners and losers. If a government serves the people and adopts those policies and programs which serves their needs, it will be returned to office. If it fails to meets those needs, it can be replaced. Although one need not be an "errand boy or girl" as a public official, it is important for public officials to remember who put them in office and who can remove them.

H. THE DEMOCRATIC PROSPECT

In Latin America, Eastern Europe, Russia and elsewhere, democracy appears to be on the rise. Given national histories and cultural differences, democracies can and will vary, but the essentials seem to be in place in many of these new democracies. Opposition political parties have arisen in place of single-party states. Free elections, at least by previous standards, are developing. Freedom of expression and religion are on the rise. Even Fidel Castro, then one of the last hard-line Communist rulers in the world, invited the late Pope John Paul II to visit his nation in 1998.

II. POWER AND THE CONSTITUTIONAL ORDER

A. WHAT IS A CONSTITUTION?

Before the 18th Century, the word "constitution" usually meant the general system of laws, customs and institutions relating to a nation. But the American and French Revolutions brought a new concept of constitution into being. The system no longer was the product of the long evolutionary process or a nation's history. It was, rather, a formal written instrument of government, a **"social contract"** drafted by a representative assembly and ratified by a special procedure for determining public consent.

A constitution was the act of a people constituting a government. The document created a Basic Law and was the source of governmental power and authority. Government, in brief, was the creature of the constitution.

To those who subscribed to the old, "developmental" view of constitutions, the American and French constitutions were disturbing departures. In 1792, Englishman Arthur Young spoke with contempt of the new view. He said that constitution is "a new term they have adopted and which they use as if a constitution was a pudding to be made by a recipe." To Young, and many other Englishmen, constitutions could not be made; they had to grow.[1]

Although the U.S. Constitution was created in the summer of 1787, it incorporated considerable political experience from the past and has been growing and developing ever since. Democratic political and constitutional systems do not remain static. England's unwritten constitution and America's written constitution have common purposes, although they differ in detail.

Both provide a governmental structure. Both authorize the powers that the government is to have and allocate them among various branches of government. Both impose limits on government. Indeed, the very essence of constitutionalism is the maintenance of a balance between liberty and authority, between individual rights and governmental power. Finally, both systems provide a means for peaceful and orderly change.

Although few Americans stop to contemplate it in the 21st Century, theirs is the oldest written Constitution in the world. The British Constitution is older, but it is unwritten. Many other democracies have gone through a series of constitutional crises and have discarded their basic framework of government time and time again. France, for example, now has its Fifth Republic, created in 1959 by General Charles de Gaulle, one of the dominant figures in modern French history. A joke popular in academic circles during the chronic instability of post-World War II France had a young man walking into a Paris bookstore and asking for a copy of the French Constitution.

"We are sorry," the proprietor replied, "but we do not deal in periodical literature."

Why has the U.S. Constitution endured longer than any other document of democracy? Several theories have been advanced, but clearly of paramount importance is the fact that our Founding Fathers deliberately made our basic law difficult to amend. By requiring that two-thirds of both House and Senate agree to propose an amendment and by requiring that an extraordinary majority of three-fourths of the states consent to ratification of amendments, they ensured that basic constitutional change would not be undertaken lightly. Change was possible, of course, and we now have 27 amendments. But the Basic Law does not permit change merely because momentary political passion carries away a simple majority of the people.

The Framers also wrote the document in such a way as to allow for modern judicial interpretation of some of its vague clauses. It often is said that a Constitution that will not bend is sure to break. Flexibility has been a hallmark of the U.S. Constitution as the courts, particularly the U.S. Supreme Court, have interpreted it in light of modern-day conditions.

Although the power of judicial review is nowhere given explicitly to judges by the Constitution, it has been with us at least since 1803, when Chief Justice John Marshall asserted it in the classic case of *Marbury v. Madison*. For the first time in our national history, an act of Congress—the Judiciary Act of 1789—was declared to be unconstitutional.

Since that time, U.S. courts have used this major instrument of checks and balances to protect individual rights against both executive and legislative usurpation. Many strong Presidents, from Jefferson and Jackson to Franklin D. Roosevelt and Richard M. Nixon, have had "problems" with the courts. In the end, the Constitution always has endured.

Constitutions are, however, what the courts say that they are. Only when a vast and excited public opinion disagrees, can such judicial findings be set aside by process of amendment.

The income tax amendment (16th) was set aside in this manner. Citizens' attempts to overturn the Warren Court school prayer decisions and the Burger Court's abortion ruling, show that excited majorities or minorities can attempt to change the Constitution through democratic procedures. But to be successful, they must convince an exceptional number of their fellow citizens that their case has merit.

Americans have great respect for their Constitution. When Franklin D. Roosevelt, one of the most popular Presidents in U.S. history, attempted to enlarge the membership of the U.S. Supreme Court in 1937 in a transparent attempt to overturn some of its findings, even his own party rebelled.

Although many Liberals of the New Deal era assailed the Hughes Court as the "Nine Old Men," most of the nation preferred the risk of judicial conservatism (then out of style) to tampering with an institution as basic as the U.S. Supreme Court.[2]

Someone always is angry with the Supreme Court, simply because in each case there is always a loser as well as a winner. If the line of decisions is consistently Liberal or Conservative and the pendulum of popular opinion is swinging in the other direction, furious public debate will result.

In the 1930s, it was the Liberals who attacked the court for its "judicial activism." Max Lerner, a syndicated Liberal columnist, referred to the court's use of judicial review to invalidate some New Deal programs as the "Divine Right of Judges." More recently, it has been the Conservatives who have been angered by the court. Decisions in such controversial areas as race relations, reapportionment, criminal procedure, school prayer and abortion have caused demands for fundamental constitutional change in the form of several amendments and for presidential nomination and Senate confirmation of judicial Conservatives—those who rule on the legal, rather than social, aspects of current social dilemmas.[3]

"Judicial activism or judicial self-restraint" always has been a debate topic in constitutional law and American government classes. Much depends on the nature of the activism. If Supreme Court rulings are attuned to public opinion, then little friction may follow. If, on the other hand, the Court is too far ahead of public opinion—as the Warren Court was in the civil rights area—fierce debate will result.

It must be strongly emphasized that under the supremacy clause (Article VI), the Constitution is the Supreme Law of the land and nothing can conflict with it. No presidential act, no congressional statute, no state or local act. Although the U.S. Supreme Court rules only in real cases or controversies and gives no advisory opinions, people often have been willing to disobey laws they regard as unjust or unconstitutional, and in most cases, they have been willing to live with the results.

Warren Court critics were so outraged by its decisions that they proposed not only the impeachment of the Chief Justice, but also a new Constitutional Convention to rewrite some of the Basic Law itself. Such a procedure is provided by Article V of the Constitution, but never has been used. Should two-thirds of the states petition Congress to call such a convention, it could do so, although it is not clear whether it would be compelled to do so if it was unwilling. Although some 32 states did petition Congress to hold a convention to force Congress to balance the budget each year, that movement has now died down. "Feeling the heat," Congress headed the move off by moving in the direction of a balanced budget on is own.

B. DO WE NEED A NEW CONSTITUTION FOR THE 21st CENTURY?

As the U.S. marked its bicentennial of independence in 1976, academic Liberals pushed the notion that a new Constitution was necessary. One of the prime movers of that movement was Rexford Tugwell, a former New Deal "braintruster" under President Franklin D. Roosevelt. Tugwell and some of his colleagues at the Center for the Study of Democratic Institutions in Santa Barbara, CA, proposed nothing less than an entirely new Constitution for the American people.[4]

Tugwell believed that the basic plan of American government should be discarded as the nation entered its third century of independence. He saw problems everywhere. Power was fragmented between the President, two houses of Congress and the courts. What was needed, he contended, was bold and innovative action to meet the needs of the next century. The structure, he argued, was too archaic to enable the U.S. to respond quickly and effectively to major problems of military and foreign policy. Too many domestic problems also went unresolved, he argued, because of structural deficiencies.

But Americans were unwilling to discard the venerable Constitution of 1787 in favor of the plan developed by Tugwell and Robert Hutchins, former "boy-wonder" President of the University of Chicago, who headed the Center.[5]

In retrospect, it is remarkable, given Tugwell's practical political experience as an adviser to FDR, that he would support such an impractical plan of government. The proposal led many to conclude that it was the product of Ivory Tower thinking of the professoriate, rather than men and women of a practical bent of mind.

Among the proposals for a new and "better" U.S. Constitution was one limiting the President to a single term of nine years. Very few political scientists supported such a proposal. Nor were many of them enthusiastic about the suggestion that we have two vice presidents, one for general affairs and one for internal affairs. The "general affairs" Vice President would succeed in the event of the death, resignation or removal of the Chief Executive.

Perhaps most intriguing—and perhaps most impractical—was the Tugwell Plan to change the Congress. Although Congress often has been the butt of jokes and although at times it may be downright laughable, few citizens or political scientists agreed with the notion that Congress should be radically transformed.

It has not been uncommon to hear demands that Congress should scrap its seniority system, sometimes called a "senility system" by its critics. Many Americans believe that congressional procedures ought to be streamlined, that congressional parties ought to be more disciplined and responsible, that legislative procedures ought to be speeded up. Senate Rule 22, the filibuster—although modified in the 1960s—still frequently comes under attack by those who believe that 51% of the people should rule.

But Tugwell would greatly enlarge the power of the House of Representatives, giving it a legislative role similar to that of the British House of Commons. He would lengthen present terms of representatives from two to three years. At the same time, he would significantly reduce the power of the Senate as an equal partner in the legislative process, making it essentially a decorative rather than a legislative body.

A bitter partisan battle between President Bush, his Republican allies and Senate Democrats—accused of "obstructionism" in blocking appointments to Federal courts—marked the 109th Congress in early 2005.

Senators, Tugwell and his colleagues argued, ought to be appointed for life. In short, he was urging a conversion of the U.S. Congress into a British Parliament, with the Senate playing a role somewhat like that of the House of Lords. Given the popular demand for more responsive and responsible government, proposals for nine-year presidential terms, lifetime Senate tenure and a powerful unicameral legislation by the House brought little public sympathy.

One of the most astounding of all of Tugwell's proposals was to reorganize the 50 states into 20 new states of equal size. Given existing rivalries and necessity of three-fourths of the states agreeing to such a change, Professor Tugwell was accused by some political writers of engaging in academic dreaming when he made this proposal.

Nor does it seem at all likely that a Senate would agree to call a new constitutional convention, which would reduce its power, prestige and influence. Certainly, two-thirds of the senators would never agree to lay such a proposal before the states for their ratification consideration.

Given the lingering Anglophobia in the U.S., the whole package smacks rather too much of a transplant of British political institutions to American soil. What works in the United Kingdom would not necessarily work here, given enormous differences in national history, institutions and circumstances.

A small island nation with a comparatively homogeneous population has few of the problems that faced a continental nation with a "melting pot" and enormous racial, religious, national, regional and cultural differences.

Tugwell's proposals are interesting as a matter of history, but there never was (or is) any real possibility that they would be adopted. The late Sen. Sam Ervin (D., N.C.), chair of the Senate Judiciary Committee, said of Tugwell's proposals at the time:

"I think those people fundamentally need to have their heads examined by a psychiatrist. We don't need a new Constitution. Ours has weathered many storms in the past 200 years. It was written to last for the ages."

"I am left with an abiding conviction that there's a great backlog of devotion to our fundamental principles of government and devotion to morality in this country," Ervin said.[6]

The Framers of the U.S. Constitution created a system of federalism largely because no other alternative was available. The first government tried in the "New World," after the American Revolution, had been found wanting. So confederation was out. Unitary government, which the British had used to oppress the colonists, was not a practical alternative, either. So Federalism was the answer.

What is a Federal system and how does it vary from unitary and confederal systems?

C. IDEOLOGIES AND CONSTITUTIONAL SYSTEMS

As the delegates to the Constitutional Convention left the hall in Philadelphia after signing the historic document, a woman approached Dr. Benjamin Franklin with her anxious question: "Well, Doctor, what have we got, a republic or a monarchy?"

Franklin replied, "A republic, if you can keep it."[7]

A Constitution is also a statement of national purpose. The original purposes of American government are stated in the preamble to the Constitution which reads: "We the People of the United States, in Order to form a more perfect Union, establish Justice, insure domestic Tranquillity, provide for the common Defence, promote the general Welfare, and secure the Blessings of Liberty to ourselves and our Posterity, do ordain and establish this Constitution of the United States of America."

D. WHAT DO AMERICANS VALUE?

Periodically, the American nation engages in an examination of its values and ideology. What does it stand for? What are the nation's goals and objectives? What assumptions have Americans made about human nature, the process of social, cultural and economic change? What role should "mass opinion," as distinct from elite opinion, play in changing American society?

During the waning days of the Eisenhower Administration, a presidential commission on national goals and values made its report. Its findings touched off a national discussion, which carried over to the 1960 presidential campaign debates between Vice President Nixon and Senator John F. Kennedy. Kennedy said that he could not think of any national purpose which would be better than that devised by the Framers of the Constitution and expressed in the preamble. Nixon agreed.[8]

Questions about fundamental national purposes continue, however, to divide Liberals and Conservatives, as well as those on the Radical Left and Radical Right.

It should be noted that democracy has come a long way historically. At one time, the notion that the people are fit to rule was considered extremely radical. The concept of **"popular sovereignty,"** associated with John Locke and Jean Jacques Rousseau, replaced the notion of **"The Divine Right of Kings,"** which held that it was both unlawful and immoral to disobey the will of the monarch. The state could and did punish opposition to the Crown. The early absolutist theory of sovereignty was developed by Jean Bodin and Thomas Hobbes. The Church could and did punish disobedience to the sovereign as sin.[9]

E. ORIGINS OF THE CONSTITUTION

The great theorists of the democratic revolutions promoted the idea that man was both the proper source and object of political power. The individual, rather than the state, became the center of their political thought. Government exists, they said, to serve the individual. The individual exists as a rational human being, rather than a mere instrument to serve the state. One's destiny was beyond being taxed, conscripted or exploited.

The British (1688), Americans (1776) and French (1789) all threw off the shackles of **autocracy** or one person rule. History was filled, they saw, with stories of rule by single tyrants, kings and queens. Who should rule? Clearly not just one person. This kind of power leads almost inevitably to abuse. Although some theorists would argue that one just and wise ruler, dedicated to the well-being of his or her people and nation, would be ideal, few such examples are found in the pages of the history books.

With the collapse of monarchies, individual dictatorships became the pattern in the 20th Century. History books are filled with accounts of the horrors of absolute rule and one-party dictatorships led by Adolf Hitler, Joseph Stalin, Benito Mussolini and others.

Another form of government is **oligarchy,** or rule by the few (elite). Early in the 21st Century, this is the most common pattern of government in the world. The oligarchy may be the military, the church or a group backed by large landowners. It has little toleration of democratic ways and processes. The Latin American junta and the Islamic Revolutionary regime in Iran are among recent familiar examples.

Those who espouse **democracy** do not assume that individuals are perfect. They are imperfect and democracy, their political invention, is imperfect, too. Yet it is better than all the alternatives. It is better than rule by one (monarchy) or rule by a few (oligarchy). Failure to attain lofty ideals, democrats say, represented merely the frailty of human nature, rather than shortcoming of the democratic system.

The Declaration of Independence, written in 1776 by Thomas Jefferson to explain and justify the American Revolution to world public opinion, was essentially a propaganda document. Few Americans think of it in that light, but Jefferson's concern was to convince the world that the colonists were justified in throwing off the yoke of British colonialism.

The small group of men who met at Philadelphia passed a resolution that formally began the revolt against Great Britain and started the "colonists" down the road to the American Revolution. Why did they rebel?

If one judges life by 18th Century standards, rather than contemporary ones, it was not bad for most Americans in 1776. There were, of course, obvious exceptions. The life of a slave or an indentured servant was hard. But it often was said that white American colonists were "freer, more equal, more prosperous, and less burdened with cumbersome feudal and monarchical restraints than any other part of mankind."[10]

American colonists were also left largely to their own devices in areas outside of trade and foreign policy, which were matters of primary concern for King and Parliament. As a result of the French and Indian War, concluded with the Treaty of Paris in 1763, Britain obtained large areas of territory in North America. The cost of defending this area was large and Parliament concluded that the colonists, the primary beneficiaries of national defense, should pay a "fair share" of the cost.

In order to raise money for defense and administration, the Parliament passed a series of tax laws. The Sugar Act (1764), also known as the American Revenue Act, extended the Molasses Act of 1733, increasing taxes on foreign refined sugar. It also placed higher import taxes on non-British textiles and forbade the American colonies from importing foreign rum and French wines. Chancellor of the Exchequer George Grenville estimated that the act would return about 45,000 pounds annually. Later taxes were imposed on official documents (Stamp Act), newspapers, paper, glass, paint and, as every schoolchild has learned, tea. Great Britain also began to enforce its trade regulations more stringently. All of these revenue measures were designed to benefit the mother country, not the colonists. That is, of course, the whole point of being a colonial power![11]

Americans resented these taxes because they were imposed on them without their having any direct representation in Parliament. "No taxation without representation" is a familiar rallying cry of the American Revolution. The colonists protested and engaged in boycotts of the taxed goods. In a symbolic act of defiance, they tossed more than 300 chests of tea into Boston Harbor. Britain responded by blockading the harbor.

In September, 1774, the colonists formed the First Continental Congress, sending delegates from each colony to Philadelphia to discuss future relations with Britain. The Continental Congress was almost continuously in session in 1775-1776. On June 7, 1776, Richard Henry Lee of Virginia moved "that these United States are and of right ought to be free and independent states."

A committee consisting of Thomas Jefferson, John Adams, Benjamin Franklin, Roger Sherman and Robert Livingston began work on a draft document to justify the declaration.

On July 2, Lee's motion to declare independence from England was formally approved. The Declaration of Independence, largely written by Jefferson, was adopted on July 4.

Ironically, many—if not most— of Jefferson's ideas were "borrowed" from the work of John Locke. Locke, the great theorist of the British (Glorious) Revolution of 1688, was clearly the most influential philosopher of democratic revolutions. Locke's theory is built upon the doctrine of natural rights. Lockean theory holds that man is a creature of God and, as such, enjoys certain natural rights which come with his humanity. Rights which are inherent in human nature cannot depend on the consent of government.

Locke is known to students of political theory as a "social contract" theorist. He argued that before governments came to be, people existed in a state of nature, where they were governed by the laws of nature. Natural law meant natural rights, among them, the rights to life, liberty and property.

Because natural law is superior to human law, it can justify revolt against tyrannical powers, including, in the world of 1776, George III. Governments, Locke said, depend for their legitimate existence on the consent of the governed. They also must be limited, that is, there must be clearly understood restrictions on the power and authority of the rulers. Indeed, the whole idea of government, according to Locke, is protection of natural rights and liberties. It was particularly important that "the preservation of property was the end of government."[12]

In order to give the Declaration a broader appeal, Jefferson substituted the term "pursuit of happiness" for property. Few colonists had much property in 1776. But the delegates to the Philadelphia Constitutional Convention were impressed by the Lockean idea of the sanctity of property.

Again, one should note that Locke wrote to justify "The Glorious Revolution" of 1688. Jefferson wrote to justify the American Revolution in 1776. But their arguments are essentially the same: people have the right to rebel against a government that does not rest on their consent. It should be noted, however, that minor injustices should be suffered and that people should resort to revolution only when injustices become intolerable:

"...whenever any Form of Government becomes destructive of these ends, it is the Right of the People to alter or to abolish it, and to institute new Government, laying its foundation on such principles and organizing its powers in such form, as to them shall seem most likely to effect their Safety and Happiness. Prudence, indeed, will dictate that Governments long established should not be changed for light and transient causes; and accordingly all experience hath shown that mankind are more disposed to suffer, while evils are sufferable, than to right themselves by abolishing the forms to which they are accustomed. But when a long train of abuses and usurpations, pursuing invariably the same Object, evinces a design to reduce them under absolute Despotism, it is their right, it is their duty, to throw off such Government, and to provide new Guards for their future security..."

Although Jefferson was influenced by other elements of revolutionary thought, Locke clearly had the most profound impact upon him. Jefferson claimed, in the Declaration of Independence, that people should rule instead of being ruled (popular sovereignty). Each person was important, created "equal" and endowed by his creator with "unalienable rights." Consent of the government was required for legitimate democratic rule. No government before had rested on these principles. That is why the U.S. sometimes has been referred to as a great "Experiment in Democracy."

Declaring a nation's independence does not necessarily make it so. Although some insist that the pen is mightier than the sword, military force is a practical consideration when staging a revolution. In 1776, the British had the finest army in the world. They had about 8500 regulars stationed in the U.S. and had hired some 30,000 mercenaries. The colonists at first had only about 5000 men in uniform. It is not the purpose of this text to explore the military history of the American Revolution. That is best left to military historians. We will focus, however, on how the new government and its successor were formed.[13]

It should be noted that the American Revolution sometimes is referred to as a "conservative" revolution, in that it did not drastically change the lifestyle of the colonists. The objective of the revolution, in fact, was to restore rights that the colonists felt were properly theirs as British subjects, but which had been denied them by the Crown and Parliament.

One cannot forget that many people died during the Revolutionary War. But it was not the "radical" type of revolution, such as the French Revolution of 1789 or the Russian Revolution of 1917. We associate them with either plenty of bloodshed or radical social change.

The American people did not seek a major political upheaval; they were not throwing off the shackles of "colonialism." Consequently, when peace came with the 1783 Treaty of Paris, there was a crucial element of stability in the new nation which was to prove invaluable.

We sometimes forget that our present national government is our second experiment in democracy. The first was that of the **Articles of Confederation**. The Continental Congress, which adopted the Declaration of Independence, was only a voluntary association of states. In 1776, the Congress called for a permanent union, titled the Articles of Confederation.

From 1776-1781, the "United Colonies," recognized only by France and the Netherlands, had no real common government, but consisted of 13 separate states.

The United States was to be a confederacy, a "firm league of friendship and perpetual union," among 13 sovereign states. There was to be a unicameral (one-house) national legislature. Each state was to have one vote, although it could send as few as two or as many as seven delegates to the legislature. There was no national executive (President). Nor was there any system of national courts.

The powers of Congress were severely limited. Members, considered state "delegates," were chosen annually. Each state paid its "delegates" and could recall them at will. Each delegation cast one vote and the approval of nine states was required for any "important" action. Clearly, most power and authority remained with the state legislatures because the leaders of the new nation feared a strong central government which would become just as tyrannical as the British.

Unanimous approval of the states was required to put the Articles into effect. They were adopted by Congress in 1777, but did not go into effect until 1781, when

Maryland finally ratified them. Meanwhile, the Continental Congress barely survived as the government went from one crisis to another.

A **confederation,** by definition, is a loose association of sovereign states, with decentralized power and authority its distinguishing characteristics. There is some common political machinery, but the real power is in the component parts of the union, not its center. Consequently, under the Articles of Confederation, Congress had little power and little money. It had no power to tax. It could only requisition money from the sometimes reluctant states. Despite constant threats from the British and Spanish, the Congress virtually disbanded the army. It had no power to regulate commerce, which severely handicapped foreign trade and the development of a strong national economy. It could not exert even limited powers over individual citizens. That was up to the states.

Perhaps the single outstanding domestic accomplishment of the Congress of the Confederation was enactment of the **Northwest Ordinance of 1787**, which encouraged the development of the Great Lakes states. It provided for the government of the territory north of the Ohio River and west of New York to the Mississippi River. Eventual statehood was promised to those parts of the territory whose populations reached 60,000. The statute established local self-government, reaffirming an act of 1785, which set up the township system of dividing land and establishing local schools. Slavery was excluded from the territory, and political and civil rights were recognized.

One could say that the national government was weak and ineffective. It could take very little action independent of the states. From the perspective of today's citizen, it may seem strange indeed that the Confederation had no power to deal directly with individual citizens.

In the post-revolutionary Articles of Confederation era, Democracy was enshrined in the new 13 states. What was happening there was clearly more important than what was happening in the Continental Congress.[14]

Democracy was becoming extended for white males. The states adopted bills of rights which abolished religious qualifications for office and expanded voting opportunities. The old, pre-Revolutionary elite saw its power erode as framers and craftsmen were enfranchised and became the majority.

Political power and authority was concentrated during this period in the state legislatures. Legislators were considered the champions of the liberties of the people. Certainly, they were closer to them than governors or judges. There was a great fear of executive authority. Governors, often selected by state legislators, were kept on a short leash. They had limited veto powers and short terms of office. Their powers of appointment were also severely curtailed. Legislators could overturn court decisions and criticize judges for making unpopular rulings.

As noted, the American Revolution was not as radical as the French or the Russian Revolutions. But it did unleash Republican impulses in the land. Americans were in process of becoming "the most liberal, the most democratic, the most commercially minded and the most modern people in the world."[15]

To members of the pre-Revolutionary elite, this was troublesome indeed. It challenged their hold on power in the "New World." They became genuinely alarmed when legislatures began to adopt policies which favored debtors over creditors. They were horrified, in 1786, when a small band of farmers in western Massachusetts rebelled at losing their land to creditors. Led by Daniel Shays, a captain during the Revolutionary War, back-country farmers staged armed attacks on courthouses to prevent judges from foreclosing on their farms.

They demanded abolition of the state Senate, which they considered a citadel of wealth. They demanded removal of the capital from aristocratic Boston to an inland city.

They urged that state lands in Maine, then a part of Massachusetts, be sold to reduce the burden of taxation. Like those in debt everywhere, they demanded legal-tender issues of paper money.

Neither the Congress nor the states stopped Shays and his followers, and only a privately-paid force was assembled to do the job. **Shays' Rebellion,** which lasted for almost a year, fueled dissatisfaction with the weaknesses of the Articles of Confederation. Ironically, after the uprising had been suppressed, many of the rebels' demanded reforms were enacted.[16]

Military concerns were present as well. Great Britain disputed the boundary line between the U.S. and Canada. The Royal Navy forced U.S. sailors into their service on the grounds that anyone who spoke English was British. France, a Revolutionary War ally, blocked U.S. trade with islands in the West Indies and demanded repayment of money advanced during the Revolution. It was difficult for the Confederation to deal with these problems, particularly when some of the states engaged in their own negotiations with foreign countries. All of these factors stimulated a desire for greater security and a central government which could better cope with these threats.

The Annapolis Convention: In 1785, the initial step toward major constitutional change followed an agreement between Maryland and Virginia, resolving problems of tariff duties, navigation rights on Chesapeake Bay and commercial use of the Potomac River. The Virginia legislature then advanced the notion that the 13 states should gather to discuss their common interstate problems. In September, 1786, a small group of continental leaders gathered in Annapolis, MD, to discuss the problems of government under the Articles of Confederation.

Although nine states appointed delegates to go to Annapolis, only five of the 13 states were represented. They waited—and waited—and waited, for three weeks—for more delegates to arrive. They finally decided to adjourn, but first issued a call for a meeting of states in Philadelphia the following May. It was important, Alexander Hamilton said in a written report, "to take into consideration the situation of the United States, to devise such further provisions as shall appear to them necessary to render the Constitution of the Federal Government adequate to the exigencies of the Union."

The Continental Congress initially ignored the project, but in February, 1787, it recommended a convention at the time and place already set, to meet for the "sole and express purpose of revising the Articles of Confederation" and of reporting to the Congress such alterations as would "render the Federal Constitution adequate to the exigencies of government and the preservation of the union. Technically, the Philadelphia Convention's status was merely that of an advisory body to Congress. It was, of course, to assume a much more significant historic role than that. It began its work in May, 1787.

F. THE CONSTITUTIONAL CONVENTION

1. Delegates

Representatives from 12 states came to Philadelphia to meet "for the sole and express purpose of revising the Articles of Confederation." Rhode Island, a stronghold of paper money interests, refused to send delegates. The delegates were hardly typical, even for their own day. Some 74 delegates were appointed, but only 55, all of them men, ever attended the sessions. They included economic and political leaders. They were men of substance, position and considerable wealth in the new nation. Their ranks included lawyers, physicians, wealthy planters and merchants. Nearly half of the delegates were college graduates, most extraordinary in the world of 1787. Most lived along the Atlantic Coast, rather than on the expanding western frontier. Most came from cities, rather than rural areas. Thomas Jefferson once referred to the delegates as "an assembly of demi-Gods."[17]

Virginia sent George Washington, who had retired to his estate at Mt. Vernon, James Madison, George Mason and Gov. Edmund Randolph. The Pennsylvania delegation included Benjamin Franklin, the oldest delegate at 82, James Wilson, John Dickinson and Gouverneur Morris. New York sent Alexander Hamilton, John Lansing and Robert Yates. Massachusetts sent Rufus King and Elbridge Gerry. Other outstanding delegates were Roger Sherman, Oliver Ellsworth and William Johnson of Connecticut, John Rutledge and the two Pinckneys, Charles and Thomas, of South Carolina.

At least 30 of the delegates had risked their necks in prominent military or civilian positions during the Revolution. Some 39 of them had served in Congress, and all were political leaders in their states. One should note, however, that only eight of the 56 signers of the Declaration of Independence attended the Constitutional Convention. Conspicuously absent were Jefferson and John Adams, who were representing the "new nation" abroad as diplomats in France and Great Britain, respectively. This may mean simply that different abilities were required for making a revolution than for writing a nation's Basic Law.

They chose George Washington of Virginia, commanding general of the American Revolutionary forces, as their presiding officer.

The delegates were generally young men. The average age was about 43, and six were under the age of 31. Only a dozen were 55 or older.

There were no media to cover a Constitutional Convention in 1787. Some would say, "Thank God!" No one played to the TV cameras. There were no "spin doctors," no correspondents filing copy for their newspapers. The proceedings were largely secret. What we know about the work of the convention is largely due to the extensive notes kept by James Madison, whom historians have called "the Father of the Constitution."

The delegates were uncommonly well-read and launched their deliberations with a two-week debate on the philosophy of government. At times, very divisive issues threatened to dissolve the meeting. The delegates ranged in philosophy from Franklin, a strong proponent of democracy, to the aristocratic Hamilton, who had a low opinion of democracy and seldom tried to hide his contempt for it. Yet the delegates did reach a consensus on some key questions.

One item on which most delegates agreed was their view of human nature. People, they thought, were self-interested. "Men love power," Alexander Hamilton said. One of the points of agreement at Philadelphia was that government must play a key role in keeping natural self-interest of people under control.

Madison believed that the main source of political conflict was the unequal distribution of wealth. Other sources of social conflict were religion, differing views on governing and attachment to various leaders. Madison said that the principal source of conflict was factionalism—what we later called political parties or interest groups.

A majority might consist of the many who had little property, the minority those with property. Each would seek to control the government in its own interests. Factionalism must be checked.

Gouverneur Morris of Pennsylvania said the preservation of property was the "principal object of government." The delegates were property owners themselves and could not imagine a government that did not make the preservation of individual rights to acquire and hold wealth one of its principal objectives.

Man, the delegates reasoned, was avaricious and self-interested. The principal cause of political conflict is economic inequality. Either a majority or a minority faction will be tyrannical if it has too much power. Property must be protected against the tyrannical tendencies of factions.

Power must be used to counterbalance power. No one faction should be able to dominate the others. The secret of good government was "balanced" government. A limited, democratic government must also control itself. Ambition must balance other ambition. No one faction should be able to seize control of government at any one time. A complex system of checks and balances and of separation of powers would be required for a truly balanced government.

2. Practical Problems To Be Resolved

In addition to the lofty, abstract debates on political philosophy that occurred in Philadelphia, the delegates faced some practical problems that had to be resolved. These included equality, individual rights and the national economy.

Although the Declaration of Independence says that all men are created equal, the original, unamended Constitution says nothing about it. However, the delegates spent hours debating issues of equality. One crucial policy issue was how the new Congress would be constituted.[18]

3. The New Jersey Plan

One plan, put before the convention by William Paterson, is usually called the Small States or New Jersey Plan. The Convention would limit itself to considering only amendments to the Articles of Confederation, as delegates had been instructed to do. It called for each state to continue to be represented in a unicameral legislature. Each state would have equal representation, but the power and authority of the central government would be increased. Congress would have the power to levy duties on goods imported into the U.S., to impose a tax on documents, and to regulate interstate and foreign commerce. Another important change was that all Federal laws and treaties were to be the supreme law of the individual states.

Congress would choose a plural Federal executive, which would have power and authority to execute Federal laws and appoint Federal officials. It also would be responsible for direction of all military operations. The executive authority, however, would have no power of veto. The Paterson Plan also proposed a Supreme Court, appointed by the executive, which would have jurisdiction over cases involving treaties, regulation of trade and collection of taxes.

New Jersey won little support for its plan of government. Only New York and Delaware supported it.

The delegates faced a decision whether they wanted to limit themselves, as instructed, to amending the Articles of Confederation or to draw up the framework for an entirely new national government. After three days of debate, the Convention voted to work toward a stronger national government. Discussion then focused on the issue of equal versus proportional representation in the national legislature.

4. The Virginia Plan

The view of the large states was very different. Put before the delegates by Gov. Edmund Randolph of Virginia, the Large States Plan proposed a far-reaching plan for establishing a new national government. Virginia wanted to scrap the Articles of Confederation and to establish a supreme, bicameral legislature with representation in both houses on the basis of population or wealth. Although Randolph presented the plan, its chief architect was James Madison.

The lower house was to be elected directly by the people. The upper house would be selected by the lower house from nominees proposed by state legislatures.

Congress was to have sweeping powers, including the right to veto all state laws that it believed went beyond state authority. The national executive and judges of national courts were to be elected by the Congress. Together, the executive and judicial branches would constitute what was called a "council of revision" with power to veto acts of Congress.

On May 30,1787, the Convention resolved itself into a committee of the whole. It then debated the Virginia Plan until June 13, when 19 resolutions based on Governor Randolph's Plan were presented to the Convention.

5. The (Great) Connecticut Compromise

This conflict over representation was settled by a compromise, worked out by Roger Sherman and William Johnson of Connecticut. The famous **Great Compromise** created a bicameral (two-house) legislature. One chamber, the Senate, would be based on the principle of the equality of the states. Each state would have two senators. The second chamber would be chosen on the basis of population. The Congress of the United States is still organized this way.

Another major dispute had to do with slavery. It is obvious that slavery was completely inconsistent with the philosophy expressed in the Declaration of Independence. But, with the exception of Massachusetts, slavery was legal in every state. The south, it was argued, depended upon slavery for its agricultural, plantation system.

The delegates could agree only to limit future importing of slaves, banning it after the year 1808. They refused to ban slavery entirely, and even wrote a provision into the Basic Law requiring that fugitive slaves escaping to free states be returned to their owners.

The south wanted to have its proverbial cake and eat it, too. Although unwilling to recognize slaves as free persons, it wanted to count all slaves for purposes of representation in the House of Representatives. The answer was another famous—some would say infamous—compromise, the three-fifths compromise. Representation and taxation were to be based on the number of "free persons" plus three-fifths of the number of "all other persons." The other persons, of course, were the slaves.

6. Individual Liberties

The delegates also were faced with the challenge of designing a system which would protect individual liberties. They saw this as a relatively easy task because they were committed to building a system of limited government which could not endanger personal freedoms. They had separated powers among the branches of government. They had separated the powers of the national and Federal government and the state governments. Consequently, the original, unamended Constitution says little about civil rights and civil liberties.[19]

It does contain three Article I provisions limiting the powers of Congress. Section 9 forbids suspension of the writ of *habeas corpus*, except in cases of invasion or domestic rebellion. **Habeas corpus** enables persons detained by authorities to get an immediate hearing into the causes of their detention. It is a great writ of Anglo-American liberty, designed to prevent people from being imprisoned without reason and left—literally in some cases—to rot in jail, as had happened in Europe. If authorities cannot satisfy a judge or magistrate that a person is being held legally, a release order can be issued by the bench.

Section 9 also forbids Congress or the states from passing **bills of attainder,** which punish people without the benefit of a day in court. A judicial trial is imperative under the U.S. Constitution because the framers understood the sad lessons of human experience where individuals had been declared guilty of a crime, such as treason, by the British Parliament. They then were executed without ever having had their day in court.

The same section of Article I forbids Congress from enacting *ex post facto* laws, which punish people or increase the severity of punishment for acts which were not criminal when they were done. Laws which substantially alter the rules of evidence to the detriment of the defendant also are forbidden.

The Constitution also contains a provision in Article VI forbidding the imposition of religious qualifications for holding office in the national government. Such tests continued in the states until the ratification of the First Amendment and other provisions of the Bill of Rights in 1791.

Article III, which deals with the Federal judiciary, upholds the right to trial by jury in all Federal criminal cases. This provision is found in Section 2.

7. Economic Issues Facing The Delegates

Although American historians disagree—even more than two centuries later—about the state of the economy in 1787, there is no doubt that economic issues were a top priority item on the Framers' agenda at Philadelphia. They believed that the economy was in virtually complete disarray. They were concerned that the Continental Congress was unable to raise sufficient funds as the nation went through a recession.

Each of the 13 states had its own paper currency and money fluctuated wildly in value. In some states, paper money was nearly worthless, but in those states debtors often controlled state legislators, which forced creditors to accept this valueless currency.

The development of a truly national economy was severely impeded by tariff barriers, as one state after another erected tariff walls against competing products from other states.

The Framers were, historians agree, among the nation's economic elite.[20] If they were not capitalist entrepreneurs, they were creditors whose loans were being wiped out by cheap paper money. Many were merchants whose efforts to trade in interstate commerce were handicapped by tariff barriers. Nearly all of the delegates concluded that only a strong national government could bring economic stability to the nation. Clearly, one of their purposes in drafting the new Constitution was to bolster the powers of the new national government. Congress was intended to be the chief economic policy maker.

The new national legislature was granted power in Article I to raise revenues through taxation and borrowing. It was also given the authority to appropriate funds. Congress would maintain sound money policies and assume responsibility for the national debt.

Investment was encouraged as Congress was given the power to build the nation's first real infrastructure, a systems of roads and highways. It built post offices. It constructed standards of weights and measurements. It was empowered to punish counterfeiters, to ensure patent rights and copyrights as well as establish rules for bankruptcy. Perhaps most important in the long run, Congress was given the tools to regulate interstate and foreign commerce.

States were forbidden from printing the hated paper currency, imposing tariffs on goods from other states and interfering with legally contracted debts. As a result of the "full faith and credit clause," states had to honor civil judgments and contracts concluded in other states. States were guaranteed a "republican form of government" to prevent another occurrence like Daniel Shays' Rebellion.

8. Key Features of the Constitution

Among the key features of the new Constitution were separation of powers and checks and balances. James Madison is largely responsible for these ideas.

Madison explained that "ambition must be made to counteract ambition." Specifically, he believed that as much of the government as possible should be placed beyond direct control of majorities. He also thought that different political institutions (Congress, President and Federal Courts) should be separated. Articles I, II and III of the Constitution do this, so that each branch of the government can trace its authority directly to the nation's Basic Law. It does not depend upon any other branch for its political power or authority.

Finally, Madison believed that a system of checks and balances must be created to thwart the **"tyranny of the majority,"** as Alexis de Tocqueville, the great French observer of the American scene, later was to call it.

The new Constitution placed only the House of Representatives within direct control of the majority. Senators were to be elected by their state legislatures and Presidents by the Electoral College. Judges were to be nominated by the President and subject to Senate confirmation before their appointments could take effect. Should the majority take control of the House, it still could not impose its will without the concurrence of the Senate and the President.

In a bicameral legislature, no bill could become law without both houses agreeing to the identical version of a measure. To divorce majority will even further from public opinion, judges were given tenure for "life or good behavior." Senators were to be elected for six-year terms, with no more than one-third to be chosen at any one time. Members of the House were to have only two-year terms, the President a four-year term.

Madison's plan, reflected in the Constitution, imposes a system of **separation of powers**. No one branch can control the other. Executive, legislative and judicial organs of government are independent of one another. The Congress can trace its power and authority to Article I, the President to Article II and the Federal courts to Article III. Most contemporary political scientists tend to refer to this arrangement as not an absolute separation of powers, but the creation of separate institutions sharing powers.

Because power was not to be completely separate, each of the organs of government was required to obtain the consent of the others for many of its actions. This system, known as **checks and balances**, reflects the Madisonian goal of pitting power and ambition against other power and ambition to control government actions. If a dominant group or "faction" gained control of one segment of government, it could do no great harm to the system. The President, armed with the veto power, could check the

Congress. Congress would control the purse strings. It had to agree to a number of key presidential nominations before an appointee could take his job. Treaties would not go into effect without the "advice and consent" of the Senate.

The courts were not explicitly given the constitutional power and authority of **judicial review.** Although this enormous aspect of checks and balances may have been intended by the Framers, it is not clearly stated anywhere in the Basic Law. It was, however, successfully asserted by Chief Justice John Marshall in *Marbury v. Madison* (1803). This landmark case is discussed more fully in Chapter 6. It should be stated here, however, that by asserting its power to check the other two branches of government by holding their acts unconstitutional, the Supreme Court changed the balance dramatically. It greatly enlarged its own power and authority while further restraining that of the President and the Congress.

The Founders also created a Federal system of government. Most government power, under this decentralized plan of rule, was to rest in the hands of states and local communities. The Framers of the Constitution believed that this would be a further effective restraint on the powers of the national government. Federalism will be explored in greater detail in the next chapter.

9. The Ratification Debates

The Constitution did not go into effect automatically. It still had to be ratified by the states, and, given the politics of the day, that was by no means a sure thing. The Framers realized that ratification of the document could present grave difficulties. Future Chief Justice John Marshall said: "It is scarcely to be doubted that in some of the adopting states, a majority of the people were in opposition."

The Constitution itself required that nine of the 13 states approve the document prior to its going into effect. This provision was very convenient for the Framers, who totally ignored the provision in the Articles of Confederation that they could be changed only by unanimous consent of all 13 state legislatures. Rhode Island had not even sent delegates to the Convention. Sent to Philadelphia to produce a revision of the Articles, the Framers committed an *ultra vires* act, one beyond the scope of their authority. In the long run, it can be argued that it was good for the nation that they did.

America's first political parties grew out of the debates on the ratification of the Constitution. The Federalists were the party of the Constitution, its great champion. The anti-Federalists originally opposed the Constitution, then shifted the debate after ratification to how it ought to be interpreted.

Newspapers were filled with letters and articles either praising or damning the new Constitution.[21] Many of them were written under pseudonyms. Most important were the essays of three men, Alexander Hamilton, James Madison and John Jay, who wrote a series of 85 articles under the pen name of Publius. Known as *The Federalist Papers*, these newspaper articles are considered by some political scientists as among the most important works in the history of American Political Thought. They were written primarily to influence the vote in the doubtful state of New York.

Why would anyone oppose the new Constitution? The anti-Federalists were convinced that the new government was simply too strong, an enemy of the freedoms they had just fought a war against Britain to win. They questioned the motives of the Framers. They argued that the new Constitution was a document created by an elite to advance their economic and class interests. One critic said: "These lawyers, men of learning, and moneyed men expect to get into Congress themselves so they can get all the power and all the money in their own hands." Who were these "conspirators?" None other than Washington, Franklin and Hamilton.[22]

Perhaps the most widely-known criticism of the Framers' motives was expressed in a book by Columbia University historian Charles A. Beard, *An Economic Interpretation of the Constitution*.[23] Beard's thesis was that the Framers represented an economic elite and that the Constitution was intended to protect their interests. Beard tried to prove that the Framers stood to gain a great deal from the creation of a strong and stable government.

The Framers were, Beard said, professional or propertied men with extensive holdings in public securities. They also owned land and slaves, were engaged in shipping and manufacturing. Unlike the Marxist historians, to whom economics is the determining factor in the unfolding of history, Beard conceded that economic interests were only one of the factors that motivated the Framers. He did not attribute any malice to them.

The anti-Federalists had other fears. The new government would not only be run by an elite. It also would jeopardize civil liberties. Most important on their list of grievances was the absence in the new Constitution of a Bill of Rights. To answer this complaint, the Federalists promised that the very First Congress of the United States would propose such a Bill of Rights to the states for their ratification. State Constitutions commonly included Bills of Rights at the time of the Philadelphia Convention.

The Federalists later were true to their word. James Madison introduced 12 constitutional amendments in the First Congress in 1789. Ten of them subsequently were ratified and became the Bill of Rights in 1791. Curiously enough, one of Madison's other proposed amendments was ratified more than two centuries later as the 27th Amendment. It stipulates:

"No law varying the compensation for the services of the Senators and Representatives shall take effect, until an election of representatives shall have intervened."

. Anti-Federalists also worried that the new government would weaken the states—which it eventually did. States rights was an important concern at the time.

Where one stood on the economic ladder also had something to do with one's attitude toward the new Constitution. Not everyone wanted an economy which would be placed on a "sounder foundation." Creditors opposed issuance of paper money because it would be inflationary and make the payments on their loans decline in value from what they had lent. Debtors, however, favored paper money. Their debts remained constant, but if money became cheap, it would be easier for them to pay off their debts.

If the Federalists lacked majority support, they compensated for it by shrewd politics. They understood that some state legislators might lose power under the new Constitution. Therefore, they specified that the new document be ratified by special conventions called in each of the 13 states, rather than by state legislatures.

Delaware was the first state to ratify the document. Within six months, New Hampshire became the ninth, which put the Constitution into effect. Virginia and New York quickly joined the fold. North Carolina and Rhode Island insisted that a Bill of Rights be added to the Constitution as a prerequisite for their joining the new union of states.

Had a unanimous vote been required to make the Constitution effective, it is probable that the entire effort would have failed.

G. KEEPING THE U.S. CONSTITUTION "ALIVE"

The United States is nearing the second decade of the 21st Century. The world of the late 18th Century no longer exists. Enormous political, economic and social changes have occurred in the land since the Constitution was ratified. Technology today far exceeds anything that even the brilliant Thomas Jefferson could have imagined. Inventions have made life more comfortable, yet more complex in many ways. We have progressed from the horse and buggy era to the age of the automobile, the jet airplane and the exploration of space. Communications have undergone revolutionary changes. We live not only in an age of newspapers, books, and magazines but also an era of radio, television, communications satellites and the internet!

Medical science has advanced far beyond anything the Framers of the Constitution could have envisaged. Population has grown many times over. Today, we are a nation of nearly 310 million people, largely urban, industrial or post-industrial. When the Constitution was born, the U.S. was rural, agricultural and pre-industrial.

The role of the Federal government has been radically transformed. Its budget today is measured in trillions of dollars. The United States is the leader of the Western World, a major player on the world stage. Like it or not, internationalism, rather than isolationism, has been thrust upon us. Domestically, the American people demand much more of their government than ever before. The values of the 20th Century welfare state were unknown at the time of the Philadelphia Convention.

How is a nation able to govern effectively in the 21st Century with an 18th Century document as its basic law?

One answer to that question is that the Framers were wise and astute enough as politicians to avoid drafting a document which was too detailed. Their basic purpose was to stick to fundamentals and allow the legislature to deal with specifics at a later date. Many of the clauses of the Constitution are deliberately vague.

Clearly, change is the law of nature, even constitutional change. An old saying in comparative government is: "A Constitution that will not bend is sure to break." The U.S. Constitution has not broken—to a large degree because it has the built-in flexibility to accommodate change. The Framers, knowing that they could not predict the future, created a document that has been amenable to change by both formal amendment and informal constitutional interpretation.

The Constitution provides a formal mechanism for changing the Basic Law. But the Framers deliberately made that very difficult. Article V spells out two methods for formal amendment, proposal and ratification. Each stage has two possible avenues.

Proposal: An amendment may be proposed either by a two-thirds vote in both houses of Congress or by a national Convention called by Congress at the request of two-thirds of the states' legislatures. Only the first method ever has been used.

Ratification: An amendment may be ratified either by the legislatures of three-fourths of the states or by special conventions called in three-fourths of the states. Although the President is given no voice in the process, his support for or opposition to change can be a major factor in its success or failure. But he cannot "veto" an amendment.

All but one amendment to the Constitution have been proposed by Congress and ratified by state legislatures. The exception was the 21st Amendment, which repealed the 18th or Prohibition Amendment. That Amendment is referred to as the "noble experiment." The nation attempted to legislate virtue by banning the manufacture, sale and consumption of alcohol. What it got was "vice," organized crime in the form of mobs, like Al Capone's in Chicago, an era of rum-running, violence and bloodshed.

In 1933, newly-elected President Franklin Roosevelt urged Congress to propose the 21st Amendment. But he knew that rural legislatures, then dominated by "dry" interests, would not ratify it. So he asked Congress to stipulate that the amendment be ratified by conventions in each of the states. This would enable delegates to run as "wet" or "dry" and for the nation to have a true referendum of the issue. This is the only time in U.S. history where an amendment has been ratified by conventions rather than by state legislatures.

During the 1980s, Conservatives championed the cause of a balanced budget amendment which would require the Congress to balance its books each year, except in cases of war or national emergency. But the states have been the moving force behind this proposal. Some 32 of them have petitioned the Congress to call a national convention to consider the balanced budget amendment. Although Conservatives are only two states short of the required 34, no new state has joined the cause in nearly two decades.

Sometimes, however, Congress gets the political message. A balanced budget agreement was concluded by President Bill Clinton and the Republican-controlled 105th Congress.

Without doubt, formal amendments have made the Constitution more democratic. The original, unamended constitution stressed economic issues. This is balanced by amendments stressing equality and the ability of majorities to control the government. Although thousands of proposals have been discussed on the floor in House and Senate, only 33 have been endorsed by both houses. Some 27 of them have been adopted, and now are part of the nation's Basic Law.

The first 10 Amendments are referred to collectively as the Bill of Rights. They were proposed by the First Congress to fulfill a Federalist party pledge to the people, made during the ratification debates. Then, the absence of a Bill of Rights was perhaps the anti-Federalists' strongest argument against the new document.

The 11th Amendment provides: "The Judicial power of the United States shall not be construed to extend to any suit in law or equity, commenced or prosecuted against one of the United States by Citizens of another State, or by Citizens or Subjects of any Foreign State."

It was intended to reaffirm an old principle that a state cannot be sued without its own consent and grew out of the Supreme Court decision in *Chisholm v. Georgia.* 2 Dallas 419 (1793). South Carolina creditors sued Georgia to recover confiscated property. Protests from the legislatures of Georgia, as well as other states, led Congress to propose the amendment in 1794. It was ratified in 1798.

The 12th Amendment grew out of the disputed election of 1800, in which Thomas Jefferson and Aaron Burr received an identical number of Electoral Votes. At the time, there was no separate ballot designation for President and Vice President. Jefferson was the intended Presidential candidate, and Burr the candidate for Vice President. However, the tie in the Electoral College forced the election into the House of Representatives, then controlled by the Federalist Party.

Ironically, Alexander Hamilton, Jefferson's old opponent, threw his support to him, helping to defeat Burr. This was the beginning of a tragic story. Burr wrote to Hamilton in June, 1804, after Jefferson's re-election, demanding that the former Treasury secretary retract a slur upon his character, reported in the press. Hamilton refused, Burr challenged him to a duel and Hamilton accepted. On July 11, 1804, he fired a fatal shot into Hamilton's chest.[24]

To prevent a situation similar to the Jefferson-Burr episode of 1800, the 12th Amendment requires each elector to designate his or her choice for President and Vice President on separate ballots.

Three amendments were proposed and ratified during the Reconstruction Era. The 13th Amendment abolished slavery, constitutionalizing Lincoln's Emancipation Proclamation and freed those slaves, primarily in the border states, who had not been covered by it.

The 14th Amendment guaranteed "equal protection of the laws" for all Americans and made "due process of law" binding on state governments. It categorically rejected the Confederate doctrine of state sovereignty and had the effect of overturning a U.S. Supreme Court decision in the Dred Scott case. The Taney Court had ruled in *Scott v. Sanford* 19 Howard 393 (1857) that Blacks could not be considered "citizens" of the United States under the Constitution.

The 15th was designed to enfranchise the Black male in the southern states. It forbids states from denying a person the right to vote because of race, color or previous condition of servitude. After withdrawal of Union troops in the South, however, southern states developed a number of devices to circumvent the 15th Amendment. Not until the "Civil Rights Revolution" of the 1960s did southern Blacks win a meaningful right to vote. This was achieved primarily by passage of two landmark statutes, the Civil Rights Act of 1964 and the Voting Rights Act of 1965.

The 20th Century saw 11 formal amendments added to the Constitution. Congress proposed the 16th Amendment to overturn a Supreme Court ruling in *Pollock v. Farmers' Loan & Trust* Co., 158 U.S. 601 (1895), which held that the income tax violated Article I, section 9, and was, therefore, unconstitutional. It authorized Congress to impose a Federal income tax.

The 17th Amendment was part of the Progressive Movement and made the election of U.S. senators direct and by the people, rather than by state legislators.

The 18th Amendment, as noted previously, prohibited the manufacture, sale or trans-portation of intoxicating liquors and gave Congress and state legislatures concurrent power to enforce the amendment. It later was repealed by the 21st.

The 19th Amendment gave women the right to vote in those states where they were not already enfranchised.

The 20th Amendment changed the date of the President's inauguration from March 4 to January 20. It also stipulates that terms of newly elected representatives and senators begin on January 3 rather than on March 4. The newly elected Congress must meet two months after its election, instead of 13 months afterward, as had been the case previously.

Presidents are limited to two full terms by the 22nd Amendment, ratified in 1954. It formalizes what had been an American tradition, established by George Washington. This "two-term tradition" was shattered in 1940 and 1944, when Franklin D. Roosevelt was elected to third and fourth terms.

The 23rd Amendment gives residents of the District of Columbia, if otherwise eligible, the right to vote in presidential elections. In presidential elections, voting in the Electoral College is by states. Because the District is not a state, a constitutional amendment was required to enfranchise its residents. The District was given three electoral votes, equal to the number of the least populous U.S. states.

The 24th Amendment forbids denial of a citizen's right to vote in any Federal election because of failure to pay a poll or any other tax. It was ratified in 1964.

The 25th Amendment deals with presidential disability and succession, as well as the permanent filling of the office of Vice President in the event a vacancy occurs there. It is discussed extensively, along with provisions of the 22nd amendment, in Chapter 4.

The 26th Amendment, ratified in 1971, gave the right to vote to youths between the ages of 18-21 who had not yet been enfranchised by their states. It was proposed after the Supreme Court ruled in *Oregon v. Mitchell*, 400 U.S. 112 (1970) that provisions of the Voting Rights Act of 1965 were unconstitutional, insofar as they related to state elections.

The most recent amendment added to the Constitution, the 27th, was ratified in 1992, more than 200 years after it was first proposed. It stipulates that no law varying the compensation for the service of Senators and Representatives shall take effect, until an election of Representatives shall have intervened.

One could argue, and most political scientists and American historians do, that the overall effect of the formal amendments to the Constitution has been to expand freedom and equality of opportunity in the United States.

Even popular amendments, however, may not succeed. It is very difficult to get two-thirds of the members of both houses of Congress to propose an amendment. It may be even more difficult to get three-fourths of the states to ratify the proposals. The Framers of the Constitution wanted to create a stable political system and to prevent temporary majorities from changing basic political and legal arrangements.

One example of the difficulty encountered in getting an amendment added to the Constitution is the Equal Rights Amendment. Originally proposed in 1923, the ERA waited almost half a century until 1972, when it formally was proposed by Congress and sent to the states. It stated simply that "equality of rights under the law shall not be denied or abridged by the United States or by any state on account of sex."

The amendment sailed through Congress and many state legislature soon after it was proposed. But it never was ratified. Southern states opposed it, as did some of the states of the Rocky Mountain West, where the influence of the Mormon Church—which opposed the amendment—was profound. The U.S. system of checks and balances gives a veto power over amendments to 13 states![25]

Time Limits for Amendments: When it proposes an amendment, Congress may impose a time limit within which the amendment must be ratified. When this is done, the time limit is commonly seven years, as in the cases of the 22nd (presidential tenure) Amendment or the proposed Equal Rights Amendment. In the latter case, there was a good deal of political maneuvering and Congress voted to "extend the deadline" beyond seven years. This was too much for Sen. Sam Ervin, (D., N.C.), chairman of the Judiciary Committee, who argued that such action was unconstitutional. Ervin and several of his colleagues threatened a lawsuit in the event that the ERA was ratified within the extension period, but it never was.

In 1978, Congress proposed a constitutional amendment that would have given citizens of Washington, D.C., full voting representation in Congress. Only 16 states had ratified it when it expired in 1985.

One also should note that states can change their minds after rejecting a proposed amendment. They later may vote to approve it, although the contrary is not true. Once a state ratifies a proposal, it may not rescind its ratification, despite the fact that several states did precisely that in the case of ERA.

Perhaps the strangest ratification story involves the 27th Amendment, which prevents members of Congress from voting themselves immediate pay increases. Proposed originally in 1789, it languished until 1982, when Gregory Watson, a student at University of Texas, stumbled upon it while doing research for a term paper. Only eight states had ratified the amendment, but Watson took up the cause. In May, 1992, Michigan provided the decisive vote and the amendment was ratified more than two centuries after it had been proposed.[26]

Informal Constitutional Change: It may be argued that even though the formal amendments have greatly changed the nature of the American constitutional system, many meaningful changes have occurred without changing a single word of the Constitution. In short, the Constitution changes informally, as well as formally, as the process of historic and cultural change occurs. Judicial review has been of great significance in keeping the Constitution up to date. Some scholars call the U.S. Basic Law a "Living Constitution."

The possibility of gradual changes in constitutional meanings to meet new conditions of life is one of the main reasons why the U.S. has not often resorted to formal amendments.

Disputes occur constantly about the meaning of vague phrases of the Constitution. What is "due process of law" in a specific case or controversy? Someone has to decide and the U.S. Supreme Court has become the final arbiter of the meaning of the Constitution, as it exercises its power of judicial review.

The Constitution has come to mean what the Supreme Court says that it means. Not everyone agrees with this. Both Liberals and Conservatives have argued that this amounts to "The Divine Right of Judges." While Liberals attacked the Court for vetoing much of Franklin Roosevelt's early New Deal, Conservatives later were appalled by Warren Court decisions in areas such as race relations, national security, reapportionment, school prayer and criminal law.

The Burger Court came under fire for its abortion decision, *Roe v. Wade*, 410 U.S. 113 (1973), that held that a woman had a legal right to an abortion during the first two trimesters of pregnancy when the fetus is not viable outside the womb. This was an issue that the Framers never could have imagined! And even some members of the Court dissented vehemently, arguing that this was a matter that they should never be called upon to decide.[27]

Evolving Political Factors: Although they are not mentioned anywhere in the Constitution, political parties have played a major role in the evolution of the Basic Law. Political parties, as we know them today, did not exist at the time of the Philadelphia Convention. Both Washington and Madison warned against the effect of "factions." In time, however, those "factions" evolved into our modern parties.

America's original parties developed over differences about the new Constitution. Federalists supported it and anti-Federalists opposed it. Once the document was ratified, debate shifted to how the new document ought to be interpreted. Federalists, led by Hamilton, believed in a strong national government with vigorous presidential leadership. The anti-Federalists believed in strong state governments, a national government of very limited role and congressional leadership.

By 1800, Jefferson was leading what became the Democratic-Republican Party, a party which took over control of the government from the Federalists that year. As the years passed, the term Republican was dropped and competition was between Democrats and Whigs (successors to the Federalists), then after 1860, between Democrats and Republicans.

Partisan politics has made an enormous difference in how the American Constitutional System works. The evolution of parties meant a great change in the Electoral College. Originally expected to include the "wise men of the community" as electors, its function was reduced to an essentially clerical one with the emergence of the party system. In 1796, the first election in which George Washington's name was not on the ballot, electors split their votes between 13 candidates. By the time of Jefferson's victory (1800), the country was split into two parties, both of which required electors to pledge in advance that they would support the candidate who had won the state's popular vote. This made the Electoral College largely, but not entirely, an automatic device.

In the 21st Century, electors are generally viewed as nothing more than rubber stamps. But that is not quite true. Nothing in the Constitution prevents an elector from voting for anyone he or she chooses to support. Occasionally a "faithless elector" will do exactly that. In 1976, for example, although President Ford had carried the state of Washington, one Republican elector decided to cast his vote for Ronald Reagan. Mr. Reagan, who was elected President four years later, had to be content with that single electoral vote in 1976.

The President's cabinet also has no formal constitutional status. Dating back to George Washington, it has been used by Presidents largely for their own purposes. At the beginning, Washington sought the advice of his secretaries of Treasury (Hamilton), State (Jefferson) and War (Knox). Presidents used the cabinet throughout much of the 19th Century as an advisory body.

Most 20th and 21st Century Presidents, however, have not relied on it as an important source of ideas for public policy, preferring instead the counsel of their close, long-term political advisers. Unlike the British cabinet, which has formal legal authority under the British parliamentary system, the American cabinet is powerless, unless the President chooses to make it otherwise.

Many students have heard the story of President Abraham Lincoln asking his Cabinet for advice and then taking a vote on an issue. After a unanimous 7-0 vote, he announced, "Seven nays and one aye, the ayes have it." The aye vote, of course, was cast by Lincoln and was the only one that counted.[28]

The Constitution, Ideology and the March of Democracy: Early proponents of constitutional democracy had different definitions and expectations of what the new regime would mean to them. The march of time has brought great, extra-constitutional change in the U.S. and the opportunity for much greater popular participation in the political process.

Consider for a moment the matter of voting. In early America, it was considered folly to suggest that those without property ("the irresponsible") should vote. Blacks were "property," not citizens, and were therefore excluded from the franchise until the post-Civil War period when the 13th, 14th and 15th Amendments were adopted.

It was considered nonsense at the beginning of the Republic to suggest that women could possibly know anything about something as "serious" as politics. Why should the "weaker sex" have a role in political decision-making? It was too much for die-hard male chauvinists of an earlier age when a number of territories like Wyoming and states like Kentucky began to permit unmarried school teachers to vote.

In 2009, the U.S. Senate has only 17 female senators. Yet, in 1982, it had only two. So progress has been made, if slowly. The House of Representatives includes 73 females among its members in the 111th Congress, the largest number in history. One of them, Nancy Pelosi of California, is the first woman chosen as House minority leader by her party. Congress has a smaller percentage of Blacks, Hispanics and Asians than there are in the general population. Nonetheless, it is a more "democratic" body than in the past. In the words of some of its critics, however, "It still doesn't look like America."

The nation also has made progress in the number of female and other minority governors, state legislators and local government officials. It was not until the 1970s that the late Ella Grasso of Connecticut and Dixie Lee Ray of Washington state became the nation's first two female governors, elected in their own right. Prior to that time, several women had served as governors after their husbands had died in office. This was described as the "widow's mandate." But as more women and others have run for public office, more of them have been elected. In some cases, the problem has been to convince other women to vote for them.

Civil rights laws enacted in the 1960s, especially the Civil Rights Act of 1964 and the Voting Rights Act of 1965, have extended political and economic opportunities to both females and Blacks. While much remains to be done in the war against discrimination, these statutes represented giant strides forward on the path to a more egalitarian society.

The election of Barack Obama as President of the United States in 2008 would not have been possible had it not been for the civil rights legislation passed during the Lyndon Johnson administration.

American youth—one of the noisiest protest groups during the 1960s—won the right to vote as the result of the 26th Amendment. The opportunity to "change the system" was there for young social critics who were sincerely interested in electoral politics. They did, however, face the challenge of convincing older citizens of the merits of programs and policies they advocated.

Freedom of speech, vital to election campaigns, never has meant the freedom to be taken seriously if policies championed are unattractive to most of the electorate! Voters in a democracy are free to accept or reject candidates and policies as they see fit.

Some candidates and their supporters who "demand" a long laundry list of fundamental reforms and criticize the people and nation when these "demands" are rejected, may be seeking only self-aggrandizement and narrow self-interests, rather than the general welfare.

Dr. Reo Christenson, professor of political science at Miami University of Ohio, in his excellent little paperback, *Heresies, Right and Left,* suggested that the real threat to American democracy may come from decline in self-discipline and the erosion of confidence in our historical moral values.[29]

There is not much question early in the 21st Century that the term "democracy" has great appeal. Heated debate occurs, however, over the meaning of the term. Some Americans would argue that Western nations, such as Britain, the U.S. and Canada, are genuine democracies, while categorically rejecting the notion that the People's Republic of China, the former Soviet Union or former Eastern European satellites are "democracies."

Americans tend to equate certain practices with democracy. If a society lacks competing political parties, free and frequent elections, freedom to offer alternative policies and candidates and lacks due process of law, then, we say, it is not really democratic. China and other Communist regimes of the past have argued that these "procedures" are not really important and that Western nations are "sham democracies" of people living under the oppression of capitalism.

Liberals, Conservatives, Radicals and Moderates: One of the more difficult tasks in studying American politics is to sort out the meaning of terms which are used loosely by most Americans. Who is radical? What is the Radical Right? Radical Left? What is a Liberal? A Conservative? What is an extremist group?

Students understandably may be confused when they hear political activists or professors talk about Liberal Conservatives or Conservative Liberals, centrists or moderates. Why do these terms mean? Can they really be given precise meaning?

It sometimes is argued by Conservatives that they have a very hard time getting a fair hearing on most of the nation's campuses or in the major media. Studies of the "elite media" by Robert Lichter of Indiana University and others have shown, for example, that reporters and editors of papers like The *New York Times*, The *Washington Post,* the major wire services and major broadcast networks are "not like the rest of us" in their political, economic and social values.[30]

The Conservative cause, it is argued, is handicapped on campuses by Liberal professors, particularly in the social sciences, and Liberal-left student organizations Free speech for Conservatives was threatened on campuses during the 1960s and 1970s, in particular, when even physical intimidation was not uncommon.

Liberals are not immune from attack. During the academic year 1997-98, Secretary of State Madeleine Albright was virtually booed off the platform at Ohio State University while trying to defend President Clinton's foreign policy.

Some critics of Conservatism portray it as an ideology which simply seeks to defend the *status quo*. Although the late Clinton P. Rossiter, a noted student of American Political Thought, considered the "stand pat" Conservative merely one small group, some generalize that all Conservatives are nay-saying, 19th Century thinkers. While it may be true that Conservatives are more inclined to say no to change than are Liberals, one must keep in mind that every change is not necessarily for the better.

England's Lord Macaulay once wrote: "We find everywhere a class of men, sanguine in hope, bold in speculation, always pressing forward, quick to discern the imperfections of whatever exists, disposed to think lightly of the risks and inconveniences which attend improvements and disposed to give every change credit for being an improvement."[31]

Conservatives oppose the "welfare state." They do not believe that the function of government is to make its citizens happy. They note that increased taxes usually hit middle-income families harder than others. Although the pursuit of happiness is an ideal, recognized in the Declaration of Independence, government can never guarantee that the pursuit will be successful. Some Conservatives have even dared to question whether happiness is the central purpose of life. What matters, some suggest, is not happiness, but whether one's existence has made any difference. President Ronald Reagan often said, for example, that the citizen had a better chance to achieve happiness if government got out of the way.

The late Walter Lippmann, never accused of being a Conservative, once observed in his book, *The Public Philosophy:* "The radical error of the modern democratic gospel is that it promises, not the good life of this world, but the perfect life of Heaven." Lippmann also noted that "the harder they (Liberals) try to make Earth into Heaven, the more they make it into a Hell."[32]

Looking at the U.S. as the 21st Century nears its second decade, Conservatives are apt to raise serious questions about unrestrained majority rule, excessive concern with ideal, rather than real, aspects of life and misinterpretations of equality. Equality under law and equality of opportunity are respective and cherished Conservative ideals. But equality of result and "forced equality" of those who are not equal bothers contemporary Conservatives.

Denial of economic freedom by the New Deal and post-New Deal efforts to regulate the economy also bothers Conservatives. They view man as naturally competitive, aggressive and capable of bettering his condition. Economic Conservatives do not favor plans to redistribute market-determined incomes to produce greater social equality. Historically, they have viewed growing costs of welfare and Social Security programs with great dismay.

Many ask for "accountability." What benefits have we received from these social programs of the past 75 plus years? Can anyone, they ask, seriously argue that the welfare system has worked?

Conservatives are inclined to accept social classes as natural. Most do not particularly regret the existence of hierarchy or elites. They point to the mobility of American life, where people have "made it" through their own hard work and ability. Excessive taxes, from the Conservative standpoint, make the system less mobile, destroy incentive and interfere excessively with the workings of the market mechanism. People should be free to succeed or fail, depending upon their own abilities. Most Conservatives are strong individualists, stressing the paramount importance of self-discipline.

Their highest values include liberty and authority. Respect for tradition and the social order also are important ingredients in the Conservative philosophy. The late Sen. Robert A. Taft (R., OH), speaking to a gathering of Republicans in Plymouth, MA, expressed this view:

"What is the liberty which the Pilgrims established and which during these...years has gradually built this country up to be the greatest and happiest and most powerful in the world today?

It is not just free enterprise. It is the liberty of the individual to think his own thoughts, and to live his own life...liberty of the local community to determine how its children shall be educated...liberty of local self-government, without which in a country the size of the United States, there can be no liberty at all...

It is liberty of men to choose their own occupation, and liberty of men to establish their own businesses and run them as they think they ought to be run, as long as they do not interfere with the rights of other people to do the same. And finally, the liberty to worship God which the Pilgrims sought as their first end. It is these liberties which have given dignity to the individual in this country."[33]

While Conservatives are willing to accept necessary social change, they view Liberal efforts to "over-legislate" with disdain. Many problems cannot be solved by making laws, they complain.

Moderate Conservatives, such as President Eisenhower, have argued that self-discipline may be an answer to economic problems. Eisenhower often suggested "belt-tightening" measures to deal with inflation. President Ford suggested, in 1976, that New York City consider factors other than "how to spend money" when formulating its budget policies.

Indeed, the suggestion of then New York Mayor Abraham Beame that the U.S. government "bail out" the city was greeted with disdain by Conservatives, already upset by what they regarded as the excessive "nationalization" of problems in the post-World War II period. Community control and community responsibility still are important concepts to them.

Contemporary Conservatives are inclined to reject the excesses of "participatory democracy," a favorite phrase of the "New Left." They see eternal wisdom in the warning of the French philosopher de Tocqueville against the "tyranny of the majority."

There has been a debate for many years, primarily within the Republican Party, over who is and who is not Conservative enough. Conservatives, of course, resemble Liberals in one respect. They come in many different types and different stripes. President Ford, who was far "too Conservative" for Liberals, was not "Conservative enough" for those far right of center. *National Review* publisher William Rusher called in 1976, for example, for the formation of a third party with Ronald Reagan and George Wallace as its nominees. At the time, such notions were rejected by practical

Conservative politicians who felt that realities of the American political system made such a ticket impossible.

"Mainline" Republicans were surprised, in 1976, when Reagan mounted a strong challenge to Ford and nearly wrestled the nomination away from him. But most Conservatives were willing to close ranks and fiercely oppose the ideas associated with the McGovern-Kennedy Liberal wing of the Democratic Party.

Jimmy Carter was elected in 1976 because he was an "outsider." The nation was sick of Watergate and all that the term implied. Trust in government, politics, politicians and virtually all other American institutions fell in its aftermath. Carter, a former governor of Georgia, was a born-again Southern Baptist, a Sunday school teacher who did not drink and whose language was much less salty than that of Lyndon Johnson, last Democrat to serve in the White House.

When Reagan ousted Carter in 1980 and ushered in 12 years of Republican control of the White House, Conservatives were overjoyed. The former California governor was clearly the most Conservative President since Herbert Hoover. Many Conservatives regarded the New Deal-Fair Deal (1933-53) as the darkest period in U.S. history, marking the beginning of an unprecedented Federal presence in American life. Federal budgets had grown larger and larger. Budgets were bloated, gigantic bureaucracies were created and the results, they concluded, were unimpressive or worse. With the possible exception of the period 1947-48, when the Republican-controlled Congress sat as a check on Truman, the nation's legislature tried to "throw good money after bad" in an effort to solve the nation's problems.

Reagan and his successor, George Bush, promised less Federal intrusion in state and local affairs, less centralization of decision-making and greater individual freedom— all cardinal objectives of Conservatives.

But what were the results of the Reagan-Bush era? The growth of Federal spending was slowed, but clearly budgets continued to grow. An examination of the first and last of these Republican budgets show that spending increased while, under Reagan, the national debt grew by leaps and bounds. In fact, the Federal deficit under Reagan was more than that accumulated by all previous Presidents from Washington through Carter. This was due, in large measure, to the President's massive tax cut at the same time that a massive increase in defense spending was undertaken to combat the power of the Soviet Union.[34]

Whether this vast increase in defense spending was worth the price is arguable. Conservatives, led by Reagan, viewed the Soviets an "evil empire" and Communism as a detestable ideology. In the minds of many Conservatives, no price was too much to combat these forces. When the Soviet Union collapsed in December, 1991, many Americans rejoiced, although they may have underestimated some of the problems that would follow.

One of the problems for Republicans was that the very success of the Reagan-Bush administrations in winning the Cold War removed their most effective issues, foreign policy and national security, from the 1992 campaign. Former Arkansas Gov. Bill Clinton hammered on one issue, the economy, and capitalized on the perception that it was in bad shape.

Clinton and his vice presidential running mate, Sen. Al Gore Jr. of Tennessee, ran in 1992, however, as "new kinds of Democrats." The implication was that they were not the Liberal-left kinds of Democrats like McGovern or Mondale, who had brought the party electoral disaster. McGovern and Mondale won only one state each in 1972 and 1984 respectively. Dukakis was overwhelmed in 1988.

Clinton and Gore had been among a number of young Democratic leaders who helped to form a new party group whose purpose was to focus on winning the White House by pointing the Democrats in a more centrist direction, rather than insisting on a left-of-center ideology which the electorate clearly did not share.[35]

George W. Bush's victories over Gore in 2000 and Sen. John Kerry in 2004, resulted, according to many political writers, in a deep ideological rift in Washington. After the 2000 presidential contest, ultimately decided by the U.S. Supreme Court, many Democrats were embittered. Some even contended that the election had been "stolen."

After the terrorist attacks of September 11, 2001, on New York City's World Trade Center and the Pentagon, there was a brief show of national unity and bipartisan support for a wartime President.

But fundamental policy differences between Conservative Republicans and Liberal Democrats resulted in a heated 2004 campaign. Bush's victory was "close, but clear." The President took it as a "mandate" to undertake such fundamental changes as Social Security/Medicare reform, a revision of the tax code and a fight for Conservative judicial nominees that most Democrats opposed.

By mid-2005, partisan wrangling over Senate filibusters of presidential judicial nominees, the war and occupation of Iraq, and the direction of economic policy seemed to reflect a permanent ideological conflict in Washington political life.

In 2006, the Republicans lost control of Congress and President Bush's success in getting his programs enacted into law declined dramatically. When the GOP controlled Congress, Bush was able to get 75% of his recommendations enacted into law. By 2007, his success rate was less than 40%.

Popular discontent with the war in Iraq, high unemployment and $4 a gallon gasoline prices led the electorate to turn sympathetic ears to the Democrats' promise of "change." When the economy virtually collapsed in September, 2008, it became apparent that Sen. John McCain, who led in the polls after the Republican National Convention, was unlikely to overcome the voters' focus on the pocketbook issue. Bill Clinton virtually ignored foreign policy when he ran against President George Herbert Walker Bush in 1992. "It's the economy, stupid," a sign in his campaign headquarters said. In 2008, it may have been the same idea: "It's still the economy, stupid."

III. AMERICAN FEDERALISM: DIVIDING POWER
BETWEEN STATES AND NATION

A. POWER DISTRIBUTIONS

American Federalism is a form of political organization in which power is divided in a written constitution between two levels of government. Power is shared between the states and the national government as a matter of right. The Framers of the Constitution were well aware of their own historic legacy and colonial practice of government. Local governments were permitted considerable autonomy. Compromises, noted in Chapter 1, were necessary because of the split between delegates who wanted a charter establishing a strong central government and those who wanted merely to improve the existing Articles of Confederation.

Basically, there are three ways to organize a political system: unitary government, confederation and federalism. In a **unitary system**, the national government has ultimate legal authority over its citizens. Contemporary examples include France, the United Kingdom, Sweden and Israel. Local governments play a role, but that role is defined by the national regime.[1]

In a **confederation,** illustrated by America's first post-revolutionary regime, the powers of the national government are granted to it by state governments. In theory, the states can reclaim those powers at any time. The central government cannot regulate the actions of its citizens because it has no direct authority over them. Confederations are very rare in the contemporary world, although Switzerland is a confederation of 23 sovereign cantons.[2]

Perhaps the most familiar example of a political organization which works like a confederation is the United Nations, where real power remains in the hands of the member nation states, rather than in the organization itself. There is some common political machinery, but the UN is powerless to act without the support of its members, particularly the "Big Five," the United States, China, Russia, United Kingdom and France.

Under **federalism,** neither nation nor state has absolute power and authority. Political power is divided between them, usually in a written constitution. We sometimes use language imprecisely. The word "Federal" refers to an activity of institution of the U.S. government, whereas federalism refers to a system in which functions and decisions are divided between these two levels of government. In the American brand of federalism, each unit of government can make decisions separately from the other in its specific areas of authority.[3]

Unlike the situation in unitary states, American states are more than mere administrative entities that manage programs devised by the central government.

At the 1787 Philadelphia Constitutional Convention, a strong national government could be created only by taking power away from existing state governments and delegating them to the central government. Thus, the U.S. often is referred to as a government of **"delegated powers."** The most significant enumeration of powers delegated to Congress is found in Article I, Section 8, ranging from punishment of counterfeiting to the declaration of war. The powers of Congress were stated very broadly.

In domestic affairs, the most important of powers delegated to Congress are the authority to tax and spend and the power to regulate interstate commerce.

Article I stipulates in part: "Congress shall have power...to lay and collect taxes, duties, imposts and excises, to pay the debts and provide for the...general welfare of the United States."

Under the so-called spending clause, Congress uses its taxing authority not only to raise revenue, but also to regulate certain kinds of products. Federal taxes on tobacco and alcohol are designed to regulate behavior, as well as fill the Treasury Department's coffers. Congress also can use its taxing authority to "encourage" the states to change policies it regards as undesirable.

The power to regulate interstate commerce has had a major impact on American life. Courts have distinguished between interstate, or between-state commerce, which Congress is empowered to regulate and intrastate or within-state commerce, which only the states have authority to regulate.

In the 19th Century, the Supreme Court defined interstate commerce very narrowly. In *United States v. E.C. Knight Co.* 156 U.S. 1 (1895), it held that Congress could not break up a sugar monopoly that had a nationwide impact on the price of sugar because the company refined its sugar within the borders of Pennsylvania. The fact that the sugar was sold nationally was, the tribunal ruled, only "incidental" to its production.

The *Knight* case denied the Federal government authority over a large part of the nation's economic activity and remained the dominant legal precedent until the 1930s. When Franklin D. Roosevelt campaigned against President Hoover in 1932, he ran on a platform which pledged to use national power to combat the Great Depression.

After FDR's victory, the Democratic-controlled Congress enacted a wide variety of new Federal programs. Historians refer to these measures collectively as the New Deal. The phrase came from Roosevelt's acceptance speech at the Democratic National Convention, in which he promised a " New Deal" for the American people.

Many congressional Republicans opposed the New Deal because they believed that it violated established American principles of federalism. At first, the Supreme Court ruled against expansion of Federal powers, but after the election of 1936, in which FDR won 46 of the 48 states, the Court began to change its position.

During Roosevelt's second term, the Supreme Court interpreted Federal power more broadly, upholding new government regulation of the economy. This had an enormous impact on business corporations, labor unions and American farmers.[4]

In 1935, Congress wrote the **National Labor Relations Act**, also known as the Wagner Act, after its principle sponsor, Sen. Robert Wagner of New York. The statute gave working men and women the legal right to join a union and to bargain collectively with their employer over terms of their employment. It created the National Labor Relations Board (NLRB) to administer the act.

Collective bargaining imposes an obligation on both unions and employers to bargain in good faith over wages, hours and working conditions and to conclude a written contract detailing the agreements reached.

Hailed by labor unions as their Magna Carta, the Wagner Act brought to an end the legal fiction that negotiation between an employer and an individual employee was sacred, under liberty of contract. How much "freedom of contract" did a worker have in negotiating his or her own contract with the emerging American industrial corporate giants?

Despite the fact that the law regulated labor-union relations within a state, the Supreme Court upheld its validity. Chief Justice Charles Evans Hughes, speaking for the court in *NLRB v. Jones & Laughlin Co.*, wrote: "When industries organize themselves on a national scale, …how can it be maintained that their industrial labor relations constitute a forbidden field into which Congress may not enter?"[5]

Relations between labor and management, once declared local, suddenly became a part of interstate commerce as a result of this decision.

Because of his long tenure as President, Roosevelt had the opportunity to virtually reconstitute the Court. As a result, its definition of commerce continued to expand.

The Court upheld the **Fair Labor Standards Act of 1938**, also known as the Wages and Hours Act. This statute put a floor under wages by establishing the first federally guaranteed minimum wage (25 cents an hour). It also put a ceiling over hours by establishing the 40-hour work week as the standard in interstate commerce.[6]

In 1942, a farmer violated crop quotas imposed under the New Deal legislation by planting 23 acres of wheat. The Court upheld the law as a valid regulation of interstate commerce, despite the fact that the farmer was feeding all the wheat to his own animals. The Court reasoned that the farmer, by not buying the wheat, was depressing the worldwide price of grain.[7]

This extremely broad construction of the commerce clause made it appear that nothing was local anymore and that Congress could regulate virtually anything. This broad interpretation of law remained unquestioned until 1995, when a case shocked many Liberals and professional Supreme Court followers.

Responding to a number of widely-publicized crimes on public school grounds, Congress passed the Gun-Free School Zones Act in 1990. The law made it a Federal offense to carry a gun within 1000 feet of any school. Nearly every state already had outlawed such conduct.

Critics said that Congress simply was reacting to political pressures to "do something" to stop school violence. Prime time national television news was covering the story—"kids killing kids"—and the media had aroused the public's rightful indignation. These acts, while horrible, were strictly state and local problems, and, it was argued, state and local officials could deal with them under existing laws. They saw the Federal statute as unnecessary and a violation of the principles of federalism.

Those who supported Congress argued that it clearly could use its power to regulate interstate commerce to control the presence of weapons in public places.

Soon after the law was passed, one Alphonso Lopez, a teenager, took a 38 caliber handgun to school. A U.S. district attorney, rather than leaving the matter to local officials, prosecuted the youth under the new Federal statute. Lopez was convicted and sentenced to six months in Federal prison. His lawyer appealed the conviction on grounds that the Gun-Free School Zones Act violated Texas sovereignty. The Supreme Court agreed, and Lopez was freed.

Speaking for a badly divided Supreme Court (5-4), Chief Justice William Rehnquist said: " … Congress may not use a relatively trivial impact on commerce as an excuse for broad general resolution of state and private activities."[8]

Four justices dissented on grounds that "guns in the schools significantly undermine the quality of education in our nation's classrooms…education has long been inextricably inter-twined with the nation's economy…"

The public accommodations title of the **Civil Rights Act of 1964** was justified by the commerce clause as well. Congress outlawed discrimination in hotels, motels and restaurants. Because both customers and the food they serve move across state boundaries, discrimination handicaps the free flow of interstate commerce. The new statute was quickly challenged by Lester Maddox, an Atlanta restaurateur, who refused to serve Black customers. The Supreme Court upheld the law in *Heart of Atlanta Motel v. U.S.*, 379 U.S. 241 (1965).

Many acts have been made Federal crimes under the commerce clause. If a kidnapper takes a victim across a state line, it becomes a Federal matter. So do crimes involving the use of the mails, or the use of interstate telephone lines in conducting fraudulent businesses activities. Crossing state lines to engage in illegal occupations, such as interstate gambling or interstate prostitution, are matters which may involve the Federal Bureau of Investigation (FBI), as well as state and local police.

B. IMPLIED POWERS

Congress also was given general authority in the final clause of Article I, Section 8, "to make all laws which shall be necessary and proper for carrying into execution the foregoing powers." The relationship of this clause to the enumerated powers preceding it quickly became the subject of major political debate between Federalists and Jeffersonians. The Jeffersonians wanted strict construction of the new Constitution; the Federalists preferred broad construction. The first issue to touch off a major debate was Secretary of the Treasury Alexander Hamilton's plan for a national bank, which was presented to the very first Congress.

Although there was no clear or specific authorization anywhere in the Constitution for Congress to create such a bank, President Washington signed the bill into law. Hamilton persuaded Washington to sign the measure because of his strong arguments for a broad and liberal interpretation of congressional power.

In 1819, in one of the most significant cases in the history of American Federalism, Chief Justice John Marshall gave a definitive statement of the Hamiltonian view in the case of *McCulloch v. Maryland*. Congress had created the Bank of the U.S. and it had been incorporated by statute in 1816. Marshall found implied congressional power to establish a bank in the expressly granted powers to collect taxes, to borrow money, to regulate commerce, to declare and conduct a war.

The Chief Justice analyzed the necessary and proper clause at length. He rejected the strict Jeffersonian interpretation which, he said, "would abridge, and almost annihilate the useful and necessary right of the legislature to select the means." His famous conclusion, widely-quoted in history texts, is as follows: " ...Let the end be legitimate, let it be within the scope of the Constitution, and all means which are appropriate, which are plainly adapted to that end, which are not prohibited, but consistent with the letter and spirit of the constitution are constitutional."[9]

The necessary and proper clause is also called the **elastic clause** because it provides the constitutional system with flexibility. It gives to Congress all those powers that can reasonably be inferred but that are not specifically enumerated in the Constitution. The clause has enabled the national government to deal with problems which the Framers of the Constitution could not possibly have anticipated.

Constitutional lawyers are interested in another category of national powers that have been called **inherent powers** of the national government. These powers are considered to derive from the nation's sovereign authority to ensure its own survival and to achieve the purposes for which it was created. Although there is some disagreement among constitutional scholars, a number of them regard inherent powers as a third kind of national government power, distinct from both expressed and implied.

The View of the States: The 10th Amendment to the Constitution makes it clear that powers not specifically delegated to the national government are to remain with the states and the people. In the original draft of the Constitution, no effort was made to insert such a stipulation because it was regarded as obvious. During the ratification debates, however, assurances were demanded and these demands were met by formally proposing what became the 10th Amendment. It specifies: "The powers not delegated to the United States by the Constitution, nor prohibited by it to the States, are reserved to the States, respectively, or to the people."

It is clear that the 10th Amendment was not intended to limit Federal powers, for its excepts from its effect "powers…delegated to the United States." Nevertheless, those hostile to Federal authority have sometimes tried to erect barriers to Federal action authorized elsewhere in the Constitution.

Chief Justice Roger B. Taney, appointed by President Andrew Jackson, developed the doctrine of **"dual federalism,"** which asserted that the two levels of government were coequal sovereigns and that authority delegated to the national government was limited by the powers reserved to the states in the 10th Amendment. Although dual federalism is no longer operational, some political analysts suggest that it is what President Reagan sought, at least rhetorically, during his eight years in office.

James Bryce, a British scholar who later became a Lord, visited the U.S. in the 1880s and described dual federalism as he saw it: "The characteristic feature and special interest of the American Union is that it shows us two governments covering the same ground, yet distinct and separate in their action. It is like a great factory wherein two sets of machinery are at work, their revolving wheels apparently intermixed, their bands crossing one another, yet each doing its own work without touching or hampering the other…"[10]

Concurrent Powers: are those which can be exercised by both state and Federal governments. The most frequently cited example is the power to tax and spend. States can and do impose taxes on individuals and businesses within their borders. They could not function without the ability to finance their activities. Other concurrent powers include the power to borrow money, to take private property for a public purpose (**eminent domain**) with just compensation, to establish a judicial system and to enforce the laws.

States exercise concurrently with the national government any power that is not specifically delegated to the national government by the Constitution and does not conflict with national law. It is, of course, imperative that governments have enough power to perform their functions.

Concurrent powers reflects the **doctrine of dual sovereignty**, which holds that both national and state governments are sovereign in their own sphere. As noted in the preceding chapter, The Federalist Papers argued that liberty could best be preserved by division of power. It is best that power not be concentrated in any one place. By dividing power between state and nation, the possibility that any one faction would be able to control all centers of political power was reduced.

C. THE SUPREMACY CLAUSE

The U.S. Constitution establishes ground rules for the Federal system by allocating authority to the two levels of government. But conflicts over the division of power and authority are inevitable and debates still occur over whether state or nation should perform certain functions of government. To make Federalism work, an "umpire" was needed to decide contests between states and nation over their respective roles.

The main rule set forth in the Constitution is found in the **"supremacy clause"** of Article VI: "This Constitution, and the laws of the United States which shall be made in pursuance thereof; and all treaties made, or which shall be made, under the authority of the United States, shall be the supreme law of the land; and the judges in every state shall be bound thereby, anything in the Constitution or laws of any state to the contrary notwithstanding…"

The effectiveness of this section was demonstrated in *McCulloch v. Maryland,* previously discussed. Chief Justice Marshall based his opinion on the supremacy clause: "…If any one proposition could command the universal assent of mankind…we might expect it would be this: that the government of the Union, though limited in its powers, is supreme within its sphere of action…no state has any power to retard, impede, burden, or in any manner control the operations of the constitutional laws enacted by Congress."[11]

A more recent example of the Supreme Court acting as an umpire of the Federal system is found in *Philadelphia v. New Jersey,* 437 U.S. 617 (1978). A New Jersey statute forbade bringing into the state "any solid or liquid waste that originated or was collected outside the state." The Court declared the law unconstitutional under the commerce clause, which forbids one state from setting up discriminatory laws designed to isolate itself in the stream of commerce from a problem shared by all.

The commerce clause also prohibits a state from taxing interstate transactions. If you purchase an item by mail from an out-of-state firm, and many people do, you do not have to pay a sales tax on the transaction unless the company has stores in your state. Such a tax would amount to illegal state regulation of interstate commerce.

When Congress legislates in an area in which it has the constitutional authority to act, its laws void all state regulations to the contrary. As a practical matter, it is not always clear that Congress has preempted a given area, since Federal laws seldom stipulate whether all local rules on the matter are suspended. Ultimately, it is up to the Supreme Court to play the role of umpire and define the relationship of Federal and state laws.

Chief Justice Earl Warren tried to codify the tests which the Court has used to guide such decisions. In *Pennsylvania v. Nelson,* 350 U.S. 497 (1956), the Supreme Court developed a three pronged-test. First, is the scheme of Federal regulation so pervasive as to make it a reasonable inference that Congress has left no room for the states? Second, do Federal laws touch a field in which the interest of the national government is so dominant that it must be assumed to preclude state action on the same subject? Third, does enforcement of the state law present a serious danger of conflict with the administration of the Federal program?

In *Nelson,* the Pennsylvania Supreme Court had reversed a conviction under the state sedition act on the ground that the Federal sedition act (the Smith Act of 1940) had superseded state law. The Warren Court agreed. Using the three criteria just described, Warren concluded that Congress, in passing the Smith Act, had assumed sole responsibility for protecting the Federal government from seditious conduct. The Court reached this conclusion, although no express intention to exclude the states was stipulated in that law.

The U.S. Supreme Court enforces the principle of Federal supremacy, as stipulated in the provisions of Article VI. The First Congress, in the Judiciary Act of 1789, further spelled out the tribunal's powers to review decisions of state courts. Section 25 of the law provides judicial review of final judgments of state courts in three categories of cases:

(1) - where the validity of a Federal law of treaty was "drawn into question" and the decision was against its validity;

(2) - where a state law was questioned as repugnant to the Constitution, treaties or laws of the United States, and the decision was in favor of its validity;

(3) - where the construction of the Federal Constitution, treaty or statute was drawn into question and the decision was against the title, right, privilege, or exemption claimed.

These three categories were all based on the principle that, if the Constitution and the laws of the United States were to be enforced, the Supreme Court would have to review decisions of state courts that ruled adversely on asserted Federal rights.

Courts in some states, notably Virginia, did not agree that their decisions were subject to review by the Supreme Court. However, the Supreme Court's authority was firmly asserted and established in two landmark early decisions, *Martin v. Hunter's Lessee* (1816) and *Cohens v. Virginia* (1821)

In *Cohens*, 6 Wheaton 264 (1821), the Supreme Court found that state court decisions are subject to review by the nation's highest court if the case involves a question of Federal law, treaties, or the Constitution, even though the state is a party to the suit. An appeal brought to a Federal court by a defendant convicted in a state criminal court does not constitute a suit against the state, contrary to the 11th Amendment.

Prior to *Cohens*, the Supreme Court held in *Martin v Hunter's Lessee*, 1 Wheaton 304 (1816), that it has the right to review state court decisions involving suits between private individuals when a Federal question is involved. In both cases, the Court stressed that Federal jurisdiction is necessary to establish uniformity of decision throughout the United States on the interpretation of Federal laws, treaties and the Constitution. Otherwise, each state would be supreme, rather than the national government.

D. STATE RESISTANCE TO FEDERAL AUTHORITY

The nature of the Federal Union has been a source of controversy from the very beginning. Ultimately, it brought on the tragedy of the Civil War. In 1861, the issue was slavery, but earlier there had been a number of controversies that led to the development of theories of state resistance to Federal authority.

One controversy was the result of the enactment of the **Alien and Sedition Acts** in 1798. These laws, passed by the Federalist Congress, were aimed at the opposition Jeffersonian party and at aliens who supported the bloody French Revolution. The President was authorized to deport "undesirable aliens" and Congress made it a crime to criticize the government or its officials.

In fact, some 25 persons were jailed for criticizing President John Adams. These laws contributed to Adams' defeat in the election of 1800. Jefferson, the winner of that election, pardoned those convicted under the statutes. This episode was not one of the bright moments in the history of the First Amendment, free speech or free press.[12]

Jefferson and Madison attacked the Alien and Sedition Acts by drafting the Virginia and Kentucky Resolutions and won their adoption in the legislatures of those two states.

In the **Kentucky Resolutions**, Jefferson argued that the states had an "equal right," with the Federal government, to interpret the Constitution and that they could nullify acts passed by Congress which they deemed unauthorized. In the **Virginia Resolutions**, Madison suggested that the states could "interpose" their authority to prevent the exercise by the Federal government of powers not granted by the Constitution.

The use of terms like nullification and interposition sounds very radical and they may have been more threatening to people than Jefferson and Madison intended. But the two future Presidents were certain in their own minds that the Congress had passed legislation forbidden by the Constitution and they set out to resist it. Jefferson's election as President in 1800 was due in part to popular resentment over the **Alien and Sedition Acts**. This conflict ended after Jefferson entered the White House.

Another major challenge to Federal authority was launched by John C. Calhoun in 1828. Calhoun voiced southern opposition to the continual increase in tariff rates between 1816 and 1828. Alarmed by open talk of secession in the South, he offered the **doctrine of nullification** as a substitute, contending that this plan was merely a logical extension of the Virginia and Kentucky Resolutions.

Calhoun maintained that the Constitution was a compact formed by "sovereign and independent communities." The Federal government was not a party to the compact, but an emanation from it, he said, "a joint commission, appointed to superintend and administer the interests in which all are jointly concerned, but having, beyond its proper sphere, no more power than if it did not exist."

Apparently, Calhoun thought that mere recognition of the **right of interposition** would probably "supersede the necessity of its exercise, by impressing on the movements of the Government that moderation and justice so essential to harmony and peace, in a country of such vast extent and diversity of interest as ours."[13]

In 1832, however, South Carolina translated this theory into action by passing a law which "nullified" Federal tariff acts of 1828 and 1832. President Andrew Jackson immediately challenged this action, saying that the power of nullification was "incompatible with the existence of the Union, contradicted expressly by the letter of the Constitution, unauthorized by its spirit, inconsistent with every principle on which it was founded and destructive of the great object for which it was formed."

President Jackson sent Federal ships into Charleston Harbor to enforce the tariff, but when Congress passed a compromise tariff bill with lower rates, South Carolina withdrew its nullification law.

In the years before the War Between the States, southern leaders shifted their ground from nullification to secession. With controversies over slavery and the tariff swirling on around them, the south saw secession as a final remedy to preserve states' rights. John C. Calhoun argued that after a state had interposed its authority to prevent Federal action, the Federal government could appeal to the amending process. If three-fourths of the states upheld the Federal claim, the matter was settled as far as those states were concerned. But the dissenting state was not obliged to acquiesce in all instances. Calhoun said: "That a State, as a party to the constitutional compact, has the right to secede, acting in the same capacity in which it ratified the Constitution, cannot, with any show of reason, be denied by any one who regards the Constitution as a compact, if a power should be inserted by the amending power, which would radically change the character of the Constitution, or the nature of the system."[14]

The debate over the legality of secession ended with the Civil War and the Union victory over the Confederacy. But after the war, the Supreme Court took the case of *Texas v. White* (1869). It considered the question whether or not Texas had ever left the Union. The governor of Texas sued to recover possession of U.S. bonds, acquired in 1850, that the secessionist state legislature had sold to purchase supplies for the Confederate Army. The Court ruled that Texas could recover the bonds. When entering the Union, a state becomes party to an indissoluble relationship. Therefore, ordinances of secession and all other acts intended to give effect to it are null and void. The Court found: "The Constitution, in all its provisions, looks to an indestructible Union composed of indestructible States...Whereas the states, being the parties to the constitutional compact, it follows of necessity that there can be no tribunal above their authority to decide, in the last resort, whether the compact made by them be violated; and, consequently, they must decide themselves, in the last resort, such questions as may be of sufficient magnitude to require their interposition."[15]

E. U.S. OBLIGATIONS TO THE STATES: VERTICAL FEDERALISM

The Constitution imposes on the Federal government a number of obligations to the states. Only one, however, has actually involved any significant Federal action, the responsibility of the U.S. to prevent domestic violence.

Article IV, section 4, reads as follows: "The United States shall guarantee to every State in this Union a Republican Form of Government, and shall protect each of them against Invasion; and on Application of the Legislature, or of the Executive (when the Legislature cannot be convened) against domestic violence."

The U.S. used its military forces to oppose an invasion only in the early years of its national history. That was during the War of 1812 when the British invaded Washington, D.C., and, as every schoolchild knows, set fire to the White House. The British also invaded Baltimore and New Orleans during that conflict. Andrew Jackson's victory over the British in the Battle of New Orleans catapulted him forward as a national hero, a man who eventually was to be elected President of the United States.[16]

The states have asked Federal aid in putting down domestic violence some 16 times. Congress has delegated this responsibility to the President. One of the most notable cases in modern U.S. history occurred in 1967 when Michigan Gov. George Romney asked President Johnson to quell the Detroit riots.[17]

A request from the state is not necessary when domestic violence threatens the enforcement of Federal laws. Article I, Section 8, authorizes Congress to provide for calling forth the militia to execute the laws of the Union, suppress insurrection or repel invasion.

Acting under this authority, President Cleveland sent troops into Chicago in 1894, during the Pullman strike, to keep the trains running. President Eisenhower, in 1957, sent Federal troops to control violence in Little Rock, AR. They were sent to enforce a Federal court order to desegregate the local high school. In 1962, President Kennedy used U.S. marshals and the National Guard to put down violence at the University of Mississippi campus when James Meredith became the first Black student to enroll at "Ole Miss."

Kennedy also called the Alabama National Guard into Federal service in the summer of 1963 and ordered it to enforce a Federally-ordered integration at University of Alabama. In a symbolic act of defiance to Federal authority, Gov. George C. Wallace stood in the doorway, blocking the way of Black students Jimmy Hood and Vivian Malone until the Commander of the Guard asked him to please step aside.[18]

The Federal government has a number of other obligations toward the states. It is to maintain equal representation of the states in the U.S. Senate. It is to guarantee each state "a republican form of government." The Supreme Court, however, has always refused to become involved in issues arising under the **guarantee clause**. It views such disputes as non-justiciable or political. Consequently, they must be decided either by the Congress or the President.

In *Luther v. Borden* (1949), the Supreme Court considered a case which arose in the aftermath of the 1841 Dorr Rebellion, during which two rival governments existed in Rhode Island. One had been elected by residents who met long-standing property qualifications for voting.

The other (Dorr's) was based on an informal election under universal manhood suffrage. At the request of the "regular" government, President John Tyler ordered militia into the state and Dorr's regime collapsed.

In interpreting Article IV, section 4, of the Constitution, the Supreme Court refused to rule on which government was "republican" in form or whether or not President Tyler had been justified in suppressing "domestic violence." The Court ruled instead that these were "political questions" which should be resolved by Congress and/or the President.[19]

The Court, in 1912, refused to decide whether provisions of the Oregon Constitution, which permitted "direct democracy" by the people through procedures known as the initiative and referendum, denied the state a republican form of government. The phone company had asked the Supreme Court to invalidate an Oregon tax measure enacted by popular initiative, contending that the initiative had made the government unrepresentative and therefore not republican.[20]

Obligations of the States to the Union: The Constitution imposes few obligations on the states toward the Union. As noted above, they must maintain a "republican form of government" and preserve peace within their borders. They must also conduct elections for members of Congress, fill congressional vacancies when they occur and choose presidential electors. Finally, under provisions of Article V, they must consider proposed constitutional amendments.

F. INTERSTATE RELATIONS: HORIZONTAL FEDERALISM

Under the Constitution, each of the 50 states has certain obligations in its relationships with sister states. States are required to extend the same **privileges and immunities** to citizens from other states that their own citizens enjoy. Out-of-state residents have the right to make contracts in the state, own property and have access to the courts, as do the state's own citizens.

However, the privileges and immunities clause in Article IV, Section 2, does not prevent a state from treating citizens of other states differently when there are good reasons why the two groups should be placed on different footings. Practice of such professions as law and medicine can be restricted to those licensed by the state. Persons moving into a state from outside can be prevented from voting until they have resided in the state for a certain period. Students from outside a state can be charged higher tuition in a state university than residents of the state.

It should be noted, however, that the Supreme Court ruled, in *Vlandis v. Kline,* 412 U.S. 441 (1973), that a Connecticut law which required students admitted to state universities as nonresidents to pay nonresident tuition for their entire four years was an unconstitutional violation of due process. A Washington state law requiring a year of residence in the state to qualify as a resident for tuition purposes was upheld in *Sturgis v. Washington* (1973).[21]

Another obligation is that each state must give **full faith and credit** to the public acts, records and judicial proceedings of every other state. A court ruling in one state can, if properly authenticated, be enforced in another state. Divorces granted in one state are generally recognized in all other states. Before the advent of the "no fault" concept, which made divorce easy in the 1970s, Nevada was the divorce capital of the nation. People with means could fly to Nevada, establish "residence" by living there for six weeks, and shed a spouse. In most states, divorce was based on an adversarial procedure, where "fault" had to be established. Grounds for divorce varied widely. In New York state, there was only one ground for divorce and that was adultery.

When Gov. Nelson Rockefeller of New York, widely considered a leading Republican presidential possibility at the time, decided to obtain a divorce from his wife of some 31 years, it was necessary for Mrs. Rockefeller to fly to Nevada, establish residence and divorce the governor. It would have ended Rockefeller's political career for his wife to sue in New York on grounds of adultery. In those days, of course, it was not "gentlemanly" to divorce one's wife; she divorced you.

Governor Rockefeller later remarried and the second Mrs. Rockefeller gave birth to a child on the eve of the California presidential primary in 1964. Rockefeller and Arizona Senator Barry Goldwater were battling it out for the GOP nomination. The birth of a child, usually a "happy event," reminded voters of the messy Rockefeller divorce and caused one political pundit to say that: "Nelson Rockefeller is the first man in American political history to turn motherhood into a liability!" Goldwater won the nomination, but was the victim of President Johnson's landslide victory.

As a result of changing mores and a more tolerant attitude toward divorce, Rockefeller eventually emerged in a position of national prominence. President Ford, acting under authority granted by the 25th Amendment, named Rockefeller, in 1974, as the first appointed vice president in U.S. history.[22]

The full faith and credit clause seldom has been at the center of controversy. It was taken virtually word for word from the Articles of Confederation. But, in 1996, the clause became the center of a heated public debate over same-sex marriages. A court in Hawaii held that it was illegal to deny persons of the same sex the right to marry under the state constitution.

People in other states feared that the decision in Hawaii would cause gay couples to travel there, marry, and upon returning to their home state, seek to have the marriage recognized under the full faith and credit clause of the U.S. Constitution.

No state except Hawaii then recognized same-sex marriages, although several do in 2009. More than a dozen states have enacted statutes specifically declaring that they would not acknowledge such marriages, even if they were sanctioned in another state.

After extensive debate, Congress exercised its power under Article IV, Section 1, which provides that Congress "may by general Laws prescribe the Manner in which such (state) Acts, Records and Proceedings shall be proved, and the Effect thereof." **The Defense of Marriage Act,** passed in the fall of 1996 and signed by President Clinton, provides that no state shall be required to give effect to any same-sex marriage that is treated as a marriage under the law of another state.

A state, however, is free to grant such recognition if it chooses to do so.

Extradition: Article IV, Section 2 provides that: "…A person charged in any State with Treason, Felony, or other Crime, who shall flee from Justice and be found in another State, shall on demand of the executive Authority of the State from which he fled, be delivered up, to be removed to the State having jurisdiction of the Crime."

Although this language may seem clear enough, the Supreme Court has held that the Federal government cannot force a state official to take such action, and governors sometimes do refuse to honor extradition requests. Three examples:

Michigan Gov. William Milliken refused to extradite Paul Branzburg to Kentucky. That state sought the return of a former *Louisville Courier Journal* reporter, found guilty of contempt of court for refusing to surrender his notes to a Clay County, KY, Grand Jury. Branzburg had written a series of articles on drug dealing in the Louisville area.

Branzburg wanted to protect his news sources for both ethical and practical reasons. He knew that "burning a source" would destroy his credibility as a reporter. But the courts rejected the argument that reporters had a "privileged relationship" with a source. After exhausting all of his appeals in Kentucky and losing in the U.S. Supreme Court, Branzburg had limited options.

He could comply with the court order, go to jail or stay of out Kentucky. He chose the latter option and got a job as a reporter on the Detroit *Free Press*.[23]

Several years ago, the governor of Indiana refused to extradite Indiana University basketball coach Bobby Knight to Puerto Rico, an American territory. Knight had been convicted *in absentia* by a Puerto Rican court of assaulting a police officer during the Pan American Games. The governor of Puerto Rico dropped the matter, rather than pursue it in the courts.

More recently, and on a much more serious life-and-death matter, Oklahoma Gov. David Walters demanded that New York Gov. Mario Cuomo perform his "moral duty" to extradite convicted killer Thomas Grasso from New York to Oklahoma. Grasso had been convicted of a second felony in New York and was serving a sentence of 20 years to life in Sing Sing prison. Walters said that Cuomo, an outspoken opponent of the death penalty, was trying to prevent Oklahoma from exercising its right to capital punishment. After Cuomo's defeat in 1994, Gov. George Pataki, a supporter of the death penalty, extradited Grasso to Oklahoma, where he was executed by lethal injection on March 20, 1995.

Most criminal law is state law. Usually people who murder, rape, steal or commit arson are not breaking Federal laws. When states seek extradition of these kinds of fugitives, governors ordinarily are happy to comply with the requests. They do not wish to harbor fugitives from justice. Nor do they wish to have their own future extradition requests denied.

One should also note that Congress has made it a Federal crime for a fugitive from justice to flee from one state to another with the intent of avoiding prosecution or imprisonment.

Federalism in Theory and in Practice: The constitutional provisions discussed thus far establish a framework in which the Federal system operates. Actual relationships between nation and state will vary from one era of U.S. history to another. Different popular demands and expectations are translated through the American political process into government decisions. Over the broad sweep of U.S. history, there is a clear trend in the direction of placing greater power and authority in the hands of the Federal government.

During the 20th Century, two world wars, the Cold War and the Great Depression have all been major contributing factors toward this development. The New Deal-Fair Deal of Presidents Roosevelt and Truman set the stage for the growth and development of the Welfare State in America. This was sharply accelerated during the administrations of John F. Kennedy and Lyndon Johnson. The latter's Great Society added to popular expectations of what government could and should do for the American people, or at least a segment of the American people.

Yet there have been periods during which the centralizing trend was reversed. The central-local relationship is the product of political conflict, compromise and consensus.

We have had competitive theories of federalism for almost 150 years. The basic question has always been the same: which level of government should have the most power? The adoption of the Constitution was itself a major victory for those who favored the Hamiltonian dream of a **nation-centered federalism**. Washington, Hamilton and Chief Justice John Marshall all emphasized national supremacy. They believed that the new Constitution embodied the will of the American people and that the national government, created by the people, should have the greatest legal authority to serve the people's needs. They also believed in **broad interpretation of the Constitution**.

But the Jeffersonians, who advocated **state-centered federalism**, won the election of 1800 and ultimately destroyed the Federalist party. Jefferson and John C. Calhoun argued that the Constitution was the result of state action. States sent delegates to the Philadelphia Convention, and it was the states which ratified the document and made it the law of the land. State-centered federalism rests on the assumption that the Federal government is one of enumerated powers and that these powers should be interpreted as narrowly as possible. If government goes beyond its enumerated power and authority, it is infringing on the legitimate power of the states.

Like so many Presidents who have followed him, Jefferson never let his "principles" get in the way when the public interest required a major decision which conflicted with ideology. One of the things for which Jefferson is best remembered is the **Louisiana Purchase**. The territory, which gave the U.S. a tract of land of some 828,000 square miles, was purchased from Napoleon's France for about $15 million.

Although he could hardly reconcile that deal with "strict interpretation" of the Constitution, strong Federal action here was clearly in the lasting public interest of the United States. Ideological consistency was totally absent in the case of the purchase. Jefferson took a strict, rather than broad, constructionist view of the Constitution. The Federalists took precisely the opposite view. In this case, both sides reversed positions. The most significant thing was that the U.S. Senate ratified the treaty, 24-7, and the United States concluded one of the best real estate deals in its history.[24]

Despite the fact that they disappeared as a major factor in national politics by 1816, the Federalists were able to keep their ideology alive as John Marshall and the Supreme Court broadened constitutional interpretations of Federal power. However, when Chief Justice Roger B. Taney succeeded Marshall, the pendulum swung back in the direction of state powers.

After the Civil War, the nation witnessed the development of sectional politics. The Republican Party emerged as the dominant force, representing the views of the east and midwest. The Democratic Party became the voice of states' rights and the advocate of the south. So much so that from the time of Reconstruction until 1928, not a single southern state ever cast an electoral vote for a Republican presidential candidate.

After Woodrow Wilson's victory in 1912, however, the Democrats began to rethink their position. The necessity of using the powers of the Federal government to "wage war successfully" greatly contributed to the growth of Washington's influence on American life. The trend was accelerated by the Great Depression and the advent of Franklin Roosevelt's New Deal.

The notion of dual federalism, in which governmental functions are divided between Washington and the states, dominated until the age of FDR. It clearly was supported by the Supreme Court until the late 1930s.

Since the New Deal, we have seen the evolution of **cooperative federalism**. The system has been modified in an attempt to deal more effectively with problems of an urban, industrial society. States and local governments have often been hard-pressed financially, and have been either unable or unwilling to meet the costs of many public services. Americans have come to expect and demand more, in areas such as education, health care, transportation and social welfare.

From the perspective of the states, the national government has preempted the most productive revenue source, the personal income tax. As national wealth increases, so do Federal tax revenues. The states rely on a variety of sources to finance their activities. These include small personal and business income taxes, sales taxes and excise taxes on products like alcohol and tobacco. Community governments have historically depended on the real estate taxes.

There are great disparities of wealth in the individual states. Some, like Mississippi, Alabama and Arkansas, are poor. Others, like Connecticut and Delaware, are relatively wealthy. There are also regional economic differences within states, where some cities and counties are relatively well off and others relatively poor.

For most of the 20th Century, this fiscal dilemma of federalism has been clear. People want more public services at the state and local level. These are expensive, and state and community governments lack the tax base to finance them. Federal government, on the other hand, has a much greater tax base and relatively few basic domestic programs that it is constitutionally required to finance.

Political leaders have tried to resolve this dilemma by a system of cooperative federalism. This concept views states and the national government not as antagonistic competitors for power, but rather as cooperating partners in carrying out public service. The system is characterized by joint operations of Federal and state governments and the expanded use of grants-in-aid.

A **grant-in-aid** is money given by a higher level of government to a lower level to be used to pay for some specific program, such as highway construction or law enforcement. The emphasis is on cooperation between state and local governments and the U.S. in achieving goals set by the national government.

Congress, one should note, has no direct constitutional authority to regulate public health, safety or welfare. But it does have the enormous power of the Federal purse strings. It can use its authority to tax and spend for the general welfare to induce states to carry out programs desired by Congress.

During the New Deal, cooperative federalism was the dominant theory. Several programs that required both financial and administrative cooperation between U.S. and state authorities were undertaken. Most New Deal programs were financed by grants-in-aid and all of them were **categorical.**

As the term suggests, Federal money was to be used for specific, narrowly-defined purposes. They also were considered **matching grants**, that is, state and local governments were required to pay some of the costs of the project. From 1932-52, Republicans generally criticized the New Deal-Fair Deal and Dwight Eisenhower pledged to reverse the centralization trends.[25]

Kennedy and Johnson created new and expanded roles for the Federal government. Federal aid to education, begun during the Eisenhower Administration with the **National Defense Education Act of 1958,** was accelerated.

One of the major accomplishments of the Johnson years was the **Elementary and Secondary Education Act of 1965**. Johnson's administration also championed enforcement of voting rights and many other new civil rights measures. It probably is not an overstatement to say that LBJ changed the nature of American politics, as well as the relationships between Washington and the states. This was particularly the case as far as the border and southern states were concerned.

When Congress passed the **Civil Rights Act of 1964**, many southern states deserted the Democratic Party and voted for Republican presidential nominee Barry Goldwater. The south also resisted the Voting Rights Act of 1965. In fact, South Carolina filed a suit in the Supreme Court, arguing that the statute violated "reserved powers" and the 10th Amendment's guarantee of rights to the states and the people. Nonetheless, the Court upheld the law.[26]

Johnson saw not only major social legislation enacted during this presidency, but also the beginning of a new form of federalism. It was characterized as **centralized federalism** and entailed tighter controls over grant-in-aid money by the U.S. Johnson used the proverbial "carrot" to induce state and local communities to initiate programs that they otherwise might not have undertaken.

Although some leaders in both parties applauded some of Johnson's social programs, others disliked Washington's growing power. Johnson made no bones about it: Washington would define the agenda and set national goals. State and local roles in defining national problems were to be minimal. In effect, what was called centralized federalism was really centralized government. Some of the President's critics even suggested that American federalism was moving in the direction of unitary government.

Richard Nixon ran as a Conservative in 1968. He pledged to reduce centralization in Washington. After he took office, Nixon made some progress in this direction. He announced a **"new federalism"** designed to restore the balance of power between the Federal government and the states. The centerpiece of his program was **general revenue sharing**. This was a system of financial aid in which a portion of Federal tax money was returned to the states and cities with no strings attached.

The Nixon Administration also made greater use of the **block grant**. A block grant is a sum of money given by the U.S. to state or local governments to be used for a broad, general purpose. If a city received a Federal block grant for law enforcement, it then could decide for itself whether to buy more squad cars or computers, or improved communications systems. This, many Conservatives said, was ideal in that the government closest to problems was best able to decide how to use money to solve them.

Revenue sharing lasted until 1986, when President Reagan ended it.

During its 14-year existence, revenue sharing had distributed some $83 billion to state and local governments. But the growing, enormous Federal budgetary deficits of the Reagan Administration resulted in erosion of support for the program in Congress.

During the Nixon years, Congress passed legislation which imposed minimum wages and overtime provisions on state government employees who performed governmental functions. States protested that this infringed on their sovereignty and violated the 10th Amendment to the U.S. Constitution. The matter was not decided by the Supreme Court until 1985, when it gave its approval to this highly centralized federalism by backing congressional authority to enact such laws. The Court held that the rights of the states are protected through their representation in Congress and by their role in the election of the President, not by the Supreme Court or the 10th Amendment.[27]

The Nixon Administration, Conservative in theory, was not always that in fact. It set up a national price control system, in 1971, in order to control inflation. It also advocated national assumption of the welfare burden and a national system of medical insurance, neither of which the Democrats, who controlled Congress, would enact.

Ronald Reagan clearly was the most Conservative President since Hoover. He understood some of the problems of the states, given his years in office as governor of California. In his first inaugural address in January, 1981, Reagan said that states had primary responsibility for governing in most policy areas. He promised that he would "restore the balance between levels of government."[28]

Reagan hoped to increase the flexibility of the Federal grant-in-aid system and reduce Federal involvement in state domestic affairs. He tried to achieve this by combining existing categorical grant programs into larger, more loosely defined block grants, and by dividing major responsibilities between the U.S. and state governments.

At bottom was Reagan's philosophical opposition to huge Federal domestic spending programs. This forced a cutback in spending for state and local governments during the 1980s, and shifted some responsibility for policy back to the states. Reagan clearly preferred the older concept of dual federalism.

Initially, some governors, particularly those who were Republican Conservatives, applauded the new President's ideas. But they soon realized that they were going to get less money from Washington while they were asked to assume more responsibility for government programs. Congress did block some of Reagan's proposals, such as elimination of Federal grants for Aid to Families with Dependent Children (AFDC).

One of the great myths of American politics is that President Reagan sharply reduced spending for domestic programs. Not true! Although total costs for Federal grants did decline during his first year in office, the cost of grant programs increased throughout the rest of his two terms. During fiscal 1982, for example, the Federal government spent about $88 billion on state and local grants. By fiscal 1989, the amount had increased to about $124 billion.

President Bush, who succeeded Reagan, made no effort to curtail Federal spending and the amount of Federal aid to the states grew throughout his term.

During the 1994 mid-term congressional elections, the Republicans made welfare reform a major item on their national agenda. After they achieved what a *Washington Post* headline called a political "Earthquake," the GOP passed three welfare reform bills. President Clinton, who had promised, in his 1992 campaign for the White House, to "end welfare as we know it," vetoed the first two, but in August, 1996, signed the third bill.

It was the first time in 40 years that the Republican Party had captured control of both houses of Congress. In 1996, President Clinton won re-election over Senate Majority Leader Bob Dole of Kansas. But the GOP maintained control in both House and Senate.

The new welfare statute, effective October 1, 1996, required Congress to appropriate about $16 billion a year to the states, through the year 2002. The states were to receive the funds in the form of block grants based on the number of welfare recipients in the state. This was matched, in part, by the states. The law established a five-year limit on the length of time individual clients could receive welfare benefits.

The major goal of the law is to move people off welfare rolls and on to payrolls. States are given considerable latitude to establish their own programs to achieve this objective. The new law requires welfare clients to work. They must find work within two years. It was estimated that the new system would save about $55 billion over a six-year period. Some $27 billion of this was in food stamps alone.

Basically, the Federal government has shifted the burden of the welfare system back to the states. Until the Great Depression, welfare had been considered the primary responsibility of state and local governments, rather than the national government. Herbert Hoover, in fact, was slow to act after the collapse of the stock market because he believed that he lacked the constitutional authority to do so.

It may be too soon to conclude that, because of the welfare reform bill of 1996, federalism will take a different path in the 21st Century than it has in the past 75 years. Public opinion is notoriously fickle. Today, the public may be dissatisfied with centralized government. Many state governors and legislatures may prefer more freedom from Federal controls. But one cannot be certain that the political pendulum will not swing back tomorrow.

One of the favorite ideas of President Reagan and many of his Conservative Republican colleagues on Capitol Hill was **"devolution."** Essentially, the concept means that activities which have long been undertaken by the national government ought to be returned "where they belong," to state and local authorities.

The concept took hold in the 1990s, with the devolution of responsibilities to state and local governments. This is compatible with a long-established, earlier American tradition. Nearly a century ago, James (Lord) Bryce commented on the major role played by community governments in the American Federal system. He wrote: "It is the business of a local authority to mend the roads, to clean out the village well or to provide a new pump, to see that there is a place where straying beasts may be kept until the owner reclaims them, to fix the number of cattle each villager may turn out on the common pasture, and to give each his share of timber cut in the common woodland."[29]

The American experience suggests that ideologies and Supreme Court decisions, while not irrelevant to the march of our Federal experiment, may well be of secondary importance. Wars, urbanization and "revolutions" in transportation and communication all have created problems. The national government has been considered best equipped to deal with them, as well as to promote a growing and stable economy.

For most of American history, nation and state each remained supreme within its own sphere. The national government, for example, had clear-cut control over military and foreign policy, the post office and monetary policy. States had the primary, if not exclusive responsibility, for education, law enforcement and highways. The oft-used analogy was that of a layer cake. Layers of government were distinct and proponents of dual federalism urged that the powers of national government be interpreted narrowly.

From the era of Franklin Roosevelt until today, most political scientists have argued that dual federalism is out of date. They characterized the current system as one of **cooperative federalism**. Rather than the layer cake, they see a marble cake, with blurred distinctions and mingled responsibilities between state, nation and local community.

Costs may be shared, with both Washington and state and local governments paying a part of the bill. Municipalities and states can get Federal money for such things as airports, sewerage treatment plants and many other purposes. However, they must agree to bear their share of the costs involved. Administration may also be shared with state and community officials working under Federal guidelines. Each year, the Labor department gives billions of dollars to the 50 states to retrain unemployed workers. How they train them may be up to the states. But when these programs don't work, there is also plenty of blame to share.

Professors in introductory economics courses usually tell their students that there is no such thing as a "free" lunch. Most Federal grants to states and municipalities come with strings attached. Congress can and does attach strings to such things as grants for state highway construction. If you want the money—and billions of dollars are involved—you must pass legislation at the state level raising the drinking age to 21. Then you must enforce the law.[30]

G. THE CASE FOR FEDERALISM

Why do we have a Federal system of government? As noted in the preceding chapter, the delegates to the 1787 Philadelphia Constitutional Convention did not really have any other choice. The Articles of Confederation had been tried, and had been found inadequate to the needs of the new nation. Unitary government was simply out of the question. It was characterized by centralization of power and authority, and was associated with the British abuse of power, which brought on the Revolution. The American people also had grown attached to their state governments and disliked the prospects of centralized rule. Federalism was the only viable alternative.

The Federal system is largely the result of a compromise between the delegates to the Constitutional Convention. Advocates of a stronger national government clashed with proponents of states' rights. But both sides had political pragmatists in their midst. Without federalism which retained state power while establishing a strong national government, there could be no new Constitution,

It may be difficult for today's students to contemplate the world of 1787. One should remember that both travel and communication were slow. The 13 states were larger than England and France. Too much centralization was impractical because it could take weeks for all of the states to be informed of a political decision.

One should keep in mind that the Federal form of government has many advantages. They include the following:

1. National Unity with Diversity

The national motto of the United States is *"E Pluribus Unum."* It means essentially, "one from many." Political scientists, especially those who specialize in Comparative Government, often have cited federalism as the ideal form of government when a nation is large and diverse. The American nation was and is composed of a heterogeneous people. They are spread over a nation that is continental in size.

Political scientists long have held that federalism is most appropriate where different cultures, languages, religions and ethnic backgrounds are present. Yet sometimes this is not enough for **separatists.** The Canadian province of Quebec is a good illustration of the problems of cultural diversity. Most residents of Quebec speak French and have a French culture. For years, they have sought more freedom from the Canadian Federal government. In 1995, these separatists who wanted Quebec to "leave Canada" and deal with the world as a sovereign nation nearly won their goal. They failed by only a few thousand votes when the question was put to the Canadian nation in a referendum.[31]

There is a great advantage, as Thomas Jefferson suggested long ago, in having people who are closest to a problem deal with it. "The closer the government to the people, the better" is an old motto. Simply put, the national government can "farm out" governmental functions to state and local communities.

Thousands of citizens are involved each day in the activities of their state and local communities. They serve on school boards, city councils and county boards, neighborhood associations and a wide variety of local boards and commissions. They are gaining experience in "grassroots democracy" and serving an apprenticeship for possible higher office.

Nonetheless, state and local governments are training grounds for future national leaders. Many council members and mayors have later served in Congress, as governors or even on the U.S. Supreme Court. But while they are local officials, they very likely believe that they know best what needs to be done in their communities.

Historically, state governors have proved to be excellent presidential candidates. Within the past generation, Jimmy Carter of Georgia, Ronald Reagan of California, Bill Clinton of Arkansas, and George W. Bush of Texas have used the governor's chair as a springboard to the White House.

In a Federal system, the President and Congress do not have to deal with every state and local problem. Issues such as marriage and divorce laws, legalized gambling, financing of public education and capital punishment all are fought out on state and local political battlegrounds. Washington, according to this line of reasoning, has enough to do.

State legislatures, county court houses and municipal buildings may be the appropriate places for citizens to deal with their problems, rather than running to Washington to seek solutions to every problem of modern life.

One should also note that there are many subcultures in the U.S. They divide along the lines of race, religion, ethnicity, wealth, education, sexual preferences and other factors. The political subcultures often are able to influence state and local officials more readily than they can the national government.

2. The Laboratory Argument

Another argument on behalf of federalism is that state and local governments can serve as **centers for experimentation**. Try a new program or policy and see if it works. If it does, fine. Then other states, or perhaps even the President and Congress, can follow the example. If not, the negative impact is not as great as if the "experiment" had been tried on the entire nation. In short, states serve as proving grounds for public policies.

Unemployment compensation did not originate in Congress, but rather was pioneered by the state of Wisconsin. Georgia decided it was worthwhile to permit 18-year-olds to vote during World War II. Some critics suggested that the intellectual requirements for shooting and voting may be different, but a few other states followed suit. Kentucky, Georgia, Alaska and Hawaii all permitted youths under the age of 21 to vote before the ratification of the 26th Amendment.

The state of California has been at the forefront in many experiments, some of which have been adopted later by the national government. Examples include air pollution control and auto emission standards. Today some states, like Hawaii and Oregon, are pioneering new health care delivery systems.

Nebraska has pioneered in the use of a unicameral legislature. No other state has seen fit to follow its example, although some states (California and Minnesota) have had discussions about it.

Oregon today is permitting its electorate to cast ballots by mail. Nevada is the only state to permit statewide legalized gambling, although more than half of the states permit some aspects of legalized casino gambling. Are these good ideas? Bad ideas? The answer to these questions depends upon one's own system of values, but in a Federal system, such experiments can be tried and evaluated before other state and local governments follow. Or the people and public officials observing these experiments may choose simply to brush them off as "local eccentricities."

One should note that there are more than 86,000 governments in the U.S. There is only one national government and 50 states. The largest number of public officials clearly operate at the level of county, municipality, township, special districts and school districts. The potential for new ideas and experiments is enormous.[32]

3. Check on Arbitrary National Power

One argument which carried some weight in 1787 was that federalism would check the power and authority of the central government. The national regime was to have only delegated or enumerated powers. The states were still to be of first importance. The tradition of strong state and local governments is deeply rooted in the American past.

The Framers of the Constitution feared that a single interest might capture control of the national government and attempt to suppress the truly national interest. They hoped that the very size of the nation and the great diversity of interests within it would check these factions. James Madison, in *The Federalist, Number 10,* stressed the fact that a Federal system would serve as a check on the power of the national government.

One might note that national histories and cultures vary enormously throughout the world. Although Americans tend to believe that federalism serves to check national power, such has not always been the case. While some unitary governments (but not most of them) are democratic, some Federal systems are totalitarian. The former Union of Soviet Socialist Republics was one of the most totalitarian police states in world history under the tyranny of Joseph Stalin and some of his successors.

When the U.S.S.R. proclaimed a new basic law in 1936, called the **Stalin Constitution**, it even gave Union Republics (in theory analogous to American states) the right to secede. This was pure Soviet propaganda, contrasting it to the experience of the U.S. and the Confederate states. When Stalin was asked what would happen if, in fact, a Soviet Republic attempted to withdraw from the Soviet Union, he replied, "Well, of course it wouldn't want to."

After the collapse of the Soviet Union in 1991, the Russian Republic became its successor state, again adopting the Federal form. In this instance, one of the main reasons was to attempt to prevent the rise of a new dictatorship and to protect ethnic minorities.

Following the defeat of Hitler and the Nazis in World War II, West Germany created the Federal (Bonn) Republic. It was designed to prevent the rise of another tyrant and to protect liberty in the infant democratic state. Included in the Constitution of the Bonn Republic was judicial review, one of the few original American contributions to the art of government.

Given the fact that Hitler and the Nazis used German courts to rubber stamp their atrocities, the founders of the Republic readily agreed to incorporate this check on executive and legislative authority in their new Federal system. After the collapse of Communism and the East German Peoples Republic, a Soviet satellite regime, Germany reunited under a democratic Federal system.[33]

Federal systems differ greatly. As we have seen, under the U.S. Constitution, the national government is one of delegated or enumerated powers. The states, under the 10th Amendment, exercise reserved powers. In the Canadian system, the constitutional distribution of powers is precisely the opposite. The provinces (equivalent to states) have delegated powers. Powers not specifically delegated to them are reserved to the national government.[34]

H. THE CASE AGAINST FEDERALISM

1. Inadequate Resources and Public Services

Not all political scientists admire federalism. They point out that most governments in the world today are unitary states. Decentralization of power and authority bring problems, not the least of which is that state and local communities may lack sufficient resources to provide adequate public services to their citizens. In other cases, they have the resources, but not the will, to spend tax dollars on schools, highways and other necessities.

The quality of education a child receives depends on the accident of birth. Where did his or her parents reside? Some states spend considerably more money on public education than others. In 1993, for example, New Jersey spent nearly $10,000 on each school child within the state. Utah, on the other hand, spent only a little more than $3200.[35]

One of the major fiscal problems of state and local governments in recent years has been that of **unfunded mandates**. This is the imposition of Federal regulations on state and local communities without appropriating enough money to cover their costs. It may be well and good to require equal access to public facilities by disabled persons, but who is going to pay the construction costs to bring old facilities into compliance?

Clean air is highly desirable, but who is going to pay the cost of reducing air pollution? Perhaps there also is a need for an increase in Medicaid services to the poor, but should the Federal government require states to provide them without giving them the funds?

Between 1931 and 1960, Congress passed only 11 unfunded mandates. During the next 20 years, it passed more than 50, a trend that continued at the end of the 20th Century and the beginning of the 21st.

President George W. Bush came to office as a former governor of Texas and spoke fondly of devolution, restoring power to the states. He was a bit inconsistent; witness the No Child Left Behind Act, enlarging the Federal role in education. But more than anything else, it was the events of September 11, 2001, when national power became his focus.

Political philosophy sometimes yields to pragmatism when parties want to win elections. Rigid ideologues don't win many votes. After the nation's economy failed in September, 2008, the President, despite his philosophical reservations, pushed for a national bailout. Many congressional Republicans fought their President on this. Eventually, however, the Secretary of the Treasury was authorized to rescue financial institutions buried under a mountain of bad debt.

The Obama administration has intervened as perhaps no other since the Great Depression. Economic stimulus programs and government dictation of terms for bailouts by banks and auto companies became topics of heated debate in Barack Obama's "First 100 Days."

2. Inadequate Public Interest and Participation in State and Local Government

Thomas Jefferson is associated with the statement, "The closer the government is to the people, the better." A modern corollary to that may well be: "The closer the government is to the people, the less likely they are to pay attention to it."

Many studies have been undertaken of political participation at various levels of government. They all show basically the same thing. Participation is greatest in presidential elections. It is next largest in congressional and gubernatorial contests. It is smallest in local contests.

This is not to suggest that local government is unimportant. Far from it. It may, however, be suffering from general neglect. The obvious exception to this occurs when a change in tax structure is suggested. If a city council concludes that it may have to impose a new municipal income tax, citizen interest level picks up. The same may be said of a decision by the county board or the state legislature. When a tax measure is placed on the ballot in the form of a popular referendum, turnout soars.

But the work of cities, counties, townships, villages and other local governments is not all that interesting to most people. The press typically pays little attention to it, other than brief reference to meetings in its "calendar of events." Although issues such as the environment are of great significance, few reporters want to write stories about sludge problems and fewer newspaper subscribers care to read them.

Few citizens ever have attended meetings of their city council. Fewer still have attended meetings of the county board. Charles Adrian refers to county government as "the lost continent of American Politics" in his textbook, *State and Local Governments*. Adrian writes: "…in America there is frequently a great deal of difficulty in getting a public position filled. Not only is there no competition for the job, but there is sometimes no one who will even allow himself to be drafted for it.

The small town, the township, the suburb and the school district often present scenes, not of strident conflict, but of citizens putting pressures on other citizens to accept jobs that need to be done. These are positions that carry not a little prestige but involve the budgeting of a considerable amount of what would otherwise be leisure time for the individual."[36]

3. Domination of State and Local Government by Powerful Interests

Business, labor and agricultural interests often find it easier to dominate state and local governments than to have their way at the national level. Interests vary from state to state, but clearly some are able to exert vast influence in the states. Oil and natural gas producers have been dominant forces in the politics of states like Texas, Oklahoma and Louisiana. Tobacco farmers have had a profound impact in states like Virginia, North Carolina, Kentucky and Tennessee. Copper mining interests have "been heard" in Montana. Labor unions have historically been strong in Michigan, while dairy farmers and beer barons have had a significant impact in Wisconsin.

Federalism permits concentrated interests to gain substantial influence in the election of public officials at both state and congressional levels. These "pressure groups" promote policies not only in state capitals, but also in Washington, D.C., where they are "represented" by members of House and Senate from states in which they are dominant.

Although they may not like the labels used by media, members of Congress have been singled out for their representation of special interests. The late Henry Jackson (D., WA) was called the "senator from Boeing," reflecting the fact that the aircraft industry was dominant in Jackson's home state. A Liberal in domestic policy, Jackson never met a defense contract, particularly for a new bomber being built in Seattle, that he did not like.

Political opponents have always liked to trade barbs. Michigan Republicans have sometimes called Democratic senators from that state, "the senator from the UAW." Democrats have countered by referring to past Republican senators as "the senator from General Motors."

James Madison saw nothing wrong in this system of checks and balances. Neither did former Harvard economist John Kenneth Galbraith, a Liberal Democrat who describes the process of **"countervailing power"** in his book, *American Capitalism.* Pluralism of interests is valued in a nation as large and diverse as the American Republic.[37]

4. Move toward Centralization

Some critics of American federalism argue that it has evolved in a way contrary to the intent of the Framers since the 1930s. Federal systems, some political scientists agree, tend to move in one of two directions. They either move toward centralization, resembling unitary governments, or they tend to break down and resemble confederations.

Conservatives in particular lament the expansion of national power and authority at the expense of the states. In an 1981 address to the National Conference of State Legislatures in Atlanta, President Reagan said:

"The Founding Fathers saw the federalist system as constructed something like a masonry wall. The States are the bricks, the national government is the mortar…Unfortunately, over the years, many people have increasingly come to believe that Washington is the whole wall."

IV. PRESIDENTIAL POWER AND AUTHORITY

A. PRESIDENTIAL ROLES

What are the major tasks—traditional and modern—of the American President? What roles must he play, what powers must he have? Merriman Smith, late White House news correspondent for United Press International, once wrote that a President "is many men." He wears, in short, a number of hats and plays a number of different roles.[1]

Although political scientists may use slightly idiosyncratic jargon to enumerate some functions which they consider more important than do some of their colleagues, there is a consensus that six roles are vital to the "job description." What are they?

1. Chief Executive

Article II of the U.S. Constitution provides that "the executive power shall be vested in a President of the United States of America." It also stipulates that he shall take care that the laws be faithfully executed. Under this grant of power, the President runs the executive branch of the Federal government. When we say that the President is the Chief Executive, we mean that he is the head of a vast bureaucracy. The executive branch of government numbers roughly three million civilian employees. About another million and a half are in the armed forces.

He is responsible for the operations of the executive branch with its many departments, bureaus and agencies. He executes the laws, whether he likes them or not.

Former President Truman had a sign on his desk which said, "The Buck Stops Here." This is a clear view of responsibility, although no President really can control that many people. Presidents must be willing to delegate much of their administrative authority. They can, however, set a tone and clearly define what is expected of executive branch employees. Presidents, however, must depend upon their subordinates.

Like Chief Executive Officers (CEOs) of major corporations, Presidents are assisted by staffs which advise them. White House staffers who long have been close to the President are the ones most likely to have his ear. Cabinet secretaries often are viewed as being advocates for their department's point of view. In some cases, that may be too narrow for the President.

During the Cuban Missile Crisis of 1962, for example, President Kennedy rejected the advice of the Defense Department leaders, preferring instead to listen to the counsel of his diplomatic advisers and his most trusted aid, Robert F. Kennedy, his brother and attorney general.[2]

Sometimes the White House is thought of as a palace court, in which assistants who persist in offering unwanted advice are weeded out. That, in fact, can be a major problem. President Johnson often was accused of preferring to surround himself with "yes men." In fact, whenever an answer to a problem seemed "too pat" to LBJ, he called in veteran presidential adviser George Ball, who could quickly develop strong arguments to support opposing viewpoints. This gave the Chief Executive alternative policy options.

The President, under Article II, Section 2, of the Constitution, has the authority to make appointments to the executive branch with the advice and consent of the U.S. Senate. The Supreme Court also made it clear in *Myers v. United States,* 272 U.S. 52 (1926), that the President has broad removal powers. Only those individuals willing to carry out the administration's policies remain in office. When subordinates sometimes forget this, they are ousted. This "gun behind the door" makes it possible for the President to have a "team" that will carry out his will.

Scandals and scoundrels fill the pages of history. Many Presidents have had subordinates who have betrayed his confidence in them. Truman, a personally honest man, had many influence peddlers in his administration and the Republicans swept to victory in 1952 on the slogan "Korea and Corruption." Dwight Eisenhower, the commanding general who led the Allies to victory in Europe over the forces of Hitler and Mussolini, pledged that his new administration would be "as clean as a hound's tooth." But it was embarrassed when Sherman Adams, the White House Chief of Staff, was forced to resign. Adams' ethics and judgment were questioned when it was revealed that he had accepted gifts from New England textile manufacturer Bernard Goldfine. This at least created the impression of improper influence.[3]

More recently, Nixon was forced to leave office because of Watergate—and related political scandals. Carter had problems with White House staffers and his budget director Bert Lance. Reagan had the Iran-Contra scandal. The Clinton Administration spent much time deflecting criticisms of how the executive branch was being run, as well as trying to defend the President's own character and personal morality.

Media made famous such names as Gennifer Flowers, Paula Jones and Monica Lewinsky. Whether the public has a "right to know" about the personal life of a President is hotly debated in media circles. Bill Clinton, some would argue, was elected to be President, not a saint. One syndicated columnist, Cynthia Tucker of the *Atlanta Constitution,* once wrote that the people trust the President to handle the economy, but probably would not trust him with their daughter.

Before Watergate, media did not write about the personal lives of the Presidents. Franklin Roosevelt, Kennedy and Johnson all had affairs, and the latter two were notorious womanizers. Yet reporters did not bother to write about it at the time. The rules have changed in the past generation.[4]

The President sets the tone for integrity in the Executive branch. Any hint of scandal, such as has occurred in nearly every administration since World War II, is his responsibility.

That is one reason why modern Presidents must choose major policy makers carefully. The Cabinet, although primarily an advisory group in the American system, nonetheless consists of individuals who head the great executive departments of government. To control management of the professional bureaucracy, the President must choose people who are supporters of his programs and policies. He must do this at the beginning of his administration if he hopes to get firm control.

In short, the focus should be on appointing people who are "in sync" with the President, rather than those who have connections with groups that were essential to the President's election. Some political scientists would argue that this is unrealistic, and it is not unusual to reward interest group representatives for their support. However, if program execution is primary, then attention must be paid to appointing "loyalists."

The role of Chief Executive also involves execution of the laws. When the President takes his oath of office, he places his hand on the Bible and swears to enforce the Constitution and the laws of the United States.

Courts can issue orders, but lack the muscle to enforce them. When, for example, a U.S. Circuit Court in Arkansas ordered Central High School in Little Rock, AR, to integrate its student body by admitting Black students, Gov. Orval Faubus, in 1957, ordered the National Guard to prevent the integration of the school. President

Eisenhower, acting as Chief Executive, gave meaning to the court order by sending U.S. paratroops to Little Rock to enforce the law.

President Kennedy sent U.S. marshals to Oxford, MS, to enforce a court order integrating the University of Mississippi in 1962. Kennedy also sent the Alabama National Guard (which he had federalized as Commander-in-Chief) to the Alabama campus to integrate the 1963 summer session of the University of Alabama. A court order had been challenged by Gov. George C. Wallace, whose motto was "segregation now and forever."

2. Chief Legislator

Modern Presidents are expected to do more than execute the law. They must be "Chief Legislators" and have political programs that they try to translate into public law. The Executive branch formulates policies to solve a variety of social problems or to achieve desired ends. It then lobbies the legislative branch to enact these policy preferences into law. Article II, Section 7, also gives the President the authority to veto bills.

Congress was, for most of the 20th Century, largely a reactive body. It tended to await key presidential messages—the State of the Union, the Budget Message, the Economic Report—before going to work on the nation's problems.

In the age of political television (some call it polivision), the President can use his **message power** not only to outline his programs to Congress, but also to appeal to the American people. He can use the media to build a base of public support. He also can exercise his **veto power** to block ill-considered or unconstitutional bills (in his view) from becoming law. The veto is a powerful weapon of public policy. The mere threat of a veto is often sufficient to force Congress to modify legislation so that the President will not block it.

Once a bill has passed both House and Senate in identical form, it goes to the President's desk. He can sign it, in which case it becomes law. Or he may prevent it from becoming law in a number of ways. He may send it back to Congress with a veto message, stating the reason why he objects to the bill. If it is the end of the congressional year, the President need do nothing. If he has not acted on the bill within 10 days of the adjournment of Congress, the bill dies. This constitutes a so-called **"pocket veto"** and Congress can do nothing to override his objections. Pocket vetoes are fairly common because many bills are rushed through Congress in the days just before it adjourns. Sometimes a President knows that his veto will not be sustained. In that case, he simply does nothing. If Congress is in session, it becomes law without his signature. He has, however, clearly indicated that he does not support the new law.

Although Congress can override a presidential veto with a two-thirds margin in both houses, this seldom is easy to do. Even with large Democratic majorities, Congress was able to overturn only five of President Nixon's 43 vetoes and 12 of President Ford's 66 vetoes.

Franklin D. Roosevelt, who held the office longer than any other Chief Executive in U.S. history, vetoed 633 bills. Congress overrode only nine of them. Democrat Grover Cleveland used the veto power to block legislation 584 times. Bill Clinton vetoed 37 measures and only two became law over his objections.

President George W. Bush did not veto a single bill during his first term, making him the first Chief Executive since John Quincy Adams to complete a full term without vetoing legislation. Bush did not use the veto during the first half of 2005.

Bush, however, used the threat of a veto on a number of occasions to keep Congress in line. He has threatened to veto major spending and defense bills which were out of line with administration proposals. He headed off congressional efforts to fund international family planning groups involved in abortion.

He also blocked congressional efforts to require Iraq to pay back part of the $18.6 billion earmarked for reconstruction of that nation.

Republican congressional leaders were willing to side with the President; party solidarity, given GOP control of both House and Senate, made it unnecessary for the President, unlike his father, to use the veto as a weapon in partisan battles with Congress.

President George Herbert Walker Bush (1989-2001) never had a Congress controlled by his own party. As a result, he wielded the veto some 44 times during his single term.

In recent years, taxpayers have been angered at the apparent inability of the Congress to discipline itself insofar as spending is concerned. A favorite Conservative cause was the **line item veto.** In 1994, it was part of Speaker Newt Gingrich's *"Contract With America."*[5]

Until 1997, the President had no line item veto, which permits an executive to strike specific provisions of an appropriations or tax measure. Presidents were put in a "take it or leave it" position. They had to either veto a spending bill, perhaps "shutting down the government," or sign an appropriations measure they did not want. The latter policy option, although not a good one, was preferable to the horrid practical result of a veto.

Governors of nearly all of America's 50 states have a line item veto power, envied by the President. In 1996, Republicans, whose platform had long called for the measure as a way to curtail wasteful government spending, granted it to Democratic President Bill Clinton. Clinton was happy to sign it because it enlarged his power and authority in dealing with Congress. He praised the statute as one which would allow future Presidents to battle "special interest boondoggles, tax loopholes, and pure pork." **Pork-barrel legislation** refers to government programs that may benefit a member's state or district (they are bringing home the bacon to the folks back home).

The law was not to go into effect until 1997, as the GOP-controlled Congress hoped that Senate Majority Leader Bob Dole, their presumptive presidential nominee, would be the first Chief Executive to use it.

The line item veto authorized the President to veto specific appropriations and all provisions of tax laws that benefit fewer than 100 persons. When the President decided to exercise this new power, he had to inform Congress within five days after signing a tax or spending measure.

The 1996 law did authorize any member of Congress, or anyone else adversely affected, to challenge the law's constitutionality. Such a suit, of course, was predictable and the law also required the U.S. Supreme Court to expedite any lower court decision on the measure. Early in 1997, six members of Congress, led by Sen. Robert Byrd (D., W.V.), sought an injunction against use of the new statute. They argued that the new statute unconstitutionally shifted power over taxing and spending from the Congress to the President. Such a transfer of power and authority could be accomplished, they argued, only by a constitutional amendment.

In April, 1997, Federal District Court Judge Thomas P. Jackson sided with Senator Byrd and his colleagues, ruling that the power to make the laws of the nation "is the exclusive, non-delegable power of Congress." Judge Jackson's holding that the

President's line item veto authority was unconstitutional immediately was appealed to the U.S. Supreme Court.

The Supreme Court heard the case in the spring of 1997 and overruled the lower court. It held that the six members of Congress "have alleged no injury to themselves as individuals. Therefore, they lacked standing to sue."[6]

The item veto is a power exercised by 48 of 50 governors of U.S. states. It allows the Chief Executive to "red-line" specific provisions of an appropriations or tax bill while accepting remaining provisions of the law. American Presidents have never had such constitutional power and authority. They had been confronted with the choice of shutting down parts of the government, which they never enjoyed contemplating. Therefore, American Presidents had to sign money and tax bills, despite the fact that they objected to parts of them. U.S. Chief Executives had sought the item veto since the days of Ulysses S. Grant. President Ronald Reagan popularized the idea in recent years.

The truly remarkable thing about the 1996 law was its timing. It was enacted by a Republican Congress intent on reasserting its power, particularly with Democrat Clinton in the White House. Nonetheless, the item veto had been part of the 1994 GOP "Contract With America," designed to bring fiscal discipline and responsibility to a Congress that frequently could not control itself.

It passed Congress easily, with 69 senators and some 290 House members voting for it.

In 1997, Clinton used the item veto 10 times, cutting out 82 spending provisions. Congress did override his veto of a $287 million military construction bill, involving 38 projects. Some Conservative Republicans joined Democrats in complaining that Clinton had killed "worthy projects" in their home states or districts.

In June, 1998, the U.S. Supreme Court ruled, 6-3, in *Clinton v. City of New York* (118 S.Ct.209), that Congress had unconstitutionally given to the President the power to rewrite legislation. The Constitution, the Court held, establishes the President's veto power, and Congress cannot alter the system through the exercise of its ordinary legislative power. In short, a constitutional amendment would be required to change the "rules of the game." Writing for the majority, Justice John Paul Stevens said: "…This act gives the President the unilateral power to change the text of duly enacted statutes…the functional equivalent of partial repeals of acts of Congress…There is no provision in the Constitution that authorizes the President to enact, to amend or to repeal statutes…The Line Item Veto Act authorizes the President himself to effect the repeal of laws, for his own policy reasons, without observing the procedures set out in Article I," he added.

Concurring, Justice Anthony M. Kennedy wrote, "Failure of political will does not justify unconstitutional remedies...Abdication of responsibility is not part of the constitutional design…Liberty is always at stake when one or more of the branches seeks to transgress the separation of powers."

The Supreme Court quoted George Washington, who presided over the Constitutional Convention and later wrote that a President must "approve all the parts of a bill, or reject it in toto," but cannot modify the text of legislation presented to him by Congress.

Justices Antonin Scalia, Sandra Day O'Connor and Stephen G. Breyer dissented. Scalia and O'Connor concluded that Idaho potato growers lacked standing to sue because they had not shown that they were harmed. The three dissenters agreed that the line item veto should have been upheld.

The majority ruled that both New York City hospitals and the Idaho potato growers had suffered an "actual injury." Justice Stevens noted that the line item veto, by creating a potential liability of at least $2.6 billion for New York, could harm the city's financial strength and borrowing power.

Stevens also noted that the Supreme Court was expressing "no opinion about the wisdom of the procedures authorized by the Line Item Veto Act." But, he said, if Congress wants to establish such procedures, it must amend the Federal Constitution.

In his dissent, Justice Scalia wrote, "There is not a dime's worth of difference between Congress authorizing the President to cancel a spending item and Congress's authorizing money to be spent on a particular item at the President's discretion. And the latter has been done since the founding of the nation."

Justice Breyer, in his dissenting opinion, wrote that the line item veto was an acceptable experiment. He said, " In sum, I recognize that the act before us is novel. In a sense, it skirts a constitutional edge. But the edge has to do with means, not ends. The means chosen do not amount literally to the enactment, repeal or amendment of a law. Nor, for that matter, do they amount literally to the line item veto. That the act's title announces. Those means do not violate any basic separation of powers principles. They do not improperly shift the constitutionally foreseen balance of power from Congress to the President. Nor, since they comply with the Separation of Powers principles, do they threaten the liberties of individual citizens. They represent an experiment that may, or may not, help representative government work better. The Constitution, in my view, authorizes Congress and the President to try novel methods in this way. Consequently, with respect, I dissent."

Predictably, Clinton, who was traveling in China when he got the news of the Supreme Court's ruling, was upset. "The decision is a defeat for all Americans. It deprives the President," he said, "of a valuable tool for eliminating waste in the Federal budget and for enlivening the public debate over how to make the best use of public funds."

Sen. Robert Byrd of West Virginia, a former Democratic majority leader, disagreed. Byrd, the foremost opponent of the line item veto, a man some consider the "all-time pork barrel champion of the Senate," said: "This a great day for the United States of America, a great day for the Constitution of the United States…Today we feel that the liberties of the American people have been assured. God save this honorable court."

Sen. Byrd did not let the moment pass without expressing his dismay at Justice Breyer's opinion. This was, he said, a remarkable position to take. Bryd quoted Sir William Blackstone, the 18th Century English jurist, who wrote: "In all tyrannical governments, the supreme magistracy, or the right of both making and enforcing the laws, is vested in one and the same man, or one and the same body of men. And whenever these two powers are united together, there can be no public liberty."

Sen. Carl Levin (D., MI) said that Congress "tried to bend the Constitution but the Court said it will not allow this to happen."

Sen. Daniel P. Moynihan (D., N.Y.) also rejoiced at the decision. "In the history of Congress," he said, "we have never had an issue of such importance for the powers of the executive and legislative branches. Liberty has prevailed."

As a result of the ruling, New York was able to keep all the Federal money it received for the care of poor people under Medicaid. Idaho potato farmers kept the tax break they had received from Congress. Under the Line Item Veto Act, the President could cancel tax breaks that benefited less than 101 persons.

Although the Framers of the U.S. Constitution created separate institutions of government to share power, a common political party affiliation has often served to bridge the gap created by the principle of separation of powers. A President may appeal to party loyalty or resort to a variety of "carrot and stick" techniques to line up support for his program. Franklin D. Roosevelt and Lyndon Johnson were legendary for their abilities in this respect.

In the age of mass media politics, however, we have seen the decline of party and the rise of personality politics. The Democratic Party would not have chosen young Sen. John F. Kennedy of Massachusetts for President in 1960, had it been left to the "king-makers" or party bosses to make that decision. It was only through a strategy of selecting carefully a number of primaries and winning all of them that Kennedy was able to capture the nomination.

Senator Lyndon Johnson clearly was the choice of Democratic Party leaders in Congress. Others preferred candidates like New York Gov. Averell Harriman, Sen. Stuart Symington, former secretary of the Air Force, or former Illinois Gov. Adlai E. Stevenson—already a two-time loser to Dwight Eisenhower in 1952 and 1956.

Kennedy, however, was a candidate who took advantage of television. He was young, handsome, energetic and had a very attractive family. He also had money, organizational skill and the support of party leaders, like the legendary Mayor Richard Daley of Chicago. Kennedy came to the presidency with a legislative program, called **The New Frontier**. But in his brief tenure of about 1000 days in the White House, he failed to move Congress to enact Civil Rights legislation, the War on Poverty or other key measures.

All of these measures were passed into law after Johnson—the former majority leader of his party—became Chief Executive. Kennedy originated many of the ideas of Johnson's **"Great Society"** program. However, he was ineffective as "chief legislator," failing to convince the congressional leadership to support those policies.[7]

American voters often choose a President of one party and a Congress controlled by the opposition. In the post-World War II period, Truman faced a Republican Congress. Eisenhower had to work with a Democratic Congress for the last six years of his presidency. Nixon and Ford never had a Congress controlled by their own party and Reagan did only briefly, when the GOP captured the Senate on his coattails in 1980. Clinton saw a Democratic Congress in control only in the first two years of his first term.[8]

3. Chief Diplomat

Despite the fact that the Constitution gives Congress some important foreign policy-national security powers, the President often is called the Chief Diplomat. Although assisted by the professionals in the Department of State, the President has the primary constitutional responsibility for formulation and implementation of U.S. foreign policy. This role is particularly important today because history has seen the U.S. move out of its isolationist tradition. World War II showed the folly of "playing ostrich" and burying one's head in the sand, "ignoring" the aggressive acts of Hitler, Mussolini and Tojo.

The U.S. emerged in the postwar period, along with the Soviet Union, as the only remaining world powers. Whether they liked it or not, history had thrust upon the shoulders of the American people the role of leader of Western democracy.

The President alone can recognize or decide not to recognize a foreign regime or government.

It took Truman only a few minutes after the Israeli Provisional Government announced its existence as a state in 1948 to grant it full diplomatic recognition. This indicated clear-cut U.S. approval and support for the State of Israel, although many diplomats considered it premature, considering the Arab states responded by going to war with the infant nation. It was not at all clear that the Jewish state would survive.[9]

By way of contrast, Wilson rejected traditional criteria of the international law of recognition in 1917. The new Soviet regime came into being after overthrowing the democratic, provisional government of Alexander Kerensky. Until then, most Presidents simply asked three questions:

(1) - Can you look at a map and identify a specific territory?

(2) - Is the territory inhabited by people?

(3) - Does the government control the people and territory?

Wilson, however, approved of only one form of government: democracy. He refused to recognize a regime that had come to power by bullet, rather than by the ballot. He was consistent in this view, also refusing to recognize the revolutionary government in Mexico.[10]

Wilson's Republican successors—Warren G. Harding, Calvin Coolidge and Herbert Hoover—carried on this policy, not so much because of their love for democracy as an abstract idea, but rather because they disapproved of a Communist regime. It was only when Franklin Roosevelt became Chief Executive, in 1933, that the U.S. ended 16 years of isolating itself from one of the most populous nations in the world.[11]

The recognition question arose again after the overthrow of the Chinese Nationalist regime of Chiang Kai-Shek, in 1949, by the Communist forces of Mao Tse-Tung. Presidents Truman, Eisenhower, Kennedy and Johnson all refused to recognize Maoist China.

It was only when Nixon became President that conditions had changed sufficiently to explore the possibility of recognition. Nixon made a dramatic trip to China in 1972, where his meetings with Mao and Chou En Lai changed the climate of Sino-U.S. relations. Later, President Ford also visited China and commercial, diplomatic and cultural exchanges were advanced.

In 1979, President Carter, acting under authority granted by Article II, Section 2, to "receive Ambassadors and other public Ministers" from foreign nations, extended U.S. recognition to the Peoples' Republic of China, the most populous nation in the world.[12]

In 1989, Eastern European Communist regimes collapsed, one after another, in what media characterized as "the year of falling dominoes." President Bush immediately extended U.S. diplomatic recognition to many of these new regimes. In 1991, Bush extended U.S. diplomatic recognition to Latvia, Lithuania and Estonia, Baltic states which had been absorbed into the Soviet Union by dictator Joseph Stalin, just before World War II. When the U.S.S.R. broke up in 1991, Russia was recognized as the successor state to the Soviet Union.

During his first term in office, President Clinton extended diplomatic recognition to Vietnam, some 20 years after the end of war with what had been an enemy state. He agreed to exchange ambassadors with one of the few remaining Communist regimes in the world. One dramatic human interest story which highlighted "normalization" of relations between the two nations was the appointment of a U.S. ambassador who had been held as a prisoner of war in the infamous "Hanoi Hilton."

Although some international lawyers questioned it, the U.S. and other major world powers in the United Nations—China, France and the United Kingdom—decided that Russia would have the uncontested right to the Soviet seat on the Security Council.

No one with power could question that decision, given the unanimity of the major powers on the issue.

Presidents also can sever U.S. diplomatic relations with other countries. Eisenhower, for example, cut off U.S. relations with Cuban dictator Fidel Castro. The two nations still have no formal ties 40 years later.

An important aspect of the President's power as chief diplomat is his authority to appoint, with the advice and consent of the Senate, ambassadors and other diplomats to represent the nation abroad. Foreign diplomats are appointed to represent their governments in Washington and do so by being "received" by the President. New ambassadors are expected to present their credentials to the White House.

Presidents can negotiate and conclude treaties, but those agreements become effective only with the advice and consent of at least two-thirds of the U.S. Senate. Sometimes this is very difficult, as when the Panama Canal Treaty passed the U.S. Senate by a margin of one vote during the Carter Administration. Although the Senate has rejected about 20 treaties, it is in a constitutional position to require amendments to a pact before it gives it consent.

In 1977, for example, the Senate forced the Carter Administration to clarify several matters with Panama, prior to approving the Canal Treaty. The Senate supported a reservation by Sen. Dennis DeConcini (D., AZ) who asserted the right of the U.S. to send troops into Panama to keep the canal open. But the U.S. turned over the canal to Panama in the year 2000.

New Presidents often will ask for the support of former Presidents in foreign policy matters. Carter, for example, was deeply in trouble on the Panama Canal Treaty. He asked for and received the support of former President Ford and former Secretary of State Henry Kissinger during the Senate debate. Bipartisanship is a strong tradition in U.S. foreign relations.

It is assumed by many Democrats and Republicans that partisan politics should end at the nation's borders. There should be, tradition holds, no Democratic or Republican foreign policy, but one U.S. foreign policy. Some scholars, however, suggest that this tradition has diminished in recent years and that foreign policy differences between the major parties now are sometimes significant.[13]

Clearly, the U.S. invasion of Iraq and Bush foreign policy was a hotly debated topic in and out of Congress during the election of 2004. Parties were deeply divided on this, the occupation, the war on terrorism and the Patriot Act early in the 109th Congress (2005-2006).

Diplomatic agreements between the U.S. and foreign regimes can take a number of forms. Most commonly, these pacts are either in the form of treaties or executive agreements. A treaty, negotiated by the professional diplomats in the state department, once concluded by the parties, must still be approved by the Senate. The Constitution requires the advice and consent of two-thirds of that body before it can be signed by the President and be effectively ratified. The Senate also can make reservations that effectively force the President to enter into new negotiations with the other party to the pact.

Although the Senate usually will ratify a treaty, it does not always do so. Sometimes a nation will not follow its President. The most famous—some would say infamous—rejection of a treaty occurred when the U.S. Senate rejected the Treaty of Versailles after World War I.

The most important part of the pact was the creation of a League of Nations, dedicated to world peace, a dream of President Wilson. But the nation was in a mood to reject idealism and return to its isolationist tradition. This U.S. refusal to ratify the treaty probably sealed the League's fate. Historians still argue whether World War II could have been avoided, had the Senate followed Wilson's leadership.

Historically, Presidents sometimes have attempted to circumvent the Senate by entering into **executive agreements**. Not expressly mentioned anywhere in the Constitution, these pacts, reached by the President with foreign heads of state, do not require Senate approval and have been upheld by U.S. courts since the days of George Washington. In *U.S. v. Belmont,* 301 U.S. 324 (1936), the nation's highest tribunal held that executive agreements are equal to treaties and thus enjoy that status of "supreme law of the land." They are concluded under the President's general power and authority as Chief Diplomat and Commander-in-Chief. Such agreements can be weakened by Congress or rejected by subsequent administrations, although in practice they are usually honored.

The executive agreement has proved to be an effective tool, enabling the President to enlarge his power and authority vis-a-vis the Senate during the 20th Century. Since speed may be of paramount importance in foreign policy-national security matters, quick and decisive action by the Chief Executive is of vital importance. Treaty-making is sometimes painfully slow. From 1789-1988, the U.S. adopted nearly 1500 treaties. Nearly 13,000 executive agreements were negotiated by Presidents during the same period.

One also should note that secrecy is vital in national security matters. Franklin Roosevelt, in 1940, traded some 50 over-age U.S. destroyers to British Prime Minister Winston Churchill in return for naval bases in British Western Hemispheric possessions. This action probably would have been impossible in a Senate split evenly between isolationists and interventionists. Other important examples of executive agreements are those made with Stalin's Soviet Union by Presidents Roosevelt and Truman at Yalta and Potsdam, respectively.[14]

Some senators dislike efforts to bypass them and commit the U.S. to important international obligations without obtaining the Senate's advice and consent. Efforts to limit the President's power to conclude executive agreements, led by isolationist Sen. John Bricker of Ohio, the Republican vice presidential nominee in 1944, failed by the margin of only one vote. The idea that the President should be "cut down to size" lives on, as reflected in the 1973 War Powers Act.

But executive agreements remain an important presidential option. This has been especially true in the post-World War II era.

It often has been said that strong Presidents, like Wilson and Franklin D. Roosevelt, were their own secretaries of state. Kennedy is said to have chosen Dean Rusk as his secretary of state after being impressed by an article Rusk published in *Foreign Affairs* magazine. Rusk indicated clearly that the President was the sole organ of the U.S. in foreign policy and the secretary had to know the limits of his role.

Some secretaries of state have been fired because they took too much on themselves. When Wilson was incapacitated by a stroke and Robert Lansing called a cabinet meeting to discuss foreign policy and other pressing business, Wilson fired him for "usurpation" of presidential authority. Harry Truman fired Secretary of State James Byrnes after Byrnes made speeches which were not consistent with Truman's foreign policy. There can be no confusion about the nation's foreign policy objectives.[15]

Some Chief Executives, however, have relied heavily on professional diplomats for advice. John Foster Dulles clearly was the architect of the Eisenhower Administration's foreign policies. Kissinger had a major influence on the thinking of

Presidents Nixon and Ford. William Rogers, Nixon's first secretary of state, was primarily an adviser and administrator at the State Department. Kissinger was not only an adviser on international issues. He also had broad authority to formulate U.S. foreign policy. Reagan's "style" was to delegate policy areas to members of his cabinet, particularly Secretary of State George Schultz and Defense Secretary Caspar (Cap) Weinberger, key members of his foreign policy-national security "team."

At the dawn of the 21st Century, the world was a much more complicated place than it was a century earlier. We live in a global economy, an era of jet travel, the internet, satellites and intercontinental ballistic missiles. In the words of Canadian scholar Marshall McLuhan, we have become a "global village."

The new technology means that Presidents now are more involved in "personal diplomacy" than were their predecessors. They frequently meet with heads of government and heads of state. Foreign leaders also use the same technology. They are free to travel and negotiate, just as the American President does. But no other world leader can speak with the authority of the President, given the nature of U.S. military and economic power.

4. Commander-in-Chief

"The President shall be Commander in Chief of the Army and Navy of the United States, and of the Militia of the several States, when called into the actual service of the United States." –Article II, Section 2.

One of the most important constitutional roles given the President is that of Commander-in-Chief. He alone can order the use of nuclear weapons, as President Truman did when he ordered the first atomic bomb dropped on Hiroshima, Japan, on August 6, 1945. Three days later, another A-bomb was dropped on Nagasaki. The President announced the surrender of Japan on August 14, and World War II was over.

Although the use of the A-bomb in Japan is debated by some revisionist historians of today, the decision was not very controversial at the time. Truman's approval rating was the highest ever recorded in the history of the Gallup Poll, a figure that held until George Bush topped it after the Persian Gulf War in 1991.[16]

Presidents have the final authority for the conduct of U.S. military policy. They outrank admirals and generals, irrespective of how distinguished they may be. Sometimes generals and admirals forget who the boss is, and Presidents must remind them. Civilian control over the military is built into the U.S. Constitution. So Lincoln fired Gen. George McClellan during the Civil War and Truman removed General Douglas MacArthur as U.S. and UN Commander in Korea after a public uproar over war strategy.

Truman wanted to keep the war limited to the Korean peninsula and he wanted to keep it fought for limited objectives. MacArthur wanted permission to bomb Chinese bases and to pursue Chinese aircraft into China. When the President refused, the two men had a public disagreement. Because the President is the boss, MacArthur—perhaps a great general—had to go. This, of course, had profound political consequences. General MacArthur, a great Pacific Theater commander during World War II, was a hero in the U.S. Truman's approval rating sank to 24%, the lowest in the history of the public opinion polls. But the authority of the President and Secretary of Defense over the top officers in the armed forces is necessary to guarantee civilian control of the military, an important basic principle of American Constitutional Law.[17]

Popular disgust with how wars are conducted can be politically ruinous to Presidents. Failure of the Truman Administration to end the war on favorable terms caused Dwight Eisenhower, hero of World War II, and the man who commanded the armies which expelled the Nazis from Europe, to enter the contest. In January, 1953, Eisenhower, who had never voted, became the first Republican President since Hoover. By July of that year, the war ended in a truce.

It should be noted that the Constitution gives the power to declare war only to Congress. That is largely academic, however, given that only five wars have been declared in the nation's history and none has been declared since World War II. The President, by way of contrast, has involved the U.S. military in more than 200 instances of combat. Sometimes the Congress has given explicit approval by passing resolutions or by appropriating funds to support the military action. More often—in an estimated two-thirds of the cases—the President has acted without such support.

One must constantly keep in mind the fact that senators and representatives, above all else, are political animals. Robert A. Taft of Ohio, dubbed "Mr. Republican" by the media in the early 1950s, originally praised Truman's intervention in Korea. It was a case, Taft said, of a courageous President standing up against Communist aggression. When the war turned into a prolonged stalemate, and as the election of 1952 neared, Taft, a leading contender for the GOP nomination, changed his tune. Korea, he now said, was a case of a President exceeding his authority.[18]

A more recent and historic debate over the President's power as Commander-in-Chief came as the result of the Vietnam War. The U.S. had been involved in South Vietnam since the Geneva Agreement partitioned old French Indochina into the new states of North and South Vietnam, Laos and Cambodia. This effectively removed the French from Southeast Asia.

But Eisenhower and Secretary of State Dulles were determined to prevent the Communist regime of North Vietnam from taking over all of the area. Eisenhower and Kennedy committed a small number of American advisers to the area. The latter sent troops to help with logistics and training of the South Vietnamese Army. But a major escalation of the war during the Johnson years changed U.S. history.[19]

When Kennedy was assassinated in Dallas, Texas, on November 22, 1963, the U.S. had about 16,000 troops in Vietnam. In August, 1964, Johnson reported that an unprovoked attack by North Vietnamese torpedo boats on two U.S. destroyers in the Gulf of Tonkin had occurred. He asked Congress to pass a joint resolution of support to bolster his hand. Sen. J.W. Fulbright of Arkansas, then chairman of the Committee on Foreign Relations, steered the measure through the Senate. The House followed suit in its support. The **Gulf of Tonkin Resolution**, passed August 7, 1964, supported "the determination of the President, as Commander-in-Chief, to take all necessary measures to repeal any armed attack against the forces of the United States and to prevent further aggression."[20]

Johnson later relied on the resolution to justify the major escalation of war operations in Vietnam. Many members of Congress, including Senator Fulbright, argued that there had been no intention to approve such a major escalation and that they had been manipulated into a corner where they either had to approve the resolution or appear to create an impression of national disunity. The Great Society domestic programs became a casualty of the war in Vietnam. By the time Johnson left office and Nixon succeeded him in January, 1969, about 540,000 U.S. troops were in Vietnam.

Johnson saw the nation deeply torn by supporters of the war effort, called "hawks," and those who passionately protested against it, called "doves." Some senators and academics, calling themselves "owls," suggested that wisdom was what was most needed. U.S. national interest should always be paramount in foreign and national security policy, they said.

On March 31, 1968, the President, challenged in Democratic primary contests by Senators Eugene McCarthy and Robert Kennedy, addressed the nation in a prime time television broadcast. He said: "For 37 years, in the service of our nation, first as a Congressman, as a Senator, as Vice President, and now as your President, I have put the unity of the people first, I have put it ahead of any divisive partisanship...There is a division in the American house now...Fifty-two months and 10 days ago, in a moment of tragedy and trauma, the duties of this office fell upon me. I asked then for your help and God's that we might continue America on its course, binding up our wounds, healing our history...What we won when all of our people united just must not now be lost in suspicion and distrust and selfishness and politics among any of our people. And believing this as I do, I have concluded that I should not permit the Presidency to become involved in the partisan divisions that are developing in this political year...Accordingly, I shall not seek and I will not accept the nomination of my party for another term as your President...."[21]

After Nixon expanded U.S. military efforts into Cambodia in 1970 without any prior consultation with Congress, a major national upheaval took place. Anti-war protesters reacted violently and many of the nation's college campuses, including the University of Michigan, were forced to close their doors early that spring. Ohio National Guardsmen, called to the Kent State campus, fired on students and four were killed.

Congress repealed the Gulf of Tonkin Resolution later that year, but the action had no practical effect because the official justification for continued military operations was the need to protect American GIs until they could be withdrawn from Vietnam. Congress ordered the bombing of Cambodia stopped by August 15, 1973.

Some anti-war dissidents even filed lawsuits, charging that the war was unconstitutional since it had not been declared by Congress. The U.S. Supreme Court, however, rejected all efforts to enter the "political thicket" which the political branches of the Federal government would have to resolve.

Nixon's policy of phased withdrawal and "peace with honor" resulted ultimately in the 1973 Paris Peace Accord. But when the North Vietnamese violated the accord and invaded the South, the South Vietnamese Army collapsed. Congress was in no mood to invest further blood or treasure and the war ended in 1975, with what some call the first military defeat in U.S. history.[22]

One of the consequences of the Vietnam conflict was congressional frustration that eventually produced the **War Powers Act of 1973**. Passed by Congress largely in response to military policies of Presidents Johnson and Nixon, the law provides that the President may commit American troops to battle only if:

(1) Congress declares a state of war.
(2) Congress specifically authorizes use of force.
(3) Armed attack on the U.S. or its armed forces creates a national emergency.

If the third condition occurs, the President is charged with the responsibility of reporting to Congress immediately. If Congress does not declare war within 60 days, the President must withdraw the forces unless he certifies to Congress that military conditions require, for the safety of U.S. troops, an additional 30 days.

After 90 days, Congress may, by concurrent resolution, not subject to presidential veto, require the President to disengage all troops involved in hostilities.

The War Powers Resolution was intended to avoid prolonged presidential wars such as those fought in Korea and Vietnam. Clearly, it reduced the power of the White House to involve the U.S. in protracted conflicts abroad without the support of Congress and the American people.

President Nixon vetoed the measure, asserting that it was an unconstitutional and dangerous restriction on the power of the Commander-in-Chief to respond to emergencies. But Congress passed the measure over his objections. Lawyers may debate the constitutionality of the measure, which never has been tested in court, but most would agree that it is politically realistic. Prolonged military action without the support of the people and the Congress cannot succeed.

One should note that no President has accepted the act as a direct limitation on his power and authority to function as Commander-in-Chief of the nation's armed forces.

More than a generation after enactment of the statute, it is clear that Congress has failed to effectively limit the President's war-making power. Before the Persian Gulf War, President Bush ordered the U.S. military into Panama in 1989. The U.S. invasion ousted Panamanian dictator Manuel Noriega, who was arrested, taken to Miami, FL, tried, convicted of drug trafficking and sentenced to 40 years in prison.

Bush sent U.S. forces into Somalia in 1992 as part of a United Nations peacekeeping force. Reagan had sent Marines to Lebanon in 1982 and had invaded and captured the Caribbean island of Grenada in 1983. Reagan bombed Libya in 1986 and sent the U.S. Navy into the Persian Gulf in 1987 to protect Kuwaiti ships from attacks by the Iran's revolutionary Islamic regime. Reagan also conducted a covert war against Nicaragua's leftist regime throughout much of his presidency.

In 1990, Congress gave its support to President Bush after he had decided on a large-scale involvement of U.S. forces in the Persian Gulf.[23]

Although some congressional critics demanded a larger role for Congress as the troop buildup took place, Bush rejected the notion that the Congress had any constitutional power or authority to participate in military decision-making involved in **Operation Desert Shield** (1990) and **Operation Desert Storm** (1991).

Senator Edward M. Kennedy of Massachusetts predicted that 700 American GIs would die every week in a long and bloody land war. He and other administration critics eventually looked a bit foolish when the conflict ended rapidly and decisively after massive U.S. air attacks on military targets in Iraq and the liberation of Kuwait.

In fact, President Bush won the highest approval rating ever given to an American Chief Executive when some 91% of poll respondents approved of the job he was doing as President. This topped the prior record of President Truman, whose approval rating on V-J (Victory Over Japan) Day was about 87%.

President Clinton also asserted this position in 1995, when he committed some 20,000 American troops to join with those from 25 other nations in maintaining the peace agreement reached by the presidents of Bosnia, Croatia and Serbia. A year earlier, Clinton had ordered American GIs to Haiti.

Congress is clearly at a disadvantage in competing with the President for control of foreign and national security policy. In the age of intercontinental ballistic missiles, Congress seems somewhat archaic in its procedures and ability to operate quickly during a period of national crisis. How effective the War Powers Act will be in the 21st Century remains to be seen.

The presidential seal depicts both the olive branch of the peacemaker and the arrows of the warrior. The roles of Chief Diplomat and Commander-in-Chief clearly overlap.

5. Chief of State

The American President is not only the head of government. He also is the ceremonial Chief of State. He ranks in international protocol ahead of mere heads of government, such as the British Prime Minister. He is on a level with kings and queens, the symbol and personification of the nation. George W. Bush, like him or not, is the spokesman for nearly 300 million Americans.

Gordon Brown is head of the United Kingdom's Cabinet system of government. Elizabeth II is Chief of State. The British, as well as other constitutional monarchies, have divided the roles which Americans combine in the person of one individual—the President.

Much of the President's time is spent in ceremonial roles. He welcomes foreign leaders to the White House on behalf of the American people. He throws out the first ball to open the baseball season. He invites national champion football, basketball, baseball and U.S. Olympic teams to the White House. He receives delegations of Boy Scouts and Girl Scouts. He issues countless proclamations. He opens great national charity drives. In a televised ceremony, he lays a wreath at the Tomb of the Unknown Soldier at Arlington National Cemetery on Memorial Day. He awards medals to military heroes, holds state dinners and lights the nation's Christmas tree.[24]

That is why, as one views films of the state funerals of Franklin D. Roosevelt and John F. Kennedy, one sees genuine grief reflected in the faces of men and women on the streets of Washington, D.C. Americans tend to identify with the President and most of them, except pathological partisan types, want him to succeed. What he does is too important to all of us to hope that he will fail.

Successful Presidents can inspire the American people, particularly in periods of national crisis, when patriotism is a necessary national virtue. Republicans, as well as Democrats, rallied around the leadership of Franklin D. Roosevelt during the Great Depression and World War II.

Some Presidents fail, as Richard Nixon did. After he was forced to resign his office in disgrace after the national nightmare of Watergate, many Americans feel a sense of tragedy. They welcome a transition in an orderly, constitutional manner.

President Ford seemed, in August, 1974, like the "common man" to many of his fellow citizens. They breathed a sigh of relief to read in their newspapers that the new Chief Executive got up and made his own breakfast. This, they could see, was not an "Imperial President." When Jimmy Carter was inaugurated in January, 1977, he left the traditional motorcade and, arm-in-arm with his wife Rosalyn, walked from Capitol Hill to their new address at 1600 Pennsylvania Avenue.

But some Presidents apparently have let the pomp and ceremony go to their heads. The arrogance of power is always a potential problem at the White House.

George Reedy, who served Lyndon Johnson as press secretary before "seeking refuge in academe" as dean of the Marquette University School of Journalism in Milwaukee, wrote a book entitled *The Twilight of the Presidency*. He commented:

> "The life of the White House is the life of the court. It is a structure designed for one purpose and one purpose only—to serve the material needs and the desires of a single man. It is felt that this man is grappling with problems of such tremendous consequence that every effort must be made to relieve him of the irritations that vex the average citizen. His mind, it is held, must be

absolutely free of petty annoyances so that he can concentrate his faculties upon the great issues of the day.

To achieve this end, every conceivable facility is made available, from the very latest and most luxurious jet aircraft to a masseur constantly in attendance to soothe raw presidential nerves. Even more important, however, he is treated with all the reverence due a monarch. No one interrupts presidential contemplation for anything less than a major catastrophe somewhere on the globe. No one speaks to him unless spoken to first. No one ever invites him to 'go soak your head' when his demands become petulant and unreasonable.

The distinction between President as head of the Executive branch of government and head of state helps to explain much of the mystery and dignity that historically have attached to the office. He is, as Theodore Roosevelt once said, both 'a king and a prime minister.' "[25]

Not all Presidents relish the pomp and circumstance that goes with being Chief of State. Eisenhower thought many of the tasks were a waste of time and delegated a good bit of the ceremonial role to Vice President Nixon, especially after his heart attack and stroke. Bush often joked that he had attended more funerals of foreign dignitaries than any other Vice President in history because Reagan delegated that job to him.

Presidents, however, cannot forget that, if performed properly, the role as Chief of State can be used to cement their power, authority and political popularity.

Who can become President of the United States? Under Article II, Section 1 of the Constitution, "No person except a natural born citizen...shall be eligible for the office of President." The meaning of the phrase "natural born" is not clear, although it excludes naturalized citizens. If one is born in another nation, one will never become President. Some scholars argue that the limitation includes only persons born in the U.S. Others contend that people born abroad of parents who are U.S. citizens are covered. This seldom comes up, although the late Michigan Gov. George Romney, the GOP presidential front-runner early in 1968, was born in Mexico of Mormon missionary parents. Most scholars did not consider that a problem for Romney.

The Constitution imposes few other legal qualifications for office. The President must be at least 35 years old and a resident of the U.S. for 14 years. As a practical matter, very few presidential candidates are under 50. Only four men, Theodore Roosevelt (42), John F. Kennedy (43), William J. Clinton (46), and Barack Obama (47), entered the Oval Office before their 50th birthdays.

In 1972, political "amateurs" who were left-of-center, seized control of the Democratic National Convention, nominated George McGovern and wrote a party platform which was about 180 degrees removed from what most Americans thought public policy should be. Some other delegates forgot the constitutional age requirement when they placed the name of Julian Bond, first Black ever elected to the Georgia legislature, in nomination for the presidency. Bond then mounted the rostrum, thanked the delegates for their support, and withdrew—because he was only 32.[26]

Ronald Reagan was the oldest President (just three weeks short of 70) when he was sworn in on January 20, 1981.

But presidential candidates must do considerably more than meet minimal prescribed constitutional qualifications. They must be able politicians. Experience is important. Most Presidents have served as governors of their states or as members of the Congress. A few have been military heroes. Since the era of John F. Kennedy, nearly all successful presidential candidates have been at least competent in their use of political television. In order to win votes, one must be attractive to the public on TV. Kennedy and Reagan had charismatic personalities. They were made-to-order candidates for TV. Bill Clinton, like him or not, was a very able politician, although he has lost some elections, such as a campaign for Congress in 1974 and a re-election bid as governor of Arkansas in 1980.[27]

6. Party Leader

Who is the current leader of the Democratic Party? Barack Obama plays that role as President of the United States. Whoever wins his party's presidential nomination is called upon to serve as party leader. He is the party's spokesman during the election, and, if successful, after taking office. Although this role is not mentioned in the Constitution, it is a further source of political power and authority.

Obama, like his predecessors, tries to build a popular program which will transfer to other candidates wearing the party label in national, state and local elections. Because his success or failure depends largely on the political makeup of Congress, the President tries to help elect those candidates who will support him and his programs.

The President controls the national party organization. He can install his choice as national chairman and, unless he loses control of his party, a first-term President ordinarily can demand re-nomination if he wants it. Quadrennial national party conventions which nominate incumbent Presidents are more coronations than deliberations. Indeed, most of the mystery has gone out of these quadrennial events. By the time delegates assemble, it usually is a foregone conclusion who the convention will nominate.

Before 1972, outgoing Presidents could dictate the choice of their party's nominees as Theodore Roosevelt did in 1908 (Taft), Truman did in 1952 (Illinois Gov. Adlai E. Stevenson) and Johnson did in 1968 (Vice President Hubert Humphrey).

The rise of the presidential primary has complicated the picture. A candidate no longer can win the nomination without showing ability to survive marathon primary and caucus tests. But being endorsed by the President doesn't hurt, even today.

If, however, an incumbent President is unpopular, as George W. Bush was in 2008, the party nominee may not involve him in the campaign. Sen. John McCain paid a visit to the White House after winning the GOP nomination to receive the endorsement of the President. McCain, however, chose not to have Bush actively campaign for him.

Presidents also often play key roles in mid-term congressional elections, particularly those involving candidates in tough, competitive races. They may intervene in an attempt to help long-standing close or powerful political friends, particularly those whose support is vital on key administration bills. Some Democrats were horrified when Bill Clinton flew to Chicago to endorse Dan Rostenkowski, powerful chairman of the House Ways and Means Committee. Why?

Chairman Rostenkowski's support was essential for Clinton's tax reform measures. The President needed him. But the powerful legislator was under Federal indictment and eventually was to spend time in a Federal prison, rather than as chair of the tax writing panel. He was sentenced to 17 months for mail fraud and putting "phantom employees" on the public payroll in 1996.

If the course of political events should cause the Chief Executive to fall from grace with the American people, then congressional and other candidates may prefer for him to stay out of their state or district. Clearly this was the case in 1966, when President Johnson was a political liability in many constituencies. In 1974, President Nixon was unwelcome when a number of special House elections were held to fill vacancies prior to the President's August resignation. Nixon's disgrace hurt his party badly in 1974. Democrats, for example, carried President Ford's old "safe" (Grand Rapids, MI) Republican district in the aftermath of Watergate.

Clinton's relatively weak approval rating midway through his first term hurt the Democrats in the 1994 mid-term congressional elections and Republicans captured control of both houses of Congress for the first time since the campaign of 1946. But Clinton, called "the comeback kid" by the media, won an easy victory over Republican Senate Majority Leader Bob Dole in 1996. The Democrats, however, failed to regain control of Congress.

In 1998-2000, Clinton spent much of his time at party fundraisers. In one evening, a President can appear at a gathering of well-heeled party faithful and raise nearly $1 million, as Mr. Clinton did in one Chicago-area gathering in May, 1998. It is important to appear and speak at fundraisers and party rallies. It also is vital to try to maintain some semblance of party unity in a notoriously undisciplined American party system.

The President still has some patronage to dispense, even in the age of civil service. He is expected to appoint deserving partisans to diplomatic posts, to Federal judgeships and to important cabinet or sub-cabinet positions in the administration.

The President's control over his party stems from the fact that party needs him. It needs him to voice its policies to the nation. It needs him to raise money for its candidates for public office. It needs him to push the party agenda through the Congress, if the President's party controls Congress. This is virtually impossible when the opposition party holds power.

There are limits to how effective the President can be in this role. American parties are essentially coalitions of state and local organizations that come together every four years to nominate presidential and vice presidential candidates and to write a party platform. This general statement of principles is usually so phrased as to mean whatever one reads into it. When platforms are rigid, as was the case of the Republicans in 1964 or the Democrats in 1972, electoral disaster follows.

Party members often hold conflicting views, reflecting differences in the sections and interests that they represent. Partisans may disagree with some aspects of the President's programs. The President then will resort to the "carrot and the stick." Lyndon Johnson, a master wheeler-dealer in his relations with Congress, knew exactly what legislators wanted. He knew their weaknesses. He was willing to give his backing to local projects that a senator or representative was anxious to get for his state or district. All that he wanted in return was support for "Great Society" legislation. Other Presidents do the same thing. Few, however, have been as successful as Johnson was in getting his domestic programs enacted in 1964-65.[28]

Who is the leader of the Republican Party in 2009? Sen. John McCain, Republican presidential nominee in 2008, is the **titular head** of the party. But who will be its leader when it prepares to launch the presidential campaign of 2012? No one can say with any degree of certainty.

Clearly, there are a host of would-be candidates.

But no one can agree on any one person. Only after the Republican Party nominates a candidate in 2012, will it unite around a clear-cut leader.

In short, the American system does not provide for a clear choice of leader of the opposition, as do many parliamentary systems. In England, there is not only a government. There is also a shadow government. The British people know who their future leaders would be in the event of a change in administrations.

B. THEORIES OF PRESIDENTIAL POWER & AUTHORITY

One of the classic topics of American political debate centers around the question of presidential power and authority. How do Presidents use or abuse their constitutional power and authority? Indeed, how much power does Article II of the U.S. Constitution give to the nation's Chief Executive?

If one studies the history of the presidency, he or she is struck by the diametrically opposed theories of presidential power held by some of the nation's Chief Executives. Most Presidents, however, fit one of two models, the strong or the weak.

1. The Stewardship Theory

The so-called **"stewardship theory"** holds that a strong President must lead, if not dominate, American government and politics. It is associated with Theodore Roosevelt, who wrote in his *Autobiography:* "My view was that every executive officer, and above all, every executive officer in high position, was a steward of the people, bound actively and affirmatively to do all he could for the people, and not to content himself with the negative merit of keeping his talents undamaged in a napkin...My belief was that it was not only his right but his duty to do anything that the needs of the Nation demanded, unless such action was forbidden by the Constitution or by the laws...I did not usurp power, but I did greater broaden the use of executive power. In other words, I acted for the public welfare, I acted for the common well-being of all our people...I did not care a rap for the mere form or show of power; I cared immensely for the use that could be made of the substance."[29]

In brief, TR believed that the President must use the powers of his office to promote the well-being of the American people. The Constitution empowered him to do anything not specifically forbidden. Given such an "elastic" interpretation of presidential powers, it hardly is surprising that TR's administration was characterized by vigorous executive leadership and dominance of the Congress.

2. The Constitutional Theory

William Howard Taft dissented strongly from this view. He believed that the President had no broad unspecified grant of power, but was confined to doing those things specifically authorized by the Constitution or at least clearly implied by it.

Taft, who had been hand-picked by T.R. as his successor, later disappointed Roosevelt. In 1912, Roosevelt attempted a political comeback, trying to wrest the Republican nomination away from the incumbent Taft. When he failed to do so, he and his supporters bolted the GOP, went off to Chicago and held a secessionist party convention, where Roosevelt became the nominee of the Progressive Party. The net result was that the GOP was badly split, which enabled Woodrow Wilson to win the presidency. The two never forgot or forgave one another for that defeat. Taft, who later was appointed by Warren G. Harding as Chief Justice of the United States, wrote his memoirs years later and clearly stated his position—known as the **"constitutional theory"** of presidential power and authority as follows: "The true view of the Executive function is, as I conceive it, that the President can exercise no power which cannot be fairly and reasonably traced to some specific grant of power or justly implied and included within such express grant as proper and necessary to its exercise…There is no undefined residuum of power which he can exercise because it seems to him to be in the public interest."[30]

Wilson, who had a Ph.D. in Political Science from Johns Hopkins and was president of Princeton University before going into politics and becoming governor of New Jersey, once remarked: "The President is at liberty in law and in conscience to be as big a man as he can. His office is anything he has the ability and force to make it."

3. The Prerogative Theory

Perhaps the strongest statement on the need for presidential leadership was made during the election of 1940 by Franklin D. Roosevelt, Theodore Roosevelt's cousin.

Hitler had overrun Europe and only Great Britain stood between the Nazi dictator and complete conquest of Europe. Fighting for her very existence as a nation, Britain, through Prime Minister Winston Churchill, appealed to FDR. The Roosevelt Administration responded, as most historians feel was necessary, by giving England 50 U.S. destroyers in return for long-term leases on naval bases in the Caribbean. At the time, this was considered useful in any U.S. defense of the Panama Canal.

But isolationists were outraged, and predicted the U.S. was headed for war. They insisted that FDR had violated the Neutrality Act.

In brief, the so-called **"prerogative theory"** holds that the President should do whatever the national interest requires, even if this involves violation of the laws. Such a view brought storms of protests from Conservatives who called FDR "King Franklin I."[31]

President Truman described his power and authority as follows: "…people talk about the powers of a President, all the powers that a Chief Executive has, and what he can do. Let me tell you something—from experience.

The President may have a great many powers given to him in the Constitution and may have certain powers under certain laws which are given to him by the Congress of the United States; but the principal power that the President has is to bring people in and try to persuade them to do what they ought to do without persuasion. That's what I spend most of my time doing. That's what the powers of the President amount to."[32]

Like Taft, Eisenhower believed that the powers of the President could not be expanded. He said: "The principle of separation of powers required the President actually to impose restraints on himself because of the overwhelming power that the Presidency has acquired; and…a belief that the incidental influences flowing from the Presidency itself should not be exploited to promote causes beyond those assigned to the President by the Constitution."[33]

The use of presidential power, particularly the war-making power, led some political scientists to take a new look at what had been orthodox in their graduate school training. The dominant idea of the 1950s and early 1960s clearly was that only a strong President could lead the nation. Congress was too large, unwieldy, inefficient and filled with parochial perspectives to effectively cope with the nation's major foreign and domestic problems.

Among those who held this idea was Harvard historian Arthur Schlesinger, Jr. But Johnson and Nixon, in Schlesinger's opinion, had abused their power. He was inspired to write a best-selling book of the era, *The Imperial Presidency*, in which he said: "What the country needs today is a little serious disrespect for the office of the Presidency; a refusal to give any more weight to the President's words than the intelligence of the utterance, if spoken by anyone else, would command; an understanding of a point made so aptly by Montaigne: 'Sit he on never so high a throne, a man still sits on his bottom.'"[34]

The "New Orthodoxy" stressed the need for checks and balances—particularly congressional checks of executive power and authority.

Liberals who had once cheered the presidency as the center of the U.S. political system, now cheered congressional efforts to "cut the President down to proper size."

Sen. William Fulbright (D., AR), chair of the Foreign Relations Committee, held hearings questioning the Johnson Administration's intentions in Southeast Asia. Not only anti-Vietnam War activists applauded, so did those who felt that the presidency had grown too bloated in power, prestige and authority. Many felt that now was the time for Congress to reassert its proper role in the U.S. system of separation of powers and checks and balances.

Fulbright was joined in his anti-war, anti-Johnson stance in the Senate by other Democrats. One of them, Sen. Frank Church of Idaho, had long been asking the President's help in getting a dam on a river in his state. But Church was constantly making speeches on the Senate floor attacking the Vietnam War and, far worse, the President himself. He often quoted Liberal, syndicated columnist Walter Lippman, who had covered the Washington scene since the era of Woodrow Wilson. When Johnson held a White House reception for senators and Church moved through the receiving line to shake LBJ's hand, the President said to him, "Frank, that dam you want in Idaho? Ask Walter Lippman to build it for you."[35]

Watergate: If Vietnam was one major argument for balance of power and authority, another major one developed in what is loosely called **"Watergate."**

Watergate itself is a hotel-apartment, office complex in Washington, D.C. It also was the site of Democratic National Committee headquarters, chaired in 1972 by Larry O'Brien. A group of seven men, associated with the Committee to Re-Elect the President, were caught breaking into O'Brien's office.

The resulting cover-up of a large number of illegal acts committed by Nixon Administration officials led ultimately to the resignation of the President and the succession of Vice President Ford as Chief Executive. The national trauma has been condensed into one word, "Watergate." Over time it has taken a larger meaning and now refers to political crimes and bureaucratic corruption.

Among the illegal acts included within the term were bribery of public officials and illegal use of the Federal Bureau of Investigation (FBI) and Central Intelligence Agency (CIA). "Watergate" also referred to income tax fraud, White House staff use of an unofficial "plumbers group" to spy on private citizens and use of "dirty tricks" during the 1972 campaign. Finally, the term meant illegal campaign contributions and the use of campaign money for personal purposes.[36]

After Watergate, scholars began to re-examine their attitudes toward the presidency. During the New Deal-Fair Deal years of Roosevelt and Truman, the emphasis had been on concentration of power and authority in the executive branch.

Watergate was a "wake-up call," a reminder of Lord Acton's famous dictum: "power tends to corrupt and absolute power tends to corrupt absolutely."

In response to a request from the Ervin Committee (Senate Select Committee on Presidential Campaign Activities), a special committee of the National Academy of Public Administration provided a detailed indictment of the Nixon Administration's abuses of executive and administrative power. It urged educational institutions to "focus more attention on public sector ethics."

The committee, chaired by Frederick C. Mosher, also recommended more effective codes of conduct and standards for public administrators.[37]

There is nothing new in efforts by Congress to "trim the President down to size." Congress often has tried to reclaim authority and reassert itself after delegating special emergency powers to the President during periods of war and depression. "Watergate," however, was unparalleled in American history. No American President ever had been driven from office by such a scandal. After major Executive-Legislative battles between Nixon, Ford and the Democratic-controlled Congresses (1969-77), the election of former Georgia Gov. Jimmy Carter in 1976 brought an end to the Watergate saga.

But Carter's failures to lead Congress caused Tip O'Neil, Democratic Speaker of the House, to complain that the new President simply did not understand how Congress works. It cannot, he said, "do everything in one year." Presidents cannot overload it with requests. They must "prioritize." They must work with party leaders. Carter got low grades from Democratic congressional leaders in both of these categories.

After California Gov. Ronald Reagan won the presidency in 1980, political writers began to suggest that perhaps efforts to reduce the "swelling of the presidency" had been short-sighted and, in the long run, potentially disastrous.

Those scholars—probably a minority—who had been intellectually consistent during the turbulent 1960s and 1970s, argued that Schlesinger and other critics of the "Imperial Presidency" were inconsistent. As long as one of their own—a Harvard Liberal like FDR or Kennedy—occupied the Oval Office, they championed a strong presidency. When Lyndon Johnson and Nixon moved into 1600 Pennsylvania Avenue, their viewpoints changed.[38]

Clearly, most modern Presidents can be classified as strong. The two Roosevelts, Wilson, Truman, Kennedy, Johnson, Nixon, Reagan, both Bushes and Clinton all fit that model. International problems in the world of the late 20th and early 21st Centuries have forced the American President to play a leadership role.

Although it is far too early to judge President Obama, the enormous financial and foreign policy crises he faces make it virtually certain that he will follow the Roosevelt model. Indeed, few contemporary Presidents would advocate the restricted views of Taft, given the challenges of our times.

Although the statement was made at the beginning of the nation's history, Alexander Hamilton's support of strong presidential leadership is perhaps as true today as it was in the formative years of the Republic. Hamilton wrote in *The Federalist*: "Energy in the executive is a leading character in the definition of good government. It is essential to the protection of the community against foreign attacks; it is not less essential to the steady administration of the laws; to the protection of property against those irregular and high-handed combinations which sometimes interrupt the ordinary course of justice; to the security of liberty against the enterprises and assaults of ambition, of faction and of anarchy…A feeble executive implies a feeble execution of the government. A feeble executive is but another phrase for a bad execution; and a government ill executed, whatever it may be in theory, must be, in practice, a bad government."[39]

C. PROBLEMS OF TENURE, DISABILITY AND SUCCESSION

There are a number of major problems associated with the institution of the presidency. The problems of selection and the politics of the Electoral College is dealt with elsewhere. Among other recent concerns have been issues of tenure and disability and succession, which produced the 22nd and 25th Amendments, respectively.

1. Tenure and the 22nd Amendment

Fear of a strong President was partially responsible for the 22nd Amendment, which limits the Chief Executive to two terms in his own right. Although Franklin D. Roosevelt was the only President ever to be elected more than twice, Congress proposed and the states ratified an amendment which takes this possibility out of the hands of the American people.

Many, including former President Truman, have opposed the 22nd Amendment. They have argued that it tends to make the Chief Executive a "lame duck" during his second term. A number of scholars agree, but given the perceived abuses of power by the Johnson and Nixon Administrations, there is little likelihood of repeal in the near future.

2. Disability and Succession

The Framers of the Constitution recognized the vitally important role of the President and they provided in the Basic Law for transfer of presidential power and authority in the event that was necessary. Article II stipulates that: "...in case of the removal of the President from office, or of his death, resignation or inability to discharge the powers and duties of said office, the same shall devolve on the Vice President." Initially, it was not clear whether the vice president was to become only "acting President" or whether he actually became President. John Tyler, the first vice president to acquire the office upon the death of President William Henry Harrison (1841), resolved the matter by insisting that he was legally entitled to the full powers of the office.

Events which occurred during the Eisenhower Administration underscore the importance of the problems of presidential disability and succession. As President, Eisenhower suffered three major disabling illnesses in a little more than two years. He suffered a heart attack in September, 1955, while vacationing in Colorado. In June, 1956, he underwent serious, emergency surgery. The President, then 67, suffered a stroke—which temporarily affected his speech—in November, 1957. Each of these ailments created a temporary power vacuum.

Earlier in U.S. history, other Presidents suffered from physical disabilities. James Garfield, felled by an assassin's bullet, was confined to bed for some 80 days with a bullet in his spine. Vice President Chester Alan Arthur declined to act in Garfield's behalf because the cabinet believed that once Arthur assumed the role of acting President, it might be legally impossible for Garfield to get it back. Ultimately, Garfield died and Arthur became President.

Even more serious was the case of President Woodrow Wilson, who suffered a stroke in 1919 while touring the nation, trying to build political support for the League of Nations. For more than nine months, the Chief Executive was virtually an invalid.

The President's personal physician, Dr. Edward Graham, told Edith Wilson, the First Lady, to avoid bringing the President problems. That, Dr. Graham said, would be like turning a knife in an open wound.[40]

During the Wilson disability crisis, the **Treaty of Versailles** was being debated in the U.S. Senate and the nation was reconverting from a wartime to a peacetime economy. Secretary of State Robert Lansing called the cabinet into session to discuss urgent business. After learning of this "usurpation" of presidential power and authority, Wilson promptly asked for and received Secretary Lansing's resignation. At the time, there was no constitutional provision for declaring a President disabled and unable to perform the duties of his office.

Wilson thought about resigning his office. Some historians think that he should have done so. But it was a precedent that he did not wish to establish.

Both Garfield and Wilson were pre-nuclear Presidents. The U.S. government today plays a much larger role in the international community than it did then. It must defend itself in a world where the potential adversary is only minutes away by Intercontinental Ballistic Missile (IBM). The role of the Federal government in the lives of the American people, for better or worse, has grown enormously. We no longer can afford the luxury of presidential disability and lack of vice presidential initiative producing a lag in decision-making.

The concern raised by President Eisenhower's ailments, noted above, led directly to a precedent-shattering memorandum of understanding between the Chief Executive and his Vice President, Richard M. Nixon. Under terms of the agreement, made public in March, 1958, the President would serve as "acting President," exercising the powers and duties of the office until the inability has ended. Then the President "would resume the full exercise of the powers and duties of the office." Presidents Kennedy and Johnson entered into similar agreements with Vice Presidents Johnson and Humphrey, respectively.

If the President were unable to communicate the fact of disability (such as in case of a stroke or coma), the Vice President would, after consulting with appropriate leaders of Congress and Cabinet, assume the role of Acting President on his own initiative, again giving up the office when the Chief Executive recovered.

This agreement, with some modifications, is essentially what is provided by the 25th Amendment's disability clauses. The Amendment, ratified in 1967, contains detailed provisions for the transfer of presidential power and authority to the Vice President. It stipulates: "The Vice President shall become President in the event of the removal of the President from office or of his death or resignation."

The amendment also provides that, should the President become disabled, he may submit to the Speaker of the House and the president pro tempore of the Senate a written declaration that he can no longer fulfill his duties. The Vice President then becomes Acting President. Ronald Reagan wrote to the Congress in 1985, for example, that he was going to undergo surgery and would be incapacitated. Vice President Bush was to serve during that brief period as Acting President.

The disability provisions of the 25th Amendment also cover the possibility of disagreement between President and Vice President (perhaps ambitious and anxious to keep the job) over the state of the President's health. The Vice President and a majority of members of the Cabinet or an agency established by Congress, such as a panel of physicians, would submit a written statement to Congress declaring that the President is disabled.

In such a case, the Vice President would immediately become Acting President. But the President can regain his office after the disability is ended. He will reassume his powers and authority after transmitting to Congress a written statement that the disability no longer exists. This presidential claim can be challenged by the Vice President and a majority of members of the Cabinet or a panel created by Congress.

Congress then must decide by a two-thirds vote that he still is unable to perform his duties. If a two-thirds vote is obtained, the Vice President remains Acting President. Only an extraordinary majority could deny presidential power to the man or woman elected by the American people.

Eight American Presidents have died in office. Four of them—Lincoln, Garfield, McKinley and Kennedy—have been assassinated. The U.S. Constitution provides for an orderly transfer of power to the Vice President upon the death of the Chief Executive, a definite advantage to the nation, given the plight of some other societies who have failed to provide for this kind of orderly transition.

After the deaths of Lenin and Stalin, for example, the former Soviet Union was torn by bloodshed and violence until Stalin and Khrushchev, respectively, emerged as leaders.

The Kennedy assassination focuses the spotlight on another aspect of presidential succession. Who should succeed to the office of Chief Executive after the Vice President?

A false report was carried by an American wire service after the death of President Kennedy. It said that Vice President Johnson had suffered a heart attack. Because Johnson had a medical history of coronary problems and had previously suffered a heart attack while Democratic Majority Leader of the U.S. Senate, there appeared to be some basis in fact for the report. Millions of Americans, already shocked by the tragic events in Dallas, asked themselves, "What now?"

The **Presidential Succession Act of 1947** is the present controlling law in this matter. But it is the third succession act in our history. Before 1947, the line was different with the Secretary of State and Chief Justice of the United States next in line.

Current (1947) law provides that the Speaker of the House, Nancy Pelosi (D., CA), and then the President Pro Tempore of the Senate, Robert Byrd (D., W.VA), follow the Vice President in the scheme of succession. After that, (unlikely except in case of all-out nuclear war) would come senior cabinet members—Secretaries of State, Treasury and Defense, then other cabinet heads, essentially in order of the creation of their departments.

Millions of Americans learned in November, 1963, that John McCormack of Boston and Carl Hayden of Arizona were next in line behind Lyndon Johnson in the succession plan. McCormack, the 72-year-old Speaker, never had presidential qualifications and claimed none. He said, in fact, that he would have resigned his office had the burden fallen upon him and permitted the House to elect a new Speaker, knowing that in so doing they would be electing a President. Senator Hayden, then 86, had been in Congress since his state was admitted to the Union in 1912.

After waiting a "decent" amount of time after the assassination and not wishing to offend Speaker McCormack—whom he dutifully kept briefed on foreign and national security matters—President Johnson proposed to Congress that it consider a constitutional amendment, permitting the President to name a new Vice President in the event that the office became vacant.

Ultimately, Congress agreed, adding a section to the 25th Amendment that gives the President authority to nominate a Vice President, who then must be approved by a majority vote of both House and Senate. President Johnson could have had no way of knowing that the new procedure would be invoked twice within less than a year.

In October, 1973, Vice President Spiro T. Agnew resigned his office and was fined for tax evasion. President Nixon chose House Republican leader Gerald R. Ford of Grand Rapids, Michigan, as our first appointed Vice President. When Nixon was forced to become the first President ever to resign his office, Ford succeeded to the Oval Office and invoked the 25th Amendment, nominating former New York Gov. Nelson A. Rockefeller as Vice President.[41]

The net result of the 25th Amendment is that between August, 1974, and January, 1977, it gave the American people a President and a Vice President, neither of whom had been elected in a national election. At the time, some critics argued that it should be repealed and perhaps replaced by one calling for a special election to fill any vacancies that might arise.

The amendment's defenders note that it provided an orderly constitutional procedure which "got us through Watergate."

Some political writers argue that the U.S. was better served by its pre-1947 line of succession in which the Secretary of State and Chief Justice of the United States were next in line to the White House after the Vice President. President Truman, who urged Congress to enact the 1947 law, argued that it was better to have an elected official (Speaker of the House) immediately in the line of succession, rather than an appointive one, such as the Secretary of State or Chief Justice.

Other political leaders, political scientists and journalists are quite pragmatic about the whole matter. Why, they ask, change something on the basis of an event that has happened only once in the nation's entire history and may never happen again?

D. PRESIDENTIAL CHARACTER

Not all questions about presidential character involve accusations of Nixon and Lyndon Johnson's lying or Clinton's womanizing.

Duke University's James David Barber, a former President of the American Political Science Association, has published *"The Presidential Character,"* a book which suggests that patterns of behavior, some of which may be traced to childhood, can help to explain presidential behavior.[42]

Barber enumerates four presidential character types. They are based largely on (1) the degree of enjoyment a President finds in his job (he is either positive or negative about it) and (2) the energy level the president brings to it (he is either active or passive in his job efforts).

Barber concludes that **active-positive** Presidents have been the most successful. They have, he suggests, generally enjoyed happy childhoods. As a result, they are happy individuals open to new life experiences. They approach their White House job with enthusiasm. They want to lead and are confident in their leadership abilities. They are flexible and adaptable. They love being President and using the power and authority inherent in the office. Above all, they are goal oriented. They have ideas about what the public good requires and have no hesitation to push Congress and the nation to support their policies.

They are not ideologues. They are pragmatists, realizing that politics is "the art of the possible." They understand the importance of timing and the limits of what can be accomplished within a relatively short period.

Barber labels the following Presidents as active-positives: Franklin D. Roosevelt, Truman, Kennedy, Ford, Carter, Bush and Clinton.

The worst Presidents, Barber thinks, are **active-negatives**. They spend a great deal of energy in being President, but unlike their positive counterparts, do not appear to enjoy being President.

They use power for its own sake, rather than for the public good. Some of them appear to have been obsessed with power. They have sometimes viewed opponents as "enemies" to be not only defeated, but also humiliated or punished. This, Barber suggests, is due to lack of self-esteem and painful childhood experiences.

Active negatives are sometimes convinced that morality is on their side. They are frequently unwilling to compromise, exhibiting a rigidity that works against them in dealing with Congress and factions within their own party who disagree with their policy objectives. Barber concludes that they are doomed to failure and are also a danger of the nation. Barber puts four 20th Century Presidents—Wilson, Hoover, Lyndon B. Johnson and Nixon—in this category.

Barber theorizes that **passive-positive** Presidents find themselves reacting to circumstances and fail to use presidential power and authority effectively. They enter politics not for the love of power and authority, or the trappings of office, but rather because they like people and want to contribute to "public service." Barber believes that passive-positive types have a superficial optimism about life. They tend to let others set goals for them and sometimes have trouble making up their minds. They have a low sense of self-esteem.

The problem with passive-positives, according to Barber, is that they sometimes allow the ship of state to drift. Three 20th Century Presidents who illustrate this type are, he says, Taft, Harding and Reagan.

Passive-negatives combine two personality characteristics which one might not expect to find in an American President. These are a lack of job satisfaction and a lack of energy spent on the duties of being the nation's Chief Executive. These are men who have become President because they have considered public service their "duty," something that they ought to do—rather than something they really want to do. Barber includes among this type Coolidge and Eisenhower.

Professor Barber's theory is highly controversial. Many historians do not agree with his assessments and evaluations. Some suggest it is too partisan, because Barber considers most Liberal Democrats as outstanding Presidents and many Conservative Republicans as less than successful Chief Executives.

Like all social scientists, political scientists are trained in the specialties of their discipline. They are not psychologists. Clearly, they have not attended medical school and become experts in psychiatry. Examination of a President's psychological characteristics, while perhaps interesting, is of doubtful value.

Specialists in the mental health profession will tell you that they cannot evaluate a person's character or mindset if they have not examined the patient. In some cases, prolonged examination and consultation with a subject would be required to reach conclusions contained in presidential psycho-biographies. Wilson was the topic of one such book, written by Sigmund Freud and William Bullitt.[43] The book was not to be published until after the deaths of all involved. But it goes far beyond what some psychiatrists might consider ethical.

Later volumes have been written about Lyndon Johnson, Nixon and Carter by social scientists who attempt to probe presidential personalities, mental states and childhood experiences. These subjective and uncertain studies go far beyond the boundaries of traditional political science.

E. RATING THE PRESIDENTS

Most American citizens have their own ideas of who the great Presidents were. They also are quick to tell you who they think failed miserably in the White House.

Selective perception is always with us. Democrats are inclined to look at Jefferson, Jackson, Wilson, Franklin Roosevelt, Truman and Kennedy as great Chief Executives. Prior to the escalation of Vietnam War, many considered Lyndon Johnson great. Probably few contemporary citizens would put that label on Carter or Clinton, but history teaches us that the worst judges of Presidents and their performances are their contemporaries.

Republicans are inclined to think that Lincoln, Teddy Roosevelt, Eisenhower, Ford, Reagan and the first President Bush were outstanding or great. Democrats would agree with them only on the first two listed. We obviously lack the historical perspective necessary to rate any recent or incumbent Chief Executives, such as George W. Bush or Barack Obama.

There is a great difference between professional historians and average citizens. Historians clearly know more about Presidents and the presidency. That is their business, how they make their living. Many men and women in the street would be hard-pressed to name more than a handful of the nation's Chief Executives.

But scholars also suffer from selective perception. An estimated 75% of social scientists who have a party preference prefer the Democratic Party. Although they must be objective or at least "fair" in their assessments of presidential performance, some of them are not.

Harvard historian Arthur Schlesinger, in 1948, polled U.S. historians, who rated six Presidents as "great." They were Lincoln, Washington, Franklin D. Roosevelt, Wilson, Jefferson and Jackson. Note that Lincoln is the only Republican on the list. A 1962 Schlesinger poll had the same result, except that Jackson was dropped from the list. One can only imagine what "Old Hickory" had done between 1948-62 to deserve being dropped..

In 1982, The *Chicago Tribune*, a newspaper with long-established Republican Party editorial page preferences, took a poll in which it asked 49 prominent historians to rate the 10 best and 10 worst Presidents. Their findings listed the 10 best as:

Lincoln (the best), Washington, Franklin Roosevelt (hated while he was in office by *Tribune* publisher Colonel Robert McCormick), Theodore Roosevelt, Jefferson, Wilson, Jackson, Truman (also on McCormick's list of least favorite Presidents), Eisenhower and Polk.

The 10 worst on the *Tribune*'s list in 1982 were as follows:

Harding (the worst), Nixon, Buchanan, Pierce, Grant, Filmore, Andrew Johnson, Coolidge, Tyler and Carter.

In 1995, the Chicago *Sun-Times*, historically a paper which has endorsed Democratic candidates, listed the 10 best Presidents as Lincoln (best), Washington, Franklin D. Roosevelt, Jefferson, Theodore Roosevelt, Wilson, Truman, Jackson, Eisenhower and Polk. The 10 worst: Harding (worst), Nixon, Buchanan, Pierce, Grant, Filmore, Andrew Johnson, Coolidge, Tyler and Carter.

Remarkably, the *Sun-Times* and the *Tribune*, on opposite sides of the political fence, came to virtually identical conclusions.

In February, 2005, a Gallup Poll found Americans rating Ronald Reagan as the greatest president in history, followed by Bill Clinton, Lincoln, FDR and Kennedy. Some scholars believe that the poll indicates how little people know about presidential history.

In his 1998 book, *Star Spangled Men: America's 10 Worst Presidents,* Nathan Miller focuses on the negative and comes to these conclusions: character, political skill, vision and integrity are important qualities, contributing to the making of a good President. The lack of political skill, moral integrity and character and a sense of purpose contribute to the making of presidential failures. Most significant, Miller says, is how much harm (wars, depressions, crime and human rights violations) a President inflicted on the nation. Franklin Pierce and James Buchanan were so inept, Miller says, that they helped plunge the nation into Civil War.[44]

Andrew Johnson, the only President until Bill Clinton ever to be impeached by the House of Representatives (although the Senate failed by one vote to remove him from office), was intent on preserving the white power structure in the South after the Confederacy's defeat.

Harding and Coolidge pursued policies which led to the Great Depression.

Miller considers Nixon the worst of all Presidents, a highly controversial conclusion. Conceding that Nixon had the stuff to be a good President and that he did achieve a "solid record of accomplishments in both domestic and foreign affairs," Miller nevertheless concludes that Nixon's blatant violation of the Constitution merits being chosen as worst. His tragic character flaws forced Nixon to resign his office in order to avoid impeachment.

Most historians have reserved the "worst of the worst" honor for Harding, who accomplished little during his tenure in the White House. Harding ran Washington like a political boss in New York City ran Tammany Hall, location of the famous, or infamous, 19th Century Democratic machine.

Miller lists a recent Democratic President (as well as Republican Nixon) as a member of his presidential "Hall of Shame." Jimmy Carter, considered by many one of the most honorable men ever to serve in the White House, is rated 10th worst.

Carter had the lowest approval rating in the history of the polls (18%) after an abortive effort to rescue American hostages in Iran in 1980. He left office with a Gallup approval rating of 34%. In 2006, however, 61% of Americans approved of the job he had done as Chief Executive.

Soon after Barack Obama took office in January, 2009, Carter said that history might be kinder to President George W. Bush than were his contemporaries. Like Carter, Bush left office with a dismal 34% approval rating.

Carter said that as time goes by, it's likely that the negative ratings would improve. Bush will see his popularity go up, he concluded. Both Carter and Bush, however, had better ratings than Harry S. Truman, who had a 32% score and is today regarded by many historians as an outstanding President.

F. THE VICE PRESIDENT

The Founding Fathers paid little attention to the office of Vice President. Originally, he was to be only an immediate stand-in for the President, in the event of the death of the Chief Executive. Later in the constitutional debates, the delegates decided to make the Vice President the President of the Senate, but gave him the "power" to vote only in case of a tie.

History tends to remember only those Vice Presidents who became Chief Executive. The phrase, "just one heartbeat away from the presidency," reminds us of the President's mortality. Harvard historian Arthur M. Schlesinger, Jr. has suggested that this may have caused some early conflicts between President John Adams and Vice President Jefferson. In an article in *Atlantic* (May, 1974), Schlesinger commented: "The Vice President has only one serious thing to do: that is to wait around for the President to die. This is hardly the basis for a cordial and enduring friendship."[45]

During the administration of George Washington, Vice President John Adams remarked: "My country has in its wisdom contrived for me the most insignificant office than ever the invention of man contrived or his imagination conceived."

Texan John Nance Garner, who served as Speaker of the House, prior to being chosen as Franklin D. Roosevelt's running mate in 1932 and 1936, once said: "The vice presidency isn't worth a pitcher of warm spit."

Other examples of self-effacing vice presidential humor are easy to find.

Theodore Roosevelt, who served as Vice President until the assassination of President William McKinley, told the story of the mother who had two sons. One joined the U.S. Navy, went to sea and was never heard from again. The other son went into politics, became Vice President of the United States and suffered the same fate, Roosevelt said.

Until recently, Presidential candidates have chosen as their running mates individuals who "balanced the ticket." This meant that, if the nominee at the top of the ticket was from the East, for example, geographic balance dictated that someone from the Midwest or West, be chosen for the second spot.

In the case of the Democrats, southerners often were chosen as running mates, given the south's historic attachment—until recently—to the Democratic Party. It also was considered a good idea to have a running mate from a state with a large block of electoral votes, necessary to winning the supreme prize of American politics, the White House.

Republicans, in 1948, thought that they had a "dream ticket" with governors from the two largest states, New York's Thomas E. Dewey and California's Earl Warren, as their team. But Dewey's inept campaign and Truman's victory, perhaps the biggest presidential election upset of the 20th Century, made that dream a nightmare.

In 1960, John F. Kennedy from Massachusetts chose Lyndon B. Johnson of Texas as his running mate. Sectionalism was important and Kennedy had to get religious balance on the ticket. No Roman Catholic ever had been elected President of the United States. Kennedy needed Johnson to minimize anti-Catholic bias in the south, where the Ku Klux Klan was still an influence, and to keep Texas—the largest of the southern state—from bolting into the Republican column.

Ideological balance has been important in the past. Typically, if a Liberal Republican wins the nomination, he will choose a more Conservative running mate. Eisenhower, whose nomination was engineered by Eastern Liberal Republicans, chose Sen. Richard Nixon of California as his running mate in 1952. Nixon had great appeal to

Conservative Republicans as a leader in the "fight against Communism." The fact that East and West balanced nicely didn't hurt.

This "balancing the ticket" made many citizens cynical about politics. Did it make sense to have a Conservative next in line if a Liberal President died in office? Perhaps it can be argued that it did, given the Kennedy-Johnson case.

Before he was chosen as Kennedy's running mate, Johnson was regarded as a pragmatic, Conservative Democrat, reflecting the views of his Texas constituents. If students could see tapes of the 1960 Democratic convention, they could hear the Liberal, Democratic governor of Michigan, G. Mennen "Soapy" Williams, shouting, "NO, NO, NO!" when the announcement was made to the delegates that Johnson was Kennedy's choice. Once he had a new, national constituency, Johnson's perspective changed. Historians regard his domestic program, much of it enacted in 1964-65, as a continuation of the New Deal.

Clinton broke most of the old "balance" rules of American politics in winning the 1992 and 1996 presidential elections. In choosing Sen. Albert Gore Jr. of Tennessee, he violated the rule of geographical balance because Tennessee borders Clinton's home state of Arkansas. Religious balance? Both are Southern Baptists. Clinton said that the most important thing was to have a running mate who would be an able successor, should that need arise. It is traditional for presidential candidates to say that, even if they don't mean it. But perhaps Clinton did.

Gore and Clinton also were from the same ideological wing of the Democratic Party. Both were among the founders of the Democratic Leadership Council, a group of party "moderates" who were tired of losing elections to Republicans. "A New Kind of Democrat," Clinton's theme in 1992, suggested that he was less Liberal than defeated Democratic candidates like Walter Mondale (1984) and Michael Dukakis (1988).

Five Vice Presidents have become President since the World War II era: Truman, Johnson, Nixon, Ford, and Bush. In 2000, Al Gore nearly became number six. Being a Vice President has both its advantages and disadvantages. Clearly, Gore got plenty of national exposure to the issues. But he always had to remember his place and could not "upstage" the President.

Recent Vice Presidents have been members of the National Security Council. President Clinton assigned Gore the task of reviewing the Federal bureaucracy in a highly-publicized "re-inventing government" initiative. He was active in Clinton's efforts on behalf of the "information superhighway." Most reporters concluded that he bested Jack Kemp, Bob Dole's GOP vice presidential running mate, in a TV debate in 1996. He also took on the troublesome Ross Perot in a debate on the North American Free Trade Agreement and received high marks for his performance by those who did not have a vested interest in the outcome.

George W. Bush chose Richard Cheney of Wyoming as his vice presidential running mate in 2000 and in 2004. Cheney became a lightning rod for critics of the Bush administration, strongly supporting post-September 11, 2001 measures, characterized as the "war on terrorism."

Among these were the PATRIOT Act, expanding wiretapping to detect terrorists, and the prison camp at Guantanamo Bay, Cuba, where "enemy combatants" were held indefinitely. He also backed military tribunals where alleged terrorists could be tried without the benefits of legal protections of civil trials.

Before becoming Vice President, Cheney had served in the U.S. House of Representatives as President Ford's White House Chief of Staff and as Secretary of Defense in President George H.W. Bush's cabinet during the first Persian Gulf War. In short, his considerable national government experience was expected to offset George W. Bush's lack of experience at the Federal level.

In 2008, Barack Obama selected U.S. Sen. Joe Biden of Delaware as his running mate. Biden had served 30 years in the Senate, was a former contender for the Democratic presidential nomination and had chaired the Senate Foreign Relations Committee, an area that some considered an Obama weakness.

Republican John McCain's choice of Alaska Gov. Sarah Palin was applauded by party conservatives. Palin was strongly pro-life on the abortion issue, had a reputation as a reformer and, McCain hoped, would appeal to women, angry that Hillary Clinton had been denied the Democratic Party's presidential nomination.

Her lack of foreign policy experience, combined with McCain's age, proved to be a negative in the long-run.

The 2000 Presidential Election: The election of 2000 was the most unusual in more than a century. Nearly all political writers and pollsters expected a close presidential vote, but no one predicted that the outcome of the election would ride on a U.S. Supreme Court decision. Many Americans will recall the high drama and the intensity of the struggle, which remained in doubt for 36 days.

It has always been troubling to some people that the Electoral College makes it possible for the winner of the popular vote to lose the election. Indeed that now has happened four times in the nation's history.

John Quincy Adams (1824), Rutherford B. Hayes (1876) and Benjamin Harrison (1888) all lost the popular vote. But they became President and Andrew Jackson (1824), Samuel Tilden (1876) and Grover Cleveland (1888) were losers because of the Electoral College system. In 2000, however, the electorate was not prepared for what happened: Vice President Al Gore won more than a half a million votes more than Texas Gov. George W. Bush. Bush, however, became President because a majority of the Electoral College voted for him, rather than Gore.

Although the drama began on election night, the legal and political struggle was to continue for more than a month as the American public attempted to understand what was happening and what had happened in Florida.

The Electoral College has always given an edge to the candidate who carries the big states. It's not how many states one wins that matters. It's winning the majority (today that's 270) of the 538 electoral votes. Gerald Ford, in fact, lost to Jimmy Carter in 1976, although he had won 26 states. Had Ford won about 4000 votes more in Hawaii and 3500 more in Ohio, he would have carried those states and their electoral votes. Although Carter won the "popularity contest" by a margin of about 1.7 million votes, he could have lost with a change of about 7500 in two states.

In 2000, Vice President Gore won victories in key states of the East (New York, Pennsylvania) and Midwest (Illinois and Michigan). It soon was obvious that Bush had to win Florida to become the nation's 43rd President.

Gore would not have needed to win Florida, had he taken his own state, Tennessee, President Clinton's home state, Arkansas, or West Virginia, which nearly always votes for the Democratic presidential candidate.

Election night was not an example of the American news media at its best. NBC announced at 7:50 p.m. that Gore had won Florida, despite the fact that the polls had not yet closed in the Western part of the Sunshine state, in a different time zone. Other networks followed NBC's example. But by 9 p.m., they began to back off on their predictions.

At 2:15 a.m. on Wednesday, all of the networks declared Governor Bush the winner in Florida.

Vice President Gore called Governor Bush and conceded, offering his congratulations and best wishes for a successful administration. Bush thanked the Vice President for his call and, according to reporters said, "You're a good man," adding that he understood how hard this was for Gore. Bush extended his best wishes to Tipper and the Gore children.

The Vice President then got into his car and his motorcade moved through the rainy streets of Nashville, TN, toward the War Memorial where he would concede. Gore removed the concession speech from his pocket and he was preparing to read it.

Michael Feldman, Gore's chief of staff, felt his pager quiver. Field director Michael Whouley was watching the Florida Board of elections web site. National campaign chairman William Daley said the Bush margin was shrinking quickly. Daley told Feldman to grab Gore and prevent him from going on stage, saying "You're only 500 votes behind, don't concede."

At 3:45 a.m., Gore placed a second telephone call to Governor Bush and withdrew his concession. It was, according to media reports, not the most polite or pleasant of conversations. It ended abruptly.

Additional returns from Florida showed that Bush's lead continued to erode. The broadcast networks took back their call of a Republican victory and said that the election was too close to call. The official vote tally in Florida declared Bush the winner by 1784 votes out of about 5.8 million cast. However, state law requires an automatic recount. in a contest that close. After the recount, Bush's lead was only 300 votes, although absentee ballots increased it to 930.

What transpired next was a maze of lawsuits filed by Democrats in Florida state courts and by Republicans in the Federal courts. Democrats charged that there had been irregularities in voting procedures in several Florida counties. They also alleged that the forms of the ballot used in some counties had confused voters and that not all of the legal votes had been counted.

The Florida Supreme Court barred Republican Secretary of State Katherine Harris from issuing a final certification of the Florida vote. It further granted three counties, all heavily Democratic, an additional 11 days to recount their presidential ballots. Only one of them, Broward County, managed to complete its work within the allotted time.

The outcome of the vote still left Governor Bush ahead by 537 votes and the Secretary of State then acted to certify the Texas governor as the winner of the Florida presidential election. With Florida's 25 votes in hand, it appeared that George W. Bush would be the new President of the United States.

However, Democrats won a ruling from the Florida Supreme Court, ordering Miami-Dade County to hand count about 9000 votes on which voting machines had not detected a vote for either Bush or Gore. County officials were ordered to determine if there was a legal vote, "one in which there was a clear indication of the intent of the voter." Florida's highest court also held that results of recounts that had not been completed by the end of the court's initial deadline, be included in the final count.

This recount added 215 votes from Palm Beach County and 168 from Miami-Dade to Gore's total, reducing Bush's lead as Miami-Dade's 9000 uncounted ballots were to be tabulated.

Gore supporters pinned their hopes on the ordered recount in the three heavily Democratic counties. Republicans quickly appealed the Florida Supreme Court ruling to the U.S. Supreme Court, which granted a hearing.

Governor Bush's attorneys, led by Theodore Olson, argued that Florida's vote counting procedure, ordered by the state supreme court, violated both Federal law and the 14th Amendment's Due Process and Equal Protection clauses.

On December 12, 2000, the Supreme Court issued its ruling. Seven justices found that the Florida Supreme Court's order violated the U.S. Constitution. Three of the seven also found that the state Supreme Court had violated an act of Congress that governed presidential elections.

Two dissenting justices believed that the case presented no substantial issue that required the Federal courts to intervene and that the Florida Supreme Court decision should be upheld.

The U.S. Supreme Court ruling in *Bush v. Gore* marked the end of the presidential contest of 2000. But one step remained.

A week after the ruling, members of the Electoral College met in their respective state capitols to cast their ballots. George Bush won 271 electoral votes, one more than the minimum required to be chosen President of the United States. Gore won 266, one less than he should have. This was because an elector from the District of Columbia, angered that the District has not been granted statehood, cast a blank ballot.

On January 20, 2001, George W. Bush was inaugurated as the nation's 43rd President.

In 2004, Bush, running for re-election as a wartime President, fought off the challenge of Sen. John F. Kerry of Massachusetts, winning 51% of the popular vote to his opponent's 48%. In so doing, he became the first President to win a majority of the popular vote since his father defeated former Massachusetts Gov. Michael Dukakis in 1988.

Bush won 286 electoral votes, 16 more than the majority required by the U.S. Constitution.

Only three states deviated from their recent political behavior. Bush won New Mexico and Iowa, won by Gore in 2000. Kerry took New Hampshire, which the President had previously captured.

Had he carried Ohio's 20 electoral votes, Senator Kerry could have won the election, although he lost the popular vote by a margin of about 3.5 million Bush carried the Buckeye state by about 120,000 votes. But, as 2000 reminded American voters, the Constitution requires an absolute majority of the electoral vote, not a popular vote majority.

Some 12 million more ballots were cast in 2004 than in 2000, perhaps because of the sharp differences between the candidates. Both parties also focused their efforts on voter registration and getting their supporters to the polls on November 2. Bush won more votes than any other presidential candidate in U.S. history. Kerry compiled the second largest vote total ever recorded.

But, as one cynical political writer put it: "Close only counts in horseshoes and hand grenades."

The Presidential Election of 2008: History was made in 2008 when Senator Barack Obama, known to few Americans outside of Illinois four years earlier, won a series of highly contested primaries and caucuses to become the Democratic Party's presidential nominee. He then went on to defeat Republican John McCain by a wide margin.

As the year 2007 began, political pundits had anointed Sen. Hillary Clinton of New York and former New York Republican Mayor Rudy Giuliani as front-runners for the Democratic and Republican presidential nominations, respectively.

No less than five current or past U.S. Senate Democrats sought their party's nod. In addition to Obama and Clinton, there was Joe Biden of Delaware, Christopher Dodd of Connecticut and former Sen. John Edwards of North Carolina, the party's 2004 vice presidential nominee. Also running were New Mexico Gov. Bill Richardson, former Alaska Gov. Mike Gravel and Rep. Dennis Kucinich of Ohio.

The Republican field of contenders eventually grew to 10. Besides McCain and Giuliani, there were former governors Mitt Romney of Massachusetts, Mike Huckabee of Arkansas, and Tommy Thomson of Wisconsin.

Also Sen. Sam Brownback of Kansas, former Sen. Fred Thompson of Tennessee and Congressmen Ron Paul (Texas), Duncan Hunter (California) and Tom Tancredo of Colorado

Giuliani's campaign made the gross tactical error of skipping the first six primaries. The reasoning was that the crowded GOP field would split the vote and Giuliani could score a major victory in Florida.

Huckabee surprised, however, by winning the Iowa caucus and McCain edged Romney in New Hampshire, a severe setback. Romney did win the Michigan primary by stressing his ties to the state where his father had been governor, promising to help the state with the nation's highest unemployment rate.

McCain, however, continued to win primaries and media attention. He defeated Huckabee, Romney and Thompson in South Carolina, and Giuliani in Florida. The next day, the former New York mayor quit the contest and only McCain, Huckabee and Romney remained.

McCain won nine contests on Super Tuesday. Romney withdrew two days later and endorsed the Arizona senator. On March 4, McCain beat Huckabee in four states and the former Arkansas governor ended his campaign.

President Bush endorsed Senator McCain, who visited the White House the next day.

On the Democratic side, Senator Clinton failed to win endorsements from former presidential candidates Al Gore or John Kerry. At first she campaigned as if her nomination was virtually inevitable. But the Iraq War was unpopular and Obama had opposed it as early as 2002, while Clinton had voted in favor of a Senate resolution favoring action against Saddam Hussein. Polls indicated that Clinton was losing ground to Obama, who also was raising record sums of money for his campaign.

Although Obama and Clinton were viewed as the major candidates, Governor Richardson and former Senator Edwards were also considered viable candidates by the media, which paid little attention to the rest of the field.

Obama defeated Clinton in the Iowa caucuses, scoring 35% to her 25% and Edwards' 24%. It was a stunning result, suggesting that Obama could defeat Clinton with the support of white voters.

Throughout the campaign, Obama dominated the caucus states and Clinton did better in primaries. Clinton won a close victory in the New Hampshire primary.

Richardson quit the campaign on January 10 without endorsing a candidate. Kerry endorsed Obama.

Michigan was, along with Florida, a peculiar case in 2008. Democratic Party leaders challenged the rules of the Democratic National Committee by moving their primaries ahead of dates permitted. All the leading Democrats agreed not to campaign in those states, but Clinton did not have her name removed from the ballot. When she won 55% of the vote in Michigan, she touted this victory, although it was questionable that any of Michigan or Florida's delegates would be seated at the Democratic National Convention.

Although Clinton scored a rare caucus state win in Nevada, Obama won the South Carolina primary. That contest introduced Obama's race into the Democratic contest for the first time. Bill Clinton, playing the role of "attack dog," said that South Carolina was unimportant because Jesse Jackson twice had won there. Some Democrats openly questioned whether Bill Clinton was more of a handicap than a help in his wife's presidential campaign. Sen. Ted Kennedy endorsed Obama. Clinton won the Florida primary with 50% of the vote. Edwards dropped out the next day without endorsing anyone.

Super Tuesday on February 5 appeared to be of critical importance. Obama won 12 states to Clinton's nine, but she won larger industrial states, California, New York and Massachusetts. Of critical importance – Obama's delegate count was only 55 votes ahead of Clinton, 931-876.

The rest of the month belonged to Obama, who won Louisiana, Nebraska, Washington, Maine, Virginia and Maryland. When he won the Wisconsin primary, he neared the nomination.. On March 4, Clinton won in Ohio and Texas and the two candidates split Vermont and Rhode Island.

It became obvious that the primaries and caucuses had produced almost a dead heat and that votes of party "superdelegates," as well as the fate of Michigan and Florida delegates, would be critical.

Iraq began to recede in importance as the campaign progressed with the success of the "surge." Newspaper headlines focused not on Baghdad, but on the mortgage crisis, rising inflationary pressures and a weak stock market.

Although Clinton won the Pennsylvania primary, because of proportional representation, Obama's delegate lead was reduced by only 12.

In May, the Democratic National Committee decided to award Michigan and Florida delegates each one-half vote. This resulted in a gain of only 24 votes for Clinton.

The final primaries were on June 3, when Clinton won South Dakota and Obama won Montana. This put him over the top. .A few days later, Clinton endorsed Obama for President.

The general election featured fundamental political conditions which favored the Democrats. The war in Iraq was unpopular. President Bush had extremely low approval ratings. Some political observers said that Obama was running more against Bush than against McCain.

The excitement produced by the Obama-Clinton contest for the nomination resulted in more Democratic Party registrations and voter turnout. These paid handsome dividends as more than 130 million voters cast ballots in 2008.

Either way, the Democratic Party was going to make history in 2008. It would nominate the first woman candidate for President or choose the first biracial candidate, the son of a Kenyan father and a white mother from Kansas who met at the University of Hawaii in their student days.

Some political analysts believe that Republicans showed less enthusiasm for McCain. In many cases, conservatives did not think of the Arizonan as "one of our own." Moderates were upset by his choice of Alaska Gov. Sarah Palin as his running mate, given her lack of experience in foreign policy. Given McCain's age and health history, many were troubled by the idea that Governor Palin would be only a heartbeat removed from the presidency.

Media predictions of an inevitable Obama victory also may have discouraged some GOP voters.

Another major advantage for Obama was money (the "mother's milk of politics"). McCain accepted Federal financing of his campaign, which limited him to spending $84 million. Obama built a huge campaign treasury, raising more than $500 million from private sources in the fall alone.

The televised debates also may well have helped to make Obama President. People could—and did—get comfortable with the idea of the first candidate of mixed racial ancestry becoming their Chief Executive.

To some extent, McCain was the victim of bad luck. The year 2008 saw the first major crash that ever occurred before a presidential election. Some forget that the Republican nominee, perhaps enjoying a post-Republican National Convention "bounce," led Obama in the polls in early September.

But the economic panic of that month destroyed McCain's hopes, as well as those of many Republicans running for Congress. In American politics, voters long have been most concerned about two issues: war and peace and the economy. Although Iraq was an unpopular conflict, it was not the paramount issue in fall, 2008. It was the pocketbook issue, the Great Crash, that was ruinous to the GOP.

As the economy sank, Obama's fortunes rose. Even had he run a faultless campaign (he did not), McCain probably could not have won, given economic conditions in the U.S. at the time. He was crushed by the Crash.

The numbers show that the Obama-Biden ticket won by almost 10 million popular votes. They took 53.7% of the two-party vote. The Electoral College vote favored Obama, 365-173

V. CONGRESSIONAL POWER AND AUTHORITY

A. THE ROLES OF CONGRESS

Article I of the Constitution enumerates the powers and provides a blueprint for the organization and operation of the U.S. Congress. It is no accident that the very first article of America's Basic Law concerns itself with these matters, because the legislature was viewed in late 18th Century America as the "champion of the people."

The legislative Article provides simply that "all legislative Powers herein granted shall be vested in a Congress of the United States, which shall consist of a Senate and House of Representatives." The Constitution establishes the principle of a bicameral (two-house) legislature rather than a unicameral (one-house) system. But bicameralism was not the legislative system desired by all of the Framers of the Constitution in 1787.

After considerable skirmishing among the delegates at the Philadelphia Convention, notably between Governor Edmund Randolph of Virginia and William Paterson of New Jersey, the famous **Connecticut Compromise** was struck, establishing a two-house Congress. Randolph reflected the view of the large states when he presented his plan to the convention. Paterson mirrored the view of the small states which feared being harmed by a new system of government that treated them as less than equal partners in a new national union.

The Randolph, or **Virginia Plan**, called for a system of government based on European models in which the national government dominated and was considered to derive its power directly from the people rather than from the states. Virginia wanted :

1. A strong central government with three branches of government: executive, legislative and judicial.

2. A bicameral system with one house elected directly by the people and the other chosen from candidates nominated by state legislatures.

The Paterson, or **New Jersey Plan**, offered another concept of government. Small states like New Jersey were not entirely sure that a new government was needed. Indeed, the delegates to the Convention were instructed only to revise the Articles of Confederation, not to establish a new governmental system. The New Jersey Plan proposed the following:

1. Revision, not replacement of the Articles of Confederation.

2. Creation of a one-house (unicameral) legislature with each state being equally represented with one vote. Representatives would be chosen by state legislatures.

3. Giving the new Congress power to impose duties to raise revenue and creating a national post office system.

When the disagreement between the Randolph and Paterson Plans on representation in Congress appeared to deadlock the convention, Connecticut offered a compromise, embracing concepts from both the Virginia and New Jersey Plans.

States were to be considered equals in terms of Senate representation, each getting two senators. But in the House, representation was to be on the basis of population, with every state guaranteed at least one seat.

The House was to have power to originate all money bills. Senators were to be chosen by state legislatures, rather than directly by the people.

One very troublesome problem remained unresolved. How would state populations be counted in determining their representation in the House? The south wanted to count slaves, but they could not vote. After prolonged debate, the convention decided that population would be determined by adding the "whole Number of Free Persons" to "three-fifths of all other Persons." All other Persons was the delegates' way of referring to slaves.

Known as the **Three-Fifths Compromise**, this formula was based on the then-common belief that slaves were only three-fifths as productive as white men.

Nearly two centuries after this compromise, the original Constitution was called a "racist document" by Thurgood Marshall, Associate Justice of the U.S. Supreme Court, and the first Black ever to sit on the nation's high tribunal.

One must keep in mind, however, that the world of 1787 was far different from the contemporary world. Many of the Framers were strongly opposed to slavery and considered it morally repugnant. But they were also practical politicians who understood that any effort to restrict slavery in the short run would result in the walkout of the southern states' delegates and the end of efforts to create a new national union.

Finally, all states at the Convention agreed to the Great Compromise. Small states were satisfied that they were equally represented in the Senate. Large states were pleased that they won proportional representation in the House. Small states might be able to dominate the Senate but the large states could control the House. In a bicameral legislature, a law cannot be enacted without both houses agreeing to the exact version of a bill. In essence, the delegates created a "double veto" in which it became much more difficult to pass laws than to defeat them.

Today, states like California (53), New York (29), Texas (32), Florida (25) and Pennsylvania (19) have large delegations and considerable influence in the House, while states like North and South Dakota, Wyoming, Montana, Vermont, Delaware and Alaska have only one seat. Some states—Hawaii, Idaho, Rhode Island, New Hampshire and Maine—are represented equally in the House and Senate, with two seats in each chamber. The net result is rural overrepresentation in the U.S. Senate.

As noted in Chapter 2, the Constitution establishes governmental institutions on the separation of powers principle. Legislative, Executive and Judicial functions are given to three distinct branches of government.

President and Congress are independent of each other in that they are each elected by separate electoral processes for specific terms of office. The President cannot dissolve Congress, shorten its term or remove any of its members. Congress, even when controlled by the opposition party, cannot remove the President from office except by **impeachment.** It is no accident that only two Presidents—Andrew Johnson and Bill Clinton—were impeached by the House. Neither, however, was removed by the Senate.

Federal judges, although appointed by the President and confirmed by the Senate, are independent in that they enjoy tenure for life or good behavior. The power and authority of Federal courts to enforce the Constitution on both the President and Congress is not subject to any meaningful debate.

The term "separation of powers" is useful in describing the American system when contrasted with parliamentary systems, such as the English, where authority is concentrated in the hands of the legislature (Parliament). The English Executive is plural—a Council of Ministers—headed by a Prime Minister. It is, in effect, a committee of the majority party in the House of Commons. The English courts have great prestige and security, but they have no power or authority to challenge the legitimacy of acts of Parliament.

Some political scientists contend, however, that the term "separation of powers" is a bit misleading. It would be, they conclude, more accurate to describe the U.S. Constitution as creating a government of separated institutions sharing power and authority. The process of government requires that these three separate institutions work together effectively to promote the common good of the American people.

The institutional separation of President and Congress is exaggerated by their diverse electoral bases. In choosing to create a bicameral system, the Founding Fathers wanted to ensure that checks and balances operated, not only between the three major branches, but also within Congress itself.

Most Americans assume that the primary responsibility of Congress is to pass law. But it has non-legislative roles as well as legislative ones. Ask a member of Congress what takes most of his or her time. Chances are the answer is that the non-legislative roles, particularly constituent service, are most demanding of one's efforts.

1. Non-Legislative Roles

a. Amending the Constitution. Under Article V, Congress, providing that two-thirds of its members in both Houses "deem it necessary," may propose constitutional amendments to the states. It may, under the Constitution, also call a new constitutional convention, if two-thirds of the states so request. It can impose a time limit within which amendments must be ratified, if it so chooses. It can prescribe the method of ratification to be used by the states. Three-fourths of the states must ratify an amendment before it can go into effect. Ratification can be either by state legislatures or by state conventions. State legislatures have ratified 26 of 27 amendments. In the case of the 21st Amendment (repeal of Prohibition), Congress mandated that conventions be called in each of the then-48 states to consider the merits of the proposal. Why?

Given the rural and "dry" domination of state legislatures, President Franklin D. Roosevelt and the Democratic Congress knew that the so-called "Noble Experiment," put into effect by the 18th Amendment, would be retained unless state conventions were used. Conventions could focus on a single issue, candidates seeking election as delegates to these state conventions would run as "wet" or "dry" and the electorate would have a clear choice to make.[1]

b. Judicial roles. At times, Congress performs certain judicial functions. The House sits in judgment during impeachment proceedings or during challenges to the proper election of its own members. Impeachment, which simply means accusation, is solely the responsibility of the House. If it votes Articles of Impeachment, the Senate sits as a trial court. Only if two-thirds of the Senate votes to convict, can certain public officials, such as Presidents or Federal judges, be removed from office.

If a President is on trial, then the Chief Justice of the United States presides.

Only two Presidents, Andrew Johnson and Bill Clinton, were impeached. The former "survived" his Senate trial by a single vote, that of Sen. Edmund Ross of Kansas, who voted for Johnson, although it meant the end of his political career. John F. Kennedy included a chapter on Senator Ross in his Pulitzer Prize winning book, *Profiles in Courage*.[2]

Some historians had thought that the vindictive partisanship of the "Radical Republicans" during the Reconstruction Era had so discredited the impeachment process that it would never again be used against a President.

The U.S. Constitution refers to impeachment several times. Article II, Section 4, provides that "The President, Vice President and all Civil Officers of the United States, shall be removed from office on Impeachment for, and Conviction of Treason, Bribery, or other High Crimes and Misdemeanors. Article I, Sections 2 and 3, stipulate how the process is to be carried out. The House and Senate play clearly defined, if different, roles.

The authority to impeach (accuse or charge) is vested in the House of Representatives. Formal impeachment proceedings must begin there. A representative must list the charges against the President, Vice President or other Civil Officer. The charges then are referred to either the Judiciary Committee or a special investigating committee. If a House majority favors impeachment—as in the Clinton case—then Articles of Impeachment are drawn up, which establishes the basis for the removal of the executive branch officer.

The actual trial occurs in the Senate, where all members sit in judgment. The Chief Justice of the United States presides. A 2/3 vote of senators present is required for conviction. The only punishment that Congress can impose is removal from office and disqualification from holding any other Federal office. President Clinton's accusers were unable to muster a 2/3 vote on either of the charges against him.

The different roles played by House and Senate in the impeachment process illustrates the Founder's view that the frequently fickle and volatile will of the people (reflected in the House) needed to be balanced by the more stable view of the Senate. With a six-year term and removed from popular influence (until ratification of the 17th Amendment in 1913), the so-called "Upper House" was expected to restrain the potential "tyranny of the majority."

The Impeachment of William Jefferson Clinton. In September, 1998, Independent Counsel Kenneth Starr, a former Federal judge on the U.S. Court of Appeals, sent the findings of his investigation on the charges of perjury and obstruction of justice to Congress. The House Republican majority then began to organize for the possible impeachment of the President. On December 11-12, after the 1998 elections, the Judiciary Committee presented four charges to the House for its consideration.

The Impeachment Resolution began:

"Resolved, that William Jefferson Clinton, President of the United States, is impeached for high crimes and misdemeanors, and that the following articles of impeachment be exhibited to the United States Senate:

"Articles of impeachment exhibited by the House of Representatives of the United States of America in the name of itself and the people of the United States of America, against William Jefferson Clinton, President of the United States of America, in maintenance and support of its impeachment against him for high crimes and misdemeanors."

The House considered the specific charges against Clinton. Article I stipulated:

"In his conduct while President of the United States, William Jefferson Clinton, in violation of his constitutional oath faithfully to execute the office of President of the United States and, to the best of his ability, preserve, protect, and defend the Constitution of the United States, and in violation of his constitutional duty to take care that the laws be faithfully executed, has willfully corrupted and manipulated the judicial process of the United States for his personal gain and exoneration, impeding the administration of justice.

On August 17, 1998, William Jefferson Clinton swore to tell the truth, the whole truth, and nothing but the truth before a Federal grand jury of the United States. Contrary to that oath, William Jefferson Clinton, willfully provided perjurious, false and misleading testimony to the grand jury concerning one or more of the following:

(1) the nature and details of his relationship with a subordinate Government employee, (2) prior perjurious, false and misleading testimony he gave in a Federal civil rights action brought against him, (3) prior false and misleading statements he allowed his attorney to make to a Federal judge in a civil rights action and (4) his corrupt efforts to influence the testimony of witnesses and to impede the discovery of evidence in that civil rights action.

In doing this, William Jefferson Clinton, by such conduct, warrants impeachment and trial, and removal from office and disqualification to hold and enjoy any office of honor, trust or profit under the United States."

The House approved Article I, 228-206.

Article III charged that the President "...has prevented, obstructed and impeded the administration of justice, and has to that end engaged personally, and through his subordinates and agents, in a course of conduct or scheme designed to delay, impede, cover up and conceal the existence of evidence and testimony related to a Federal civil rights action brought against him in a duly instituted judicial proceeding."

Clinton was charged with seven specific acts under Article III. These included:

(1) encouraging a witness to execute a false affidavit that he knew was perjurious, false and misleading,

(2) encouraging a witness in a Federal civil rights action brought against him to give perjurious, false and misleading testimony if and when called to testify personally in that proceeding,

(3) encouraging a scheme to conceal evidence that had been subpoenaed in a Federal civil rights action brought against him,

(4) intensifying and succeeding in an effort to secure job assistance to a witness in a Federal civil rights action brought against him in order to corruptly prevent the truthful testimony of that witness in that proceeding at a time when the truthful testimony of that witness would have been harmful to him,

(5) corruptly allowing his attorney to make false and misleading statements to a Federal judge characterizing an affidavit, in order to prevent questioning deemed relevant by the judge (such false and misleading statements subsequently were acknowledged by his attorney in a communication to that judge),

(6) relating a false and misleading account of events relevant to a Federal civil rights action brought against him to a potential witness in that proceeding in order to corruptly influence the testimony of that witness and

(7) making false and misleading statements to potential witnesses in a Federal grand jury proceeding in order to corruptly influence the testimony of those witnesses. The false and misleading statements made by William Jefferson Clinton were repeated by witnesses to the grand jury, causing the grand jury to receive false and misleading information.

In all of this, William Jefferson Clinton has undermined the integrity of his office, has brought disrepute on the Presidency, has betrayed his trust as President and has acted in a manner subversive of the rule of law and justice, to the manifest injury of the people of the United States.

Wherefore, William Jefferson Clinton, by such conduct warrants impeachment and trial, and removal from office and disqualification to hold and enjoy any office of honor, trust or profit under the United States.

Article III was approved by the House, 221-212.

Counts 2 and 4 were rejected. Count 2 charged, "The President provided perjurious, false, misleading testimony in the Jones case in his answers to written questions and in his deposition." **(Vote was 229-205.)** Count 4 said, "The President misused and abused his office by making perjurious, false and misleading statements to Congress." **(Vote was 285-148.)**

Shortly after the new Congress convened in January, 1999, the Senate received Articles of Impeachment from the House. The trial then began with Chief Justice William Rehnquist presiding. Although all senators took an oath to act impartially and do justice, what followed was not, in the judgment of many political analysts, impartial. With few exceptions, it was clearly partisan.

After an initial presentation to the Senate, Clinton's team of defense lawyers moved to dismiss the charges for lack of evidence. Some 41 senators, all Democrats, voted to dismiss. That number made it apparent that it would be virtually impossible to get 67 senators to vote to convict and remove the President from office.

On Friday, Feb.12,1999, the Senate voted.

"Senators, how say you?" Chief Justice Rehnquist asked after each article was read aloud by the clerk. "Is the respondent, William Jefferson Clinton, guilty or not guilty?"

Silence fell over the Senate chamber as members' names were read in alphabetical order by the clerks. One by one, senators stood and answered, "guilty" or "not guilty."

Article I, charging perjury, was defeated, 45-55, at 12:21 p.m. Only 18 minutes later, Article II, charging obstruction of justice, failed by a tie vote of 50-50. The Senate was far short of the required two-thirds majority to remove William Jefferson Clinton.

It should be noted that five Republican senators voted with 45 Senate Democrats to defeat the charges. They also voted against Article I. All from the Northeast and identified as political "moderates," they were Senators James M. Jeffords of Vermont, Arlen Specter of Pennsylvania, John H. Chafee of Rhode Island, Olympia J. Snowe of Maine and Susan Collins of Maine.

Another five Republican senators voted against the perjury count but favored conviction on obstruction. They were Senators Slade Gorton of Washington, Ted Stevens of Alaska, Richard C. Shelby of Alabama, Fred Thompson of Tennessee and John Warner of Virginia.

Michigan's two senators split along party lines, with Republican Spencer Abraham favoring removal and Democrat Carl Levin favoring acquittal.

Shortly after the Senate's acquittal votes, a bipartisan majority tried and failed to get the Senate to pass a non-binding resolution censuring Clinton for "shameful, reckless and indefensible" conduct. Although the Senate voted, 56-43, to consider censure, it fell short of the two-thirds vote necessary to suspend Senate rules.

Sen. Tom Daschele (D., SD) who led the Democratic effort which rescued the Clinton presidency, spoke of the "sense of betrayal" he experienced because of the President's actions.

Two hours after the Senate removal vote, Clinton emerged from the White House to make a brief statement, telling the nation that he was "profoundly sorry" for his actions and the "great burden they have imposed on the Congress and on the American people."

The Nixon Case. President Nixon never was impeached. When the House Judiciary Committee, then chaired by Rep. Peter Rodino, (D., NJ), reported out three specific charges for their colleagues to consider on the floor, Nixon resigned. "Political heat" also had been put on the President by the Senate Select Committee on Watergate, chaired by Sam Ervin, (D., NC). The story of the President's involvement in the Watergate scandals began to unfold. The Committee's hearings became a television spectacular during the spring and summer of 1973.

Former White House counsel John Dean testified that Nixon was intimately connected to the cover-up and it was later revealed that there existed tape recordings of the President's conversations with White House aides. Ultimately, this caused Nixon's resignation.

At first, Nixon refused to surrender tapes of conversations in the White House. They had been subpoenaed by Federal Judge John Sirica for trials of several Watergate defendants. When special prosecutor Archibald Cox continued his efforts to get the tapes, Nixon ordered Attorney General Elliott Richardson and Assistant Attorney General William Ruckelshaus to remove him. Both refused to do so, preferring to resign their positions instead. Robert Bork was summoned to the White House, named Acting Attorney General and agreed to accept the task. Bork, in a two-paragraph note, carried out the presidential order to fire Cox. The news media referred to events of October 20, 1973, as "the Saturday Night Massacre."[3]

Two major issues were considered by the Rodino Committee. One was the meaning of the language in Article II, Section 4, providing impeachment for "treason, bribery, or other high crimes and misdemeanors."

Some of Nixon's supporters argued that the President could be impeached only for serious, indictable crimes. Critics argued that the Founding Fathers intended for impeachment to be used as a remedy for major abuses of executive power.

Another major issue was whether there was any limit on the investigative powers of the House Judiciary Committee as it conducted its probe. Committee lawyers argued that the impeachment power of Congress is very broad. It is the sole judge of what is relevant evidence and, consequently, can command the President to produce it.

Nixon disagreed, arguing that preservation of the integrity of the presidency required that he decide what evidence was relevant to the investigation. He later refused to obey court orders for tapes demanded by the committee. The President did, however, submit edited versions of several tapes to the public.

After months of closed hearings, the committee went on television in July, 1974, and voted three articles of impeachment against Nixon. The committee charged obstruction of justice by the Watergate cover-up and voted, 27-11, to support the charge. A second count was abuse of presidential power by misuse of the FBI, CIA and other government agencies. It was adopted, 28-10. The third charge against the President was contempt of Congress because he had refused to obey the committee's subpoenas. That vote was fairly close, but passed, 21-17.

The committee rejected two other charges. It would not accept the notion that secret bombing of Cambodia and Nixon's tax policies constituted impeachable offenses.

Some Nixon loyalists insisted that, although unlawful acts had taken place, the President's responsibility for them had not been established. They demanded a "smoking gun" before they would charge the President with high crimes and misdemeanors.

"The smoking gun" evidence was soon forthcoming. The U.S. Supreme Court, in *Nixon v. U.S.*, unanimously held that the President must turn over White House Watergate-related tapes. The President complied, revealing that he had been involved in the cover-up less than a week after the break-in at Democratic National Committee Headquarters in the Watergate Complex.[4]

Nixon's own words proved that he had obstructed justice. Public opinion, both in and outside the halls of Congress, turned overwhelmingly against the President. A Senate trial on the impeachment charges could have tied up the nation in a divisive debate while major problems remained unsolved. The President said that, because he wanted to spare the nation that ordeal, and because he no longer enjoyed the confidence of the Congress or of the nation, he would resign his office effective August 9, 1974. He became the first Chief Executive in American history to leave office by resignation.

On August 8, 1974, at 9 p.m., Nixon announced his resignation as President in a televised address to the American people. He said, "…In all the decisions I have made in my public life, I have always tried to do what was best for the Nation. Throughout the long and difficult period of Watergate, I have felt it was my duty to persevere, to make every possible effort to complete the term of office to which you elected me.

In the past few days, however, it has become evident to me that I no longer have a strong enough political base in the Congress to justify continuing that effort. As long as there was a base, I felt strongly that it was necessary to see the constitutional process through to its conclusion, that to do otherwise would be unfaithful to the spirit of that deliberately difficult process, and a dangerously destabilizing precedent for the future.

But with the disappearance of that base, I now believe that the constitutional purpose has been served, and there is no longer a need for the process to be prolonged.

I would have preferred to carry through to the finish, whatever the personal agony it would have involved, and my family unanimously urged me to do so. But the interests of the Nation must always come before any personal considerations.

From the discussions I have had with Congressional and other leaders, I have concluded that because of the Watergate matter, I might not have the support of the Congress that I would consider necessary to back the very difficult decisions and carry out the duties of this office in the way which the interests of the Nation would require.

I have never been a quitter. To leave office before my term is completed is abhorrent to every instinct in my body. But, as President, I must put the interest of America first. America needs a full-time President and a full-time Congress, particularly at this time with the problems we face at home and abroad.

To continue to fight through the months ahead for my personal vindication would almost totally absorb the time and attention of both the President and the Congress in a period when our entire focus should be on the great issues of peace abroad and prosperity without inflation at home.

Therefore, I shall resign the Presidency, effective at noon tomorrow. Vice President Ford will be sworn in as President at that hour in this office…

…To have served in this office is to have felt a very personal sense of kinship with each and every American. In leaving it, I do so with this prayer: May God's grace be with you in all the days ahead."[5]

Vice President Ford, appointed to the Vice Presidency under terms of the 25th Amendment, then became the nation's first President who never had been elected to national office before assuming command in the White House.

To date, only seven Federal officials have been both impeached and removed from office. All of those removed were lower Federal court judges. The last removals took place in 1989, when Florida Federal District Court Judge Alcee K. Hastings and Mississippi Federal District Court Judge Walter Nixon Jr. were ousted. Ironically, after being removed from the Federal bench, Hastings, a Democrat, later ran for a seat in the same House of Representatives which had impeached him. Perhaps even more ironically, he was elected in 1992 from the 23rd District of Florida and has been re-elected eight times, most recently in November, 2008. Most ironically of all, Hastings voted (against) in the House impeachment of Bill Clinton.

Members of Congress sit in judgment on the qualifications of their own members, although their discretion in this matter has been limited somewhat by the U.S. Supreme Court in the Adam Clayton Powell case. In essence, the Court held that a duly elected member could be denied his seat only for failure to meet qualifications required in the Constitution, such as age, citizenship and residence.[6]

When the Senate failed, in 1975, to decide the winner of the closest election in Senate history, it decreed that the voters of New Hampshire should try again. Ultimately, Democrat John Durkin defeated Republican Louis Wyman by a more decisive margin than the 10 disputed votes a recount produced.

Sometimes the Senate may be on the verge of expelling a member, something it hates to do to a colleague. In 1980, Harrison Williams, a New Jersey Democrat, avoided expulsion—by resignation. But he then reported to Federal prison to begin a sentence for taking a bribe in the "Abscam" scandal.

c. Electoral Roles. The House of Representatives performs an important electoral function if the Electoral College fails to choose a President. The Constitution requires that a candidate win an absolute majority of the Electoral College vote to be chosen as Chief Executive. If that should not occur, the House then chooses the President from the three candidates with the most electoral votes. In this procedure, each state gets one vote and a majority of 26 states is required to elect a President.

In the event that no candidate for the vice presidency wins a majority of the Electoral College votes, the Senate chooses the Vice President from the two candidates with the most electoral votes.

Congress also canvasses the election returns for President and Vice President. The President of the Senate (Vice President of the United States) has the ceremonial duty of opening certificates of the electors and the votes are counted before a Joint Session of House and Senate. Ironically, Vice President Nixon presided in January, 1961, and announced that John F. Kennedy had defeated him for the office of Chief Executive.

d. Rules. Congress also has rule-making powers and both House and Senate may change their rules whenever they please. Because it is a "continuing body" with a six-year term rather than the two-year term of House members, the Senate tends to have greater stability in its rules. Specifically, Article I, Section 5, provides:

"Each House may determine the Rules of its Proceedings, punish its Members for disorderly Behaviour, and, with Concurrence of two-thirds, expel a Member.

Each House shall keep a Journal of its Proceedings, and from time to time publish the same, excepting such parts as may in their Judgment require Secrecy; and yeas and Nays of the Members of either House on any question shall, at the Desire of one-fifth of those Present, be entered on the Journal.

Neither House, during the Session of Congress, shall, without the Consent of the other, adjourn for more than three days, nor to any other place than that in which the two Houses shall be sitting."

e. Executive Roles. The Senate also shares certain executive functions with the President. Article II, Section 2, of the Constitution provides that nominations of cabinet members, Federal judges, ambassadors, military officers and certain agency heads require the "advice and consent" of the Senate. The Senate has refused on 28 occasions to confirm Supreme Court nominees.

It is most unusual for the Senate to reject a presidential cabinet nominee, the theory being that Presidents ought to be able to choose the people they work with intimately in their administrations. Only twice in the past 30 years has the Senate rejected cabinet nominees

It is not at all uncommon, however, for the President to withdraw a nomination from the Senate after it runs into political opposition. President Clinton got off to a rough start during his first term when Senate opposition forced him to withdraw the nominations of two candidates for Attorney General, Zoe Baird and Kimba Wood. Both Baird and Wood had failed to pay Social Security taxes for women caring for their children. This was hardly appropriate behavior for the potential U.S. chief law enforcement officer. The press labeled the affair "Nannygate."[7]

Barack Obama had problems constructing his cabinet in 2009. New Mexico Gov. Bill Richardson, nominated as Secretary of Commerce, asked that his nomination be withdrawn. A Federal investigation into a state government contractor who contributed $100,000 to Richardson's political committees created problems. Richardson himself denied any wrongdoing, but said that he had no wish to have the probe bog down the nomination process of an Obama cabinet member.

Former U.S. Senate Majority Leader Tom Daschle, nominated to be Secretary of Health and Human Services, also withdrew after media reports of his "problems" with his Federal Income taxes. He reportedly owed $140,000, which he paid just before his nomination.

That also was a problem for Treasury Secretary Timothy Geithner, who the Senate nonetheless confirmed. Obama said that Gaither was a vital player in his efforts to restore economic stability to the financial and banking industries Some 34 senators voted against the nomination, however.

Under the Constitution, the Senate also must ratify treaties by a two-thirds vote before they go into effect.

f. Constituent service. Many members of Congress, when asked, say that they spend most of their time "servicing constituents." Helping a voter in one's state or district to untangle bureaucratic red tape takes time, whether it's a complaint involving one's Social Security check, veterans' benefits or a complaint about a surly civil servant who thinks people work for him rather than the other way around.

It also takes time to process the mail, and e-mail, effectively, but political survival in "doubtful" states or districts demands that this be given a high priority. Some congressmen and women estimate that they spend about 80% of their time doing "casework."

One member of Congress said, " I thought I was going to be Daniel Webster and I found out that most of my work consisted of personal work for constituents."[8]

But how should a member of Congress act as a representative? There are a number of varying opinions about this, but some political scientists suggest that three of them are most important. They are as follows:

1. Delegate perspective. A member believes that his role is to act as a representative of the constituency back home, be it state or district. There is, of course, an element of political wisdom in the notion that one ought to be loyal to the folks who "hired" (elected) you to look out for their interests. This view sometimes is challenged as being excessively parochial. What is in the interest of one's state or district, for example, may not necessarily be in the national interest. There also are problems of **pork barrel legislation** ("bringing home the bacon" for one's constituents) and **logrolling** (trading votes), which are associated with this perspective.

One should note, however, that no representative or senator can get too far removed from what "the folks back home" are thinking. When Sen. J.W. Fulbright, chairman of the Senate Foreign Relations Committee, came to view himself as an international statesman and principal critic of the administration's Southeast Asian policy, voters in Arkansas retired him for failure to consider their needs, rather than those of the "global community."

2. Trustee perspective. Another view holds that one owes nothing to his constituency except his own best judgment and his conscience. This perspective is associated with Edmund Burke, a late 18th Century British political philosopher.

Burke, a member of Parliament from Bristol, argued that the representative was not intended to be a puppet whose strings were pulled by those who had elected him. Rather, he should be a substantial person in whom the electorate was willing to place its confidence. He was to represent their interests, but only insofar as he understood those interests through the application of his own reasoned judgment as a member of the legislature. Clearly, Burke believed that he must also represent the interest of the whole nation.

Such a "trustee perspective" may surprise contemporary Americans, inclined to favor not representative democracy, but "participatory" democracy. They may be repelled by the notion that leadership and democracy are compatible, or that it is right for a representative to reject constituents' views in favor of his own best judgment. Some "democrats" fear the idea that a representative body might develop a will of its own, apart from that of the people it represents.

While Conservatives are fond of the trustee view, there are practical problems with it. Most important, a legislator risks losing his seat, as Burke did, in the next election.[9]

Many would argue, however, that losing an election is not as bad as losing one's principles. President Johnson tried to convince some southern members of Congress to vote for Civil Rights legislation because it was "the right thing to do." Almost all of them rejected that argument, maintaining that political survival was the issue and that the President could not ask them to commit political suicide.

In the real world, it might be argued that both trustee and delegate positions have some merit. Democratic government, while insisting that representatives be responsible to the electorate, also must have leadership if it is to resolve modern public policy problems.

Let us consider for a moment the role of the electorate. How well informed is John Doe or Jane Roe? What does he or she know about problems on the agenda? Economic policy dilemmas? Monetary and fiscal policy problems? Trade problems? Balance of payments and balance of trade problems? What does the average citizen know about foreign policy problems?

Either through a lack of intelligence or lack of information, the average voter is unable to contribute very much to the formulation of public policies in some of these areas. It may well be that the average citizens is simply too busy with the demands of earning a living. Or he or she may have interests other than politics in a culture obsessed with sports and entertainment, rather than reflection on the public agenda.

Elected officials must provide leadership and they simply cannot rely on their constituents for instructions. Congressional leadership is not only essential, it also is unavoidable. When a member of Congress seeks re-election, the people ultimately will approve or disapprove of his or her record in office.

As we near the second decade of the 21st Century, the ideal representative may well be one who can recognize when it is best to act as a leader and when it is necessary to act as a delegate.

3. Politico. A third view is that one should go to Washington to engage in political horse trading, getting the most possible benefits for the constituency. Wheeling and dealing come naturally to many members of Congress. The, "I'll do something for your district or state if you do something for mine," mentality is common. Members understand the need for political survival, and political survival demands that one produce tangible benefits for one's state or district. Whether a new post office, highway improvement, grant for the local university or some other project is really in the national interest is a seldom-asked question.

If one were to look, for example, at the state of West Virginia, one would need a calculator to add all the things named after Senator Robert Byrd, President Pro Tempore in the 111th Congress and former Democratic Senate Majority leader. He has been labeled by the media as the "king of pork."[10]

g. Checking the Executive. Legislatures in nearly all democracies give considerable attention and effort to the job of supervising and restraining the increasingly powerful executive branch. This is essential in any system of limited, constitutional government.

Under the U.S. system of checks and balances, Congress is responsible for control of the Executive branch of government. It often can do this effectively by exercising its hold on the Federal purse strings. Congress, after all, decides the nation's priorities when it authorizes and appropriates money and enacts budget laws. Presidents prepare budgets and they recommend national priorities, but the old saying still is true: "The President proposes, the Congress disposes."

Presidents have no authority to tax citizens or to authorize or appropriate money. These powers are solely in the hands of the Congress, under Article I of the Constitution. Actual fiscal power is centered in the hands of key congressional committees, such as the House Ways and Means Committee and the Senate Finance Committee.

h. Investigatory Power and Authority. Congress can use its power to investigate any matter which it considers important to the national well-being or the honest and efficient operation of the Federal government. This power is sometimes referred to as "inherited" because it was used by the British Parliament and early American state legislatures. Theoretically, it is necessary for Congress to resolve political, economic and social problems by studying them intensely. Congressional committees can subpoena witnesses to testify, pro and con, on vital pending legislation.

To legislate wisely requires information and the best information Congress can get usually comes from "expert witnesses," many of whom represent the views of a wide array of interests throughout the nation. It has power to punish those who refuse to produce documents or answer questions.

In the age of television, certain congressional investigations have generated widespread publicity for committee members, especially chairmen.

Nearly every American family with a TV set became aware, during the Watergate crisis, of the identity of Sam Ervin and Peter Rodino. Ervin chaired the select Senate Committee investigating Watergate-related crimes while Rodino chaired the House Judiciary Committee making parallel inquiries. Rodino's panel drew up a bill of particulars in recommending that the House of Representatives impeach President Nixon.

In *Watkins v. U.S.* 354 U.S. 178 (1954), the Supreme Court warned that the doctrine of separation of powers limits congressional authority to investigate. It said, "...The power to investigate must not be confused with any of the powers of law enforcement; those powers are assigned under our Constitution to the Executive and Judiciary...Congress has no power to expose for the sake of exposure..."[11]

Witnesses before congressional committees have a Fifth Amendment right to refuse to answer questions if the answers would expose them to risk of criminal prosecution. Congress, however, could grant immunity and the witnesses then would have to testify.

2. Legislative Role

The most basic task of Congress is to enact laws which will provide solutions to national problems. But Congress shares its legislative powers with the President. The nation expects the President to lead Congress. It also expects sources external to the legislature, notably pressure groups, to play a major role in the lawmaking process. Congress provides a formal meeting ground for political parties, pressure groups and executive leadership. It tries to encourage conflict resolution and group accommodation in carrying out its legislative role. The task of Congress is to foster national unity and promote the general welfare simultaneously. In our diverse, technological, urban and often conflict-ridden society, this is no easy task.

The legislative powers of Congress are enumerated in detail in Article I of the Constitution. They have been enlarged by judicial interpretation of some vague clauses and the **"implied powers" doctrine** that if the end is legitimate, Congress may choose the means to accomplish its purpose.[12]

Court rulings have expanded the powers of Congress to tax and spend for the public welfare and to regulate interstate commerce. A wide variety of laws regulating the economy—minimum wages, maximum hours, protective laws for women and children— rest on congressional control of interstate commerce, as do some provisions of civil rights legislation.

The legislative arena has been the battleground of Liberals and Conservatives, with quite contrasting ideas of what government should, or should not do, throughout our history. It has intensified since the era of Franklin D. Roosevelt and the New Deal (1933-45). Louis Howe, a close friend and political adviser to FDR, once advised Liberal Democrats in Congress to "spend and spend, elect and elect." His advice was followed and the role of the Federal government in American life expanded considerably.

B. PRESIDENT AND CONGRESS

Although the Constitution vests "all legislative powers herein granted" in the Congress, lawmaking is a "shared function" in the U.S. constitutional system. Throughout American history, Presidents and Congress have fought dramatic battles, emphasizing differences between executive and legislative branches of our Federal government.

Separation of the two branches, provided in the Constitution, is one of the main reasons for this conflict. The struggle to maintain "separate" but "equal" status has been waged by both President and Congress at various points in U.S. history. The authors of the Constitution did not foresee the rise and development of American political parties. They could not, therefore, recognize that the Chief Executive also would be the leader of his party.

The establishment of separation of powers, of check and balances and of bicameralism has made the development of "responsible government" more difficult. Bicameralism makes it exceptionally difficult to pinpoint responsibility. Members of the two houses are elected on different bases. Senators represent states. Members of the House represent congressional districts. A party program, satisfactory to both houses, is often difficult to attain.

It is possible, under the American congressional system (unlike a parliamentary system), for opposing political parties to control the two houses. During part of President Reagan's administration, he had a Republican Senate and a Democratic House. Under these circumstances, voters can hold neither party responsible for the policies and conduct of the government. Members of each chamber are jealous of their prerogatives as senators or representatives. Cooperation between the two houses may be difficult to achieve.

Intelligent voters sometimes are frustrated by the fact that House and Senate often blame one another for failure of Congress to produce legislation. Some political scientists suggest that we revise the congressional system to make it more like the British parliamentary system. Their objective would be to tie together election of executive and legislative branches as a "team ticket" and end the current system of divided party government. Some advocate four-year terms for House members to coincide with the term of the President.

The problem with these proposals is, of course, that they would require several constitutional amendments. Inertia is one factor, lingering Anglophobia is still another. One might as well label these proposals as impractical. It is unlikely that today's students will live long enough to see them put into effect.

An American President cannot demand the support of Congress. He may ask for it, but he cannot demand it. He has weapons, however, to fight any battles which may develop with Congress. He has the enormous prestige of his office; he has control over patronage; he has the veto. In 1997, the item veto has added a new weapon to his arsenal, but it subsequently was ruled unconstitutional by the U.S. Supreme Court in *Clinton et al. v New York City, et al.*[13] If he is a strong leader and has widespread popular support, he can appeal to public opinion. Yet, in many respects, the President is at the mercy of Congress.

As Chief Executive, the President has the constitutional duty to recommend a program of legislative action. If his party controls Congress, he may succeed in seeing it enacted. Even under such a condition, however, he cannot be certain of support.

Historically, an alliance of Republicans and southern Democrats frequently has prevented adoption of Liberal measures proposed by Democratic Presidents. If the President has an "unfriendly" Congress, one controlled by the opposition party—as President Clinton did after the elections of 1994, he may expect his legislative recommendations to carry little weight. Unless, of course, for reasons of political expediency, he wants to push some measures championed by the opposition which have won popular support, and then claim political credit for them himself. "Welfare reform" during the second Clinton Administration may be a case in point.

The President has the power to appoint certain Federal officials. Patronage can be an important weapon in his dealings with members of Congress, eager to reward constituents for their support. The Chief Executive, however, must obtain senatorial confirmation for some of his major appointments. The rule of **"senatorial courtesy"** demands that the President must confer in advance with his party's senior senator in a state in which an appointment is to be made. Should the senator object to the nomination, confirmation would be virtually impossible.

The veto power is a highly effective one, especially in the hands of a "strong President." It gives the Chief Executive a voice in legislative matters virtually equal to that of two-thirds of both houses of the Congress. However, a two-thirds vote in the two chambers is sufficient to override the veto and enact any legislation, irrespective of the President's wishes. Historically, however, presidential vetoes have been sustained much more often than they have been overridden.[14]

A President may appeal to public opinion. Franklin D. Roosevelt's fireside chats had a major impact in winning public support for his programs. Even considering the critical economic plight of the nation in 1933, the legislation passed on his recommendation during the famous "100 Days," is remarkable. Yet the President is on uncertain ground when he attempts to exert his influence on the election of senators and representatives. FDR failed in his attempt to "purge" anti-New Deal Democrats in the 1938 mid-term congressional elections.

The struggle between President and Congress is often a matter of "who shall lead." Strong Presidents, such as Andrew Jackson, Abraham Lincoln, the two Roosevelts and Lyndon Johnson, have managed to win congressional approval of their domestic legislative programs. Other Chief Executives, such as Calvin Coolidge and Herbert Hoover, had neither the inclination nor the ability to exert leadership.

Major differences of political philosophy also can complicate matters. Although the dominant wings of both parties are centrist, ideological wars do occasionally erupt. Battle lines were clearly drawn during the 1930s over the issue of how to fight the Great Depression. In the election of 1932, President Hoover assured the nation that prosperity was just around the corner. Roosevelt, called by his political opponents "a man of no philosophy or principle," was the ultimate pragmatist. He believed in trying anything that might work. Few people remember today that FDR was elected, in 1932, on a platform which pledged to cut Federal spending and balance the budget.

Perhaps measures taken by FDR to combat the Great Depression and to fight the totalitarian regimes of Hitler, Mussolini and Tojo during World War II made the growth of government inevitable. But the architects of the New Deal followed an old political axiom that "nobody likes Scrooge" and many members of the Congress were anxious to "buy votes" by supporting generous spending measures. The Fair Deal of Harry Truman (1945-53) followed Roosevelt without any significant change in this direction.

Twenty years of Democratic Party monopoly on the White House ended with the election of Dwight D. Eisenhower. But that eight-year period (1953-61) of moderate

Republicanism was merely an interlude, to be followed by the New Frontier-Great Society Liberal programs of Kennedy and Johnson (1961-69). The Johnson years, in particular, saw enormous changes in American life.

Although today's generation of college students may associate Johnson primarily with the Vietnam War, historians also focus on Johnson's domestic programs, from major advances in civil rights, voting rights, the war on poverty and a rapid expansion of Federal spending. Cost estimates of what the Liberal Democratic Congress produced were far short of reality.[15]

The Nixon-Ford era (1969-77) and the presidency of Jimmy Carter (1977-81) saw continued advances in social programs and Federal spending. But the election of former California Gov. Ronald Reagan brought the ideological debate to the forefront. Reagan campaigned in 1980 on a platform which said that government was the problem, not the solution, that taxes were too high, crippling incentive to produce, and that it was time to "get the government off the backs of the American people."

The "Reagan Revolution," as those who liked to engage in rhetorical overkill called it, merely slowed the growth of Federal spending. It clearly did not reduce it. The budget grew enormously with increased outlays for defense spending, a major factor. During the Clinton Administration, the budget reached $1.6 **trillion**, a far cry from the less than $100 **billion** of the early Johnson administration.[16]

President Obama's first budget was $3.4 trillion., more than double that of Clinton.

Many of the presidential-congressional battles over legislation and programs which the Executive wants and the Congress does not, such as Clinton's national health insurance, are essentially quarrels over taxing and spending.

Only after the Federal debt reached $3.7 trillion did political pressures mount. The congressional election of 1994, which gave the Republicans control of both houses of Congress for the first time since 1947, was called a "Political Earthquake" in a *Washington Post* headline. Rep. Newt Gingrich of Georgia, the new Speaker of the House, had devised a 10-point Contract With America during the campaign. It pledged, in the area of economic policy, to work for a constitutional amendment to force Congress to balance the budget annually, except in case of war or national emergency. Clinton seemed to get the message, particularly after voters, although giving him a second term, also returned the Republican Congress. President and Congress ultimately reached some basic agreements. One gave the President the item veto and the two parties agreed that the balanced budget was a good idea. A historic budget agreement was announced in 1997.[17]

C. CONSEQUENCES OF BICAMERALISM

Any discussion of the legislative process must begin with a basic fact of political life, bicameralism. Laws cannot be passed in the U.S. Congress without both House and Senate agreeing to the identical version of a bill.

The roots of bicameralism lie in the legacy left to the American nation by its British colonial rulers. The British Parliament, which has been the primary model of democratic legislatures, developed two houses because of 13th and 14th Century refusal of peers and leading members of the Church of England hierarchy to sit with knights and commoners. The subsequent establishment of a House of Lords and a House of Commons influenced legislative organization and practice in most democracies.

The British system also embraced a system of checks and balances between members of the aristocracy and the representatives of the rest of the people. British practice gave both houses equal power and required that no bill could become law which did not pass both houses in precisely the same form. Wealth and power, therefore, had a virtual veto over the "commoners."

The Framers of the Constitution believed that the House of Representatives was more likely to be responsive to the masses. Indeed, the term "democracy" was a pejorative one at the inception of the nation. It was equated, in some circles, with "mobocracy."

The Senate originally was elected by state legislatures. Popular election of senators came only with ratification of the 17th Amendment in 1913. The Framers hoped that the Senate would restrain ill-considered, hasty actions of the House. The Federalists, the so-called "better people" of the day, believed, as Washington once said, that the Senate would act as a saucer under a hot cup of tea—cooling off hasty or ill-considered legislation, contrary to the interests of the nation.

The Senate is composed of two members from every state. Senators are elected for six-year terms. The body tends to over represent the interests of smaller states. The House of Representatives is a 435-member body whose members are apportioned to the states on the basis of population. Representatives are elected for two-year terms and tend to represent local interests, particularly those of rural areas, which, until the 1960s, had more seats than they deserved on a population basis.[18]

In the area of congressional procedure, either House or Senate may initiate legislation, although the Constitution requires that money bills originate in the House. This bicameral structure involves a good bit of duplication of committee hearings, testimony and debate before bills become law. In fact, the deck is stacked against enactment of laws. It is much easier to defeat legislation in Congress than it is to pass it. The **"survival rate"** of bills in Congress in a typical two-year session is only about 5%.

Usually, bills that do pass the Senate or House are not identical in form. It is necessary, therefore, for legislators to work out their differences. A Conference Committee, which typically consists of those members of House and Senate who have done the most work on a particular measure, negotiate and try to reconcile their differences. If a Conference Committee can agree on a compromise, it ordinarily will pass both houses. If conferees cannot agree, there simply can be no legislation.

Even if Congress enacts legislation, the President can prevent it from becoming law by using his veto power. If the President is popular, Congress faces an uphill battle in overriding his objections by the required two-thirds vote in both houses.

Franklin D. Roosevelt vetoed 635 bills during his 12 years plus in office, only nine of which were overridden. In his first term, George W. Bush did not veto a single measure when Republicans controlled Congress. After the Democrats regained power after the 2006 elections, however, he vetoed 12 measures in his last two years in office. Only four were passed over the President's objections.

D. CONGRESSIONAL LEADERSHIP

Even if the President's party controls Congress, the congressional leadership may disagree with the President's agenda or his views of what public policy should be. Members of House and Senate choose their own leaders. Any presidential interference in this process would be deeply resented. Since congressional committee chairmen are generally elected on the basis of seniority, legislators unfriendly to the administration program may be in key congressional power positions.

Historically, southern and border-state Democrats held disproportionate numbers of congressional committee chairmanships when their party controlled the Congress. Liberal Democratic Presidents often had to seek support from Republican moderates when their own party's leaders opposed their programs. Franklin Roosevelt, Truman and Kennedy all had this problem.

In Kennedy's case, one of the major roadblocks to his "New Frontier" legislative program was Rep. Howard Smith, a Virginia Democrat who chaired the House Rules Committee, one of the most powerful panels in the Congress. The Rules Committee, as its name implies, gives a rule to every bill to be considered on the floor of Congress. It also decides whether the House will even consider a bill. Smith considered Kennedy's program radical and would have none of it. Only a scheme devised by Vice President Johnson and Speaker Sam Rayburn broke the legislative logjam. The Johnson-Rayburn plan was to enlarge the House Rules Committee to give Liberals a majority and to force the chairman to at least permit measures to get on to the floor for debate, possible action and vote.[19]

It is no easy task to lead 100 senators. It is probably even more difficult to lead 435 representatives, particularly when each is responsible to no one except his own constituency. Most of the leadership role in Congress is really being an effective party leader.

Key House Leaders: By far the most important leader in the House is its presiding officer, the **Speaker**. This is the only legislative office mandated by the Constitution. In practice, the majority party chooses the Speaker, typically a senior party leader. In 1995, when Republicans took control of the House, Newt Gingrich of Georgia was chosen as the first GOP Speaker in 40 years.

He immediately began to centralize power and exercise vigorous leadership. He quickly established his authority, naming committee chairs, bypassing the seniority rule, reorganizing House committees and cutting staff. He spent most of his energy trying to fulfill the GOP campaign pledges, outlined in the Contract with America.

As noted in the preceding chapter, the Speaker is only two heartbeats away from the presidency, being second in line behind the vice president. What roles does current Speaker Nancy Pelosi of California play?

She presides over the House when it is in session. She plays a major role in deciding committee assignments, paying particular attention to trying to help party members who need a "sound base" on which to run for re-election. A representative from a rural area, for example, might seek a seat on the Agriculture Committee, and the Speaker may try to accommodate him or her.

She appoints or plays a key role in choosing the party's legislative leaders and their staffs.

She exercises some control over which bills get assigned to which committees.

When sitting in the chair as presiding officer of the House, she recognizes (or ignores) members who wish to speak. She rules on matters of parliamentary procedure.

Perhaps most important, she is the key political influence in the chamber.

When the opposition party controls the White House, she often is the voice of the party. To be effective, a Speaker must know her colleagues well. She must know their ambitions, problems and characters. She must understand the pressures under which they operate.

The principal partisan ally of the Speaker is the **majority leader**, a role that not infrequently is a stepping stone to the speakership. The current majority leader, Steny Hoyer of Maryland, helps to plan party strategy, schedules bills in the House and is responsible for rounding up votes. Party **whips** work closely with him, carrying the word to colleagues, estimating votes before they occur and "leaning" on members who are reluctant to follow the party line. The term whip comes from the English fox hunt, where the "whipper in" is responsible for keeping the hounds bunched in a pack. Whips are part of a two-way communication process, responsible for carrying messages and complaints back to the leaders. Majority whip in the 111th Congress is James Clyburn of South Carolina.

The minority party also is organized. It hopes to win the 2010 congressional elections and regain control of the House. If successful, Republicans would take over the speakership, all committee chairs and other leadership positions described above. For 40 years, the Republicans had to wait while they were the minority party, although there were five Republican Presidents during that period. The **minority leader** of House Republicans is Rep. John Boehner of Ohio. **Minority whip** is Eric Cantor of Virginia.

At the beginning of each session, each party holds a caucus of all its members to elect party officials, approve committee assignments, elect committee leaders, discuss key bills and try to develop a party legislative program.

As a result of the 2004 congressional elections, the Republicans controlled the House of Representatives, 232-202. One member, Bernard Sanders of Vermont, was an independent, aligned with the Democrats.

In 2006, the Democrats gained control, winning 235 seats. They increased their majority to 256.in the 2008 elections. Republicans had only 178 seats, a loss of 20, and one seat was vacant.

Key Senate Leaders: The Constitution makes the Vice President of the United States the President of the Senate. This is the only specific task assigned to him by the Basic Law. But there is neither power nor authority in this task. When Lyndon Johnson served as Senate president, it was the most frustrating period of his political life, although he had been majority leader for many years and had many friends in the chamber. Typically Vice Presidents leave power to party leaders and spend most of their time doing "assigned chores."

Basically, the President decides what they will do. The Vice President has no vote in the Senate, except in case of a tie. The Obama Administration will be sure that Vice President Joe Biden's "assigned chore" is to support the President on any matter before the Senate.

The real power in the Senate rests with the majority leader. Sen. Trent Lott of Mississippi held the position for several years, having succeeded Bob Dole of Kansas who resigned to run for the presidency in 1996. Dole, whose sense of humor was widely-known in the Senate, if not in the nation generally, often called himself the "Majority Pleader."

Lott and his Republican colleagues entered into an unprecedented "power sharing" agreement with the Democrats after the election of 2000. Some 34 Senate seats were contested, the remaining 66 were not. Prior to the election, the GOP held a 54-46 edge. By winning, 19-15, Democrats gained 50 seats, the same number as the Republicans. Under the agreement, the parties were to have the same number of senators on standing committees and staff budgets were to be divided equally. Vice President

Cheney had the balance of power until May 24, 2001, when a political bombshell went off in the nation's capitol.

Veteran Sen. James Jeffords of Vermont, a 67-year-old "moderate" who frequently crossed party lines on high profile issues, such as abortion, tax cuts and the environment, had what the media characterized as "strained relations" with the Bush White House. Given the fact that Jeffords voted with Senate Democrats more than 70% of the time, this may not have been surprising. Although both the President and senior Republican officials attempted to dissuade Jeffords, the New England legislator bolted his party, became an Independent, and gave control of the Senate to the Democrats, 50-49-1.

Jeffords said, " I do not approach this question lightly. I have spent a lifetime in the Republican Party and served 12 years in what I believe is the longest continuously held Republican seat in history. I ran for re-election as a Republican just this past fall, and had no thoughts whatsoever about changing parties.

...Increasingly I find myself in disagreement with my party. I understand that many people are more conservative than I am and they form the Republican Party. Given the changing nature of the national party, it has become a struggle for our leaders to deal with me and for me to deal with them... In the past, without the presidency, the various wings of the Republican Party in Congress have had some freedom to argue and influence and ultimately to shape the party's agenda. The election of President Bush changed that dramatically.

Looking ahead, I can see more and more instances where I'll disagree with the President on very fundamental issues: the issues of choice, the direction of the judiciary, tax and spending decisions, missile defense, energy and the environment and a host of other issues large and small. The largest for me is education.

In order to best represent the state of Vermont, my own conscience and the principles I have stood for my whole life, I will leave the Republican Party and become an independent. Control of the Senate will be changed by my decision.

I have informed President Bush, Vice President Cheney and (Senator) Lott of my decision. They are good people with whom I disagree. They have been fair and decent to me..."

Jefford's decision meant that Lott became minority leader on June 6, after the Memorial Day recess, and Sen. Tom Daschle of Iowa switched from minority leader to majority leader.

Perhaps even more important, all 20 standing committee chairmanships were held by the majority party. Powerful Republican chairs, like Jesse Helms of Foreign Relations, were replaced (by Sen. Joe Biden of Delaware). Jefford's defection elevated fellow Vermont Sen. Patrick Leahy, a Democrat, to the post of chairman of the Judiciary Committee (replacing Sen. Orrin Hatch of Utah).

By mid-June, 2001, the flow of legislation appeared to change. "Democratic Party initiatives" on such items as increased education spending and a patient's bill of rights, both near legislative death, were "resurrected." Sen. Edward (Ted) Kennedy of Massachusetts, one of the most Liberal senators, would head the Health, Education, Labor and Pensions Committee.

President Bush's proposed ballistic missile defense plan was in trouble with Democrat opponents in key positions. Sen. Carl Levin of Michigan, for example, became chair of the Senate Armed Services Committee, a panel which oversees about $300 billion in annual military spending.

Before party control passed to the Democrats, however, the GOP was able to accomplish two key Bush objectives, a $1.35 trillion tax cut and the confirmation of Theodore Olson as Solicitor General. Olson, who successfully argued the case of *Bush v. Gore* before the U.S. Supreme Court, won confirmation, 51-47, with several Democrats crossing party lines to support him. The Solicitor General represents the U.S. government in the Supreme Court in important cases.

The vote on the tax cut was a not-so-close 62-38. Twelve Democratic senators crossed party lines to support the President, perhaps an indication that constituent pressures are every bit as important as party affiliation.

Some scholars, who have no partisan axes to grind, noted that, under bicameralism, the Senate is powerless to act without the agreement of a Republican House and a Republican President, armed with a veto. It appeared, they concluded, that the nation was headed for more "gridlock."

Whether that is good or bad depends upon one's view. Many Americans apparently like gridlock, perhaps merely a contemporary name for the checks and balances and separation of powers devised by the Framers of the Constitution.

A largely ornamental office is that of president *pro tempore*. It usually goes to the most senior member of the majority party, who officially presides over the Senate when the Vice President is absent. Sen. Strom Thurmond, (R., SC) 98 years old, held the job during the period of Republican control. After the June, 2001, transition, the office passed to Sen. Robert Byrd (D., W.VA) , then a comparative "youngster" of 83. Sen. Ted Stevens of Alaska became President Pro Tempore in the 109th Congress, elected in 2004. Sen. Bill Frist, a heart surgeon, was the majority leader.

Frist became majority leader after Senator Trent Lott of Mississippi, scheduled to assume that position when the 108th Congress convened, praised Sen. Strom Thurmond of South Carolina at his 100th birthday celebration on December 5, 2002. It may be normal, given Senate traditions, to exaggerate the "contributions" of a retiring colleague. But Lott, appeared to be praising Thurmond's segregationist past.

Thurmond, who began his political life as a Democrat, bolted his party over its Civil Rights position in 1948 He ran for President as a "Dixiecrat," advocating "segregation, now and forever."

Lott remarked: "I want to say this about my state. When Strom Thurmond ran for President, we voted for him. We're proud of it. And if the rest of the country had followed our lead, we wouldn't have had all these problems over all these years, either."

When Lott inevitably came under heavy fire from leaders of both Democratic and Republican parties, he attempted to explain his statement as an off-the-cuff remark. He backed Thurmond's strong national defense platform.

Both Al Gore and George W. Bush denounced Lott's comment. The President said: "Any suggestion that the segregated past was acceptable or positive is offensive and it is wrong. Senator Lott has apologized and rightly so. Every day that our nation was segregated was a day our nation was unfaithful to our founding ideal."

Al Gore characterized Lott's remarks as "fundamentally racist."

Having lost the President's support, and under pressure from Senate colleagues, Lott resigned as Republican leader on December 20, 2002, and Senator Frist of Tennessee became his successor.

The job is a thankless chore and even regular Senate visitors are not likely to see the Vice President or President Pro Tempore sitting "in the chair." That task typically falls to a junior member.

In 2002, Republicans gained control of the Senate, 51-48. They increased the margin to 55-44 in 2004. Jeffords remained the only Independent, but announced in May, 2005, that he would not seek re-election in 2006.

The congressional elections of 2006 produced Democratic majorities in both House and Senate. For the next two years, they vigorously criticized the Bush Administration's policies, both foreign and domestic. Several Democratic Senators, Hillary Clinton of New York, Barack Obama of Illinois and Joe Biden of Delaware, sought their party's presidential nomination. John McCain of Arizona sought to become the GOP standard-bearer. There was little bipartisan cooperation in Washington , D.C., during the 110th Congress.

The election of 2008 produced a Democratic President and enhanced Democratic majorities in both House and Senate. In fact, 2006 and 2008 marked the first time in 50 years that a party has gained more than 20 seats in consecutive congressional elections.

The current 111th Congress has 257 Democrats in the House, up from 236. The Republicans hold only 178 House seats, down from 199 during the previous Congress. In the Senate, the election produced 56 Democrats, 41 Republicans and two Independents. Minnesota was so close that Republican Norman Coleman and Democrat Al Franken were engaged in a court challenge, expected to decide the outcome in the summer of 2009.

President Obama and the Democrats picked up a 57th Senate seat when Republican Arlen Specter announced on April 28 that he was switching to the Democratic Party. Specter, a moderate during his five terms, found that the Republicans were becoming too conservative for his tastes. He was only one of three Senate Republicans to support President Obama's $787 billion stimulus package.

Former GOP colleagues said that it was simply a case of "political self-preservation" because Specter, 79, faced a conservative challenger, former U.S. Rep. Pat Toomey in a Pennsylvania primary that he was unlikely to win. Should Franken prevail in Minnesota, the Democrats would be near a 60-vote filibuster-proof Senate majority.

Obama said the Democrats were "thrilled" to have Specter with them and promised support for his 2010 bid for the Democratic Party nomination for the Senate seat. Pennsylvania's Governor, Democrat Ed Rendell, also pledged to back Specter's bid..

E. LEGISLATIVE COMMITTEES

Most of the real work in Congress is done in committees, which dominate congressional policy making at every step of the legislative process. Committees regularly hold hearings to oversee the executive branch. They also guide legislation along the legislative path, from introduction until it leaves the Congress, headed for the President's desk. There are four kinds of congressional committees:

1. Standing committees

They are the most important committees in Congress, handling bills in different policy areas. They do most of the work on legislative proposals. Only a handful of bills introduced actually are acted on by standing committees. Those that do survive are reported to the full House or Senate. The chair of a standing committee is always a member of the majority party. At present, there are 19 standing committees in the House and 16 in the Senate.

Not all committees are equally important. Although members might not agree, students of Congress generally list the following as the most prestigious:

Senate: Agriculture, Appropriations, Armed Services, Budget, Finance, Foreign Relations, Governmental Affairs and Judiciary.

House: Agriculture, Appropriations, Budget, Government Reform and Oversight, International Relations, Judiciary, Rules and Ways and Means.

Most standing committees are split into subcommittees. They deal with specialized areas of the parent committee's jurisdiction and are created by the committee itself. The Foreign Relations Committee, for example, has several committees dealing with specific areas of the globe.

In the 110th Congress, there were 90 subcommittees in the House and 66 in the Senate.

2. Joint committees

These committees exist in a few policy areas where members are drawn from both Senate and House because Congress believes that coordinated action by the two chambers is appropriate. Such committees seldom bring legislation to the floor, but are charged with making recommendations after studying a particular policy area. Political rivalries and fear that joint committees may encroach on the "turf" of a standing committee make them unpopular. House members fear Senate domination of such joint committees.

3. Conference Committees

If there are basic differences between House and Senate versions of a bill, the chamber that first passed the legislation may request a conference. The legislation can go forward only if differences in the two bills are reconciled into identical language. About 15% of all bills go to conference. A conference committee consists of senior members of the committees that managed the bill.

Typically, conference committees are small, ranging in size from three to nine members. Members are drawn from both parties. Normally they are appointed by the Speaker of the House and the presiding officer of the Senate on the recommendation of committee chairs and ranking minority party members.

Differences usually are ironed out by bargaining over each part of the bill. If a final agreement is reached, a "conference report" is sent to the floor of each house. It cannot be amended, only adopted or rejected. If both houses agree to the report, the measure then is passed—and sent to the President.

4. Select committees

They also called special committees, appointed for a specific purpose. They look at particular issues or new areas of legislation. Although they have the same powers as a standing committee, they cannot receive bills or report legislation to the floor of the House or Senate. Most of these committees are temporary, their existence ending when the term of the Congress that created them expires. Perhaps the most widely known committee in recent history was the Senate Select Committee that investigated Watergate, chaired by Sen. Sam Ervin, a North Carolina Democrat.

F. HOW BILLS BECOME LAWS

Before a proposal can become a law, it must pass through a complex set of organizational procedures in Congress, known as the legislative process.

The American Congress, unlike many other legislatures throughout the world, is not a rubber stamp for the executive branch of government. Congressional procedures must be followed. Rules govern everything from the introduction of legislation to its submission to the President for signing. These rules influence the fate of every bill. But the route of a bill through Congress is not all that complicated.

Any member of Congress can introduce a bill. With the exception of revenue measures, which the Constitution requires to originate in the House, bills may be started in either of the two chambers. The initial step is introduction or the **"first reading."** This requires a motion in the Senate, but in the House a bill is simply dropped into a box on the clerk's desk, called the "hopper." Sometimes a senator and a representative, hoping to coordinate their efforts, may agree to introduce identical legislation. The measure then is given a number and referred to a standing committee. The number of bills introduced in any two-year term of Congress is huge. More than 14,000 measures were proposed in the 110th Congress (2007-08), but only 449 of them were enacted into law.

As a practical matter, bills supported by the majority party leadership have the best chance. They also can use their considerable power and authority to "torpedo" legislation they do not like or to punish members who have fallen into disfavor.

Most major legislation (about 80%) actually originates in the executive departments. They draft legislative proposals that embody the President's policies and then find sympathetic members of Congress to introduce them. At the beginning of each year, the President, using his message power, outlines his legislative goals and objectives. Most important of these speeches is the State of Union Address, given in January. That is followed by the Economic Report and the Budget message.

As noted above, committees sometimes change bills or draw up new ones. Committees hold **public hearings** at which witnesses may appear to speak for or against the proposed legislation. If the committee opposes the bill, it **"tables"** it (or puts it aside). In fact, this is the fate of the overwhelming number of measures. They never reach the hearing stage, they simply die quietly in committee. In the House, a **discharge petition** can be used to take a bill away from a committee, but it is rarely used. It requires signatures of a majority (218) of representatives. If the signatures are obtained, the House must then vote to approve or disapprove the motion to discharge.

If, on the other hand, a committee favors legislation, it reports it to the floor with a recommendation for passage. The measure is then added to the House or Senate **"calendar"** (the list of bills to be considered). The Senate has one calendar for all pending legislation. Routine bills are considered in the order in which they appear on the calendar. If, however, a measure is controversial, the majority and minority leaders confer with the chair of the committee which reported the bill and senators who have a particular interest in the measure.

Once a House committee reports a measure, it goes on one of three major calendars: the **Union Calendar** (for tax and appropriations legislation), the **House Calendar** (all other public bills) or the **Private Calendar.** The latter deals with bills dealing with specific individuals, corporations or localities. In addition, the **Consent Calendar** deals with bills that require little or no debate.

When a bill is reported out of committee and placed on the House Calendar, the chair of the committee will request the Rules Committee to assign the bill a rule. The **rule** takes the bill from the calendar and schedules the measure for floor action. The Rules Committee often is called the House "traffic cop." It determines the terms and conditions of debate. It may stipulate an **open rule**, with extensive debate and the possibility of amendments from the floor or a **closed rule,** with limited debate and perhaps an "up or down" vote required on the measure, without amendments, as it comes out of committee. The Rules Committee is one of the most powerful panels in the House.

When its time comes, a bill is given a **"second reading"** (usually only by title since the printed bill already has been distributed to the members). It is then debated on the floor and perhaps amended. It then is given its **"third reading"** and voted upon. If it passes, it is sent to the other chamber, where it goes through essentially the same process.

It should be noted that the Senate, because of its smaller size, usually operates under simpler rules that does the House. Bills, as noted, ordinarily are considered on the floor either in the order in which they appear on the Senate Calendar or, in the case of more controversial measures, under **unanimous consent agreements.** The agreements are worked out by Senate leaders and set the terms for consideration of the bill by placing limits on motions, amendments and debate.

Perhaps the most widely known and most controversial rule of Senate procedure is the **filibuster.** It recognizes the principle of unlimited debate. Senators are free to talk as long as they wish, and they need not speak on the issue before the floor. In 1935, for example, Sen. Huey Long, (D., LA), spoke for 16 hours against one of President Franklin D. Roosevelt's reforms. He spoke at length about recipes for Louisiana-style cooking. The record for the longest filibuster is held by Sen. Strom Thurmond, (D., SC), who in 1957 spoke for 24 hours in an unsuccessful effort to kill a civil rights bill.

The Senate, under Rule 22, can terminate a filibuster by a procedure known as **cloture.** Cloture occurs when three-fifths of the entire Senate (60 members) votes to end debate. If the Senate invokes cloture, a final vote on the measure before the chamber must be taken after no more than 30 hours of additional debate.

If both House and Senate pass the identical bill, it is signed by the Speaker of the House and the President of the Senate and sent to the President for his signature. He may sign the bill into law, or he can veto it, sending it back to the house in which it originated. He may send a formal veto message, indicating why he opposes the legislation. Congress, as previously noted, may **override** a presidential veto, but it is relatively rare for a bill to become law over the President's objections.

One of the most heated debates in Washington in recent years has been use of the filibuster to block presidential judicial nominations. Senate Democrats did not have the votes to defeat President George W. Bush's choices directly and, for several years, prevented "up or down" votes.

The dispute reached crisis proportions during spring, 2005, when Republican leaders scheduled a vote on what the press called the "nuclear option," changing Senate rules to prevent filibusters of court nominees.

Democrats clearly did not want to lose a major battle involving the "nuclear option." Republicans did not want to make filibusters the routine on judicial nominations. It was time for "reasonable" legislators to seek a compromise. Many moderates also believed that it was time to end the venomous atmosphere in the Senate, a body traditionally characterized by its civility and courtesy.

On Monday, May 23, 2005, a group of 14 "centrists," seven from each party, decided to end the ideological war that had raged for too long between Liberals and Conservatives. These senators, who held the balance of power, reached an agreement, guaranteeing "up or down" votes on five of President Bush's seven nominees in return for no change in the filibuster rule for the duration of the 109th Congress.

The two page "memorandum of understanding" did not protect two of President Bush's contested nominees, William Myers III of Idaho and Henry Saad of Michigan, who could be either filibustered or withdrawn under the agreement. Republican moderates said that they would feel free to ban filibusters if Democrats acted in bad faith.

The pact cleared the way for confirmation of President Bush's appellate court nominees. Judges Priscilla R. Owen, Janice Rogers Brown and William H. Pryor Jr. were confirmed almost immediately. Democrats, of course, were free, under the May 23 agreement, to vote against them, and most of them did, but the Republican majority ruled, and the Bush nominees took their seats on the Federal bench.

Two Michigan jurists, Richard A. Griffin and David W. McKeague, were approved for seats on the U.S. Court of Appeals for the Sixth Circuit shortly thereafter. The Cincinnati-based Sixth Circuit hears appeals from the states of Michigan, Ohio, Kentucky and Tennessee.

The Senate voted, 96-0, to confirm McKeague, a Federal District judge, and 95-0 to approve Griffin, a judge on the Michigan Court of Appeals. Bush had nominated McKeague in November, 2001, and Griffin in June, 2002.

Prior to the vote, Michigan's two Democratic senators, Carl Levin and Debbie Stabenow, spoke on the floor in favor of the nominees. Yet these two senators had blocked confirmation votes on McKeague and Griffin for years, to retaliate for former Republican U.S. Sen. Spencer Abraham's blocking of two Michigan nominees of President Bill Clinton.

The Senate moderates who broke the logjam were:

Republicans John McCain (Arizona), John Warner (Virginia), Lindsey Graham (South Carolina), Mike DeWine (Ohio), Olympia Snowe and Susan Collins (both from Maine), Lincoln Chafee (Rhode Island) and Democrats Joe Liebermann (Connecticut), Robert Byrd (West Virginia), Ben Nelson (Nebraska), Mark Pryor (Arkansas), Mary Landrieu (Louisiana), Ken Salazar (Colorado) and Daniel Inouyve (Hawaii).

Their dramatic agreement caught both Republican Majority Leader Bill Frist (Tennessee) and Democratic Minority Leader Harry Reid (Nevada) by surprise. Although Frist was disappointed that the agreement fell short of President Bush's insistence that all of his nominees deserved an up or down vote, he had no choice but to accept it. Reid was displeased that what ideologues called the "Gang of 14" had taken power from Senate leaders.

Veteran, cynical Washington political writers recalled the twisted version of the Sermon on the Mount: "Blessed are the peacemakers, for they shall catch hell from both sides."

Both Democrats and Republicans agreed that the stability of the May 23 agreement would be tested, should President Bush submit a nominee "outside the mainstream" for a Supreme Court vacancy. As the court ended its 2004 term, speculation was widespread that one or more retirements would occur.

Justice Sandra Day O'Connor informed President Bush of her retirement, effective July 1, 2005. Rumors also circulated that Chief Justice William Rehnquist could step down. The stage was set for a possible political conflict, despite the May 23 agreement, as the nation celebrated its birthday on July 4.

Subsequently, Chief Justice Rehnquist died and U.S. Court of Appeals Judge John Roberts easily won confirmation (78-22) as his successor. The nomination of U.S. Court of Appeals Judge Samuel Alito to fill the O'Connor seat was more contentious, but ultimately Alito was confirmed, 58-42.

The Alito nomination followed a failed effort by President Bush to place White House Counsel Harriet Miers on the bench as O'Connor's successor. She asked the President to withdraw her nomination because it had become a "burden on the White House."

Senators had sought internal White House documents regarding confidential advice she had given the President. This, both Miers and the President agreed, would undermine a President's ability to receive candid advice.

Both Senate Democrats and Republicans opposed Miers. Pro-life activists in the GOP opposed her. Conservatives were enraged to find that she had made contributions to Al Gore's 1988 presidential campaign and the Democratic National Committee.

More important, Miers had no judicial experience. Senators Patrick Leahy and Arlen Specter, key figures on the Judiciary Committee, called her responses to Senate questions "incomplete" and "insulting." Some political observers said the real reason for the withdrawal was to avoid the embarrassment of a Senate defeat.

G. WHAT'S WRONG (AND RIGHT) WITH CONGRESS?

Congress never is short of critics or criticisms. American humorists, like the late Will Rogers and Johnny Carson, and contemporary comedians like Jay Leno and David Letterman, have long made jokes about Congress and its members. Rogers, for example, used to say that the essential difference between a professional comedian like himself and Congress was that when Congress made a joke, it was a law.

Political scientists may not have great punch lines, but they are likely to deliver more serious charges against the institution. In recent years, they have called Congress unrepresentative (it doesn't look like America) and inefficient.

Congress is **unrepresentative,** some political scientists argue, because it tends to put the interests of the state or congressional district ahead of the interest of the nation as a whole. Although one can well understand the argument that this is necessary to remain in office, others argue that members of Congress should not be obsessed with that goal. Worse things may befall the Republic than the defeat of Senator Jane Roe or Representative John Doe, although Senator Roe or Representative Doe may not think so.

John Rhodes, a former House Republican leader, wrote in his book, *The Futile System,* that "the majority of congressional actions are not aimed at producing results for the American people, as much as perpetuating the longevity and comfort of the men who run Congress."[20]

Congress clearly does not "look like America." It is essentially an upper to upper-middle class institution. Obviously those who are middle-income or low-income Americans lack the time, money, education or inclination to run for Congress. Can their interests be represented by those who come from other social classes? Critics claim that Congress is excessively white, male, middle-aged, professionally trained and inclined to favor the *status quo.*

Can a Congress that has relatively few females and minorities among its representatives reflect their interests?

In response to the critics, many defenders of Congress argue that one need not be a member of a social class or minority group to reflect its interests. They point to aristocrats like Franklin D. Roosevelt and John F. Kennedy in the past or Sen. Edward T. Kennedy today to prove their point. The landmark civil rights laws of the 1960s were passed largely due to the efforts of a southern Democrat, Lyndon Johnson of Texas.

Yet, some of its critics argue strongly that Congress represents not the interests of the middle or lower classes, but the interests of the powerful and the privileged. The system, it is asserted, tends to respond to organized, rather than unorganized, inarticulate interests in our society. Clearly, Congress tends to listen to those who have made sizable campaign contributions to its members, although it would be rare to find actual recorded payoffs involved.

One such episode did occur early in 1980, when seven members of the House and one senator took bribes from undercover FBI agents posing as representatives of a fictitious Arab sheik. The ABSCAM (for "Arab scam") operation was only one in a series of headline stories that showed the moral bankruptcy of these legislators. The tapes later were shown on TV and Americans were witness to the sorry spectacle of legislators stuffing their pockets with cash-filled envelopes.

Rep. John Jenrette Jr., a South Carolina Democrat, was videotaped telling an FBI agent, "I've got larceny in my blood." Rep. Richard Kelly, a Florida Republican, asked, "Does it show?" as he stuffed $25,000 cash into his pockets. While accepting a $50,000 bribe, Rep. Michael Myers, a Pennsylvania Democrat, boasted, "Bullshit walks, money talks."[21]

Sen. Harrison Williams, (D., NJ), avoided expulsion from the Senate only when he agreed, at the last minute, to resign his seat. A veteran legislator, Williams apparently was persuaded by the argument of fellow senators. If he were expelled, he would lose all congressional retirement benefits. If he resigned, he could keep them. He did, however, trade his Senate seat for a cell in a Federal prison.

All of the representatives charged also were convicted. Those who showed the ethical insensitivity to seek re-election were defeated. All of those involved in "Abscam" saw their political careers come to an end.

A decade later, more serious allegations surfaced. It was charged that five powerful senators had exerted undue influence on government banking regulators to delay action against Lincoln Savings and Loan, a financial company which ultimately collapsed, costing taxpayers $2 billion. Charles Keating, Lincoln's president, had given large campaign contributions to these senators and those involved in the scandal came to be known as the "Keating Five." The senators involved were Alan Cranston, (D., CA), Dennis DeConcini, (D., AZ), John Glenn, (D., OH), John McCain, (R., AZ) and Donald Riegle Jr., (D., MI).[22]

In 1991, a Senate Select Committee found four of the senators guilty of "poor judgment" and cited the fifth, Cranston, for a serious breach of ethics. Cranston then resigned as Democratic whip and announced that he would not seek re-election in 1992. Riegle and DeConcini decided not to run again when their terms expired in 1994. Only Glenn and McCain were re-elected.

After "Watergate," Congress had tried to "clean up" an old American scandal: how we finance congressional and presidential elections. Congressional candidates now are required to report all major campaign contributions to the Federal Election Commission. Who gives how much to whom is now a matter of public record. But the activities of Political Action Committees (PACs) still are subject to considerable public debate, as noted in Chapter 7.

Critics, however, must concede that Congress is much more representative than it once was because of the Supreme Court reapportionment decisions of the 1960s and the subsequent required redistricting by state legislatures. The principle of "one person, one vote" has made a difference.

Is Congress **inefficient?** House and Senate procedures, it often is asserted, are ill-suited to advance a nation's needs in the 21st Century. This is the technetronic age, the age in which we have seen the marriage of computers and electronics.[23]

In a society which suffers from a proliferation of complex social problems, is bicameralism a sensible system? Should parallel committees of House and Senate continue to take testimony from the same expert witnesses? Should legislation be as difficult to pass or as easy to kill as it is in the American Congress? Some political scientists think not.

Presidents, of course, often are annoyed by the turtle-like speed with which Congress deals with the nation's problems. To those who want quick and decisive action, Congress gets low marks for "efficiency." But "efficiency" was not on the list of virtues held in high esteem by the Framers. They wanted legislative proposals to be considered thoroughly and for Congress to act only when the public interest required action.

In defense of Congress, one might note that it faces many difficult problems. Some of them may, in fact, not be solvable. Americans are notoriously optimistic and have operated on the assumption that every problem has a solution. That may not be the case.

But improvements can be made and some already have been. Senate Rule 22 (the filibuster) was modified in the mid-1960s and cloture now can by invoked by three-fifths, rather than two-thirds, of the chamber. Both House and Senate now have electronic voting, and their sessions are televised on C-Span. Unfortunately, viewer surveys show that few Americans bother to watch "Congress at Work."

Still, much remains to be done. Committees could be further streamlined. More computers could be used to centralize information processing. Party leadership could be strengthened. Perhaps, above all else, the budget could be handled more expeditiously.

Although modified, the seniority system still draws fire from congressional critics. Some chairs remain in their positions of power and authority long after they have passed their time.

Conservatives respond to many of these criticisms by noting that Congress is what the Framers of the Constitution intended it to be, a body that protects minority rights and restrains popular majorities.

Failure to act quickly is not necessarily bad. The bicameral system, although slow, does produce deliberation. The system of committees and subcommittees insures adequate consideration of the merits of legislative proposals. It is better to be slow and deliberative than fast and imprudent. Defenders of Congress argue that "worthwhile proposals," even if not enacted into law in a given session, will come up again if they have genuine merit.

Rapid enactment of legislation also sometimes means subsequent failure in court when laws are challenged. Many historians argue that the famous "100 Days" of the early New Deal produced this result. The Democratic Congress gave President Franklin D. Roosevelt virtually everything he wanted, but much of what it gave, the U.S. Supreme Court took away, at least in part, because measures were hasty, ill-considered and poorly drafted.

VI. JUDICIAL POWER AND AUTHORITY

A. AMERICAN LAW AND THE LEGAL SYSTEM

All societies, in order to perpetuate themselves and pursue their goals, are built on a system of rules. These rules, which may be either written or unwritten, determine the structure and operation of the governmental machinery of an organization, as well as the nature of the restraints imposed upon the conduct of its members.

Sociologists make distinctions between different kinds of **"norms."** Norms are standards of behavior that society considers typical, average or usual. They are divided into folkways, mores and laws. **Folkways** are common, customary rules of everyday behavior which make social life predictable. We see an old friend and we shake hands. We open the door for someone who has an armload of books or groceries. "Civilized" Americans are characterized by their good manners or thoughtfulness of others. It is simply a question of treating people thoughtfully, as you would wish to be treated yourself.[1]

Not every American behaves in a civil manner. Unfortunately, there are many citizens today who are so selfish that they behave as small children, thinking that the world revolves only around them. In fact, many small children behave better than some adults.

But people who violate folkways are merely labeled. We call them ill-mannered, boorish, stupid or pin some other unpleasant term on them. We do not imprison them, although we may avoid them whenever possible or maintain a good deal of "social distance" from them.

Mores involve not only violations of social rules and conventions; they involve moral judgments. A student who is ill-mannered, thoughtless or self-centered is one thing. One who steals from a roommate, fraternity brother, sorority sister or teammate is something else. As the offense is more serious, so, too, is the punishment.[2]

Both folkways and mores are the result of the process of daily living. They help people to deal with problems they encounter. We need to relate to our families, friends, acquaintances, business colleagues or fellow students. Because certain patterns of behavior have stood the test of time, we tend to accept them as legitimate ways to fulfill our needs.

Laws are much more serious and fall into a number of types or categories. In modern secular America, we think first about municipal traffic laws. We think about state laws establishing civil and criminal penalties for a wide array of anti-social conduct. The anti-social conduct can be relatively minor (a **misdemeanor**), such as disorderly conduct, or extremely serious (a **felony**), such as murder, rape or arson.[3]

But governments are not the only organizations which have laws; churches do, too. The penalty for violation of church laws are normally self-inflicted and psychological. Individuals are more likely to regulate their behavior by fear of supernatural retribution than by a government law saying, "Don't do that!"

Some young women, for example, would never think of having an abortion. Although the medical procedure has been legal in the U.S. since 1973, it also is, in their judgment, highly immoral, tantamount to killing an unborn child. Heated debate rages in America over the abortion question, the most divisive issue in contemporary American domestic politics. Americans also debate whether there is or should be a legal right to privacy. But once a person has internalized the norms (values) of a particular religious doctrine, that becomes part of her identity, part of "who she is." Consequently, what the law permits may be largely irrelevant.[4]

Virtually all social organizations have rules and regulations. Members who violate the rules can be expelled from the club. Groups "socialize" (indoctrinate) their members in the norms or values they hold dear.

What distinguishes government from other forms of social organization is its monopoly on physical force. Rules of the state are formally designated as laws and are upheld by special state judicial institutions called courts. Their "sanctity" is maintained by police and other authorities. Laws of government are thus different from those of other social organizations, although they are similar in many basic purposes.

In the past, custom, morality and religion were largely undifferentiated. Such still is the case in some simpler, less industrialized societies. But in modern, industrialized societies such as our own, morality, religion and socially approved customs are clearly distinguished from the state rules which constitute the law.

The contemporary state is so complex that its laws, although clearly identified as such by government and judicial enforcement, differ in their origin and character.

Before proceeding further, let us pause to define some basic terms that students will encounter when reading about the American system of justice:[5]

Law: a rule of conduct prescribed by a government authority and enforced by the courts.

Common Law: refers to judge-made law that originated centuries ago in England, where judges applied the customs of the people to resolve disputes. It is the basis of legal procedures in every American state except Louisiana, where the French legal tradition still is important.

***Stare decisis*:** a legal term meaning "let the decision stand." Established precedents stand unless overruled. Judges are inclined to overrule precedents only when there is compelling reason to establish a new precedent. *Stare decisis* gives stability to the legal system.

Equity: a branch of law that provides a remedy if the common law does not apply. Equity is designed to provide justice where damages may be awarded too late to be meaningful. In equity cases, judges may order that something be done (specific performance) or they may forbid certain actions by granting an injunction.

Injunction: an order in an equity proceeding to compel or restrain an act by an individual or public official. It prevents harm to an individual's property or personal rights through the power of courts to issue orders without the need of a lawsuit after damage already has been done. Judges have considerable discretion to determine the scope of an injunction.

Statutory Law: written law enacted by Congress or the state legislature.

Treaty: a formal agreement among nations. May involve two (bilateral treaty) or more (multilateral treaty) countries.

Constitutional Law: law that involves interpretation and application of the constitution. It is concerned primarily with defining the limits of governmental power and the rights of individuals. Final authority as to the meaning of the U.S. Constitution rests with the U.S. Supreme Court. The Federal Constitution is the supreme law of the land.

Administrative Law: a branch of law which creates administrative agencies and establishes their procedures. It also determines the scope of judicial review of agency practices and actions. Involves a large number of rules and regulations made by administrative agencies.

Criminal Law: today criminal law is almost entirely statutory and deals with acts that endanger the public. Because the government alone enforces criminal law, the government is the plaintiff, the party that brings the case to court in all criminal trials. The accused is the defendant. Criminal acts are of two types, misdemeanors and felonies. State laws may vary on this somewhat, but misdemeanors are considered less serious transgressions against society. Typically punishment consists of a fine or a jail sentence of less than a year. Felonies are more serious matters, anti-social conduct beyond the tolerance limits of society. Typically they are punished by sentences of more than a year in a prison. The ultimate crime is murder and some states provide the ultimate penalty, death, for this felony.

Civil Law: deals primarily with disputes between private individuals or corporations and defines the rights of parties in a dispute.

B. POWER AND AUTHORITY OF U.S. COURTS

There is a **dual court system** in the U.S. It consists of a Federal judicial system and 50 separate state court systems. State judiciaries are separated geographically, but sometimes they overlap with the Federal system. Structures of these systems are established by the Constitutions and laws of both Federal and state governments and vary considerably.

It is not our intention here to dwell upon state judicial systems. It should be noted, however, that most students who have contact with the courts will have contact with state and local courts, not Federal courts. The vast majority of both civil and criminal cases are brought in state courts. It is more likely that one will be a defendant, plaintiff, witness or juror in the state system than in the Federal one.

The concept of **jurisdiction** is the key to understanding the court system. Jurisdiction means that a court has the right to hear a particular type of case. This right is granted either by a Constitution or by a statute. Without jurisdiction, a court lacks authority to decide a dispute. Jurisdiction of state courts is very broad, while Federal courts have more limited jurisdiction. In some cases, the state and Federal courts share jurisdiction and the plaintiff can choose to sue in either system.

Article III, Section 2, of the Constitution spells out the jurisdiction of Federal courts. Jurisdiction can be based on either the subject matter or the nature of the parties in a particular case. Jurisdiction based on subject matter consists of those cases arising under the Federal Constitution, U.S. laws and treaties, or in the special area of maritime and admiralty law. Jurisdiction based on the nature of the parties includes the following half dozen categories:

- cases affecting ambassadors, other public ministers, and consuls
- cases in which the U.S. is a party
- disputes between two or more states
- disputes between citizens of different states
- disputes between citizens of the same state who claim land under grants from different states
- disputes in which one of the 50 states is a party

Disputes must fall within one of these constitutional provisions to be heard in Federal court. But Congress has established certain other limitations on Federal jurisdiction. If a case involves citizens of two different states—Ohio and Michigan, for example—the amount involved must be more than $50,000. Cases where smaller sums are involved are heard in state courts.

A court's jurisdiction may be either original or appellate. Typically, state courts are divided into a system of trial courts (exercising original jurisdiction) and appellate courts (courts of appeal and a supreme court). Titles of state courts will vary considerably from one state to another. Courts of last resort are usually called Supreme Courts, although New York calls it the Court of Appeals and Maine and Massachusetts calls it the Supreme Judicial Court.

Trial courts also vary in terms of the kinds of cases they hear. In Michigan, for example, a system of District Courts was created in the late 1960s to replace the old justice of the peace system. District courts are limited in their jurisdiction. They can try only relatively minor offenses (misdemeanors) and relatively minor civil matters. If one commits a serious crime, one may be taken before a District Court judge or magistrate for a preliminary hearing, but the judge cannot try the case. If the court finds probable cause, the defendant is then bound over for trial in Circuit Court, which can hear felony cases and large civil suits.

Above these trial courts are Courts of Appeal and the State Supreme Court, which is the final authority on the meaning of the state constitution.[6]

States also have a number of specialized courts, dealing in such things as family problems (domestic relations or family courts), wills and estates (probate or surrogate's courts) and youthful offenders (juvenile or probate courts). One also will find police courts, traffic courts and a variety of other tribunals as one travels around the nation.

At the Federal level, the U.S. Supreme Court has both original and appellate jurisdiction, but it is extremely rare for the high tribunal ever to exercise the former. Original jurisdiction is limited to cases affecting ambassadors, other public ministers, consuls and those in which states are parties. In all other cases, the Supreme Court has appellate jurisdiction. Typically, appeals go from a Federal District Court to a Court of Appeals and then to the Supreme Court. In a case involving the U.S. Constitution, a treaty or an act of Congress, an appeal may go directly to the Supreme Court from the highest state court with jurisdiction over the case.

One should note that state supreme courts have the right to make the final interpretation of the law in cases over which they have jurisdiction. They are the final authority on the meaning of the laws of their state. The U.S. Supreme Court is the final interpreter of Federal law. If a question of Federal law arises in state courts, such as the issue of Federal constitutional rights, the U.S. Supreme Court would have the final authority to rule on the issue.

C. STRUCTURE, JURISDICTION OF FEDERAL COURTS

There are two kinds of Federal courts, constitutional and legislative. **Constitutional courts** are those established by Congress under authority of Article III, Section 1, of the Constitution. It declares that "the Judicial power of the United States shall be vested in one Supreme Court, and in such inferior Courts as the Congress may from time to time ordain and establish."

The main constitutional courts are the U.S. District Courts, the U.S. Courts of Appeals and the U.S. Supreme Court. Several other constitutional courts deal with highly specialized subjects and technical bodies of law. These include the Court of International Trade (tariff law), the Court of Customs and Patent Appeals and the U.S. Court of

Appeals for the Federal Circuit, created by Congress, in 1982, to hear appeals from the U.S. Court of Customs and Patent Appeals and from the U.S. Court of Claims. Decisions of these specialized courts may be appealed to the U.S. Supreme Court.

Legislative courts are created by Congress under its authority, granted in Article I, Section 8, to "constitute tribunals inferior to the Supreme Court" and its expressed powers to legislate in specific areas. Main legislative courts are the U.S. Court of Military Appeals, which reviews court martials, the U.S. Tax Court, which settles disputes between taxpayers and the Internal Revenue Service, Federal territorial courts (Guam, Puerto Rico, Virgin Islands, Canal Zone and the Northern Mariana Islands) and the U.S. Claims Court, a trial court that hears financial claims against the Federal government.

The principal difference between constitutional and legislative courts is that judges on the former tribunals are granted tenure "for life or good behavior," while judges on the latter are to serve for a fixed number of years. Unlike Federal constitutional courts, legislative courts may give advisory opinions. The key Federal constitutional courts are the District Courts, the Courts of Appeals and the Supreme Court.

1. Federal District Courts

Federal District Courts are the trial courts, the workhorses of the Federal system. In 1995, for example, 239,000 new civil cases and 44,200 new criminal cases were filed in District Courts. This is where most Federal cases begin and end. Federal District courts are located in each of the 50 states, the District of Columbia and in U.S. territories.

The number of courts and judges depends upon the size of the population and state, as well as the volume of judicial business. Each U.S. District Court has at least two judges (Nevada), but some have as many as 28 (Southern District of New York). Boundary lines for a district never cross state lines, but a large state may be divided into two, three or even four districts, as is the case in California, Texas and New York. Altogether, there are 89 District Courts in the 50 states, plus one each in the District of Columbia, Puerto Rico and the U.S. territories (a total of 94) and 649 permanent Federal District Court judges in 1998.

All District Court judges hold office for "life or good behavior."

District Courts are the only Federal courts which operate with a jury. In fact, there are two kinds of juries at work here. One, the *petit jury,* consists of 12 jurors who decide whether, on the basis of evidence presented in court, a defendant is guilty or not guilty of a particular crime. Or, in a civil case, they rule either for or against the plaintiff (suing party) or defendant (party being sued).

Grand juries also work here. One cannot be held to answer to a criminal charge in Federal courts unless he or she is indicted by a grand jury. The function of the grand jury is simply to determine whether the government has a case. If it believes that it has, it returns what is known as a **true bill** or indictment and the individual is docketed for trial. If it believes that the state (government) does not have a case, it returns **no bill** and that— at least temporarily—is the end of it. If however, the government later develops more evidence, an indictment can be sought again. There is no double jeopardy—forbidden by the Constitution, unless there is a trial verdict.[7]

Among other things, District Courts hear cases involving crimes against the United States, suits under national laws involving use of the mails, patent, copyright, trademark and other such technical matters and civil rights laws.

On rare occasions, a case may be appealed directly from a U.S. District Court to the U.S. Supreme Court. More commonly, if an appeal is taken, the decision of the District Court is reviewed by a U.S. Court of Appeals.

Henry Abraham, a distinguished scholar and professor of constitutional law, commented in his book, *The Judiciary: The Supreme Court in the Governmental Process:* "...(Federal District Courts)...are the basic trial courts of the federal judiciary. In that role, they are the busiest of the three court layers. From some points of view, the work of the trial courts is both more interesting and more creative than that found in the two appellate tiers. The battle of the opposing platoons of counsel...takes place here. And it is here that we find the jury, that intriguing, albeit controversial, institution of citizen participation in the judicial process."[8]

2. Courts of Appeal

In the Federal system, most cases originate and end in the U.S. District Court. But, like District Courts, Circuit Courts have seen a major increase in the volume of cases on their dockets. Between 1980-1995, the number of cases brought to the Circuit Courts rose from about 23,000 to nearly 50,000. More than three-fourths of the appeals were in civil cases.

At the intermediate level in the Federal judicial system are 13 U.S. Courts of Appeal, also called Circuit Courts. The United States is divided into 11 regions or judicial circuits. A 12th court is located in the District of Columbia. The 13th, established in 1982, is the Court of Appeals for the Federal Circuit. It is a national court that primarily considers cases involving patents and tariffs. Except for this newest Federal Circuit Court, courts of appeals hear both civil and criminal cases. Appeals come primarily from District Courts located within the Appellate Court's Circuit. They also hear an estimated 14% of their cases on appeals from decisions of the Independent Regulatory Commission, such as the Federal Communications Commission or the Interstate Commerce Commission. Most of these appeals come to the appellate court that sits in the District of Columbia.

The number of Circuit Court judges varies from six to 28 permanent judges. There is a total of 179 judges. Each Court of Appeals normally hears cases in panels of three or more judges. Lawyers for the respective parties present written arguments (briefs) to the court. They also are given limited time to present oral arguments. After studying briefs, listening to oral arguments and studying trial records of the case, judges confer privately before announcing their decision. In particularly important and controversial cases, all judges may participate or sit *en banc.* Decisions of the Court of Appeals may go for review to the U.S. Supreme Court.

One should note that Courts of Appeal have only appellate jurisdiction. Therefore, they have relatively little choice regarding which cases they will decide. In most instances, the losing party in the District Court has a right of appeal. The obvious exception to this rule is in the area of criminal law, where the double jeopardy provisions of the Fifth Amendment prohibit the government from appealing a loss in a criminal case.

The Courts have considerable power and authority. Less than 1% of their decisions are reviewed by the U.S. Supreme Court. As the ideological battle heats up between Liberals and Conservatives in Congress, the policy role of Circuit Courts is being more carefully examined. The Senate also now is more inclined than formerly to give careful attention to the nominees sent to them by the President for "advise and consent."

3. U.S. Supreme Court

The U.S. Supreme Court, the only Federal court actually created by Article III, Section 1, of the Constitution, originally consisted of six justices. It is the ultimate authority of the law on all matters involving interpretation of the Federal Constitution, Acts of Congress and treaties. It has enormous power to shape the Constitution, since many cases deal with constitutional issues.

The Court begins its session on the first Monday of October each year. It normally sits until late in June or early in July. Typically, it hears arguments from Monday through Thursday, for two weeks each month. Friday is devoted to conferences at which cases are discussed and voted upon and requests (most of them denied) for appellate review are considered. The remaining two weeks of each month are spent in studying cases and writing opinions.

Congress has both reduced and increased the number of justices for political reasons. Since 1869, the size of the Court has been fixed at nine members. Efforts of President Franklin D. Roosevelt to increase the number of justices in 1937 failed.[9]

The Court is headed by the Chief Justice of the United States. His formal authority consists primarily in his role as presiding officer in Court and at conferences and in his power to assign the writing of opinions.

As noted, the Supreme Court has both original and appellate jurisdiction. The overwhelming number of cases that reach the high tribunal come there on appeal. But there are two categories of cases which can originate in the court—without prior consideration by any other court. These are cases in which a state is a party, and those affecting ambassadors, public ministers and consuls. The Court rarely accepts a suit invoking its original jurisdiction unless it feels that there is a compelling reason to do so. In its entire history, the Court has heard only about 175 cases under its original jurisdiction, most of them involving boundary disputes.

One such example was the dispute between New York and New Jersey over Ellis Island, point of entry for millions of immigrants to the United States. Originally, the island consisted of three acres of rock in the middle of New York Harbor. Since 1904, however, some 24 acres of landfill have been added to it. The island now extends into the western half of the harbor, controlled by New Jersey. The question is "who owns the landfill part of the island, New York or New Jersey?" The island is about 1300 feet from Jersey City, NJ, and about a mile from the tip of Manhattan.

In 1993, New Jersey sued New York over the issue. The case was tried in the Supreme Court under its original jurisdiction on January 12, 1998. In a 6-3 ruling on May 26, 1998, the Court held that Ellis Island is mostly in New Jersey. As a result, most of the island in New York Harbor, including part of the main immigration building, now must be considered Ellis Island, NJ. As one would expect, the attorney generals of the respective states saw the issue quite differently. New Jersey Attorney General Peter Verniero said: "We're obviously very pleased...every map-maker in the world has some work to do...The island is a national treasure that now New Jersey can rightly lay some claim to."

New York Attorney General Dennis Vacco commented: "New Jersey's attempt to turn tradition and history into a mere territorial dispute between the states cannot erase the truth, nor can the Court's ruling today deny New York's historic place in the history of Ellis Island."[10]

All of the rest of the Supreme Court's business comes to it in its appellate jurisdiction, which it exercises in the language of the Constitution, "with such exceptions, and under such regulations as the Congress shall make."

In the post-Civil War era, Congress used this authority over the Court's appellate jurisdiction to withdraw from its jurisdiction a politically embarrassing case, in which the Court already had heard arguments. The Supreme Court agreed that such action was within the congressional power.

In 1957, Senator William Jenner, (R., IN), sought reprisal against the Court's decision in certain national security cases by introducing a bill withdrawing the Court's appellate jurisdiction in five specific kinds of cases, but it failed to pass.

Most of the cases that the Supreme Court decides are brought before it by the writ of *certiorari*. This Latin word, which can be translated as "to be certified," comes from the formal language of the Old English writ of *certiorari*, by which a higher court ordered a lower court to send up the record of a case.

Certiorari is a discretionary writ—that is, the Supreme Court does not have to grant a petition for *certiorari*, and in most cases it does not. Petitions are granted only in cases in which at least four of the nine justices agree that issues of special importance are presented for resolution.

The role of the Supreme Court is to correct errors of law—that is, mistakes in defining, interpreting, or applying the law—made by courts below. But not all judicial errors are important enough to require correction the by Supreme Court. Typically, the court grants less than 10% of the petitions for *certiorari* filed each year.

The exercise of the Court's discretion in deciding whether to grant or deny *certiorari* may involve as much judicial statesmanship as the decision of a case on the merits.

Lawyers submit carefully written, detailed briefs to the justices so that they can become familiar with the facts and questions raised in the dispute. Where the court permits oral arguments, lawyers may present their arguments in person. Although it once was common in early 19th Century America for the Court to listen to these arguments for several days, the heavy workload of the Court today makes such a luxury impossible.

Typically, a case gets one hour for argument, 30 minutes for each side. Attorneys sometimes are stopped in mid-sentence as the limit is rigidly enforced. Attorneys are signaled twice by a system of lights on the lectern. They are told that they have five minutes to finish, then that time has expired.

Justices can and do interrupt lawyers to ask questions, often very pointed and barbed. Or they may wait until attorneys have concluded their arguments. Lawyers arguing cases before the Supreme Court must be patient, articulate, quick on their feet and self-disciplined. Supreme Court justices are very much individuals. Some of them appear to enjoy putting lawyers on the spot, others are more understanding and are able to ask tough questions with a soft voice.[11]

While the Court is sitting, the justices meet in closed Friday conference to discuss and decide pending cases. Doors to the conference room are locked and no one other than the nine justices is present. There is no record of the discussions. At the conference, the Chief Justice presents each case along with his views. Discussion then moves to the associate justices in order of seniority. When the vote is taken, the order is reversed, the most junior justices voting first, and the Chief last.

After the vote, the Chief Justice assigns the writing of the opinion to himself or one of his colleagues. If the decision is not unanimous and the Chief Justice voted in the minority, the senior associate justice in the majority controls the assignment of the decision. Drafts of opinions are circulated among the justices and the author may revise the final opinion on the basis of comments made by his or her colleagues.

It is no easy task to write an opinion that will win support from his or her colleagues. The author of a majority opinion cannot simply declare the decision of the Court. The opinion must also create a document that will satisfy all justices who voted with the majority. Justices sometimes reach same conclusions for different reasons and such differences must be reconciled.

Other than a **majority opinion**, two other kinds of opinion may be written, concurring and dissenting. When justices agree with the result of the case, but not the logic of the majority opinion, they may write a **concurring opinion**, stating the logical path that they followed to reach the same conclusion as their judicial brethren. A **dissenting opinion** may be written by any justice who disagrees with the majority and voted with the minority. In a widely-quoted statement, former Chief Justice Charles Evans Hughes once said, "A dissent in a court of last resort is an appeal to the brooding spirit of the law, to the intelligence of a future day, when a later decision may possibly correct the error into which the dissenting judges believe the court to have been betrayed."[12]

It is a well-established principle of Anglo-American jurisprudence that a decision by the highest court in a jurisdiction is a binding precedent on the questions of law involved in the case. The court making the decisions and all courts subordinate to it are expected to follow the precedent and to give the similar answers to similar questions whenever they arise thereafter. The Latin label for this rule is *stare decisis,* "to stand by the things decided."

Although *stare decisis* is an old and fundamental principle, the Supreme Court sometimes does not follow it. Particularly in constitutional cases, the Court may find it necessary to disregard or overrule its own prior decisions.

As the first Justice John Marshall Harlan once told a group of visiting law students, "I want to say to young gentlemen that if we don't like an act of Congress, we don't have too much trouble to find grounds for declaring it unconstitutional."[13]

If the Court will not change its interpretation of the Constitution, it can be accomplished only by a formal amendment. Justice Louis D. Brandeis once wrote, "*Stare decisis* is usually the wise policy because in most matters it is more important that the applicable rule of law be settled, than that it be settled right.

This is commonly true, even where the error is a matter of serious concern, provided correction can be had by legislation. But in cases involving the Federal Constitution, where correction through legislative action is practically impossible, this Court has often overruled its earlier decisions. The Court bows to the lessons of experience and the force of better reasoning, recognizing that the process of trial and error, so fruitful in the physical sciences, is appropriate also in the judicial function.[14]

4. Other Federal Courts

The Federal judicial system also includes such specialized tribunals as the Court of Claims, the Customs Court and the Courts of Custom and Patent Appeals. The Court of Claims hears contract claims against the government. The Customs Court deals with questions arising in the administration of the tariff laws and the Court of Customs and Patent Appeals reviews decisions of the Customs Court and the Patent Office.

On the "edge" of the judicial system are the so-called "legislative" courts, previously described above.

D. JUDICIAL REVIEW

From the time of Chief Justice John Marshall to the era of Chief Justice John Roberts, courts and judges have played an exceptionally important role in the American system of government. Like their foreign counterparts, American courts settle disputes, punish criminals and protect the rights of the innocent. But they have an additional job to perform, that of **judicial review**.

The most important responsibility of the U.S. Supreme Court is to serve as ultimate authority in interpreting of the Federal Constitution. In performing this role, the Court may have to nullify provisions of state laws or even acts of Congress as violations of the Constitution. On rare occasions, they may have to decide that the President of the United States has also violated the Basic Law.

The basic theory behind judicial review is that the written Constitution is superior law. It can be changed only by an extraordinary procedure involving both the Congress and the states. It is the Basic Law, superior to both common and statutory law. American judges are expected to enforce the Constitution as the highest law of the land and to refuse to enforce any executive or legislative act which conflicts with it.

Unlike separation of powers, checks and balances and other features of the American system, which the Founding Fathers borrowed from European experience and philosophy, judicial review is a distinctly American invention.

Was judicial review intended?[15]

Oddly enough, there is no specific provision anywhere in Article III, or elsewhere, giving Federal courts the power of judicial review. The source of the doctrine is the decision handed down by Chief Justice John Marshall in the case of *Marbury v. Madison* in 1803.[16]

William Marbury had been appointed as a justice of the peace for the District of Columbia by President John Adams. His commission was signed and sealed, but the Federalist Secretary of State—none other than John Marshall—failed to deliver it before Adams left office in 1801. The new President, Thomas Jefferson, instructed Secretary of State James Madison not to deliver it.

Marbury filed a petition for a writ of ***mandamus*** to compel Madison to deliver the commission. He filed it directly with the U.S. Supreme Court without any prior court proceedings, thus invoking the court's original jurisdiction under the Judiciary Act of 1789. A writ of mandamus is an order to a public official to perform an act required by law. The Supreme Court could have granted Marbury's petition or denied it.

If the Court issued the writ, Madison, with Jefferson's backing, would likely refuse to obey it. The Court would have no practical means of forcing him to do so. If the Court denied relief to Marbury, it would be admitting officially that it lacked any authority to control the Executive. In either case, the Federalists and the judiciary would be humiliated and the Jeffersonian would have scored a clear-cut victory.

Most historians consider Marshall's decision a masterly stroke. He ruled that the Judiciary Act of 1789, in authorizing the Supreme Court to grant writs of mandamus in its original jurisdiction, had unconstitutionally extended the Court's jurisdiction beyond that provided in the Constitution. The Court, therefore, declined to issue the writ, leaving Madison and Jefferson with nothing to defy or resist.

But the writ was refused, although not on the grounds that the Court lacked power and authority to give relief against the Executive. Rather, the highest tribunal asserted and exercised a much greater power—passing on the constitutionality of an act of Congress.

The Court initially exercised this claimed right infrequently. More than 50 years passed between *Marbury v. Madison* and *Dred Scott v. Sanford*, the landmark case which some constitutional lawyers believe was the most disastrous in Supreme Court history.[17]

Dred Scott was a slave who had been taken into a "free" state and then sued for his freedom. The court ruling that he had no standing to sue because, in essence, he was property rather than a citizen, was bad enough. But when the Court struck down the Missouri Compromise as unconstitutional, the stage was set for the Civil War. Indeed, many historians argue that the Dred Scott decision made the Civil War inevitable.

It was not until the late 19th Century that the U.S. Supreme Court began to overturn Federal and state laws regularly. Before the Civil War, it invalidated only two Federal statutes, as noted, and 20 state laws.

The doctrine of **"presumption of validity"** always has been important in this respect. In theory, courts must assume that, unless the burden of the evidence is clearly to the contrary, legislatures would not enact or executives sign into law measures which violate the Constitution. Presidents and members of Congress, governors and state legislators, local officials and others presumably take their oaths of office seriously.

After ratification of the 14th Amendment, courts found a new basis in the Constitution for declaring laws invalid. Most laws struck down in the late 19th and early 20th centuries involved a judicial finding that the statute challenged, depriving a person of life, liberty or property without "due process" of law or denied "equal protection" of the laws.

Perhaps the power of courts to declare laws and executive acts unconstitutional is most important in its restraining effect. Congress, as well as state and local legislative bodies, always must consider the attitude of courts, to the extent that they can predict those attitudes, when translating public policy into law. Above all, they must keep in mind the Court's past rulings on matters similar to those under consideration.

Some Americans do not understand that judicial review is a power exercised by all courts, Federal, state and local. State and local courts often have ruled against acts of governors, mayors, city managers and legislators. In so doing, they may apply the U.S. Constitution, as well as state and local charters of government, in arriving at their decisions.

Several Presidents, indeed most of the strong ones, have had their differences with the courts. Feuds between Thomas Jefferson and John Marshall, Abraham Lincoln and Roger B. Taney and more recently, Franklin D. Roosevelt and the Hughes Court, illustrate the point.

Once on the High Court, justices tend to become exceptionally independent, precisely what the Founding Fathers intended. Even though most of the Court consisted of justices appointed by Democratic Presidents, the Supreme Court ruled that President Truman's seizure of the steel mills was unconstitutional in *Youngstown Sheet and Tube v. Sawyer.*[18]

Although the Fathers of the Constitution had not provided specifically for judicial review, evidence supports Marshall's position. The Chief Justice cited no precedent, but state courts already had struck down state laws because they violated state constitutions.

Alexander Hamilton, in Number 78 of *The Federalist*, had argued strongly in favor of judicial review, an argument from which Marshall borrowed. Even the

Democrats voiced few objections to the doctrine at the time, although they did object to Marshall's attempt to tell Jefferson and Madison how to perform their official duties.

Proponents of judicial review argue that it is only logical for courts, which must apply the law to cases before them, to determine—in case of conflict—which laws are to take precedence. In the U.S., the Federal Constitution and the laws made under it take precedence over those which might conflict with it. It also may be argued that Federalism requires a judicial method of resolving disputes between states, between states and national government and of maintaining separation of powers between branches of government.

Civil libertarians say that courts generally have been the backbone of democracy, frequently protecting individual liberty from the "tyranny of majorities" during periods of popular excitement and inadequate legislative restraint.

In short, the Chief Justice's arguments, while debatable, were generally accepted. The notion that it was normal and logical for the Supreme Court to pass on the constitutionality of acts of Congress seems to have been generally accepted in 1803. Today it is part of the bedrock of the American Constitutional System.

In the 20th Century, judicial review was sometimes criticized as undemocratic. Some critics believe that the courts simply have become too powerful. Rather than a system of separation of powers and checks and balances, some argue that we have a system of judicial supremacy. The noted French commentator on the American scene, Alex de Tocqueville, considered judges to be the "aristocracy" of America and once remarked, "Scarcely any political question arises in the U.S. that is not resolved, sooner or later, into a judicial question."[19]

Critics, particularly those unhappy with particular Court decisions, dislike the idea of turning major questions of public policy over to a lifetime judiciary never held accountable in an election. Unquestionably, there is room for an element of judicial discretion in constitutional decision-making. It is rare in the annals of American Constitutional Law that a law is so clearly and obviously in violation of the Constitution that there is no room for justices to differ about it.

Decisions on constitutional matters are as likely to be as much a matter of economic and social philosophy as of logic and principles of law. The fact that nine justices are sitting in a "Marble Palace" in Washington, D.C., does not change that situation. Critics also contend that other democracies, notably Great Britain, have protected civil liberties without judicial review.

Many political scientists do not dispute that judicial review is undemocratic. Rather, they remind us that the U.S. Constitution creates not a direct democracy, but a republic. The Founding Fathers distrusted the abuse of power, whether in the hands of a single institution of government or in the hands of the people themselves. The "tyranny of the majority," so clearly articulated in deTocqueville's *Democracy in America*, is always a source of concern in a democracy.

Some legal scholars defend judicial review on the grounds that it is a part and parcel of our system of checks and balances. Some also argue that judicial review is not dangerously undemocratic because the Supreme Court is so weak that it cannot long frustrate the will of the people. It never has succeeded when it has tried to do so.

Congress does control some of the Court's jurisdiction, many of its powers and even the number of justices. It is the President who ultimately must execute its judgments. Students may recall the famous statement attributed to Andrew Jackson: "John Marshall has made his decision, now let him enforce it."[20] The Court lives in the real world of political and popular democratic pressures.

There have been periods in 20th Century American History when the Court was clearly handing down decisions which were out of tune with public opinion. One of the most famous of these eras was the 1930s, when President Franklin D. Roosevelt had a war with the "Nine Old Men." The Hughes Court invalidated many of the New Deal-era statutes in 1935-36. These measures had been hastily drafted, rushed through the Congress and signed into law by FDR. Clearly, the Hughes Court was blocking measures favored by majorities. One liberal news columnist, Max Lerner, accused the nation's highest tribunal of exercising "The Divine Right of Judges."[21]

In 1937, Roosevelt retaliated by sending Congress his proposal to reorganize the Supreme Court. He urged Congress to authorize the President to appoint up to an additional six justices, increasing the size of the tribunal to 15.

Although Roosevelt had won a landslide re-election over Gov. Alf Landon of Kansas, the Republican nominee in 1936, and had an overwhelming Democratic Congress, he had badly miscalculated on this one. The American people hold the Court and the Constitution in extremely high regard.

Media descriptions of the proposal as an attempt to "pack the court," and editorial cartoons portraying Roosevelt as King Franklin I stamping on the Constitution were a disaster for the most popular Democratic President of the 20th Century. The Senate rejected the proposal, but did, however, pass a generous retirement package to encourage older justices to step aside.

Within a short time, resignations enabled FDR to virtually remake the Court with new appointments. Many historians agree with the assertion that although FDR had lost the battle, in the long run, he had won the war.[22]

During the Eisenhower years, the Court again came under a storm of protest. Led by Chief Justice Earl Warren, it issued several rulings which changed American life dramatically. Of profound importance was the ruling in *Brown v. Board of Education*, which brought a legal end to segregated public schools in the U.S.[23]

Decisions in the area of national security in which the Court upheld civil rights of Communists or persons accused of being Communists were unpopular. This time it was Congress, not the President, which reacted strongly. A billboard, often seen on interstate highways during this era, read "Impeach Earl Warren, Save Our Republic."

As is the case with "bumper sticker thinking," billboard thinking is simplistic. How many Americans knew that all nine justices had agreed in the *Brown* case. Could one realistically or logically suggest impeachment of the entire Supreme Court?

E. WHO CHECKS THE U.S. SUPREME COURT?

Who can check the U.S. Supreme Court? Is it true that the only appeal from a Supreme Court ruling is an appeal to God? Not exactly. One method, although a very difficult one, that can be used to set aside a Supreme Court ruling is a constitutional amendment. The 16th income tax amendment, for example, overturned a Supreme Court ruling, *Pollock v. Farmers Loan and Trust Co.*[24] The Court had ruled that the U.S. income tax law of 1894 was unconstitutional because it was a direct tax. Congress, therefore, should have apportioned it among the several states according to population, as required in Article I, Section 9, of the Constitution.

The effect of *Pollock* was that Congress was prevented from enacting a new income tax measure until 1913, when the 16th Amendment was adopted. The Amendment dodged the issue of whether an income tax statute is a direct or indirect tax by simply eliminating any legal requirement for apportionment.

Presidents and the Senate have a "check," although not a very effective one, in the appointment process. Presidents can choose with care, although they cannot be sure that justices will be what they expect at the time of the appointment. Neither can the Senate, nor its Judiciary Committee. The committee and the Senate can reject a nomination, however, as they have done on a number of occasions in recent years.

In the past 40 years, the Senate has blocked five presidential nominations. President Johnson's promotion of Abe Fortas from Associate to Chief Justice (when Earl Warren retired) was withdrawn when it became clear the Senate did not support it. In 1969-70, the Democratic-controlled Senate rejected two of Nixon's choices in succession. Clement Haynsworth and Harold Carswell, Nixon contended, were simply victims of Senate bias against southern Conservatives.[25]

Possibly the most famous (Conservatives would say infamous) rejection of a nominee took place in 1987, when the Senate Judiciary Committee, chaired by Democratic Sen. Joe Biden, an announced candidate for his party's presidential nomination, rejected Robert Bork. Biden, Sen. Edmund Kennedy of Massachusetts and Howard Metzenbaum of Ohio announced *before* the hearings began that they were opposed to Judge Bork.[26]

Reagan submitted the name of Douglas Ginsberg to the Senate after the Bork episode, but the media then published stories that Ginsberg had smoked marijuana as a college student. Perhaps the committee could have forgiven this as a youthful indiscretion, not uncommon on campuses during the 1960s, but other stories surfaced that Ginsburg had smoked pot as a 35-year-old Harvard law professor. His support in the Senate collapsed and Reagan withdrew his name.

Although confirmed by the Senate (by the smallest margin in history), Justice Clarence Thomas ran into problems in his fall, 1991, hearings when Oklahoma Law School professor Anita Hill surfaced to charge that Thomas had sexually harassed her. The hearings became a kind of a national soap opera and included rather graphic (or pornographic) discussions of sexual matters.

The Senate has rejected 28 presidential nominees for the Supreme Court since the founding of the Republic. This is about one-fifth of the total number of nominees put before it.

A second method that Congress can use to restrict the power and authority of Federal courts is to alter or abolish all of the Supreme Court's appellate jurisdiction, change the jurisdiction of all other Federal courts, reduce the pay of future Federal judges, reduce appropriations to pay for court operations and increase the number of Federal judges.

During the 1980s, a number of bills were introduced to prevent Federal courts from hearing cases involving such issues as abortion and prayer in public schools. Other bills would have denied the Supreme Court power to review cases involving these and other controversial issues. But none of these measures had enough support in Congress to become law. Although the Congress does have constitutional authority to share the Federal courts, it seldom has used it to restrict or punish the courts.

Another method of checking the powers of all Federal judges, from trial court to Supreme Court levels, is impeachment and removal. Although tenure for "life or good behavior" usually means tenure for life or as long as a judge or justice wants to be there, bad behavior can occur. Perhaps the question is, "What is bad or what is intolerable?"

Under the Constitution (Article II, Section 4), the House can impeach and the Senate can remove a judge or justice who is convicted (by a two-thirds vote of the

Senate) of "Treason, Bribery or other high Crimes and Misdemeanors." Congress seldom has exercised this power.

Only one Supreme Court justice has ever been impeached, Justice Samuel Chase, in 1804. The Senate refused to convict him. Chase was a staunch foe of President Thomas Jefferson and may have lacked a proper judicial temperament, but he had not committed any impeachable offenses.[27]

However, there have been 12 impeachment proceedings brought against other Federal judges and 10 of them actually went to trial. Three judges were acquitted and seven were convicted and removed from office. Two judges resigned before the Senate trial, avoiding the public embarrassment involved.

The 1980s witnessed conviction and removal of three Federal District Court judges. They were Harry Claiborne, Nevada (1986), Alcee Hastings, Florida (1989) and Walter Nixon Jr., Mississippi (1989).

In one of those great ironies of American politics, Hastings announced that the chamber, which had impeached him, might have to seat him as a member. He declared his candidacy for a seat in the U.S. House of Representatives in 1993. This represented another issue for the House to decide. The Constitution stipulates in Article I, Section 3, that "officials who have been impeached and removed from office are ineligible to hold and enjoy any Office of Honor, Trust or Profit under the United States."

It was not clear whether this statement applied to service in the Congress, but the House never took any action to deprive Hastings of his seat and he has been re-elected by his Florida constituents eight times.[28]

F. JUDICIAL ACTIVISM VS. JUDICIAL SELF-RESTRAINT

Supreme Court justices understand that their power to interpret the Constitution, and particularly their power to declare acts of Congress unconstitutional, must be exercised with great restraint. Therefore, they approach constitutional questions with great reluctance, and usually decide cases on a constitutional issue only when there appears to be no viable alternative.

The simplest way for the justices to avoid constitutional issues is, of course, simply to deny *certiorari* in cases where such an issue is present, and sometimes this is exactly what the court does. The court also may delay hearing a case until the heat has gone out of a constitutional question. A number of wartime civil liberties cases were not decided until the war was over.

Furthermore, the Supreme Court has imposed a number of rules upon itself. These rules are aimed at avoiding constitutional decisions. Justice Brandeis summarized them in a concurring opinion in *Ashwander v. Tennessee Valley Authority* 297 U.S. 288 (1936). They are as follows: (1) The Court will not anticipate a question of constitutionality in advance of the necessity of deciding it, nor is it the habit of the Court to decide questions of a constitutional nature unless absolutely necessary to a decision of the case in hand. (2) The Court will not formulate a rule of constitutional law broader than is required by the precise facts to which it is to be applied. (3) The Court will not pass upon a constitutional question, although properly presented by the record, if there is also present some other ground upon which the case may be disposed. (4) When the validity of an act of Congress is drawn into question, and even if a serious doubt of the constitutionality is raised, it is a cardinal principle that the Court will first ascertain whether a construction of the statute is fairly possible by which the question may be avoided.

The Court, whether or not it always follows these rules, has outlined its general approach to judicial review. Beyond these maxims of judicial self-restraint, there are a number of technical rules applied to limit the breadth and freedom of the Supreme Court's approach to constitutional issues.

One of these is the rule that the question must be **"justiciable."** This means that the judicial proceedings must meet the tests of cases and controversies which can be resolved by courts, rather than appropriately resolved by the "political" branches, the President and the Congress.

The Supreme Court does not give **"advisory opinions,"** even if requested by the President—as Washington once did. It will refuse to consider made-up cases that are really nothing more than attempts to obtain a Supreme Court ruling on abstract questions of law, or "friendly" lawsuits where the parties on both sides have the same interests.

An important element of justiciability is **"standing to sue."** Not everyone with enough money to sue is entitled to litigate the legality or constitutionality of government action in the Federal courts. To have the standing necessary to maintain an action, the plaintiff must establish the sufficiency of his or her interest in the controversy. Courts must be satisfied that (1) the interest is one that is peculiar and personal to the individual and not one he or she shares with all other citizens generally and (2) that the interest he is defending is a legally recognized and protected right, immediately threatened by some government action.

For example, two 1974 cases held that a citizens group had no standing to question the constitutionality of members of Congress holding reserve commission in the armed forces and that a taxpayer lacked standing to sue the Secretary of the Treasury and force him to make public the budget of the Central Intelligence Agency (CIA), known only to a few key members of Congress.

Usually lawsuits are brought by, or on behalf of, specifically named individuals. However, where an interest is at stake that is widely shared—access, for example, of Black children to integrated schools—so-called **"class action suits"** may be filed by a few named individuals suing for themselves and "all others similarly situated."[29]

Sometimes the Supreme Court rejects cases that may meet the test of justiciability on grounds that they involve "political questions." Where the Court concludes that the Constitution assigns authority to make a decision to the President or to the Congress exclusively, it will refuse to interfere.

Historically, for example, it is generally agreed that the President has almost exclusive authority over foreign relations. A foreign policy question is likely to be considered a political question with which the high court does not wish to meddle. Efforts to get the court to rule that the Vietnam War was unconstitutional because Congress had not declared a state of war were uniformly unsuccessful.

The Court regards the whole process of amending the Constitution as a political question within the jurisdiction of Congress. Whether a state has a "republican form of government," guaranteed to every state in Article IV, section 4, is another political question.

Over time, the Court may change its mind about issues. In 1946, the court refused to remedy gross inequalities of population in an Illinois congressional district, where one congressman represented nine times as many people as a representative from another Illinois district. In *Colegrove v. Green* 328 U.S. 549 (1962), the majority thought it should be kept out of the "political thicket." The issue of malapportioned legislative districts, the Court ruled, was a political question and relief should be sought through the political process.

By 1962, however, it reversed this position in *Baker v. Carr* 369 U.S. 186 (1962*),* ruling that the Federal courts could review claims of malapportionment of seats in the Tennessee state legislature. The Tennessee Constitution had required reapportionment of the legislature every 10 years, but no action had been taken since 1901. As a result, districts varied greatly in population. This situation existed in many other states as well and, in general, the urban areas were seriously underrepresented in state legislatures.

In *Gray v. Sanders* 372 U.S. 368 (1963), the Court invalidated the Georgia county unit system because it intentionally discriminated against the large city populations in favor of rural areas. Each person's vote must count equally in all statewide elections. In *Wesberry v. Sanders* 376 U.S. 1 (1964), the Court ruled that congressional districts must be approximately equal in population. In *Reynolds v. Sims* 377 U.S. 533 (1964), the Court declared that the principle of equal protection of the laws required the rule of "one person, one vote" in the states, and that districts roughly equal in population must be the basis for election of representatives to both houses of each state's legislature.

G. THE POLITICS OF JUDICIAL SELECTION

The Constitution requires that Federal judges be nominated by the President and confirmed by the U.S. Senate by a simple majority vote. Because U.S. judges participate to a large degree in the policy-making process, this is a political process. Typically, Presidents will choose members of their own party for these highly-coveted lifetime judicial positions, which carry with them enormous prestige.

The nomination of a Supreme Court justice is one of the most important things that a President may do. Because they serve "for life or good behavior," justices probably will still be serving on the Court long after the President has retired from office. Presidents, therefore, usually give careful thought to the process of filling a Supreme Court vacancy.

Politics is paramount, as well as skill, in law. Presidents consider age, religion, race, sectionalism, judicial experience and philosophy. But above all else, party affiliation.

John Marshall was chosen as Chief Justice of the United States primarily because he was an able Federalist politician. Although he subsequently became one of the great jurists in Supreme Court history, his legal credentials were unimpressive and his legal education inadequate. Roger B. Taney was chosen as Marshall's successor primarily because he had been a loyal member of President Andrew Jackson's cabinet.

Presidents seldom appoint members of the opposition party to Federal Courts. Some 97% of Franklin Roosevelt's choices to serve on District and Appeals Court benches were Democrats. Harry S. Truman, Dwight Eisenhower, John F. Kennedy, Richard Nixon, Jimmy Carter, Ronald Reagan and Bill Clinton appointed more than 90% of members of their own party to the Court.

Only Gerald Ford, who filled 19% of vacancies with Democrats and George Bush, who named 11% of the opposition party to District and Circuit Courts, made even a "gesture" toward members of the opposition party.

The storm of controversy that surrounded the Warren Court (1953-1969) prompted Republican presidential candidate Richard Nixon to promise, in 1968, that he would appoint "strict constructionists" to the bench, men who would interpret the

Constitution and the laws, rather than attempt to substitute their own policy preferences for those of the President and Congress.

It is entirely too simplistic to believe that the Supreme Court is an objective, impersonal tribunal simply enforcing the Constitution, rather than its own will. It may be too much to say, as Justice Felix Frankfurter once did, "the Supreme Court is the Constitution." But the view of Justice Owen Roberts that judicial review was essentially an automatic process is equally questionable. Roberts said that all judges had to do was lay the challenged law next to the Constitution. If it "squared" with the Constitution, it was valid. If it did not, it was invalid. Some cynics refer to Justice Roberts' theory as the "slot machine" theory of judicial review.[30]

Quality is of fundamental importance on the Federal bench. Clearly, many men and women have made financial sacrifices to serve on the courts, since they could earn a good deal more money in private legal practice. But the enormous prestige that comes with a Federal judgeship, particularly the Supreme Court, is more than ample compensation to many.

For most of the 20th Century, presidential nominations to the Supreme Court were routine matters. Only one nominee failed to win Senate confirmation in the first two-thirds of the century. But Presidents, since the tumultuous 1960s, have become deeply involved in wars with the Senate over Supreme Court appointments.

President Johnson had to withdraw his nomination of Abe Fortas (already on the Court) to become Chief Justice, and the Senate never voted on his nomination of Homer Thornberry to replace Fortas. The Nixon Administration had fights over the nominations of Clement Haynsworth and Harold Carswell. When the Senate rejected them, Nixon denounced the Senate for regional prejudice against the south and ideological bias against Conservatives. The Senate later did confirm Nixon's nominations of Lewis Powell Jr., William Rehnquist, Harry Blackmun and Warren Burger as Chief Justice. President Ford's nomination of John Paul Stevens sailed through the Senate, 98-0, because Justice Stevens' qualifications apparently were beyond question.

During his 1980 presidential campaign, Ronald Reagan promised that, if elected, he would name a woman to "one of the first Supreme Court vacancies in my administration." When Justice Potter Stewart retired in 1981, Reagan made good on his promise, nominating Sandra Day O'Connor. O'Connor had a lot going for her besides gender. She was young enough (51) to have many years of service ahead on the court. She had the support of Senators Barry Goldwater and Paul Laxalt of Arizona. She had made a very favorable impression on Reagan. Less than a week after the President interviewed O'Connor, he sent her nomination to the Senate, where she was quickly confirmed.

O'Connor did have one notable foe, Rev. Jerry Falwell, president of the Moral Majority. He was afraid that O'Connor was "soft on abortion." Falwell said that all "good" Christians should be concerned about O'Connor's appointment. Senator Goldwater replied, "Every good Christian ought to kick Falwell right in the ass."[31]

When Chief Justice Warren Burger retired in 1986, Reagan elevated Justice Rehnquist to Chief and nominated Antonin Scalia to fill Rehnquist's position as an associate justice. Again, as in the O'Connor case, Reagan set a precedent. Scalia was the first Italian-American ever appointed to the Supreme Court.

When Justice Lewis Powell retired at the end of the 1987 term, Reagan had the chance to fill a third vacancy. But he was to have nothing but political trouble because the Democrats had recaptured the Senate during the mid-term congressional elections of

1986. The President nominated U.S. Circuit Court Judge Robert Bork to fill the Powell slot.

What followed was an ugly story. No one disputed Bork's brilliance or legal qualifications to serve on the nation's highest tribunal. The American Bar Association had rated him as "exceptionally well qualified." But his Conservative views were widely known because he had written so much over the past quarter century. He was, in short, a lightning rod for Liberal opposition.

Judge Bork did not believe that Americans had a constitutional right to privacy. This, he said, was a "judicially invented" right. He often spoke out against *Griswold v. Connecticut*, the 1965 decision in which the Court first found such a right to exist. Liberals feared that Bork would tip the balance of power on the Court and that it would then overrule *Roe v. Wade*, the 1973 decision which legalized abortion in the U.S. As noted above, the Senate rejected Bork's nomination, 58-42. Bork was defeated simply because the Senate Democratic majority did not like his ideology. Had Reagan nominated him when the Republicans controlled the Senate, he would likely have been confirmed.[32]

Reagan then nominated Douglas Ginsburg, who was forced to withdraw when media reported his "pot" smoking not only as a student, but also as a Harvard law professor. One cannot break the law and expect to be a justice on the highest Court in the land. On his third try, Reagan succeeded in getting the Democratic-controlled Senate to advise and consent to the nomination of Anthony Kennedy.

President Bush also had some problems with the Senate. His first nominee, Judge David Souter, was easily confirmed. But he ran into problems when nominee Clarence Thomas was accused of sexual harassment by Anita Hill, one of his former subordinates, who at the time of the Senate confirmation hearings, was a law professor at University of Oklahoma. Women's groups and other Liberals exploded in fury, although Thomas denied the charges. After three days of dramatic televised hearings, the Senate confirmed Justice Thomas, 52-48, the closest vote on a Supreme Court nomination in more than a century.[33]

President Clinton nominated two Supreme Court justices in his first five years in office. In 1993, he appointed Ruth Bader Ginsberg, the second female in history to sit on the High Tribunal. In 1994, he nominated Stephen Breyer. Neither Ginsburg nor Breyer caused much controversy.[34]

President George W. Bush did not have the opportunity to nominate a U.S. Supreme Court justice during his first term. However, on July 1, 2005, as the term of the nation's highest tribunal came to an end, Associate Justice Sandra Day O'Connor announced her retirement. Then Chief Justice Rehnquist, who had undergone thyroid cancer surgery, died.

As noted in the preceding chapter, the President was able to get the Senate to confirm John Roberts as Chief Justice Rehnquist's successor and Samuel Alito as Associate Justice.

Given their lifetime tenure, independence and enormous power, Federal judges, particularly U.S. Supreme Court justices, must be carefully screened during the appointment process. In fact, they have not always been studiously considered.

Many court watchers were stunned in the spring of 2009 when Associate Justice David Souter announced his retirement at 69, the average age of a Roberts court justice. President Obama announced on May 26 that he was nominating a successor: U.S. Appeals Court Judge Sonia Sotomayor, the first Hispanic ever to sit on the nation's highest court

Given the fact that Democrats have a sizeable majority in the Senate and that Judge Sotomayor, 54, was initially appointed as a Federal District Court Judge by a Republican President, George Herbert Walker Bush in 1992, she may well win substantial bipartisan support. She was "promoted" to the New York-based U.S. Court of Appeals for the Second Circuit by President Clinton

Because he must fill a large number of judicial vacancies, the President often does not participate directly in the selection process at the lower levels of District and Circuit Court. The Supreme Court is much more likely to find him heavily involved. Justice Department officials are usually heavily involved at lower levels.

There is, at the District Court level, what is known as the practice of **"senatorial courtesy."** Judges from particular states are selected by the President, only after consultation with the senior senator from that state if he belongs to the President's party. Thus, in 2009, President Obama would ask Sen. Carl Levin of Michigan for his advice and recommendation on appointment of a Federal District Court judge in that state.

If a state has two Democratic senators, as Michigan did during the President George W. Bush era, he would be free to consult with House Republicans or other party leaders.

Senators have the right to veto appointments in their own state and their refusal to "sign off" will effectively end any chance an individual had to become a District Court judge. Typically, senators submit a list from which the President will fill any vacancies in his or her state. Candidates are also evaluated by the Justice Department, submitted to an FBI background check and a recommendation from the American Bar Association.

The Senate Judiciary Committee plays the major role in the nomination process. Although most choices are approved routinely, the committee sometimes holds hearings at which friends and foes of particular nominees may appear to argue for or against the nomination. The committee also can resort to delay, especially just before a presidential election. Members of the opposition party hope that their candidate will be elected, which could provide an opportunity to select new Federal judges.

Presidents can only hope and venture an educated guess when they make judicial appointments. Perhaps their choice will "behave" as they hope on the bench. Perhaps he or she will be a good Conservative or a good Liberal. But with the passage of time, justices sometimes change their views. Teddy Roosevelt, for example, often regretted the day he appointed Oliver Wendell Holmes to the Supreme Court.

Felix Frankfurter, a young "Liberal" when appointed by Franklin D. Roosevelt, was later to become one of the more "Conservative" members of the Warren Court. Dwight Eisenhower is recorded as having said that his choice of Earl Warren as Chief Justice in 1953 was "the worst damned appointment I ever made as President and Brennan (Associate Justice William Brennan) was the second worst."[35]

In choosing Warren, former California governor and GOP vice presidential nominee in 1948, Eisenhower thought that he had selected a moderate. He thought the same thing about Brennan. History would prove them to be two of the most Liberal members of the court—hence Eisenhower's regrets.

Of particular importance in the selection process is how potential members of the Court see its role and their own as new justices. Should the Court defer to the judgment of the elected representatives of the American people, a policy of self-restraint? Or should it follow a policy of judicial activism, at least in the area of protecting individual freedoms against the majority?

None of these arguments is particularly new, but they are of vital importance. Courts will continue to act as a check on both the President and the Congress. The

Supreme Court, recognized as the highest authority on the meaning of the Constitution, will continue to nullify statutes or executive acts as unconstitutional. The exercise of this power has occasionally led to serious counterattacks on the Court, sometimes by even Federal judges themselves. Although the power of judicial review has been accepted as one of the valuable safeguards of American democracy, some critics continue to insist that in areas of economic regulation, civil liberties and abortion, the court simply has taken too much on itself and has become a kind of a modern-day "super-legislature."

VII. POLITICAL PARTIES AND PRESSURE GROUPS

A. WHAT IS A POLITICAL PARTY?

What is a political party? The answer to that question depends largely on the nation being studied. There are at least three major categories: single party systems, multi-party systems and two-party systems.

In some nations, parties are highly ideological. Foreign students attending American colleges and universities often remark that they are struck by the similar positions taken on issues by Democrats and Republicans.

Although dedicated Democrats and convinced Republicans see plenty of differences between the two parties, neither group favors "revolutionary change," such as the overthrow of capitalism. Both have essentially moderate agendas. They tend to exaggerate their differences, particularly during campaign years. American voters neither expect nor want their major parties to be a collection of ideologues. Whenever candidates are perceived to be "too far to the right" or "too far to the left," they court electoral disaster.

One definition of party is a group of persons who unite to promote a common purpose. In the case of American politics, that purpose is the winning of political office. One could define a major American political party as an organized attempt to gain political power. In short, the primary purpose of our major parties is to provide the personnel of government.

Americans are ambivalent about partisan politics. We do not like the word "politician." We do like the word "statesman." What's the difference between a politician and a statesman? President Truman once said that the essential difference is that a statesman is a dead politician. In short, while one is on the "firing line" in government and politics, he or she is fair game. Later on, it's the judgment of history that counts.

Delegates to the Constitutional Convention wanted nothing to do with political parties. Nowhere in the Constitution did they refer to them. The Framers apparently believed that Presidents and members of Congress could be chosen without them. At the end of his second term, President George Washington warned against the "baneful effects of the spirit of party."

The Framers understood that it was inevitable that individuals and groups would disagree about issues of public policy. But, opponents should not form permanent groups to foster their aims. Rather, they believed, groups would form on different sides of an issue until the question was settled. Then they would disappear, to be replaced by other groups as new issues emerged.

Permanent political parties, it was felt, would split the nation into factions, which could do irreparable damage to national unity. James Madison, in *The Federalist* (No. 10), argued that the new Constitution, the "most perfect document," would temper and control these political factions. He wrote: "A landed interest, a manufacturing interest, a mercantile interest, a monied interest, with many lesser interests, grow up of necessity in civilized nations, and divide them into different classes, actuated by different sentiments and views. The regulation of these various and interfering interests forms the principal task of modern legislation, and involves the spirit of party and faction in the necessary and ordinary operations of government."

Despite the hopes of Washington and the Framers, parties were not long in forming. Some contend that they appeared before the ink on the Constitution was dry.

Federalists emerged as the champions of the new government, while anti-Federalists fought against the adoption of the Constitution. In Washington's first administration, Hamilton built the foundations of the Federalist Party. By 1800, Jefferson had established a Republican Party with the beginnings of a grass roots, national organization that was characteristic of later party organizations.

Only during the Monroe Administration (1817-1825) did the Framers' hopes that there would be no contending political parties even approach realization. The Boston *Columbian Centinel* on July 12, 1817, called this the "era of good feeling." Some scholars describe this era as one of personal politics, during which voters consistently gave Democratic-Republicans control of both the White House and the Congress. Attention was focused on individual candidates, rather than on party label.[1]

The party of Jefferson had argued for strict construction of the Constitution and states' rights during their election battles with the Federalists. Once in office, Jefferson acquired the Louisiana Territory from Napoleon's France. Democratic-Republicans also enforced higher tariffs and resisted European intrusion into the New World, through the Monroe Doctrine.

The description of Monroe's two terms as an "era of good feeling" may not have been entirely accurate. Although there was no formal political opposition during the period, new political factions were developing and new contenders for power were emerging—witness the conflicts within the President's cabinet.

Party warfare erupted again during the campaign of 1824. Democratic-Republicans who supported Henry Clay and John Quincy Adams split from the rest of their party to oppose the election of Andrew Jackson of Tennessee. In 1824, no candidate was able to win a majority of the Electoral College vote and the House of Representatives chose John Quincy Adams over Jackson, despite the fact that the latter had both more popular and more electoral votes than the former. Partisan conflicts have been with us ever since.

B. HOW PARTIES, PRESSURE GROUPS DIFFER

The major difference between political parties and pressure groups is one of emphasis. Parties, as noted, want to win elections. They want to provide the personnel of government: presidents, congressional majorities, governors, mayors, legislative majorities at all levels of government and judges, where they are elected. Stands on public policy, while not unimportant, are of secondary importance.

In 1936, for example, the Republicans nominated Gov. Alf Landon of Kansas as their presidential candidate. They drafted a platform which called for the repeal of the Social Security Act, passed in the preceding year. Social Security, Landon and the GOP platform said, was an insidious piece of socialist legislation. The Roosevelt-Landon race was viewed as a referendum on Social Security. When the votes were in, Roosevelt had won 46 of the then-48 states, losing only Maine and Vermont. The people had spoken.[2]

Did the Republicans insist on maintaining the same policy on Social Security which had brought them to electoral disaster? No, Social Security became a bipartisan issue. Seldom did politicians tackle the issue. Wendell L. Willkie in 1940, Thomas E. Dewey in 1944 and 1948, Dwight D. Eisenhower in 1952 and 1956, and Richard M. Nixon in 1960, all endorsed Social Security. Some of these Republican presidential nominees promised that they would administer the system more efficiently. None of them repeated the Landon view.

But, in 1964, Sen. Barry Goldwater, the GOP presidential nominee, suggested that Social Security ought to be made voluntary. Democrats responded with a TV commercial, showing a hand ripping up a Social Security card, and the pieces fluttering down. The message was clear: Goldwater was a threat to Social Security. He won only Arizona, his native state, and a handful of southern states, angered by enactment of the Civil Rights Act of 1964, and pleased by Goldwater's vote against it.[3] Republicans and Democrats may argue details about Social Security financing. Some Conservatives, such as President George W. Bush, suggest the system ought to be privatized. Demographic changes and the pending retirements of millions of "baby boomers" in the third decade of the 21st Century make it imperative to "do something" about the system. But in this area of public policy, neither party is suggesting elimination of the system. The old saying on Capitol Hill is: "Social Security is like the third rail in the subway. Touch it and you die."

Pressure groups are interested first and foremost in public policy. More specifically, they are interested in public policy as it affects their interests. They do not, in most cases, care whether it is a Democrat or a Republican who votes on their side. Samuel Gompers, one of the great labor leaders in American history, advised members of his AFL union to "study the record, reward your friends and punish your enemies."[4]

The United States is continental in size. It is a "land of diversity" with enormous differences among people and regions. Pressure groups exist to reflect those differences and those interests.

Economic interest groups, such as unions, businesses, farm groups and trade associations, are among the most important groups. But there are many other groups whose interests are primarily non-economic. These include veterans, religious, women's, racial and ethnic groups, all of which are engaged in political activities. So are citizens who have organized into so-called "public interest" groups, like Common Cause.

Recently, American politics has seen the rise of "single interests," groups which are so committed to a particular cause that they are unwilling to compromise their values on it. Politics, being the art of compromise, has had trouble accommodating these interests. They include gun control advocates and abortion rights, advocates and opponents. They judge candidates entirely on their stand on one issue. The Sierra Club is one of a number of groups concerned with problems of conservation and the environment. Some politicians argue that single interest groups have contributed to the "fragmentation of American politics at the expense of the common good."[5]

Although pressure groups have been around since the beginning of the nation's history, it was only during the 20th Century that they proliferated. About one-fourth of the nearly 3000 interest groups with offices in Washington, D.C., were founded within the past 25 years.

We are a nation of joiners. We also are a Federal system, with separation of powers. All of these factors stimulate pressure politics.

C. PRESSURE GROUP ROLES

What major roles do pressure groups play in the American political system? The following is a list of their most important functions.

1. Lobby Executive and Legislative Branches of Government

Lobbying is a term which originated centuries ago. It referred to journalists who waited in the House of Commons to interview legislators. Today, it means trying to "sell" legislators that it is a good idea to vote for or against a particular bill in which one's group is interested.

Lobbyists also try to convince members of the executive branch, sometimes even the President, to support or oppose legislation. Although their motives may be selfish, they usually put their case in terms of national interest. Identifying one's own group with the national interest is an age-old pressure group propaganda technique.

Pressure groups often hire full-time lobbyists to represent their interest in either Washington or in state capitols. Often they are lawyers and former members of the legislature. Sometimes they are public relations specialists, who serve as **"spin doctors."** The term, of relatively recent origin, refers to the practice of putting the best possible "spin" on a news story to get good publicity for one's client or to put the best possible light on an otherwise bad situation.[6]

The fact that about 40% of those who left Congress after the election of 1992 remained in Washington as paid lobbyists creates the appearance of **conflict of interest**. Having useful contacts with former colleagues is presumably why these people were hired in the first place. But does this new role of former-legislators give unfair advantage to certain groups?

In any given year, members of Congress deal with thousands of bills and an enormous number of issues. The lobbyist has the advantage of **specialized knowledge in a particular area,** and knowledge is a form of power. He or she may be called before a legislative committee to testify as an "expert witness" and to effectively support or oppose a pending bill in which the group is vitally interested.

Most of the time, lobbyists are called upon simply to maintain friendly contacts and to be available to provide information for political leaders. Access is important, and executives and legislators are both more likely to grant access to those who are useful to them. Sometimes interest group representatives are very savvy individuals. They can help their "friends" in government with problems of political strategy, including election strategy. They can get group members to support re-election bids. They may act as political consultants to members of Congress or even the President.

Many members of Congress could truthfully say, "Some of my best friends are lobbyists."

2. Give Financial Support to "Deserving" Candidates

Pressure groups keep detailed legislative "box scores" on voting records of members of Congress and state legislatures. They study the policy pronouncements of presidential and gubernatorial candidates, as well as their records, if they are incumbents. Those judged to be "friends" are rewarded with financial contributions and endorsements in pressure group publications. Group members also may be encouraged to work for their election,

Those who are labeled "foes" are targeted for defeat, if that is possible. It may not be possible, given the fact that many legislative districts are "safe" and seldom, if ever, change political control. In a close race in a competitive district, however, the backing of an interest group can make the difference between winning and losing an election.

As a result of the past misuse of political campaign funds, Congress, in 1974, passed the **Federal Election Campaign Act**. Hailed as "by far the most comprehensive reform legislation ever passed by Congress concerning the election of the President, Vice President and members of Congress," the statute was designed to prevent so-called "fat cat" contributors from making huge donations to campaigns. It limited individual contributions to $1000, committee contributions to $5000 each and also tightened up on reporting requirements. All candidates must file periodic reports with the Federal Election Commission, a six-member bipartisan body set up to administer the new statute.

There would be no more individual contributions of more than $1 million, which J.W. Marriott gave to Nixon's 1972 campaign. There would be no $250,000 checks from individuals like Stuart Mott, who contributed that amount to McGovern's campaign. Individuals could write $1000 checks to several of their favorite candidates, but could spend no more than $25,000 per year.

The campaign reform law also established public financing for presidential primaries and general election campaigns. Presidential candidates who can raise $5000 on their own in at least 20 states can get individual contributions of up to $250 matched by the U.S. Treasury. In the general election, party nominees get a fixed amount of money for their campaign expenses.

Individual candidates are free, however, to spend as much of their own money as they wish. In *Buckley v. Valeo,* the Supreme Court ruled unconstitutional that part of the Federal Election Campaign Act which imposed limits on the amounts individuals could spend on their own campaigns. The Court found this to be an unconstitutional infringement of freedom of speech.[7]

As a result of this decision, Ross Perot was able to spend more than $50 million of his own huge fortune in 1992 and Steve Forbes more than $30 million on his unsuccessful quest for the Republican nomination in 1996.

The 1974 campaign law has stimulated the growth of Political Action Committees (PACs). Before 1974, unions and corporations were forbidden by the Taft-Hartley Act of 1947 from making direct contributions. They did circumvent the law by making indirect contributions.

Now it is open and above board. Any interest group can form a PAC and give up to $5000 to its favorite candidate. Groups still can spend unlimited amounts indirectly, if such contributions are not coordinated with a candidate's campaign.

These Political Action Committees have become very controversial in the past generation. They have proliferated in number and the amount of money spent has multiplied significantly. In the 1992 campaign, for example, nearly 4200 PACs gave almost $180 million to congressional candidates. The cynicism associated with abuses unmasked by the Watergate hearings has returned. But there is at least one vital difference from the pre-Watergate era. All contributions must be reported to the Federal Election Commission. If, as some suggest, PACs are corrupting American elections, the corruption is done openly.

Archibald Cox, a former Watergate special prosecutor, has written that PACs are "robbing our nation of its democratic ideals and giving us a government of leaders beholden to the monied interests who make their election possible."[8]

But pressure groups usually give money to their "friends." These candidates agree with group values in the first place. Right-to-life interest groups, for example, certainly are not going to contribute to the campaigns of "pro-choice" candidates. A relatively young pressure group, EMILY's List, recruits and supports pro-choice, female candidates for Congress. The acronym stands for "Early Money Is Like Yeast." Financial support in party primaries is particularly important. This is an example of an interest group seeking to elect more women—but only those women who are pro-choice.

In Michigan, Debbie Stabenow was strongly supported by this group in her bids, first for a seat in the U.S. House of Representatives, then later in her successful effort to replace incumbent Republican U.S. Sen. Spence Abraham

3. File Lawsuits

Sometimes interest groups fail to get their way in Congress or in the state legislature. The President or governor may turn a deaf ear to their views. In that case, another way in which pressure groups may be effective is by filing lawsuits. They are permitted to file *amicus curiae* (friend of the court) briefs. Groups try to persuade courts of the merits of their legal arguments on a variety of public policy issues.

Civil rights groups, for example, pursued a **"litigation strategy"** during the 1950s and 1960s. Southern Senators used the filibuster to block desired legislation. Eisenhower was not a strong supporter of their cause. But they found that they could "change things" in the courts. The Legal Defense Fund of the National Association for the Advancement of Colored People (NAACP) won landmark victories in the U.S. Supreme Court. Schools were desegregated, equal housing opportunities were won, and equal access to public accommodations was granted to all citizens, irrespective of race, color, sex or religion.

Thousands of Friend of the Court briefs are filed each year. Legal representatives of business, labor, farm, women's, racial and civil liberties groups are kept busy. More than 60 different groups, for example, filed *amicus curiae* briefs in the Supreme Court "right to die" case in 1997. In *Vacco v. Quill* and *Washington v. Glucksberg,* a variety of views were expressed by representatives of medical, religious, political and academic groups.[9]

4. Influence Public Opinion

An interest group wants the public to think well of it. But trying to capture the hearts and minds of the great American public and to persuade it of the importance of a group's values is not always easy. How do pressure groups and their public relations agents do this?

Pressure group strategies vary. Some, like Mobil Oil Corporation, regularly buy newspaper and magazines ads. Others film TV commercials. Some "plant" favorable stories about their clients with media friends who may write "puff pieces." Groups also supply favorable information about their legislative friends and "leak" embarrassing stories to the media about their foes.

Lobbyists sometimes try to pressure President and Congress, or the governor and state legislature. They understand that grassroots techniques are an important part of pressure politics.

Pressure groups try to drum up support (or opposition) from back home in the form of letters, postcards, telegrams and phone calls. In today's world, they also use e-mail and faxes! They urge constituents who share their views to express them in visits to their legislators. They may tactfully remind legislators of their past political support and suggest that the friendship may be continued in the next election. Of, if they are strong enough and the legislator is weak enough, they may even threaten opposition at the polls.

Legislators are sometimes more likely to support demands of dominant interests in their constituency than they are to back their own party's President. In 1993, when President Clinton pushed the North American Free Trade Agreement (NAFTA) in Congress, he was attacked by union groups. Some, who engaged in rhetorical extravagance, referred to Clinton as a modern-day Judas Iscariot, who had betrayed labor and jeopardized American jobs by entering into this free trade pact with Canada and Mexico.

The NAFTA agreement never would have passed Congress, had it been up to the Democrats. The principal spokesman against the pact in the House was none other than Majority Leader Richard Gephardt. Gephardt represents a district in the St. Louis area where many constituents work in auto plants. The United Auto Workers union was adamantly opposed to NAFTA. They often quoted Ross Perot's statement that there would be "a giant sucking sound" of jobs leaving the U.S., if the pact were approved.

In Michigan, every Democratic representative along the I-75 corridor voted against the agreement, including House Democratic Whip David Bonoir. Michigan's two Democratic senators, Carl Levin and Donald Riegle, also both refused to support Democratic President Bill Clinton.

Ironically, a coalition of Southern Democrats (unions are weak in the south) and Northern Republicans eventually was able to get the measure passed. George Bush, Clinton's Republican predecessor who had negotiated the treaty, and Michigan's Republican Gov. John Engler backed the President.

Not all interest groups are equally powerful. Some have the strength of large numbers and considerable wealth, while others are small and lack significant influence. Some have the strength that comes with unity and resolve of purpose. Others are split down the middle on issues because interest groups often cannot work out their differences as easily as can political parties.

What we think of an interest group depends largely on what we think of what it does. Any spokesman for liquor or tobacco interests faces a tough job today. On the other hand, it's relatively easy to sell such interests as clean air and clean water to the public. Everyone is in favor of virtue and against sin—at least in theory. It is easy to be virtuous if one is not tempted.

Congress tends to listen to groups more sympathetically when they represent basic interests of their members. If, for example, labor unions seek a higher minimum wage, a shorter work week, improved fringe benefits or greater job safety regulations, they probably will get a hearing. If the unions take positions on a variety of "social issues" and foreign policy matters, which may have comparatively little to do with workers' interests, the Congress likely will be less attentive.

D. PARTY ROLES

Having considered how parties and pressure groups differ and having surveyed pressure group functions, we now return to political parties. What principal functions do parties perform? Scholars most frequently cite the following:

1. Recruitment, Support of Candidates for Public Office

If parties are an organized attempt to provide the personnel of government, then they must recruit good candidates to staff elective offices.

This is not always easy, particularly when a party faces an uphill fight against a firmly entrenched opposition party incumbent. Sometimes offices go uncontested because individuals are unwilling to spend the time, money and energy required in a campaign which appears impossible to win.

The amount of competition involved for a party nomination varies with the possibility of success. If a candidate is vulnerable, parties can find individuals who are willing to oppose him. If it appears to be a case of "political suicide," few people are anxious to do. In party politics, however, one never can tell what will happen.

After the Persian Gulf War of early 1991, President Bush established a modern poll record of being the most popular President in U.S. history. Many of the Democratic Party "heavyweights" decided not to seek their party's nomination in 1992, reasoning that Bush was unbeatable. Governor Mario Cuomo of New York bailed out. So did others. Arkansas Gov. Bill Clinton sought the nomination, political writers said, because he felt that he could get name identification and familiarity which would serve him well in a 1996 race against Bush's successor. Clinton may have thought he could defeat President Bush, but many political writers say that he didn't think so early in 1991.[10]

2. Organizing Campaigns, Raising Funds for Elections

Although state and local governments run elections, it is the political parties that do most of the work. They conduct "get out the vote" drives and enlist recruits to work at the polls. Partisans wear out shoe leather, ringing doorbells and distributing campaign "literature." They do anything they can to drum up enthusiasm for their candidates. Perhaps most importantly, they make sure that party members get to the polls and cast their ballots.

This sometimes means organizing motor pools, providing babysitting services and helping immobile senior citizens.

In the age of mass media campaigns, running for public office is an expensive proposition. Television ads, in particular, are very costly. One of the party's jobs is to help candidates raise funds to pay the cost of their campaigns. Not all candidates are personally wealthy, although money never hurt Franklin D. Roosevelt, John F. Kennedy or Nelson Rockefeller. Staging fund raisers is an important party activity at virtually every level of government.

3. Giving the Electorate "A Choice"

Parties, despite criticisms to the contrary, do stand for something. Democrats and Republicans tend to vote together in state legislatures and in Congress. They do so because they represent constituencies who have indicated at the polls what they want and expect their officials to do.

A study of major party presidential platforms indicates that there are basic differences between the national Democratic and Republican parties on such issues as abortion, the state of the economy, health care, defense spending, education, immigration policy, taxes and the Federal deficit.

Unlike European nations, Americans do not organize a party for every interest in society. We have no Labor Party, no Catholic Party, no parties organized strictly along lines of race, ethnicity or other factors. Interest groups work within the framework of the existing two-party system. Needless to say, the two parties encourage this view, arguing that a vote for a third-party candidate amounts to throwing one's ballot away.

We do not have a National Rife Association party candidate or a candidate sponsored by the Pro-Choice party. We have had more than a century of competition between Democrats and Republicans. But who are the Republicans and who are the Democrats?

Democrats are more likely to include the following among their supporters: Blacks, Jews, Roman Catholics, union members and those with less than a high school education. Republicans are more likely to include male, White Anglo-Saxon Protestants, (WASP) college graduates, those whose occupations are "business and professional."

4. Running the Government

The party that wins the election assumes the responsibility for governing. In the case of the executive branch, it must staff the office of the President, governor or mayor. If it controls the legislature, it must plan how to enact its policies into law.

This means finding qualified, good people, willing, in many cases, to make personal financial sacrifices to take administrative jobs. It takes considerable public spirit to give up a job as Chief Executive Officer of a major corporation to head a cabinet department. But when the President of the United States asks one to do something, one does not ordinarily refuse. To a lesser extent, the same can be said when prominent people are asked to serve their state or local communities.

5. Opposing the Government

There is always a loser, just as there is a winner in an election. It is the function of the losing ("out") party, to serve as "loyal opposition" to the government. The party is loyal to democracy and democratic rules of the game. At the same time, it is opposed to the policies of the winning ("in") party government. Its responsibility becomes that of a responsible critic. This is not easy because there is always the temptation to criticize "just for the hell of it." It takes a real effort not only to oppose, but also to suggest constructive alternative policies.

6. Educating the Public

What? Yes, if one believes that supplying public information is "education," then our parties perform an educational function. It often is said by professional students of public opinion and the media that Americans know little about public policy. On details, their level of ignorance is appalling. But citizens would know even less than they do if it were not for partisan debate on issues. People who identify themselves as Republicans or Democrats view their party organizations as "reference groups." They refer to what the party says about the issues before making up their minds. In some cases, by looking to the party for a "cue," voters allow the party to make up their minds for them.

7. Party Identification

Political parties try to get voters to identify as members of their particular organization. Years ago when a pollster asked, "Are you a Democrat or a Republican?" the answer was usually one or the other. Citizens tended to identify strongly with one of the two major parties. Political scientists long have used the term **party identification** to refer to the attachment of voters to a particular party. Today, people are much more likely to call themselves independents.

In the half century between 1930 and 1980, most Americans considered themselves Democrats. Before the election of 1980, some 41% of Americans identified themselves as Democrats. Only 28% indicated a Republican Party preference. During the Reagan-Bush years, Republicans made progress in closing that gap, but Clinton's two presidential victories widened the margin again.

The most significant development of the past half century, however, has been the growth in the number of survey respondents who call themselves independents. They identify with neither Democratic nor Republican parties. During the 1940s, only one voter in five identified as an independent. In the 21st Century, nearly one-third of poll respondents give that response.[11]

Generations ago, when voters said that they were "independent," it usually meant that they didn't care much about politics or politicians. Independents were much less likely to register and vote than were partisans. Research indicates that today's independents do care who wins an election. They also study what parties have to offer voters in particular campaigns. But, as in the past, they are less knowledgeable than partisans, less active in politics and less likely to vote than party identifiers.

Political scientists, seeking to explain why this has occurred, sometimes theorize that we are going through an era of party **"realignment,"** during which voters are switching party loyalties. Eventually, the theory holds, the U.S. will have a new system of party preferences.

One example, frequently cited by "realignment" theorists, is the collapse of the "solid south" and the emergence of a competitive party system there, which now leans toward the Republicans.

For most of America's history, individuals have come to identify with a particular party because of a dominant (charismatic) personality, like Franklin D. Roosevelt, John F. Kennedy or Ronald Reagan. Or voters have developed a party preference because of a historic event, such as the Civil War or the Great Depression, which touched their lives and the lives of their families very deeply. When there are no charismatic presidential candidates on the horizon and when the issues are not earth-shaking, voters may well become apathetic.

Students of comparative government worry about the perceived weakness of the American party system. They regret the growth of **candidate-centered campaigns** in which parties seem to play a secondary role. It is not unknown for some candidates to stress their name and not even mention their party affiliation, especially when the party which has endorsed them has a record of past unpopularity in the area. During the age of **party-centered campaigns**, party label was a vital factor. Many families took pride that "no one in this family ever has voted for a Democrat." Or, "no one in this family ever has voted for a Republican." There is an epidemic of "ticket splitting" today, where voters divide their ballots between candidates of the two major parties.

It always has been difficult in the American political system to pinpoint responsibility. A Democratic President (Truman or Clinton) blames a Republican Congress for the nation's woes. Or a Republican President (Eisenhower, Nixon, Ford, Reagan or George Herbert Walker Bush) blames the Democratic-controlled Congress for the sorry state of affairs. Separation of powers creates confusion and divides responsibility. When weak political parties add to the confusion, it is even more difficult to hold a particular party responsible for the conduct of government affairs. If voters cannot pinpoint responsibility, then how can they vote intelligently?

E. PARTY ORGANIZATION: NATIONAL, STATE AND LOCAL

Political parties, as previously noted, are not mentioned in the Constitution. Their organizational blueprints are largely the result of state laws and the rules which parties themselves create. In our Federal system, parties are organized at national, state and local levels.

One of the most significant facts about American political party organization is that state and local units are independent of national Democratic and Republican parties. State and local party organizations also are stronger than the national party organization.

1. National Party Organization

National parties are the weakest in the American political organization chart. In theory, the "sovereign" party body is the national convention. But it meets only every four years to nominate a presidential ticket, draft a platform and adopt party rules. It has absolutely no authority to force candidates wearing the party label in the coming election to support its platform. In fact, congressional, state and local candidates sometimes divorce themselves from it, or at least some of its more controversial planks.

Few Democratic candidates for public office accepted the platform written by the left-of-center amateurs who took over the party in 1972 and nominated George McGovern for President. The party platform endorsed stands that Gallup Polls and other opinion surveys clearly indicated were 180 degrees removed from what the voters were thinking. It was not entirely accidental that McGovern won only one state.

The national committee is the executive authority between conventions. It usually represents states, not people or party strength. Although the Republican National Committee (RNC) still is organized in this manner, Democrats have made some reforms. In 1974, as part of its reform package, the DNC was enlarged. Each state is given members on the basis of a state's population and record of supporting Democratic candidates. Bonus points are given for electing Democratic governors, senators, members of the House, state legislative majorities and so forth. Certain groups, notably women and youth, were given special, favorable treatment.

The national chair is formally elected by the national committee of each party, but seldom emerges as a strong leader. Clearly, it is the President, in the case of the winning party, who is the party leader. The losing party's candidate becomes the party's "titular leader."

What roles do the national committee and its chair play? In an age of very expensive campaigns, fund raising has become critical. It gives financial aid to candidates for both state and national office. If a candidate is running for U.S. House or U.S. Senate, he or she can also obtain financial backing from congressional and senatorial campaign committees. Candidates need and get such assistance as money, research support and campaign materials.

2. State and Local Party Organizations

State party organizations vary greatly. Generally, members are chosen in primary elections or by local party committees. The actual power of state committees also varies considerably. Sometimes they have real power, draft the party's platform, help to screen candidates for statewide office and assist in raising campaign funds. In other states, they are nearly impotent.

The most significant local organization in most states is the county committee, which usually includes precinct officials within the county. The committee is headed by a chairman, usually chosen by the committee members. The Cook County, IL, Democratic County Committee, chaired by the late Chicago Mayor Richard Daley, was perhaps the best example of an effective local political organization. Those who didn't like the organization referred to it as the last of the urban area "machines."[12]

Daley helped, not only to raise funds, but also to select Democratic candidates in Cook County. For many years, he dominated politics in the City of Chicago, local townships, wards and precincts. His son is the current mayor of Chicago.

The most basic level of political organization is the neighborhood precinct. In some large urban areas, a precinct may have as many as 2000 voters. In rural areas, it can be very small, perhaps less than 30 voters.

Precinct workers do the basic intelligence work of political parties. They know who moves in and out of the precinct. They know who needs a job, who gets in trouble with the law. They make it a point to know a neighbor's political preference. If the voter identifies with their party, they make sure that he or she gets registered and, most important, gets to the polls on election day. They do considerable door-to-door work, calling on voters and distributing campaign literature.

But effective urban precinct workers are a dying species. They are still important in cities like Chicago where one's job, and perhaps several other family jobs, depend on "delivering the vote" for the party. The decline of "spoils" politics and the rise of civil service have, however, made "political payoff jobs" much less common than once was the case.

Today local party officials often are assisted by volunteers who usually receive no pay. For some of them, taking an active part in helping to elect a good candidate is enough compensation.

F. TYPES OF PARTY SYSTEMS

1. Single party systems

The history of the 20th Century is filled with examples of single parties which have led their nations to ruin. By definition, a highly-centralized single party system is the instrument of a dictator or an oligarchy. Clearly, it rejects the democratic principle that the people should hold responsible those who govern them.

Adolf Hitler's National Socialist (Nazi) party in Germany was a case in point. So was the Communist party of the Soviet Union. Hitler and Stalin collectively may have had more "blood on their hands" than any other dictators in world history. It was their cynical, secret treaty, the Molotov-von Ribbentrop pact, concluded in August, 1939, that made World War II possible. They agreed to partition Poland and divide up areas of influence in Eastern Europe. Both then launched attacks, starting the most horrible war in history.

Fascist parties in Italy under Mussolini, in Spain under Franco and in Argentina under Peron, are other examples of single party systems. Mao's China and the Eastern European Communist regimes, allied with the former Soviet Union, are other cases in point.

2. Multi-party systems

Many Democratic nations have multi-party systems. Ideologues prefer them because they want political parties to stand for a narrow set of clear-cut principles. If there are many parties with about the same chance of success, any group of voters can form a tightly-disciplined little party of their own and probably win some seats in the legislature. This, of course, is related to the electoral system. Multi-party systems thrive where proportional representation exists. In single-member district, winner-take-all arrangements, such as found in the U.S., minor parties soon fall by the wayside.

During the chaos of the Fourth Republic in France, there were so many political parties that it was said that three Frenchmen, having lunch, could agree to start a new group. And, perhaps, elect one of them to the National Assembly.

Small parties in a multi-party system do not need to compromise. Their policy objectives seldom change.

3. A Brief History of America's Two-Party System

A two-party system is one in which there can be more than two parties on the ballot, but only two major groups have a real chance of winning control of the government. Only once in the 20th Century did a third (minor) party have a chance in a presidential election. That was in 1912, when former President Theodore Roosevelt ran as the Progressive (Bull Moose) party candidate.

If, in fact, one examines the history of America's two-party system, one finds that there have often been periods where one party has dominated the competition. Democrats won 12 of 15 presidential elections between 1800-1860. Republicans dominated between 1860-1932, losing only four presidential contests. Between 1932-52, the Democrats enjoyed a 20-year monopoly on the White House, electing Franklin

Roosevelt four times and Harry Truman once. Since 1968, Republicans have won seven of 11 presidential elections.

A brief history of our two party system follows:[13]

Although party labels have changed over the course of our national history, we have always had a two-party system. In addition to warning of the evils of parties in his Farewell Address, Washington also said that he dreaded the appearance of "two great parties, each under its leader." Yet two of the outstanding leaders of his cabinet, Treasury Secretary Alexander Hamilton and Secretary of State Thomas Jefferson, were to become the leaders of the **Federalists** and the **Democratic-Republicans**, respectively.

Washington was less worried about the Federalists, the party of the Constitution, than he was about the Jeffersonians. Federalists consisted of banking and financial interests that favored a strong central government. Jefferson, on the other hand, attracted support from planters, slave owners and farmers. Jefferson proved to be superior in political organization to Hamilton and the Federalists. He scored a major victory when he lured James Madison into the ranks of the Democratic-Republicans.

In 1800, Jefferson was elected President. Although he proclaimed on entering office, "We are all Republicans, we are all Federalists," Jefferson aroused deep concern in the Federalist party. They feared that he would change the direction of the government as they had established it under the new Constitution. In time, the Federalists simply became so ineffective that the Democratic-Republicans candidates for the presidency won consistently. By 1820, the Federalist party disappeared from the scene.

Historians refer to the partisan battle of the Federalists under Hamilton and the Republicans under Jefferson as the **first party system**.

A major change in American party politics came with the "Age of Andrew Jackson." General Jackson, the hero of the Battle of New Orleans during the War of 1812, was convinced that a new party, organized at the "grass roots," was needed to represent the interests of the west and the frontier. He wanted to represent the common man. Fortunately for him, this was the era when the electorate was being expanded. Property owning and taxpaying no longer were required as qualifications for voting. But his constant references to the "common man" repelled some Conservative members of his own party.

Jackson's "faction" became known as **Democrats** and those who opposed him became the Whigs. The term "Whig" comes from British politics and indicates opposition to royal power and authority. Those who disliked Jackson often referred to his "autocratic" temperament and called him "King Andrew I."

The Whig party attracted many of the same groups who had earlier supported the Federalists. It included bankers, merchants and large landowners, all of whom had an acute dislike for mass democracy. The Whigs, who lacked a coherent political philosophy, were those Democratic-Republicans who sometimes called themselves National Republicans.

Led by Henry Clay of Kentucky and Daniel Webster of Massachusetts, the Whigs adopted the practice of the nominating convention as a more democratic method of choosing presidential nominees than the congressional caucus. The Democrats soon followed their example. Historians call this era of Whig-Democrat competition the **second party system**.

During the period 1840-1854, the Whigs enjoyed only mild success, capturing the White House twice. They elected William Henry Harrison in 1840. Harrison holds the record for the shortest tenure in history. Despite the fact that a major rainstorm hit Washington on March 4, 1841, Harrison insisted on giving a lengthy inaugural address.

He caught a bad cold, which developed into pneumonia and the new President died on April 4, just one month after taking his oath of office. He was succeeded by Vice President John Tyler. In 1848, the Whigs elected Zachary Taylor.

Both Whigs and Democrats suffered political strains under the burden of slavery. Both tried to compromise on an issue where ultimately compromise was not morally possible. The Democratic Party split between northern and southern factions. In 1860, the northern faction nominated Sen. Stephen A. Douglas of Illinois for President. Douglas, known as the "Little Giant," argued that the question of whether a new territory should permit slavery should be decided by the voters. John C. Breckinridge of Kentucky was nominated by the southern faction. He argued that slavery should be legalized in every territory. The northern and southern factions were so split that the relatively new Republican Party, with Abraham Lincoln as its candidate, captured the presidency, although it won only about 40% of the popular vote.

Many scholars believe that the American party system has had only one pronounced failure in all of its recorded history. That was in 1860, when the party system collapsed over the issues of slavery and the Union. It took the Civil War to resolve those issues. The legacy of that conflict persists even in the 21st Century. Major differences still divide northern and southern Democrats.

The Whigs failed to nominate attractive candidates and suffered constant defeats. After Democrat Franklin Pierce won a landslide victory in 1852, the Whig Party fell apart.

The failure of the Whigs to reach a party consensus on the slavery issue led directly to the development of another "faction," the Republicans. Historians call this the **third party system**. But the Republican Party of mid-19th Century should not be confused with the original Republicans of Jefferson. Former (Conscience) Whigs and Democrats opposed to slavery formed the Republican Party, to replace the Whigs as the major competitor of the Democrats. In 1856, they held their first national convention and nominated John C. Fremont for the presidency. Fremont lost, but in 1860, as noted, the Republicans nominated and elected Lincoln.

After the Civil War, the Republican Party entered its heyday. It completely dominated presidential politics. The only Democrat to be elected President from the Reconstruction era until the dawn of the 20th Century was Grover Cleveland.

The Democratic Party was called the "party of treason, those damned Confederates." In the North, the Grand Army of the Republic, an organization of Union Army veterans, virtually became an auxiliary organization of the Republican Party. "Vote the way you shot" was a familiar political slogan in both north and south. Increasingly, the Democratic Party became relegated to the position of a southern, regional organization. The term "solid south" was born. It referred to the fact that voters in the former Confederate states never voted for Republican presidential candidates.

After the Panic of 1893, characterized by bank failures and severe depression, a new party realignment occurred. Cleveland, who would not run for a third term, was blamed for the economic collapse and Republicans exploited that fact in the election of 1896.

The Democrats nominated William Jennings Bryan, a 36-year-old congressman from Nebraska. Barely old enough to qualify as a presidential candidate under the Constitution, Bryan was a "corn belt economist," who concluded that the gold standard was the cause of hard times and free silver the solution for all of the nation's economic miseries. Bryan electrified the Democratic convention with one of the most famous speeches in political history. He said, "You shall not press down upon the brow of labor this crown of thorns, you shall not crucify mankind upon a cross of gold." The Democratic platform urged the free and unlimited coinage of silver at the ratio of 16-1. It also condemned trusts, monopolies and the high protective tariff.

The Republicans nominated Rep. William McKinley of Ohio. They pointed to past GOP achievements and viewed with horror the "calamitous consequences" of Democratic control. They came out unequivocally for the gold standard. McKinley won easily and was re-elected in 1900 with Theodore Roosevelt as his running mate. On September 6, 1901, McKinley was assassinated and Roosevelt became President.

A personality conflict between Republican Presidents Theodore Roosevelt and William Howard Taft paved the way for the Democrats to stage a comeback. As President, Roosevelt had personally chosen Taft as his successor. But he became disenchanted with Taft's performance as Chief Executive. In 1912, Roosevelt challenged Taft for the GOP nomination and lost. Rather than accept the result, Roosevelt and his supporters went off to Chicago, formed the Progressive (Bull Moose) party and entered a three-cornered election with Taft and Democratic nominee Woodrow Wilson.

Wilson, who was nominated on the 46th ballot at the Democratic National Convention, capitalized on the split and was elected President. He was re-elected in 1916, winning a close race with Charles Evans Hughes, a former Secretary of State and Associate Justice of the Supreme Court.

After World War I, the nation turned its back on Wilsonian idealism and elected Warren G. Harding, a U.S. senator from Ohio, as its President. The decade of the 1920s ushered in what the historians, for inexplicable reasons, insist on calling the period of "Normalcy." Perhaps the nation wanted to get back to "normal." It rejected the Treaty of Versailles, turned its back on the League of Nations, retreated to isolationism and then sent Republicans Harding (1920), Coolidge (1924) and Hoover (1928) to the White House. It also introduced Prohibition, syndicate crime and the "Jazz Age." To many, that was not "normal."

The Great Depression is a watershed event in American history. Life has never been the same since the collapse of the stock market in October, 1929, the rejection of Hoover's bid for re-election in 1932 and the advent of Franklin Roosevelt's New Deal. Historians call this the **fourth party system**.

Roosevelt constructed what was called the New Deal coalition. The Democratic Party became an alliance of labor unions, southerners, ethnic minorities, Catholics, Jews, Blacks and small farmers.

Republicans appealed to more educated, higher-income, business-oriented, Protestant and suburban voters.

Those Democratic Presidents who followed Roosevelt—Truman, Kennedy and Johnson—all based their programs and policies on New Deal-era assumptions. Perhaps the most basic assumption of all was that the Federal government should use its power and authority to protect the underdog.

Until 1948, the south had been the "solid south." Only once since the Civil War, in 1928, when Gov. Al Smith of New York, a Roman Catholic, was the Democratic presidential nominee, did a southern state cast an electoral vote for a Republican presidential nominee. The Ku Klux Klan was a militant anti-Catholic force in the south at the time.

The election of 1948 broke the New Deal coalition for the first time. The South broke away on the issue of civil rights. Angered when the Democratic National Convention adopted a Liberal civil rights plank in its party platform, southerners bolted the party. They formed a new group, the Dixiecrat party, and nominated Strom

Thurmond of South Carolina for President and Fielding Wright of Mississippi for Vice President. The Democrats were split into three factions, when supporters of Henry Wallace, Roosevelt's Vice President during his second and third terms, bolted to form the "Progressive Party." Wallace was much more conciliatory toward the Soviet Union than any other candidate. For that reason, he was falsely labeled a "Communist" during the campaign.

Gov. Thomas E. Dewey of New York was the overwhelming favorite to win. Political wags later said that Dewey "snatched defeat out of the jaws of victory." Clearly, he could have written a textbook later on "How Not to Run for President." Truman scored the most surprising victory of the 20th Century. All of the polls and all of the media had predicted his defeat. Somehow, he remained in office.

A 20-year Democratic Party monopoly ended in the elections of 1952 and 1956. In both of those years, Republican Dwight D. Eisenhower defeated former Illinois Gov. Adlai E. Stevenson. In 1960, the Democrats returned to power when young Sen. John F. Kennedy of Massachusetts edged Vice President Richard M. Nixon of California by the closest popular vote margin in U.S. history, less than 1%. In 1964, Johnson, who succeeded Kennedy after the Dallas assassination, was elected President in his own right, defeating U.S. Sen. Barry Goldwater of Arizona.

The election of 1968 was another cliff-hanger, with Nixon edging Vice President Hubert H. Humphrey of Minnesota by less than a 1% popular vote margin. Nixon won re-election in 1972, but was forced to resign his office as a result of the Watergate scandal. He was succeeded by Gerald Ford of Michigan, who lost a bid for election as President in his own right in 1976 to Democrat Jimmy Carter. Carter became the first 20th Century Democratic President to lose a bid for re-election when he was ousted from the White House by former California Gov. Ronald Reagan in 1980. Reagan's victory had a "coattails effect," with the Republicans regaining control of the U.S. Senate for the first time since 1954. They retained control in 1982 and 1984, but Democrats regained the Senate majority during the mid-term congressional elections of 1986. After Reagan's 1984 re-election victory, pollsters found that more people identified themselves as Republicans than they had in several previous decades.

In 1988, Vice President George Bush defeated Massachusetts Gov. Michael Dukakis, but Democrats picked up seats in Congress. In 1992, former Arkansas Gov. Bill Clinton ousted Bush, but Democrats lost seats in the House of Representatives.

A major political change came in the mid-term congressional elections of 1994 when the Republican Party gained control of both houses of Congress for the first time since 1954. Although Clinton won re-election over former Senate majority leader Bob Dole in 1996, voters returned the Republicans to control of Congress. It was the first time since the Great Depression that the GOP had won successive congressional elections.

Republicans continued their success, maintaining control of Congress in the 1998 elections. In 2000, they held on to the House, but were able to control the Senate (50-50), only because of the tie-breaking vote of Vice President Cheney. This changed in May, 2001, when Sen. James Jeffords of Vermont became an Independent, again giving control of the Senate to the Democrats. Republicans regained control of both houses in 2002 and increased their margins in 2004.

Democrats, however, regained control of Congress in 2006. Voters turned against the President's war policy in Iraq and Republicans were blamed for mishandling relief efforts after Hurricane Katrina. This natural disaster devastated the Gulf Coast, particularly New Orleans and parts of Mississippi. The nation also was experiencing significant economic problems.

The President had to work with a hostile 110th Congress as the 2008 election neared. As discussed in Chapter IV, many Senate Democrats wanted Mr. Bush's job. One of them, Barack Obama of Illinois, got it and helped his party to enlarge its majority in the 111th Congress.

The southern "revolt" against national Democratic Party leaders reached maturity during the past two generations. Upset by enactment of the Civil Rights Act of 1964, the Voting Rights Act of 1965 and a large number of Warren Court decisions, the south reacted by leaving the Democratic Party fold. Nixon won every southern state in his 1972 landslide victory over Democrat George McGovern. Although Carter regained some southern states in 1976, he lost all of them except his own state, Georgia, in 1980, when he was unseated by Reagan.

Obama, who carried three southern states in 2008, ended a series of shutouts suffered by Democrats who failed to win any southern electoral votes in the Gore and Kerry campaigns of 2000 and 2004, respectively.

G. THE MAKING OF THE PRESIDENT: OLD POLITICS AND NEW POLITICS

We have lived in the age of the **"new politics"** since the middle of the 20th Century. Specifically, American politics has changed dramatically since the **advent of television** and **"candidate merchandising."**[14]

In the era of the **"old politics"** (before and shortly after World War II), presidential candidates were chosen at the major party nominating conventions. The convention was the center of political drama, conflict and action. The National Party Convention was a quadrennial event where governors of big states and mayors of big cities joined congressional and other party leaders to select a presidential candidate and his running mate.

But politics changed, not necessarily for the better, with the advent of television and the development of the presidential primary as the main method of choosing convention delegates.

In 1960, John F. Kennedy sought the Democratic presidential nomination. He knew that he would not be the party's nominee if he left it up to the "king makers." His strategy was to enter seven primaries and win them all, putting the Democratic Party leaders in a difficult position. They would either have to nominate him or be accused of anti-Catholic bigotry. If they did not nominate him, the Republicans were prepared to choose James Mitchell, Eisenhower's Secretary of Labor and a Catholic, as Nixon's running mate, exploiting the religious issue.[15]

In Wisconsin, Kennedy defeated Senator Humphrey of Minnesota, an adjacent state. Humphrey was called "Wisconsin's third senator" because he often voted with the state's senators on matters of common interest. Humphrey campaigned as a "Midwesterner" against the "New Englander." But when the results came in, regionalism did not matter. Kennedy was the clear winner.

Even more important was West Virginia. Kennedy set out to prove that a Catholic presidential nominee could win. Critics pointed out that Al Smith, the only Catholic ever nominated by a major party, had suffered a disastrous defeat at the hands of the Republicans in 1928, splitting the "solid south" in the process. West Virginia was 95% Protestant.

After Humphrey lost Wisconsin, many Democrats expected him to withdraw. When he remained in the West Virginia contest, Robert Kennedy was infuriated. He was convinced that Humphrey's sole motive was to destroy his brother John as a viable candidate. In the final analysis, Humphrey did Kennedy a great favor. After Kennedy's victory in West Virginia, he was the clear front runner for the Democratic Party nomination.

Belated efforts to wrest the nomination away from JFK were mounted by Senate Majority Leader Lyndon Johnson and twice defeated presidential nominee Adlai E. Stevenson. Former President Truman, who backed Sen. Stuart Symington of Missouri, asked Kennedy, "Young man, are you sure that you are ready for the country or that the country is ready for you?"[16]

The presidential contest of 1960 was historic in many ways. It ushered in the age of the "New Politics" by becoming the first election in which candidates faced one another in a series of four live televised debates. The first debate, held in Chicago, was Nixon's undoing. He had campaigned as the experienced, mature candidate. He had been a member of the House, a member of the Senate and Vice President under Eisenhower for eight years. He was ready, he said, to lead the nation as President. Kennedy, the GOP campaign theme argued, was young, immature, inexperienced and not ready for the burdens of the White House.

In one evening, the Republican campaign theme collapsed. Kennedy was sharp. He was informed. He exhibited a winning smile, a sense of humor and command of the issues. Perhaps most important, he looked good on television. Some media scholars subsequently have described Kennedy as a "candidate made for TV." Robert Kennedy later said that the debates were responsible for this brother's victory.

In television, appearances are all important. It matters what color suit and tie you wear. Today candidates all seem to wear blue suits with red ties. In 1960, Nixon wore a gray suit that blended into the set to make him appear pale. Kennedy had developed a good tan before the debate, so the contrast in appearances was significant. Nixon, some of his Republican supporters complained, looked tired, if not ill.[17]

Then there was the matter of the TV "style." Nixon stubbornly refused to wear makeup. Kennedy had "no problem" with that. Nixon was aware that he had been described as a "gutter type, street fighter." He tried to erase that image by being polite to Kennedy. This was interpreted by some of his supporters as a sign of weakness. He was urged to return to the old Nixon style in subsequent debates.

Chicago was the first of the debates, but it was the most important. First images are important and this was a historic first.

Those who were "disinterested," as opposed to those who are wildly partisan in their perceptions of the 1960 debates, said that Kennedy won the first debate. The other debates, consensus has it, saw Nixon constantly improve his performance. The Vice President, most objective analysts concluded, clearly won the last two debates which centered on foreign policy and national security matters.

But the damage had been done. Nixon lost the audience as fewer Americans watched after the first debate. Ironically, those who never saw any of the debates on television, but heard them on radio, thought that Nixon was the clear winner. An obvious lesson of the New Politics was that it mattered what you said, but it mattered more how you looked.

There were no debates between presidential candidates between 1964-1976. President Johnson was "too busy" in 1964. Besides, why give Senator Goldwater the chance to erase the popular image of "Goldwater, the Mad Bomber" and "Goldwater, would-be destroyer of Social Security" which had been the theme of Democratic campaign commercials.

There were no Humphrey-Nixon debates in 1968, no Nixon-McGovern debates in 1972.

Presidential debates resumed in 1976. A number of public opinion polls indicated that President Ford had fallen far behind Governor Carter after his pardon of President Nixon. It usually is the challenger who wants the debates and the President who is reluctant. In this case, roles were reversed. Carter accepted the challenge. It was the first time that an incumbent President ever had faced a challenger. Otherwise, with the exception of a few minor "fluffs," the three Ford-Carter debates were not particularly memorable.[18]

Ford's worst moment came when he failed to communicate exactly what he meant in the area of foreign policy. He said that Poland was not dominated by the Soviet Union, a clear factual error, when he meant to say that the Soviets could not crush Poland's spirit. "Clarifications," issued by the White House press office, came too late to correct the impression, exploited by Democrats, that Ford lacked the command of foreign affairs which voters expected of the Chief Executive.

Four years later, President Carter and Ronald Reagan held a series of debates. Although some Democrats, viewing the programs through partisan eyes, felt that Carter had won, they were the only ones who came to that conclusion. Reagan, later called the "Great Communicator," used his background as a professional actor to great advantage. Most importantly, he came over as an amiable personality, one who voters did not fear as they did Goldwater in 1964. Democratic efforts to portray Reagan as another right wing extremist just like Goldwater failed miserably. Carter became the only Democratic incumbent President of the 20th Century to lose his bid for re-election.[19]

There have been presidential debates between candidates in every election year since 1976.

In 1984, Reagan and former Vice President Walter Mondale exchanged views. Vice President Bush and Democratic challenger Michael Dukakis squared off in 1988. In 1992, it was President Bush vs. challengers Arkansas Gov. Bill Clinton and Ross Perot.

President Clinton debated Republican challenger Bob Dole in 1996. In 2000, Vice President Gore squared off against Texas Gov. George W. Bush. President Bush and Democratic nominee John Kerry offered their views on the issues in 2004.

In 2008 the nation witnessed its first "open seat contest" since 1928. No incumbent President was running for re-election and no sitting Vice President was seeking the office. Two U.S. Senators, Barack Obama and John McCain, debated the issues as voters made up their minds.

Like them or not, presidential debates appear to have become a fixture of American political campaigns.

Are presidential "debates" really debates? Many political scientists, journalists and other interested observers have argued that presidential debates are more like news conferences than genuine debates. One format consists of reporters asking questions, candidates' responses to them and a brief, closing statement by each candidate.

Although the debates or "joint appearances" could be improved, they do give the American electorate a chance to see the candidates. Voters can "size up" a would-be President's knowledge of issues, the candidate's personality and ability to "think on his or her feet."

Why Two Parties? There are a number of explanations for the existence of our two-party system. Perhaps the most widely accepted is the so-called "institutional theory." It holds that the nation's electoral system is responsible. The U.S. uses a single-member district system to choose members of the Congress, as well as state and local legislatures. Only one candidate can win, and minor parties receive nothing for their efforts. Even if they get a considerable number of votes, they generally fail.

Persistence of initial form is another theory cited to explain two-partyism. Human institutions tend, according to this line of thought, to preserve themselves.

The third and final answer to the question, "Why two parties?" is cultural in nature. Some political sociologists argue that different religious, racial, ethnic and other groups have become absorbed into our "melting pot." They have preferred to integrate into American society, rather than segregate themselves from it. Class consciousness is also much less important in the U.S. than in Europe, which still has lingering scars from its experience under feudalism.

In short, Americans do not see themselves as downtrodden proletarians who demand a workers' party, revolution and overthrow of the state. They do not want to create a party which favors a state religion or one which significantly changes the status quo. In short, although there are many minor parties on the presidential ballot, this serves merely as a "safety valve," permitting people to blow off steam. To win a presidential election or a congressional majority, a party must have a program which has broad appeal. Only moderate candidates in moderate parties can win when voters themselves are moderates.

Ross Perot ran the most "successful" third party campaign in recent years in 1992. Perot hammered away on the need to cut the Federal deficit and to save jobs of American workers. The Texas billionaire spent millions of his own dollars on what some viewed as an expensive ego trip. He won nearly 20 million votes (about 19% of the number cast) but he did not win a single electoral vote.

Perot was much less attractive to the electorate in 1996, when he won only 9% of the vote and again was shut out in the Electoral College. But perhaps his mission was not to win, but to raise questions of public policy, particularly economic policy. A noted American historian once wrote that the function of minor parties is not to win or to govern. Rather it is "to agitate, educate and generate new ideas...When a third party's demands become popular enough, they are appropriated by one or both of the major parties and the third party disappears....like bees: once they have stung, they die."[20]

H. PARTY COMPETITORS IN CANDIDATE SCREENING

Many political scientists lament the decline of political parties. Some of them are quick to place the blame for this development on the growth of "majoritarian democracy" and the new roles assumed by the American media.

Majoritarian democracy is a term which has been defined as more direct control over political outcomes than traditionally has been permitted in a representative democracy (republic). Clearly, one of the significant developments, as suggested earlier, has been the rise of the party primary. When party leaders are in charge of making a slate, or caucusing to determine who a presidential nominee shall be, they are clearly in control. When individual citizens can go to the polls and make their own choices, the rules of the game have changed.

A primary is an election in which voters decide which party candidate will face the opposition party candidate in a later general election. Sometimes no one challenges an incumbent. Sometimes there is no incumbent and several candidates emerge. Strength of competition is a critical factor. If one sees a real chance to win the primary and the general election, one is more likely to "go for it" than if he has little or no realistic chance of winning.

There are basically two types of primaries, closed and open. Most states use the **closed primary,** strongly preferred by party officials. Only those voters who are registered as party members may participate. The **open primary** permits voters who are not registered as party members to participate. The voter simply selects the ballot of the party in whose primary he wishes to participate on election day..

The so-called **blanket primary** is used in two states, Washington and Alaska. Voters may cast ballots in either party's primary on an "office type" ballot, voting for a Republican for one office and a Democrat for another.

Party leaders, as well as most political scientists, generally prefer the closed primary. It prevents the practice of **"raiding,"** in which voters who normally vote for one party in the general election invade the other party's primary, intending to help it nominate the weakest candidate. If the weak candidate wins the primary, the other party's nominee has much better prospects of victory in the general election. Political scientists tend to favor the theory of responsible government, first articulated two generations ago by Professor E.E. Schattschneider.[21] Clearly it is a violation of party responsibility to engage in raiding. Some might even question the ethics involved!

In recent decades, the State of Michigan has had many problems deciding what to do about its nomination system. In 1972, Michigan had an open presidential primary, as did Wisconsin and several other states. Richard Nixon faced no serious challenge in the state GOP presidential primary.

The Democrats, on the other hand, had a long list of would-be Presidents. Heading that list was Edmund Muskie, preferred by the state party leaders and endorsed by the Auto Workers Union. Other names on the ballot included George McGovern, Shirley Chisholm, John Lindsay, Henry Jackson, the inevitable Hubert Humphrey and George C. Wallace, segregationist governor of Alabama. Much to the chagrin of the Michigan Democratic Party officials, who prided themselves on their liberalism, Wallace won. He not only won, but he obtained a majority—not simply a plurality! Although Wallace later was removed from the 1972 campaign, suffering permanent paralysis when shot in a Laurel, MD, shopping center, Michigan Democrats were legally required to support him on the first ballot at the Democratic National Convention.[22]

The first reaction of Michigan Democrats was to blame Republicans for Wallace's victory. They concluded that GOP voters who would support Nixon in the fall of 1972 "raided" the open primary and embarrassed Democrats by choosing Wallace. The only problem with that explanation was that it did not square with the facts, as later developed by a scientific study at University of Michigan. Nonetheless, when the Democratic National Convention decreed, as part of its reforms, that it would not seat delegates from states with open primaries, many were pleased.

Michigan later dropped the presidential primary in favor of a caucus system in 1988. Primaries were too costly, given the state's desperate financial condition. Caucus systems, however, can also be embarrassing. Only "true believers" are willing to spend long hours attending precinct, county and congressional district caucuses before state party conventions finally choose delegates to the national conventions.

Neither of the winners of the Michigan caucuses was a viable candidate when the conventions opened. The state became a laughingstock when its delegates cast ballots, as required by state law, for Democrat Jesse Jackson and Republican Pat Robertson.

Subsequently, the state has returned to the primary, although there was intense partisan debate over whether it was to be open or closed. Democratic Party rules would not permit state delegates to be seated if they were chosen in an open primary. Democratic Governor James Blanchard and Democratic legislators insisted that the primary be closed. Republican governors (Milliken and Engler) wanted an open primary, as did most Republican nominees. Blanchard and his Democratic legislative majority produced a closed primary. However, Engler and the Republicans invited all comers to participate in their primary, cashing in on opinion surveys which showed that Michigan voters prefer open primaries.

Presidential primaries have changed the face of American politics. John Kennedy became the first candidate to use primaries to win his party's nomination because he could not otherwise have become the Democratic nominee in 1960. Before Kennedy, few states had presidential primaries and the ones that did permitted voters only to express a "preference," which the state's convention delegates were not required to follow. In short, a presidential primary was a political beauty contest.

In 1952, after President Truman announced that he would not seek re-election, U.S. Sen. Estes Kefauver of Tennessee entered and won a number of Democratic primaries. This no doubt was due to name familiarity. Kefauver had chaired a Senate committee investigating organized crime in 1951 and was responsible for a great increase in sales of television sets as the nation sat, mesmerized by the proceedings.[23]

But Kefauver was disliked by many of the Democratic Party "king makers," including President Truman. Truman worked behind the scenes to convince Illinois Gov. Adlai Stevenson to accept the Democratic Party presidential nomination. At first reluctant to seek the nomination, Stevenson later called Truman after the balloting began to ask for his blessing. The chairman of the Missouri delegation then read a brief telegram from the President to the delegates. It said: "If I were a Missouri delegate to the Democratic National Convention, I would cast my ballot for Gov. Adlai E. Stevenson of Illinois." Stevenson was nominated on the next (third) ballot.

The last time that a party nominated a candidate who had not entered a single primary, but who had been endorsed by the outgoing President, was in 1968. In that year, President Johnson, who controlled the party machinery and the convention, backed Vice President Hubert H. Humphrey.

Since 1972, primaries have been the test of candidates. Many political leaders have been eliminated by primaries. Some may have made good Presidents, but they were not good enough to survive the marathon we call the presidential primary.

In 2004, the Democratic Party had no less than 10 candidates seeking their nomination, eventually won by Senator John Kerry. As noted in Chapter IV, there was no shortage or candidates in either major party in 2008.

Some political scientists suggest that parties no longer offer candidates to the electorate. Rather, they accept choices made by voters in primary elections. Primaries were developed during the early years of the 20th Century as a part of the Progressive Movement.

Reformers argued that party bosses could not be trusted with the nomination process. Real democracy required popular participation, especially in those areas of one party domination where nomination was virtually equivalent to election.

A major problem with primaries is that only a small percentage of voters participates in them. As a result, **"cause people"** tend to have a disproportionate impact on the nomination process. As a practical matter, this means that the most Conservative Republicans and the most Liberal Democrats are most likely to vote. Only after a candidate is finally chosen, is he or she forced, by realities of presidential politics, to move toward the political center.

State and local communities use primaries for a long list of offices. Some states use primaries to nominate Governors, Lieutenant Governors, Secretaries of State and Attorney Generals. They are used in legislative districts and in congressional elections, as well. At the local level, one often must survive a municipal primary to be a member of council, mayor or judge. The voice of the people has been enlarged, but whether their influence is greater is debatable.

VIII. PUBLIC OPINION AND THE MEDIA

A. WHAT IS PUBLIC OPINION?

All governments, democratic and undemocratic, are based, to some extent, on public opinion. In a democracy, government rests on the consent of the governed and public opinion is enthroned. But even in dictatorships, leaders recognize the importance of public opinion. If nothing else, it must be repressed and one of the best tools of repression is a controlled communications system. History shows that one of the first steps taken by autocrats when they seize power is to control the media. A free press is not possible in a dictatorship. A state monopoly on communications and a system of censorship is used to stifle ideas which may be "dangerous" to the regime.

The focus of this chapter is public opinion and the media. In a democracy, it matters what people think. Politicians constantly are trying to influence their opinions through a variety of techniques. But the American system is one in which there is competition in what Justice Oliver Wendell Holmes called the free "marketplace of ideas." The First Amendment to the Constitution guarantees a free press. The Framers of the Constitution understood that the press must be free to report and to criticize, when warranted, the work of government. Free media and free elections are the hallmarks of a democracy.

It seems, at times, as if there are as many different definitions of public opinion as there are writers on public opinion. The term is of ancient Greek and Roman origins, but it appears that Machiavelli was the first political thinker to use it in its modern sense.

In his *Discourses*, he writes that "a wise man will not ignore public opinion in regard to particular matters such as the distribution of officers and preferment," but he apparently felt that the term was so well known and understood that it needed no defining.[1]

Some consider Jean Jacques Rousseau the first modern political thinker to make an extended analysis of public opinion. He was interested not only in relations between government policy and the opinions of individuals, but also the relationship between majority rule and representation in a democracy. He clearly recognized that all governments rest fundamentally on opinion, rather than on coercion, and that governments cannot change things very much without the support of public opinion.

Some of his comments on majority rule are remarkably modern. Considering the use of ordinary and extraordinary majorities, he says, "First, the more grave and important the questions discussed, the nearer should the opinion that is to prevail approach unanimity. Secondly, the more the matter in hand calls for speed, the smaller the prescribed difference in the number of votes may be allowed to become: where an instant decision has to be reached, a majority of one vote should be enough. The first of these two rules seems more in harmony with the laws, and the second with practical affairs. In any case, it is the combination of them that gives the best proportions for determining the majority necessary."[2]

Public opinion was of little importance to many political thinkers until the age of the democratic revolutions. Prior to the age of Locke and Jefferson, it did not matter very much what the public thought. The public also had no way of making known its opinions. But with the growth of democracy and the acceptance of the idea of popular sovereignty, public opinion became enthroned. One heard the phrase, "Vox populi, vox Dei" (the voice of the people is the voice of God).

At the dawn of the 19th Century, it was common for the educated class to use the term "public opinion." As Americans became more educated, they became more vocal in expressing their views. They also were more likely to vote. As public levels of literacy rose, so did demand for newspapers and magazines. In turn, they provided more information about government and public policy issues. Politicians became more concerned about gauging the state of opinion in order to serve the interests of their constituents, and to maintain a hold on their offices.

Not everyone was pleased by the forward march of democracy and the potential impact of public opinion on public policy. De Tocqueville associated public opinion with the dangers of a mediocre, unstable and potential "tyranny of the majority."

Some political leaders and academics, such as Woodrow Wilson and Lord Bryce, were aware of the importance of public opinion in a democracy at the end of the 19th Century. During World War I, some people argued that public opinion was unimportant. But Wilson believed that it could have an influence on international leaders. As a result, only about a week after the U.S. entered the global conflict, the President formed a Committee on Public Information (CPI).[3]

Known as the Creel Committee after its chairman George Creel, a noted editor, the panel's job was to solidify public opinion behind the war effort. It used all of the known propaganda techniques of the time. There were plenty of pamphlets and posters. Speakers used intermissions at local movie houses to urge citizens to support the war effort.

The CPI also drew up a voluntary censorship code under which editors would agree to refrain from printing stories that might aid the enemy. Creel insisted only that news of troop movements, ship sailings and other information of potential military value to the enemy be withheld.

Many scholars date the modern study of public opinion from publication of Walter Lippmann's *Public Opinion* in 1922.[4]

During the 1920s and 1930s, nearly everyone got into the act. American universities began to offer courses in public opinion, although academics disagreed about which departments should teach them. Political science, sociology, psychology and journalism all "claimed" the course.

Academics not only disagreed on where public opinion courses belonged; they also could not agree on a definition of the subject.

In *The Governmental Process*, David Truman defined public opinion as "the opinion of the aggregate of individuals making up the public under discussion. It does not include all the opinions held by such a set of individuals, but only those relevant to the issue or situation that defines them as a public."[5]

Political scientist Bernard Hennessey defined public opinion as "the complex of beliefs expressed by a significant number of persons on an issue of public importance."[6] Many other scholars have defined public opinion simply as "what the public thinks about a particular issue or set of issues at any given moment."

Perhaps one ought to remember that definitions of public opinion are only a beginning point in its analysis, rather than the terminal point.

Early in the 21st Century, many citizens still wonder what shapes public opinion. There is always the proverbial "chicken and egg" question: "Do polls influence public opinion or does public opinion drive the polls?" We shortly will focus on the media and its impact on public opinion and the making of public policy.

B. CHARACTERISTICS OF PUBLIC OPINION

Public opinion has a number of characteristics or properties. These include direction, intensity, stability, latency and salience.

1. Direction

It is possible to measure opinions in a direction along a scale. Prior to World War II, political scientists were content to record people as being "for" or "against" a particular public policy or candidate. After the conflict, public opinion became more "scientific." Analysts discovered that yes or no answers often masked wide gradations in opinion about issues of the day.

We often speak of Liberals and Conservatives as being on the "left" or the "right," respectively. We view "moderates" as being in the "center." If one thinks of Radical political opinions as being at the end of one line and Conservative at the end of the other, an individual's opinion may be located at some point along that line. A citizen may favor a program of full government health care, a program limited to government health care to the aged and needy or an entirely private health care delivery system.

2. Intensity

It is basic to know in which direction public opinion is leaning. Are people leaning "for" or against" a particular issue or candidate? But opinions have qualities or characteristics distinct from their direction character.

One of the most important of these characteristics is **intensity.** We may have very strong feelings about an issue. Collegians during the 1960s and early 1970s had strong opinions about the draft and the Vietnam War. Today some people feel intensely about the abortion issue. Under such circumstances, we say that opinion has **high intensity**. The fervor of individual opinions varies greatly. Some people are adamantly for or against gun control legislation. Others mildly support such laws, while still others mildly oppose them. Finally, some people do not care at all about the issue. In such a case, we say that opinion is of **low intensity.**

Politicians know that they cannot safely ignore certain high intensity issues on the public agenda. If, however, opinion is of low intensity, issues can be put on the back burner or ignored, at least for the time being. Many Americans care little or are extremely ill-informed about foreign policy matters. Their knowledge of geography is abysmal.

When American newspapers and TV networks carried stories daily on political problems in Haiti, few subscribers bothered to read them. They did not have strong opinions about the fate of Haitian democracy. When, however, the Haitian problem began to affect them, opinion did become intense. If it is a matter of a loved one being sent off to Haiti to maintain peace on that island, it becomes personal and highly relevant. When the policy question shifted to Haitian immigrants, militantly opposed Florida voters had a strong impact on national politics.

One of the problems with public opinion and its measurement is that it may not adequately measure intensity of opinion. In his book, *The Pollsters*, Lindsay Rogers notes that pollsters cannot tell us the loudness of the yeas and nays they say they hear. He wrote, "A public opinion poll tells us nothing about the eagerness or enthusiasm of those who wish that something be done, or about the indifference or bitterness of those who do not want it done. Until the pollsters do both of these things, they will not chart opinion or register sentiment. They may claim to count a pulse, but they cannot boast of reading a thermometer."[7]

In a notable book, attacking opinion measurement techniques, Rogers wonders whether "public opinion is ever the sum of the answers that people are willing to give to strangers." He quotes the director of Mass Observation that "public opinion is what you say out loud to anyone. It is an overt and not necessarily candid part of your private opinion."

3. Stability

Opinions may be stable or unstable, that is, they may be unlikely to change or they may be very fluid, likely to change overnight. A person may be rooted in his values. If the facts get in the way of the opinion, damn the facts. It does not matter what the evidence shows if basic, bedrock values are concerned. Or, one's opinions may change daily as he listens to public debate and is exposed to media and other influences. In this case, we say that opinion is fluid or unstable. People may have a very different opinion in June than they did in January.

Some point to the impact of historic events on opinion stability. The Civil War and the Great Depression, two watershed events in American History, illustrate the point. After the Civil War, as noted in an earlier chapter, Americans were divided politically and voted the way that they shot. The south was solidly Democratic and the north solidly Republican. That changed only after many generations. Some older Americans never have forgotten the Great Depression and, as a result, still are very conservative about money matters.

The late Professor V.O. Key of Harvard suggested that the term "stability" might not be particularly useful in the study of public opinion. He suggested the term **"viscosity,"** that is, opinions may change only slowly in response to new ideas and events in the political world. Or, he said, opinions may change rapidly and unpredictably. Key equated stability with high viscosity; instability with low viscosity. In most cases, American political opinion leans toward high viscosity. But at times, we are "fickle." In 1991, President Bush, with a 91% public approval rating, appeared destined for an easy re-election in 1992. A year later, the voters threw him out of the White House.[8]

One also should note that opinion can be either divisive or consensus in nature. When the great majority of poll respondents express the same view, we say that a **consensus** exists on the matter. When, however, the public holds widely divergent attitudes, we call this **divisive opinion**.

Perhaps the best, and certainly one of the most often cited examples of fluid opinion, is the impact of Pearl Harbor on American thinking. Prior to the sneak attack on Sunday morning, December 7, 1941, the American nation was deeply divided between interventionists and isolationists. After the attack, the U.S. was united in its determination to defeat Japan and its allies, Nazi Germany and Fascist Italy. The debate was over and there now was a consensus which enabled President Roosevelt and the Congress to do what was necessary to win the war.

4. Latency

Use of the term "latency" implies that sometimes public opinion is slumbering and exists only as a potential problem to public officials. People do not always express political opinions. When opinion is activated, it ceases to be latent. What opinion will be developed about a particular candidate? How will the public react to a particular legislative proposal? What will be the impact of a particular event and how will it effect the mood of the nation?

Political decision-makers must anticipate public reactions. Experienced leaders know that if they take certain actions, they will trigger either support or opposition from millions of Americans. David Truman spoke of the theory of "potential interest group." Any set of shared attitudes by interest groups can spark a particular reaction to political decisions. Groups have certain expectations about the "rules of the game."

Certain opinions may exist in citizens' minds without becoming activated. If, however, they are affected by a particular event, the opinion will become awakened. In a quiet, campus town, for example, there is a hostility toward violence, but it may be only a latent opinion. If, however, there is a wave of sexual assaults and murders, latent opinion will become active. Demands will be made that the police solve the crimes. If they fail to do so, aroused citizens may then demand that the police chief be removed.

5. Salience

We say that public opinion has a high degree of **salience** when it deals with issues that concern us. Put simply, an event or policy is **relevant** to us. If it does not impact our lives, we say that an event has low salience as far as we are concerned.

During the Vietnam War era, male college students were worried about the draft. It was possible for them to be conscripted, trained and sent to the jungles of Southeast Asia. Potentially, their lives were in jeopardy. Under such circumstances, it is not surprising that many male collegians actively opposed the war and the draft. They did everything they could, legal and illegal, to avoid the draft. Some, after exhausting student deferments, joined the campus ROTC, guaranteeing that they would complete their education.

Others, like future U.S. Senator Gary Hart (D., CO), enrolled in divinity schools, although they had no intention of becoming a minister. Some fled to Canada or elsewhere and did not return until President Carter declared an amnesty to draft evaders. Bill Clinton had to defend himself, during his presidential campaigns, against charges that he was a Vietnam era draft dodger.[9]

Once the war was over, this burning issue with a high degree of salience became a moot question. It no longer mattered and students turned their attention to other issues.

We are interested in issues that have an impact on our lives. Blacks are more enthusiastic about civil rights laws and affirmative action programs than are whites. Women in their child-bearing years are more interested in the abortion issue that women who no longer can conceive a child. Elderly Americans are interested in preserving the Social Security System and their retirement benefits. Today's youth is cynical about the system and is not enthusiastic about inter-generational transfer payments.

In short, age, race, religion, ethnicity and all the things that make us "who we are" determine whether an issue matters to us. There is, as one would logically deduct, a close correlation between relevant or "salient" issues and intensity. If it's irrelevant, we don't care or feel strongly about an issue. If it does concern us, we may be intensely concerned and politically active to advance or protect our interests.

The ebb and flow of events also has a major impact on how we feel about issues. During the presidencies of Nixon, Ford and Jimmy Carter, the number one worry of many, if not most, Americans, was inflation. During the late 1980s and the 1990s, we no longer considered it a major problem. We have had relatively little inflation during the past 30 years. Recently, it has been only about 3-4%.

We also were not particularly concerned at the end of the 20th Century about unemployment. We were near the target (4% or less unemployed) set by the Employment Act of 1946. This, of course, was not the case during the Great Depression, when many jobless American workers worried about how they were going to feed their families and how they were going to pay the rent. The rate has risen in the early years of the 21st Century and once again worries many Americans after the Great Crash of September, 2008. In late spring, 2009, national unemployment was the highest in two decades., just under 9%.

In the 1990s, pollsters found that Americans most concerned about crime, health care and the state of the environment. The concerns in 2009 are somewhat different. Many worry about the nation's economic future, job security, integrity of their retirement funds and unprecedented Federal deficits.

C. POLITICAL SOCIALIZATION:
HOW WE GET OUR VALUES AND OPINIONS

None of us is born with opinions about politics or anything else. We acquire them through a process that sociologists call **socialization**. This deals with the teaching of values and opinions to the next generation. As children, we learn basic cultural values from our families, our schools and our churches. Childhood is a continuous process of learning what is "good" and "bad." We are taught what to value and what to dislike. We learn specific values and develop opinions about democratic government, political institutions and processes, political parties, groups and individuals through the process of **political socialization**. Clearly, our social institutions are of paramount importance in this process. We will now briefly survey the impact of three basic institutions on the individual.

1. The Family

Very small children may think that their parents can do no wrong. The sun rises and sets on mom and dad. At this impressionable age, when parents communicate values, children tend to accept them. Some scholars believe that the "crucial period" of a child's political, social and psychological development occurs between the ages of nine and 13.

Later, when they become adolescents, the process is quite different. Not all teenagers are alike, but adolescence is often a stage of rebellion and a period in which youth searches for independence. What mom and dad say now "may or may not be true." Or, in some cases, it is certainly "false" because the values taught by parents are "so old fashioned." Later, after a bit of aging, one might well conclude that it is not so much a matter of truth and falsehood as it is a matter of preferences.

Mark Twain, the great American writer, used to tell the story of a young man who said: "When I was 18, I considered my father the most ignorant man on the face of the earth. When I was 21, I was amazed to see how much the old man had learned in the last three years."

Parents communicate all kinds of values. It is from them that we get our original religious orientation, our race, our nationality. In most cases, we also get some political attitudes. We may even get a strong sense of party identification. Many studies show that children who come from families where both parents agree about politics tend to accept the parental view of political parties and candidates.

Children growing up in Democratic families have heard many good things about Presidents Roosevelt, Truman, Kennedy, Johnson, Carter and Clinton. Conversely, they have heard bad things about Republican Chief Executives. Union families often transmit pro-labor, anti-business attitudes to their offspring. Children from Republican families have heard good things about Presidents Eisenhower, Nixon Ford, Reagan, George Herbert Walker Bush and George W. Bush. If the breadwinner or breadwinners are professionals, children may be exposed to pro-business, anti-union attitudes. In some families, the dinner table is a political classroom.

Research indicates that if father and mother are politically at odds, children tend to become independents or be "turned off" by politics, seeing it as a source of discord. Parents who are apathetic about politics also produce children who tend to be disinterested, non-voters unless some other influence intervenes. That influence often is education.

All political scientists and professional politicians are well aware that there still is a "hereditary vote." It is estimated that as many as three-fourths of first-time voters cast their ballots the way their parents did.

2. The School

Schools mold young minds. That is one of the reasons why school districts debate what should be taught (curriculum) and who should teach it. Traditionally, American schools have been "Conservative" in that they have taught support for the political system. They believe that part of their job is to turn out educated citizens who will actively take part in civic affairs.

When studying U.S. history (K-12), we view our national heroes and heroines. We study American democratic ideals, such as those contained in the Declaration of Independence and the Bill of Rights. We also learn a good deal of "myth," which later is "unlearned" in college. Did George Washington really never tell a lie? Did he throw a dollar across the Potomac River? Did Abraham Lincoln really walk many miles through rain and snow to return a library book?

We learn routine civic behaviors, such as the Pledge of Allegiance to the flag, which re-enforces respect for one's country. We learn patriotic songs, including the national anthem. We learn to respect authority, to value national honor and the dignity of the individual. At least that is what schools are attempting to communicate to youth.

College, of course, is a different matter. Students attending college tend to be more knowledgeable about politics and tend to have more Liberal attitudes than those who do not attend classes after high school. According to many studies, collegians are more concerned about civil liberties than is the general public. Research has repeatedly shown that students at the most prestigious or selective colleges are the most Liberal of all. It also matters what one intends to do in life. Pre-medical, business and engineering students are historically more Conservative than are Liberal Arts students.

During the 1980s, Republicanism and conservatism made a comeback on the nation's campuses. This may simply have been a reflection of national trends and the election of Presidents Reagan and Bush. College students of the early 21st Century may be returning to liberalism, some scholars believe. Why?

Some hypothesize that it is the effect of the Liberal Arts faculties. Republican Conservatives lament the fact that about three-fourths of social science courses are taught by Liberal Democrat professors. Where, they ask, is real "intellectual diversity" and exposure to a wide variety of ideas and philosophies? When are students ever exposed to Republican and Conservative ideas?

Others argue that it is the effect of **peer pressures** to conform to so-called "politically correct" (PC) ideas. Whatever the cause, there is considerable interest about the state of politics on the nation's campuses. This simply reflects the fact that higher education plays a major role in **adult socialization**, the shaping of political attitudes and values.

At the dawn of the 20th Century, the situation was considerably different. Only 6% of Americans were high school graduates and less than 1% held college degrees. The democratization of education in America has had a profound impact on American political life.

3. Churches and Religion

Many of our basic attitudes about morality—what is right and what is wrong—we get not only from parents, but also from our churches. We tend to "internalize" the values of our denominations if we are church-goers until they literally are a part of us. We identify strongly as Catholics, Jews, Protestants or members of some other group.

In terms of politics, there are important generalizations that we can make about religion, political party preference and political attitudes and behavior.

Historically, Protestants are more likely than Roman Catholics to be conservative on economic and welfare issues. Jews are the most liberal of all major religious groups on economic issues.

Protestants vary, of course—depending on the denomination—on certain social issues. Evangelical or fundamentalists are generally much more conservative than non-evangelicals. Presbyterians, Anglicans and Congregationalists are the most Liberal of Protestant groups.

Although one must avoid the pitfall of stereotypic thinking, generalizations still are useful. Although Jews are the most Liberal of religious groups, there are many Conservative Jewish families. There also are lots of Conservative Catholics and Liberal Protestants. One cannot predict a person's political behavior simply by knowing his or her religious affiliation, but we can study statistics, which tell us what the trends are. One should also keep in mind that an important concept in public opinion is cross-pressures. That is, individuals can be pulled in opposite directions because they belong to many groups.

We also need to keep in mind the impact of peer pressure. What happens when a college student's parents and friends disagree on basic moral values? The evidence at this point is inconclusive.

Whenever one examines basic American values, one must keep in mind that religious values, often acquired early in life, can have a profound impact on one's political views and attitudes. Questions such as abortion, physician-assisted suicide and capital punishment are but a few of many examples that may be cited.

4. Media

In the past, social scientists made confident generalizations about primary and secondary groups and their impact on the socialization process. Sociologist Charles H. Cooley developed the concept of **primary groups.** They consist of small groups of persons with whom we have frequent face-to-face contact in our daily lives. Relationships are personal and values are shared. Individuals may freely express sentiments and emotions such as love, anger and happiness. The best examples of primary groups are the family and peer groups.

Secondary groups, on the other hand, are large and impersonal. They have clearly defined, but limited, social purposes in contemporary industrial societies. Some would include the media as a secondary group; others would not.

Media in the past were presumed to have relatively little impact on the socialization of youth. But social change in the U.S. has greatly enhanced their role. We read today of television being used as a "babysitter" and a new term, "latch-key children" has been coined to refer to children who come home to no parents. They let themselves in and watch what they want on TV. Children and young adults do not usually watch the evening news. But they do spend much of their lives watching entertainment programs. and using "new media."

Networks send messages in their prime time offerings. Police and the criminal justice system are not always portrayed in a favorable light. Children growing up before television formed values from listening to radio. Then the motto was "crime does not pay" and "the bad guys" always were punished.

Critics often blast the amount of sex and violence shown on television. Major networks face enormous competitive pressures for **"audience share"** from cable industry. This has led them to air programs that never would have gotten past the censor in the past. Although censorship is not new in the U.S., increased political pressures on the TV and film industries has led to some concessions.[10]

The networks are not to air "adult" programs until late in the evening, the theory being that children should be in bed at that hour. Hollywood also has adopted a system of self-censorship, which has produced a "ratings" system. Although many parents are dissatisfied with the ratings system, it does give them some guidance on film content.

Even children's cartoon programs have drawn the critics' wrath because of the amount of violence shown. We have, they contend, desensitized our children to the human suffering involved in bloodshed and violence. Although it may be stretching the point, some critics even blame the increase in schoolyard murders on messages children get from the media.

The bottom line is that many people today are aware and concerned about the values that film and TV industries transmit, particularly to their children. We no longer agree that media are of secondary importance in the formation of values and opinions.

D. MEASURING PUBLIC OPINION

Public opinion, by its very nature, is plural. There are many different "publics" and many varieties of opinion on issues. Scholars concern themselves with the aggregate of individual attitudes or beliefs shared by a part of the adult public.

The problem of how to measure people's judgments and attitudes is not new. Anyone who hopes to win public office or hold on to it must necessarily know what is going on inside people's heads. In his classic study of public opinion, Walter Lippmann noted that each individual, in viewing distant events, tends to form "pictures inside his head of the world beyond his reach."[11]

What are those pictures and how can students of public opinion determine their nature and importance?

During the 20th Century, the emphasis in the U.S. was on making public opinion "more scientific" by the use of quantitative analysis. This means that students must have at least a basic understanding of percentages and averages. The student who fears statistics must remember that he need not be a mathematical wizard to be able to analyze public opinion.

The principal method we use to discover what people are thinking is the public opinion poll. Polls have a long history and we have learned much from the mistakes of the past.

The first step is to construct the questions to be asked. Special care must be taken to avoid "loading a question" with bad phrasing. The nature of the question may affect the nature of the response.

The second step is to select the sample. Obviously, we cannot interview every American, every voter or every resident of the city. That simply is impractical. Pollsters decide to sample the universe in which they are interested. A common technique for doing this is the **random sample.** This method of sampling gives each potential voter or adult the same opportunity of being selected for an interview. But no one usually has a list of every person in any group.

Pollsters must be careful so that their methodology does not produce unreliable results. Although it involves complex statistical analysis, random sampling is essentially like a lottery system. In a properly run lottery, each number has the same chance of being a winner.

Most national opinion surveys, such as the Gallup and Roper polls, use samples of about 1500 persons. They employ a variation of random sampling called **stratified sampling.** This method is based on census data that provides the number of area residents and their location. Pollsters split the nation into four sampling areas, then randomly select a set of counties and standard metropolitan statistical areas (SMSAs) in proportion to the total national population.

A small number, usually two dozen or less, of respondents is selected from each primary sampling unit. Small areas of the city are chosen and target families from each of these city neighborhoods are used.

Stratified sampling usually is not used by news organizations, such as The *New York Times* and *USA Today,* or by the major television networks. These media pollsters work instead on random surveys using every 10th, 100th or 1000th person or household.

As noted, polling has learned from the mistakes of the past. In 1936, *Literary Digest,* then one of the nation's most popular magazines, conducted a poll prior to the presidential election. It predicted that Gov. Alf Landon of Kansas would defeat President

Franklin D. Roosevelt in his bid for re-election. When the results were in, FDR had won 46 of the then-48 states. How could a poll be so wrong? In one word: methodology.

The 1936 presidential election had taken place during the Great Depression. Many Americans were literally struggling to survive. Food and housing were vital. Anything else was not. Relatively few Americans had automobiles. Although it may be difficult for today's youth to contemplate, many American families did not have telephones. The *Literary Digest* used auto registrations and telephone surveys. The result was that they talked to many Republicans and relatively few Democrats. In short, the sample was **biased** and **unscientific**.[12]

One of the first polling organizations was the American Institute of Public Opinion, more commonly known as the Gallup Poll. Although some scholars consider it the most reliable of today's many polling organizations, it made a serious mistake during the presidential election of 1948. In that year, President Truman was the underdog. In fact, many political writers began their stories, "…When Governor Thomas E. Dewey moves into the White House next January…" Not if, but when. It was a sure thing.

Gallup and other polls indicated that Truman was far behind. George Gallup issued a statement two weeks before the election, saying it would be a Dewey landslide. In fact, he said, it was pointless to continue to poll. On election day, the President won what some consider the greatest landslide victory of the 20th Century. Gallup had "egg on his chin." Pollsters learned to continue polling right down to election day. Last-minute changes of mind simply were not properly taken into account. Nor were the disproportionately high number of "undecideds" to split evenly, as Gallup had assumed that they would.

Today we hear a good deal about **exit polls**. Using this method, pollsters interview voters after they have cast their ballots. Initially, such polls were used to discover voter preferences in a few selected precincts. In time, journalists found that they could use exit polls to predict an election in progress.

Because TV networks and newspapers want to be first to report the results accurately, interviewers question voters throughout the day. Voters answer a variety of questions and results are entered into a computer. About 15,000 or more voters are included in the typical national exit poll, which generally has a margin of error of about 3-4%. That is, if the results are within 3-4% of the predicted outcome, the pollsters consider their work accurate.

One of the major problems with exit polls is that many voters do not wish to be questioned. It takes time to fill out a questionnaire and place it in a box, the method used in this type of polling. Unless pollsters take care to include representative numbers of voters on the basis of sex, race and age, poll results may be misleading.

Mike Royko, the late syndicated columnist of *The Chicago Tribune*, grew tired of the accuracy of the exit polls, however. He believed that it took all the fun out of elections, a favorite Windy City sport. His published advice to his readers: Have some fun, lie to the pollsters, screw up the poll results.[13]

News organizations introduced **tracking polls** during the 1992 presidential election. Taken each day, they enabled candidates to monitor short-term political developments and to assess the impact of campaign strategy on the race. Although this type of poll is plagued with reliability problems, major news organizations continued to use them in the Clinton-Dole contest of 1996.

Failure of TV news networks to accurately report the Bush-Gore contest on election night of 2000 is another example of difficulty in polling when methodology is flawed. They were considerably more careful, as well as accurate, in reporting the Bush-Kerry and Obama-McCain presidential contests in 2004 and 2008.

E. LEADERS AND PUBLIC OPINION FOLLOWERS

As we have seen in earlier chapters, there are essentially two views of power in America. The question of who has power and how it should be exercised still divides elite theorists and pluralists. Elite theorists, like C. Wright Mills, have argued that the "power elite" dominate society, including its communications systems, and that the masses simply follow along. Pluralists reject this notion. There are, they say, many sets of leaders in society and their interest groups have access to public officials. They have a real opportunity to influence public policy.

Those who believe in "republican" government, or indirect democracy, are inclined to view the role of leaders differently from those who subscribe to "participatory democracy" theories. They are, for example, much more inclined to the "trustee" theory of representation. Presidents and members of Congress, according to this view, ought not to concern themselves with the shifting winds of public opinion. Rather, they should do what the national interest requires, exercising their own good judgment. They should try to educate the public about the need for particular policies. To be a leader requires efforts to lead and shape public opinion, not merely follow it.

This apparently is often what does happen in American politics. Public opinion polls show that the political preferences of Americans often are not translated into law. Two widely-cited examples:

1. Term Limits

Polls show that the public is overwhelmingly in favor of term limits for public officials. At the Federal level, however, only the President's tenure is limited. The Supreme Court, whose members enjoy tenure for "life or good behavior," has ruled that congressional term limits can be imposed only by a constitutional amendment. This seems unlikely because two-thirds of the members of both House and Senate would have to agree to submit the matter to the states for ratification. One should note, however, that term limits have been adopted in many states. In Michigan, for example, many members of the state legislature are forced to return to private life or seek other offices. Jennifer Granholm, elected in 2002 as Michigan's first female governor, also will be the first Chief Executive of the State prohibited by law from running (in 2010) and serving more than two terms.

2. ERA

Public opinion polls indicated that the overwhelming majority of Americans favored the Equal Rights Amendment. Yet mere majorities are not enough, even if large. One-fourth of the states, plus one, can block a constitutional amendment. That is what happened in the ERA case.

Those who believe in a more direct form of democracy subscribe to the delegate theory. They argue that we have elected Presidents and members of Congress and, once in office, their mission is to follow popular will. While interesting in theory, this view may be extraordinarily difficult to implement. Americans are generally ill-informed about government and public issues. A 1996 survey reported that only one-third of

Americans knew the name of their representative in Congress. Less than one-fourth could identify both U.S. senators from their state. And, in what must have been a blow to Al Gore's ego, some 40% of the people could not identify him when he served as the Vice President of the United States.[14]

Two decades ago, University of Cincinnati researchers decided to become pranksters. Armed with a sense of humor, they set out to ask 1200 local residents if they favored enactment of the Monetary Control Bill of 1983. About one-fifth said that they did. About one-fourth said that they did not. The rest of the respondents said that they "didn't know" or hadn't thought about the merits of the legislation.

The problem with the UC poll question was that there was no such thing as the Monetary Control Bill. The Cincinnati pollsters, by the way, were simply repeating a question that had been tried on a national sample years earlier with similar results. Apparently the public is unwilling to admit its ignorance and inclined to pretend that it is informed on public affairs when, in fact, it is not.

F. WHO ARE THE MEDIA?

Media, it was said years ago, were of secondary importance as agents of socialization. They played only a relatively minor role in the formation of basic values and opinion. Clearly, they were not primary, as were the family, the school and the church. That appears to have changed, not necessarily for the better. Contemporary media have the potential to exert powerful influence over Americans, particularly young Americans. One often hears the complaint that a large segment of youth now apparently is taking its values from what is seen on television and the movie screen. Many concerned parents worry about what their children see and listen to, as well as what they read.

The term **mass media** refers to the means of communication. Broadly defined, "the media" traditionally includes newspapers, magazines, books **(print media)** and television, movies and radio **(electronic media).** The term now also includes **"new media,"** online services, the Internet, newsletters and other published material.

In the U.S., citizens take private ownership of media for granted. In some other democracies, although print media are privately owned, broadcasting is not. Because both print and broadcast media are privately owned, the American news industry enjoys more political freedom than any other nation in the world.

But private ownership means that profits are necessary to succeed, and to make a profit, "customers" (readers and viewers) must be satisfied. In short, **audience appeal** is of fundamental importance.

Political scientists always have been interested in what kinds of political messages media send. Parents, teachers, clergy and others are interested in the larger question of what kinds of social messages media are sending to our children. When we use the term media, we refer to a wide variety of communications systems. In the past, we got most of our information from print. Until the 20th Century, in fact, the press consisted only of print media. Reading was, and is, of vital importance! Yet books, magazines and newspapers, while still enormously influential, are having problems maintaining their audiences. Print media demand that one read well in order to enjoy and profit from that source of information.

1. The American Print Media

Our first newspapers date back to the colonial era and the colonists soon realized the importance of a free press. The anti-Federalists demanded an amendment guaranteeing freedom of press and speech.

The *National Gazette* was established by Jefferson to compete with the *Gazette of the United States,* founded in 1789 by Alexander Hamilton and the Federalists. Notable editors of the Federalist paper included John Fenno, Noah Webster (of dictionary fame) and William Cobbett. Perhaps most notable of Jefferson's editors was Philip Freneau, a Princeton classmate of James Madison. Freneau was lured to the capital (then at Philadelphia) to be not only a crusading editor, but also a translator for the State department.

Federalist and Republican newspapers were fiercely partisan. They not only parroted the party line; they also viciously attacked the opposition and survived on government printing contracts.

What Frank Luther Mott calls **"the dark age of the partisan press"** extended from Washington thorough Andrew Jackson.[15] Francis P. Blair, the editor of *The Globe,* Jackson's party paper, was even included in Jackson's "kitchen cabinet," a group of White House advisers close to "Old Hickory." Amos Kendall had edited the *Argus of Western America,* the Democratic Party organ, published in Frankfort, KY. He later came to Washington and became one of the President's most important political allies.

Kendall was described by one of Jackson's rivals as follows: "the President's thinking machine, and his writing machine, and his lying machine...He was chief overseer, chief reporter, amanuensis, scribe, accountant, general, man of all work - nothing was well done without the aid of his diabolical genius."[16]

During this early period, political parties were the financial supporters of the press. Treasury Secretary Hamilton gave Fenno government printing jobs and helped to secure economic support from wealthy Federalists. Jefferson, Madison and other Republicans promised financial inducements to Freneau to publish their party organ. Jackson used the patronage ("spoils") system to award public offices to friendly editors. While "Old Hickory" was in the White House, editors occupied a number of Federal jobs, including postmaster, U.S. marshal and U.S. attorney.[17]

One of the landmarks in journalism history, according to Emery and Emery, was the rise of the "penny press." *The New York Sun* first appeared on September 3, 1833. Founded by Benjamin Day, its motto was "It Shines for ALL." *The Sun* cost one cent at the news stand and stressed local news, particularly violence and triviality. It was, however, very readable and was not the voice of any political party. *The Sun* was the forerunner of the modern newspaper, built on mass circulation and advertising.[18] Another successful independent newspaper was the *New York Morning Herald,* founded, in 1835, by James Gordon Bennett.

The rise of the penny press helped to weaken party influence on newspaper editorial content. As party organizations grew stronger, they no longer felt the need to rely on the press. Congress decided it no longer would award contracts to newspapers to publish the nation's laws, and, in 1860, established the Government Printing Office (GPO). When GPO was made responsible for all government printing, presidential and congressional subsidies to partisan newspapers was a matter of history.

After the Civil War, the press became more independent, with Horace Greeley's *New York Tribune* one of the best known of the "new breed" of newspapers. Greeley and others still published one-sided editorials—that's the nature of editorials—but they were not formally allied with party organizations.

If the press became less partisan in its news stories, it did not become more respectable. To attract readers, some editors and publishers resorted to sensationalism and scandalous news.

Those who think that Bill Clinton had been treated roughly by the contemporary newspapers should go back and study the case of President Grover Cleveland. The Buffalo, NY, *Evening News* ran a story under the headline, "A Terrible Tale," which asserted that Cleveland, while sheriff of Buffalo, had fathered an illegitimate child. Cleveland accepted responsibility and paid child support. Not to be outdone in the campaign of 1884, the *Democratic Sentinel* ran a story that James G. Blaine, the Republican presidential nominee, and his wife had had their first child just three months after their wedding.[19]

This kind of peep-hole, yellow journalism was followed by a circulation war between Joseph Pulitzer and William Randolph Hearst. One sensational story followed another. Hearst, who had established himself as editor of the *San Francisco Examiner*, purchased the *New York Morning Journal* in 1895. Pulitzer, who had made his mark as publisher of the *St. Louis Post-Dispatch*, had developed the *New York Sunday World*.

The role of Hearst's Journal in fostering the Spanish-American War of 1898 is well-known. It worked hard to create public opinion for war. Some journalism historians, in fact, refer to the conflict as "Hearst's War." Particularly important was Hearst's publication of a private letter from Dupay de Lome, Spanish ambassador to the U.S., to a Spanish newspaper editor visiting Havana. The letter, purloined by a Cuban junta member, characterized President William McKinley as "weak and catering to the rabble, and besides, a low politician." American opinion of the Spanish government hit a new low and less than a week later, the American battleship *Maine* blew up in Havana harbor. The explosion of the *Maine* led the press to demand war. Pulitzer and Hearst led the charge.[20]

Theodore Roosevelt referred to some journalists of the age as the "muckrakers." He used the term in a pejorative sense, comparing sensational writers to the Man with the Muckrake in *Pilgrim's Progress,* who did not look up to see the celestial crown but continued to rake the filth. The muckrake was a special instrument used to collect manure.

Muckrakers were associated primarily with magazine journalism, such as *McClure's*, founded in 1893. It published many of the most famous articles in American journalism history. Included were Ida M. Tarbell's famous "History of the Standard Oil Company," an exposure of the unfair business practices of John D. Rockefeller. *McClure's* also published Lincoln Steffens' series, "The Shame of the Cities," which exposed corruption in St. Louis, Minneapolis, Pittsburgh, Philadelphia, Chicago and New York.[21]

One of the great changes in journalism came with the invention of the telegraph and the advent of the wire services. Associated Press could not slant its stories when it had both Republican and Democratic newspapers as clients. Playing it "straight" became the norm in reporting and the era of "objective journalism" was born.

Technological changes always have had major impacts on newsrooms. The advent of the telephone changed things dramatically. High-speed presses and cheaper paper prices made possible the era of the mass circulation metropolitan daily. Publishers shifted emphasis. Most of them were no longer primarily interested in serving as an instrument of a political party. They were concerned primarily with profit-making. Rather than being critics of the establishment, they joined it.

In recent decades, competition from radio and television has caused the deaths of many big city newspapers, particularly afternoon papers. Social habits have changed as many people now come home from work, sit in front of the TV set and watch the evening news. They used to come home and read their afternoon newspaper. Their primary source of information, until 2004-05, was Tom Brokaw, Dan Rather, Peter Jennings or CNN. Some broadcasters wonder if the role of the network "anchor" will change with the retirements of Brokaw and Rather and the death of Jennings.

At the turn of the century, New York had 29 papers and Chicago 18. Today, New York has only three papers left and Chicago has only two. Few major cities have competing daily newspapers. Another trend, decried by many, is the growing concentration in the news industry. Local, family-owned newspapers are a disappearing breed. Firms like Gannett have been buying these publications and changing their character for decades.

U.S.A. Today enjoys the largest circulation of any American newspaper, selling about 2.3 million copies each day. *The Wall Street Journal* has a circulation of about two million. The only other American newspaper with a circulation of a million is T*he New* Y*ork Times.*

2. Broadcast Media

Broadcast media first came on the American scene in the 1920s with scratchy-sounding crystal sets and headphones. Some 80 years later, we had FM and stereophonic reception. It is arguable which was the first radio station to regularly broadcast the news. Pittsburgh's KDKA began operating on November 2, 1920, broadcasting returns from the Harding-Cox presidential contest. A Detroit experimental station, 8MK, began operations under the sponsorship of the Detroit News on August 20, 1920, and shortly thereafter, broadcast results of a Michigan election.[22]

Radio had a major political impact during the Great Depression, when President Roosevelt used it to address the nation in a series of **"fireside chats,"** assuring the nation that all would be well. Television is the product of the post-World War II era and has had an enormous impact on American culture. Indeed, some social critics complain that families no longer "communicate" with one another because they are so involved in watching their favorite "communications medium."

One should note that broadcasting is not as fully protected by the First Amendment as is the print press. Licensing of newspapers clearly is forbidden. But in the early days of radio, it would have ensured complete chaos to let just anyone go on the air and start broadcasting. In fact, by early 1927, when there were more than 700 radio stations on the air, frustrated listeners found them jumping around the broadcast band to avoid interference.

To bring order out of this chaos, Congress passed the **Radio Act of 1927,** first in a series of licensing laws. First radio, then television, came under the jurisdiction of the Federal Communications Commission. Although it clearly is not in the business of censorship, the FCC does have the authority to grant or deny licenses and license renewals.

Under the **Communications Act of 1934** and its successors, the FCC is charged with the responsibility of regulating broadcasting in the "public interest, convenience and necessity." The law assumes that the airwaves belong to the public. The FCC, therefore, tries to promote equity in political broadcasting. It has adopted an **equal time rule,** which requires that all stations that sell air time to a candidate for public office must offer to sell it to his or her opponents. There is one notable exception to this rule. Stations are not required to include all minor party candidates in political debates.

Another important FCC rule guarantees the **right of rebuttal** to any person who is attacked on a radio or television station. The target of the attack must be given the opportunity to respond. This rule grew out of the case of *Red Lion Broadcasting Company v. FCC.395 U.S.367 (1969).* The U.S. Supreme Court held that Fred Cook, author of a book about Sen. Barry Goldwater, the 1964 Republican presidential nominee, must be given the chance to reply to an attack aired by a Pennsylvania radio station.

Television, of course, does have an enormous potential to create an informed public. There are more than 200 million TV sets in America's homes. But that potential never has been fully realized. Entertainment is vital to the economic success of the medium and news programs generally take up a small segment of a network's air time.

Newton Minnow, a former chairman of the Federal Communications Commission, described TV as a "vast wasteland" in a famous 1961 speech. Contemporary critics point to the presence of mindless sitcoms and "trash television" shows that "pollute" the airwaves. Those who defend TV programming argue that one person's trash is another person's treasure.[23]

News and public affairs offerings are still available to the interested citizen. The three "major" networks, CBS, NBC and ABC, air news programs that reach a total audience of about 35 million each night. Millions of other viewers tune in Cable Network News (CNN), the Public Broadcasting System (PBS) and Fox. Some viewers watch C-Span and other cable and satellite systems.

In the realm of politics, television has changed the system, as noted previously. We now expect televised debates between presidential candidates. We expect to **see** the President, congressional and other political leaders at work. Appearances are all-important, or as one popular contemporary phrase has it, "appearance is reality." Many political news events are staged for prime time evening network news.

Campaigns are now characterized by brief 15-45 second commercials. Although many scholars deplore this, studies indicate that Americans get a good deal of information from these **"sound bites,"** slanted as they may be. To be a successful presidential, congressional or gubernatorial candidate at the beginning of the 21st Century, one must be reasonably good on television. He or she must also be skilled in short and direct communications.

Until recently, the three major television networks, CBS, NBC and ABC, dominated the evening news, capturing more than 90% of the viewing audience. Today, their dominance appears at an end. Americans have alternative sources of information, notably those provided by cable television. About 25% of Americans say that they are regular viewers of Cable Network News (CNN) and some 40% say they regularly watch network prime time new magazine shows.[24]

Prior to the Persian Gulf War of 1991, some major network employees sarcastically referred to CNN as the "Chicken Noodle Network." Due to its first-rate, professional job of covering that conflict, CNN made major inroads into the networks' regular viewing audience. The major networks never have fully recovered from it.

The average American home has a TV set turned on for an average of about seven hours each day. In our affluent society, most homes have at least two sets. Although many Americans are more interested in sports and entertainment programs, they do watch news programs as well. Historically, television has had a strong influence on public opinion. Pictures of the fighting, suffering and dying helped to turn public opinion against the Vietnam War. When CBS news anchor Walter Cronkite, then rated the "most trusted" figure in American media, returned from Vietnam and said the war was not winnable, President Johnson knew that the proverbial goose was cooked.

The televised Watergate hearings, in 1973, played a significant role in making voters aware of the magnitude of that scandal. Voters had paid little attention to the "third-rate burglary," as it was characterized by the White House, during the campaign of 1972. Today, TV coverage of congressional hearings, political debates and national party conventions conveys an immediacy that no other medium can match.

Television technology now enables us to see instant news from around the world. We see at first hand the horrors of Bosnia or of Belfast. We see bombings and hostage crises, plane crashes and earthquakes. We view natural disasters and man-made disasters alike.

Media critics who prefer "hard news" regret the advent of magazine-type news programs which focus on features and entertainment. These programs sometimes are called **"infotainment."**

Walter Cronkite, who, during the 1960s, was the dominant anchor on network television, has expressed his professional dismay at the programs featuring "happy talk" between news anchors. Cronkite has called it "vaudeonews," a combination of old time vaudeville and news programming.[25]

Cronkite, who was a print reporter for United Press before going into broadcasting also has been candid about television's inability to "educate" viewers.

TV news, he says, is nothing more than a headline service. The day's top news story probably will get two to two and a half minutes of air time. Most stories are more complicated than that. Cronkite argues that to be "educated" about public affairs, citizens must read newspapers for more detail. If they really are interested in a topic, he concludes, they should read books about it or take classes on the subject.

Americans will never forget the TV images, firmly "planted" in their heads by the terrorist attacks of September 11, 2001, or the invasion, conquest and subsequent "resistance" to the U.S. military in Iraq.

The television industry is highly competitive and time is literally money, lots of money. Ratings mean everything. Prices that networks can charge for commercials are dictated by the strength of their viewing audiences. Perhaps it is pandering, but "realists" in broadcasting will tell you that economic survival is what counts. Programs featuring arch-conservative icon Rush Limbaugh, Larry King and Oprah Winfrey are popular, if not preferred, by many media critics.

Network television reached its zenith in the 1980s, when about 85% of all local stations were affiliated with one of the three major networks. After government de-regulation of the cable industry in the 1970s, Americans began to change their viewing habits. By 1995, about two-thirds of American homes were receiving cable TV programs. The networks lost about 25% of their prime time viewing audiences. Despite this relative decline, network TV remains the largest single source of information for many Americans.

3. New Media

Before the presidential election of 1992, candidates were most likely to be seen on major network TV news programs. But in that year, candidates Bill Clinton and Ross Perot made major use of the so-called new media. Perot, in fact, announced his presidential candidacy on "Larry King Live." Clinton was angry at the major networks because they focused unduly, in his view, on allegations of adultery and draft dodging. Perot did not do well under sharp questioning from veteran network reporters. He came across as an antagonistic personality whose knowledge of current issues was limited.

To counteract this, Perot developed a 30-minute "infomercial" in which he lectured the nation, complete with pie charts, on the problem of the Federal deficit and other economic issues. Using this format, he did not have to answer any questions..

Clinton made extensive use of the "town meeting" format which excluded reporters, but gave citizens the opportunity to question the Democratic candidate on the issues of the day. He also appeared on Larry King's program and even played the saxophone on the Arsenio Hall show.

President Bush thought that this was "pandering," but, trailing in the polls, decided to also appear on 20/20 and a number of talk shows.

Recent presidential contenders have used entertainments programs to get their "messages"across. Giuliani declared his candidacy on the *Larry King* show. McCain and Obama were frequent guests on late night talk shows. Hillary Clinton, like the eventual major party presidential nominees, appeared on *Saturday Night Live.*

We cannot be sure where technological changes will take us in the future. It already is clear that the nontraditional media are changing the way Americans communicate information, including political data, to one another. The enormous popularity of the Internet and the World Wide Web may have an unforeseen impact on politics in the 21st Century.

The Obama campaign organization used the internet in 2008 as both a fund-raising and networking tool. It raised an estimated $750 million from more than three million contributors. It also developed an e-mail list of 13 million addresses and sent a billion messages. Obama also used You Tube effectively. His sophistication with new media gave him an advantage over McCain..

It may not be an overstatement to say that Obama created a new style of technology politics in 2008.

G. LOCAL AND ELITE MEDIA

One should note that there are important differences between local and so-called elite media. The latter refers to those reporters and editors who work for the major wire services, major newspapers (like The *New York Times, Washington Post* and the *Wall Street Journal*) and major broadcast networks.

There is an enormous range of quality and quantity in American newspapers. Major metropolitan dailies are able to pay their staffs well. They can and do attract the best talent in American journalism. Others papers publish in middle-sized and smaller markets. Some of them have better talent than they deserve. In part, this is because journalism is an overcrowded field. The old saying was "reporters are a dime a dozen." One editor recently disagreed. "No, they are only worth a nickel a dozen now," he said.

Typically, neophyte journalists "pay their dues" on smaller publications. If they have the ability and dedication, they may move up to a larger metropolitan publication. If not, they fall by the wayside, enter other occupations, or remain in what some journalists call the "minor leagues."

Major metropolitan dailies benefit from this. They are able to hire people who have experience and ability and have "made their mistakes elsewhere."

The same generalization may be made about broadcasting. Large stations in metropolitan areas can command the best talent and pay the best salaries. Middle and smaller market communities may have to settle for people with less talent and less experience. As is true with print news people, radio and TV news broadcasters tend to be highly mobile, moving "up the ladder" when opportunity presents itself.

One should note that many of the stories in major metropolitan dailies are written by the paper's own staff. Small and middle-sized publications may be inclined to rely on wire service copy to "fill the news hole."

Not infrequently, small market television stations advertise the 11 p.m. newscast as "local news," but then proceed to include several minutes of inconsequential "filler" material aired earlier in the day by the major networks. This, of course, saves them money. Assignment editors do not have to "dig" hard for local stories. They need not send reporters and camera crews out to cover the local community. But knowledgeable media consumers (news sophisticates) are not pleased by this kind of performance.

H. IS REPORTING BIASED?

Some critics contend that the press is biased. They also argue that it is inaccurate and unfair in its reporting of public issues. Some of this type of criticism stems from Conservatives who believe that the press is too Liberal and anti-establishment in its orientation. Conservatives argue that most working journalists (as distinct from their publishers) hold left-of-center perspectives that color their presentation of the news. Journalists are viewed as ideologically committed political actors whose reporting reflects their Liberal Democratic convictions.

In the past, Liberals complained that the press was guilty of a Conservative bias. In his 1952 campaign for President, Democrat Adlai E. Stevenson blasted the "one party, Republican press."

The press also has its left-wing as well as right-wing critics. They see the privately-owned American press as the "mouthpiece of corporate capitalism" who support big business domination of society. The major role of media, Michael Parenti writes, is "to continually recreate a view of reality supportive of existing social and economic class power." Parenti suggests that journalists are "mind managers," whose stories favor the powerful over the powerless and the Conservative establishment over outsiders who challenge it.[26]

In short, partisans and ideologues do not want their candidates or viewpoints portrayed in an unfavorable light. Reporters who write or broadcast "negative" stories are singled out for criticism. They are judged guilty of carrying ideological bias into the news-gathering process. Social scientists often speak of "selective perception." Briefly, the concept means that we see what we want to see, and reject information that does not conform to our own pre-existing bias. In the case of media critics, this concept is particularly relevant.

Is there any validity to the charges of bias? "Bias," as indicated, is like "beauty." It is largely in the eye of the beholder. In the newsroom, bias is one of the worst of dirty, four-letter words. But scientific studies are available on the issue. They indicate clearly that the press is more Liberal than the general public.

The *Los Angeles Times* did a nationwide survey of 2703 news and editorial staff members of 621 daily newspapers and 2993 members of the general public in 1985. The results were reported in an article by William Schneider and I.A. Lewis, "Views on the News," in *Public Opinion*.[27]

Less than one-fourth (23%) of the general public identified itself as "Liberal" to 55% of the press. Some 29% of the public said it was Conservative, while only 17% of journalists identified themselves with that label. Ronald Reagan enjoyed a 56% favorable rating with the public, while only 30% of journalists approved of the job he was doing as President. Some 60% of the press gave Reagan negative ratings, compared to only 27% of the public.

On social issues, journalists (82%) favored allowing women to have abortions, to 49% of the general public. While 74% of the public favored prayers in the public schools, only 25% of journalists did. Two thirds (67%) of journalists were opposed to permitting prayer in schools, to only 19% of the public.

On the issue of capital punishment, 75% of the public favored it; only 47% of journalists did. On the question of hiring homosexuals, 89% of the press agreed, while 55% of the public supported non-discrimination on the basis of sexual preference. On handgun controls, 78% of the press favored stricter laws, to 50% of the public.

The *Los Angeles Times* survey was only one of many such studies. Analysis of voting behavior of hundreds of reporters and broadcasters show that they cast ballots, in overwhelming proportions, for Democratic candidates from 1964-1980. Another (1992) study of 1400 journalists found that 44% of them identified with the Democratic Party and only 16% identified themselves as Republicans.[28]

More recently, a 2004 survey was undertaken by the Pew Research Center for the People and the Press in collaboration with the Projection for Excellence in Journalism and the Committee of Concerned Journalists.

It found that 34% of national journalists view themselves as Liberals, while only 9% called themselves Conservatives.

The American public appears to believe that the media are too Liberal. A Gallup Poll of September, 2004, asked:

"In general do you think that the news media are too liberal, just about right, or too conservative?"

Some 48% of respondents said, "too liberal." Another 33% said, "just right," while only 15% said, "too conservative."

A more important question than a reporter's "bias" is whether his or her news stories are biased. Anyone who has spent time working on a major metropolitan daily newspaper knows that editors constantly tell reporters to "keep yourself out of your copy."

Reporters' stories are placed under a microscope every day and, although complete "objectivity" may not be humanly possible, professionalism demands that journalists strive for accuracy. One also might note that editors tend to be more Conservative than reporters and sometimes "tone down" reporters' liberalism. They also are the "gatekeepers" who decide what goes in the paper and what goes on the air. In that sense, they have significant control over the public agenda.

Many members of the viewing and reading public do not view the media as merely a neutral bystander in the process of reporting news about government and politics. Reporters and editors are seen as a part of the political process. Because of its power, the press today has come under fire from government, politicians and their followers.

One of the highlights of the 1988 presidential campaign was a sharp exchange between Vice President Bush and CBS anchor Dan Rather. The Vice President was asked pointed questions about his role in the Reagan Administration's Iran-Contra scandal. Bush responded very aggressively. Shortly after their nine-minute clash, Rather drew heavy fire from Republicans and others. The attempt of some media to portray Vice President Bush as a "wimp" may have been one of the reasons for Bush's strong response. He came out of the broadcast as "Rambo" and went on to defeat Michael Dukakis.

President George W. Bush was the subject of a Rather report which resulted in the anchorman's "retirement." CBS aired a story, which did not meet its own standards for "sourcing." The President was accused of failing to meet his military obligations while a member of the Texas Air National Guard. Forged documents were a part of the controversy, which resulted in an independent (outside) panel investigating the matter.

Although contemporary journalists view themselves as professionals, critics disagree, pointing out that professionals must be licensed, as are physicians and lawyers. Even some journalists concede that they are not paid professional salaries. In its April 25, 1998, edition, *Editor & Publisher*, the newspaper trade journal, had an article headlined "Milking Cows Pays More Than Reporting." The reference was to pay levels of neophyte journalists.[29]

Whether journalism is a profession or a trade is debatable. Some could say it is an art form. But there are norms connected with every job and journalism is no exception. Critics sometimes forget this. Journalism students are taught in introductory reporting courses to be sure to include the five "Ws" in their copy, along with the one "H" (How) All stories should include who, what, when, where and why. Editors and reporters constantly decide what makes a story **"newsworthy"**. A story generally must be **timely.** If it's 24 hours old, it isn't news anymore. The "when" element in a story is of central importance. Sometimes newspapers and broadcasters neglect the "follow-up" story. A major Supreme Court decision may be a one-day story unless thoughtful editors and reporters follow up on it by getting legal experts and those impacted by the decision to comment on it.

The usual or routine is not news. As the old saying has it, dog bites man is not news; man bites dog is news. In American politics, media love the unpredictable, fast-breaking story. When Gary Hart, former divinity student, U.S. Senator and candidate for the 1988 Democratic presidential nomination, was revealed to have engaged in an extramarital adventure with model Donna Rice, that made "good copy." Pictures of Ms. Rice sitting on the candidate's lap on a yacht named Monkey Business appeared in several publications. It is **unusual,** to say the least, for would-be Presidents to engage in such reckless behavior in the post-Watergate era. "What" happened is basic to this and almost any other story. Although some accused the media of "unethical" conduct for reporting this "private" matter, others said the press did the right thing. Clearly, Senator Hart's judgment and character were appropriate topics of public debate. The bottom line was that his chances of becoming President were irreparably damaged. Some would say that was a good thing.

Drama and **conflict** make good news stories. Dramatic stories attract readers and viewers. Television, in particular, is well equipped to show the human element in fires, explosions, plane crashes and natural disasters. Beginning journalism students are taught that conflict is an important element in a news story. As in a novel, where antagonists are clearly identified and a confrontation follows, the story is more compelling. In politics, the conflicts between President and Congress are often institutional. But the media love to personalize the conflict and wrote about President George W. Bush and Congressional, particularly Senate, Democrats engaged in mortal political combat. After his "honeymoon" period is over, Obama may have the same problem, even if his party controls Congress.

Personalization is another key element of news. News is the story of people. The "who" element in journalism is basic; "names make news." The fact that a celebrity in politics, government, business, or entertainment may be involved in a story gives it an added dimension. *People* is one of the most widely read magazines in the nation today. Certain people are always newsworthy simply because of the positions they occupy. The President is newsworthy, as the leader of any government is to his nation's press. Pope Benedict XVI is news. So are many actors and actresses and professional athletes. In many cases, these people owe their celebrity to the media.

Famous individuals can make a story, but so can human interest. Stories in 1981 about returning American hostages, such as Terry Anderson, held captives by Iran for some 444 days, focused on their families and their adjustments to freedom.

The "where" element in news is important, so **proximity** is another criterion for news. The closer to home, the more likely a story will be covered. Often national news, unless of unusual importance, will be displaced by local stories in daily newspapers and local TV and radio stations.

Perhaps the one form of bias which is usually overlooked by the public is local "institutional bias." Newspapers often protect hometown industries. General Motors announced, in the early 1980s, that it was going to close a plant in Flint, MI, resulting in the loss of about 3600 jobs in the community. Flint already had been hard-hit by auto industry layoffs. But the *Flint Journal* "buried" the story deep inside another article which said that the Buick Division of GM was going to build a new small car in Flint. Unfortunately, this meant very little in the way of job opportunities for UAW members.[30]

Another professional norm which influences news judgment is the "why" element in the story. Since the 1960s, there has been a great increase in interpretative and investigative reporting. Purely objective reporting stressed "just the facts." Reporters often did not put the facts in context. Readers were expected to form their own conclusions from facts presented. That all changed in the 1960s, when news "analysis" was customary and expected.

The press not only reports what happened, but now interprets the meaning of events. In short, stories are placed in context and reporters speculate about the consequences of news events. How the news is interpreted is subject to much debate, as noted.

In the 1960s, as Professor Doris Graber points out in her book, *Mass Media and American Politics,* abortion was regarded almost universally as murder. The abortionist was a villain and, if a licensed physician, one who could and should lose his license to practice medicine. The physician also was subject to criminal prosecution and a possible prison sentence for committing this felony. The pregnant woman involved was considered an accomplice in a heinous crime. Today the media pictures the pregnant woman as one who is merely exercising a constitutional right to control her body and protect her health.

Why did public opinion change from this traditional portrait?

Graber retells the dramatic story of TV personality Sherri Finkbine, who had taken the drug thalidomide during her pregnancy. When Finkbine took the drug, its horrible effects on the fetus were unknown. Once she learned of the potential harm, and fearing a severely malformed baby, she had an abortion in 1962.[31]

Rather than reporting the action as murder, as had been customary, news media defended Finkbine's decision to terminate her pregnancy. By suggesting causes and relationships of events, media may shape opinions without telling their audiences what to believe. The way the Finkbine story was framed had much to do with public reaction to the event.

Later, of course, some states, like New York and Nevada, began to "liberalize" abortion laws. The issue began a topic of debate and was put on the ballot in several states, including Michigan, where voters, in 1972, rejected liberalized abortion by a margin of about 2-1. A year later, the U.S. Supreme Court legalized abortion in *Roe v. Wade.*

I . MEDIA ROLES AND IMPACT ON POLITICS

Historically, the mass media have been called upon to play a number of different roles in American society, although scholars differ in their listings and evaluation of these functions. The most basic media roles include the following:

1. Informing the public

Historically, classical liberalism has supplied the foundation on which Anglo-American press theory was built. This credo assumes that only a free press can enable citizens to discover and know the Truth. To have the Truth, citizens must have access to all available information and ideas. Out of the variety of information which news media provides, rational citizens can distinguish Truth from falsehood in the news of the day.

While readers will find falsehood among Truth, democrats (accepting the premises of the Enlightenment), conclude that if man is faithful to his reason, Truth will win any competition in the free marketplace of ideas. Democracies will make progress only through a process of free inquiry, discussion and persuasion, rather than from force and violence.

The authors of the First Amendment believed that it was unnecessary to restrict what the press could publish. Few reporters and editors will abuse freedom in their honest search for Truth. Some, inevitably, will distort the news. Some may even lie, but all ideas and all information will be put to the test of reason. Classical liberalism assumed that it was unnecessary to demand that the press pay the price of responsibility in exchange for its freedom. Most of the press, they reasoned, will be responsible without being asked. The rest can do no great harm.

2. Educating the public

Newspapers, magazines, the Internet, radio, television and films all play educational roles. We may not read print media or use electronic media primarily to be educated. The media clearly are no substitutes for books, libraries or classrooms. But the public does extend its intellectual horizons because we learn something new every day by being media consumers.

Readers and viewers need factual information from which they may reach rational conclusions about public policies and candidates.

Long ago, political leaders saw the press as a vehicle that they could use to educate the people about the democratic process. It was vital, they believed, to guarantee the success of the infant Republic. George Washington, in an address to Congress, stressed the importance of facilitating the circulation of "political intelligence and information" through the press. Congressional and other political leaders set postal rates for newspapers at minimal levels. Exchanges of newspapers between editors through the mails were allowed free of charge. Jefferson said that the best way to prevent unwise decisions by the public was to "give them full information of their affairs through the channel of the public papers, and to contrive that those papers should penetrate the whole mass of the people."[32]

Newspaper editors are fond of quoting Jefferson on the wisdom of a nation having a free press. In a widely-quoted letter, written in 1787 to Edward Carrington, Jefferson said, "The basis of governments being the opinions of the people, the first object should be to keep that right; and were it left to me to decide whether we should have a government without newspapers, or newspapers without a government, I should not hesitate a moment to prefer the latter. But I should mean that every man should receive those papers and be capable of reading them."[33]

Jefferson made many optimistic assumptions about human nature, as did most democratic philosophers. He would be overjoyed at literacy statistics in the U.S. today, compared to the early 19th Century. He would be delighted at the number of high school and college graduates turned out each year. But he might well be horrified to discover that most Americans just don't know much about politics.

Democratic government rests broadly on public opinion and it presupposes a well informed citizenry. But learning about public affairs is largely an individual responsibility. Information about public affairs is readily available to those who want it.

3. Critic of government and protector of liberty

The Constitution gave American publishers freedom because the Framers assumed that a free press would be a worthy handmaiden of liberty. Government, they believed, was the principal enemy of freedom and the "infant press" should be free to protect individual liberty against governmental infringements. A free press, they believed, would permit citizens to be censors of government.

Jefferson believed that the press should be a check on the government. Because individual liberty is the core of democracy, government must never be permitted to infringe the rights of citizens. The press, therefore, must perform important functions. It must safeguard personal liberties, serve as a watchdog and voice alarm whenever the rights of individuals are threatened or trampled.

As a result, public officials who rule arbitrarily can be deposed peacefully by public opinion rather than violently by revolution. In a letter to Washington in 1792, Jefferson wrote: "No government ought to be without censors; and where the press is free, no one ever will be. If virtuous, it need not fear the fair operations of attack and defense." In 1816, Jefferson wrote, "If a nation expects to be ignorant and free, in a state of civilization, it expects what never was and never will be. The functionaries of every government have propensities to command at will the liberty and property of their constituents. Where the press is free, and every man able to read, all is safe."[34]

Many of Jefferson's statements can be found on the mastheads of today's American newspapers, particularly his letter to Carrington.

Contemporary media have what is called an "adversarial relationship" with the government. Sometimes reporters become angry because government has lied to them. The question then becomes, "Why did the government lie?" If the motive is "pure," to protect military or intelligence operations, for example, the press may be forgiving. In fact, some publishers have withheld stories from publication at the request of Presidents in this area (JFK-*NY Times*, Bay of Pigs Invasion).

If, however, the motive is to cover up wrongdoing, to conceal a foreign policy mistake, or to gain partisan advantage by putting a favorable spin on the news, then the media reacts fiercely and the result may well be a lowering of public confidence in government, political leaders and political institutions.

4. Advertising

Publishers would list another economic function of the press, advertising, as of basic importance. Many of them, in fact, would place it first in importance because it helps them to make a profit. Failing that, they go out of business. Some media critics argue that many publishers place entirely too much emphasis on the amount of advertising lineage carried and too little emphasis on the number of columns of news. They argue that informing the public, educating it and promoting an understanding of American democracy all should supersede the advertising function. While some publishers would agree, many would not.

Some publishers are first and foremost hard-headed, bottom-line businessmen. They have grown up on the advertising or circulation side of the operation and tend to regard editorial departments as "non-productive," that is, non-revenue producing. While every reporter would deny the validity of this perspective, it remains true that many publishers are more concerned about advertising and circulation departments than they are the editorial department.

One cannot minimize the importance of the business end of the news business. In a free market economy and in a system of private ownership and operation of the press, it is indispensable. But it cannot perform many of the basic media roles which are so vital that the Framers of the First Amendment gave the news business its special, constitutionally-protected status.

5. Entertainment

Entertainment news is also important. Readership surveys indicate that comic strips, crossword puzzles, sports, gossip and advice columns all have higher readerships than do editorial pages. Features play a role in a well-balanced newspaper or television program. The current problem, in the view of some media critics, is that there are too many "fluff pieces" (features) and not enough "hard" news.

On any given day, editorial news space is limited. Various section editors vigorously compete for it at daily "budget" meetings, where city and metro editors debate the merits of their offerings with news, business and sports editors. Managing editors usually play referee. When the news hole is "tight," fluff should not win out.

Educators and others often express shock and dismay when told that average adult Americans spend about 30 hours each week in front of their television sets. Children spend even more time watching their favorite programs. And what do they watch? Any examination of TV ratings, such as the Nielsen system, shows clearly that it isn't education that's keeping the tube going.

College professors complain that today's students are the TV generation, but so was their parents' generation. It is commonly charged that today's collegians don't read as much as students of yesterday and that they complain when given two-thirds or three-fourths of the work assigned to students a generation ago.

J. THE FOURTH BRANCH OF GOVERNMENT?

The "power of the press" is very real. Presidents and presidential candidates respect and may even fear it. Members of Congress are aware that their policies, politics and character can all be put under a microscope. Not only their policies, but their motives can be questioned. Even Federal judges and the Supreme Court is not immune from press criticism.

This is precisely what the Framers of the Constitution intended. It was not so important for the press to be responsible as it was for the press to be free. Some political writers have referred to the power of the press as so real that it constitutes "the fourth branch of government."[35]

1. The President

In the world of political journalism, the President is clearly first among equals. Baraack Obama is news. The major networks all maintain full-time White House correspondents. He can address the nation whenever he wishes and usually the networks will give him free air time to do so. Presidential news secretaries have daily briefing sessions for the media.

From the media perspective, it is much easier to focus on one individual than on an institution like Congress, with its 535 individual egos and personalities. In short, the President is without peer in his ability to command press coverage. If skilled in the arts of communication and persuasion, the contemporary President can use print and TV media to publicize and advertise his administration and its programs.

There are enormous publicity powers in the White House. If it calls a news conference, hundreds of reporters will hurry to the scene. Such meetings have changed greatly over the years. Today, they are a far cry from the days of President Hoover, who insisted that reporters submit their questions to him in writing and in advance of the conference. Hoover said: "The President of the United States will not stand and be questioned like a chicken thief by men whose names he does not even know.[36]

Franklin Roosevelt revolutionized the news conference. He promised reporters two press conferences a week and delivered them, despite the Great Depression and World War II. He also was the first Chief Executive to permit "direct quotes." Truman lacked FDR's charismatic personality, but got along well with the "working press." His dislike of Republican publishers, however, was widely known.

Eisenhower believed that news conferences were to be endured, not enjoyed. His rambling syntax was a source of constant frustration to reporters, as was his habit of referring questions to subordinates.

Kennedy introduced the "live, televised news conference." No President since has departed from it, although few have done as well as JFK. His TV personality and sense of humor always won him high marks with the White House press corps. Johnson and Nixon were less inclined to meet the press very often, particularly after the escalation of the Vietnam War and, in Nixon's case, the Watergate crisis.

Ford and Carter broke relatively little new ground, but Reagan and the first President Bush began to take "the show" on the road. They concluded that hometown editors and reporters were less hostile than the White House Press corps and preferred to get to America's heartland and out of the Washington "Beltway" on occasion.

One veteran Washington reporter described this saturation coverage of the White House "beat" as follows: "...No television idol, ax-murderer, or foreign head of state lives in the glare of continual publicity that is the accepted fate of our President. His ordinary habits of work and play are the grist of ever-fresh "news" from the White House. His most minor indisposition turns the place into a mecca for journalistic pilgrims prepared to maintain a 24-hour-a day vigil until the sickness passes. Even the bowel movements of an ailing Chief Executive (Eisenhower) has been considered fit subject for a press communique."[37]

All Presidents, from George Washington to Barack Obama, have tried to influence the news. Lyndon Johnson, prior to the escalation of the Vietnam War, hugged reporters to his bosom and overwhelmed them with facts he wanted them to print. John F. Kennedy often used a variety of forms of "social flattery." Richard Nixon was so angered at his press coverage that he developed an "enemies list." On the list were such names as *Washington Post* publisher Katherine Graham and NBC anchor David Brinkley.

In its December 2, 1968, issue, *U.S. News & World Report* (pp. 39-40) ran an article by Crosby S. Noyes of the *Washington Evening Star* headlined "Will the Press Be Out To Get Nixon?" This was less than a month before Nixon's inauguration as President. Noyes wrote, "When it comes to its treatment of Presidents, the American press is a monster...An important segment of the press apparently has come to feel that it has a God-given mission to frustrate, hamstring and finally destroy the men...chosen to lead the nation...the greatest problem and hazard of them all confronting the Nixon Administration probably will be the American press."[38]

Some Nixon apologists insist that the Noyes' prophecy came true because the press "got Nixon." The view of most Americans is that Nixon, through criminal acts associated with Watergate, was the one who got Nixon.

Presidents are concerned about the media because it does set the political agenda. It may not tell us what to think, but it often tells us what to think about. How? It does this simply by choosing to focus on certain public issues and ignore others. Presidential ability to lead the nation is related to the state of public opinion. Opinion, in turn, is related to what issues the media choose to emphasize.

Theodore Sorenson, speech writer and adviser to President Kennedy, once wrote, "...A President...must remember that public opinion and public interest do not always agree. The value to this nation of a foreign aid program, for example, is not determined by its popularity...

...The President) has a responsibility to lead public opinion as well as to respect it—to shape it—to inform it, to woo it, and win it. It can be his sword as well as his compass...

...Every President must...be a keen judge of public opinion. He must be able to distinguish its petty whims, to estimate its endurance, to respond to its impatience and to respect its potential power. He must know how best and how often he can appeal to the public—and when it is better left undisturbed."[39]

Presidents are not always able to live in harmony with the press. Indeed that may be impossible, as suggested by Pierre Salinger, former news secretary to Presidents Kennedy and Johnson. Salinger comments, "No two institutions in the country have a more important relationship than the government of the United States and the press. Each is powerful and each has almost inexhaustible resources.

Despite periodical phases of relative calm, the government and the press, in the last analysis, cannot expect to live happily together. No President in our history has emerged from his term or terms of office without having some major disagreements with the press. And no President in our history has escaped the periodic attacks of an outraged press.

The basic reason for the controversy between press and the President is the fact that the objectives of the two institutions collide. The press, rooted in American history, and a tradition of freedom, attempts to find and report every single piece of information. The government naturally wishes to present its programs and positions in the best possible light. It therefore resists—sometimes rightly and sometimes wrongly—the pressures brought on it by the press. The struggle between government and the press becomes more difficult in the areas of national security[40]

Kennedy and his successors had trouble with the press in the area of national security. When the *New York Times* became critical of JFK's Vietnam policy, Kennedy sarcastically referred to the conflict as "Halberstam's war," implying that David Halberstam's stories from the war front were inaccurate. The Times stood firm and eventually it was proved that information given the public by Halberstam was more accurate than that given by the White House.

Johnson and Nixon's difficulties with the press in its reporting of the escalating Southeast Asian story are well known. The Nixon Administration even went to the U.S. Federal courts in an effort to prevent the *New York Times* and the *Washington Post* from publishing the "Pentagon Papers." That was extraordinary in that it involved a case of **prior restraint.**

The Pentagon Papers were classified Defense Department documents stolen by one Daniel Elsberg and leaked to the *Times.* These secret government documents outlined the history of U.S. policy in Vietnam and showed that the Johnson Administration misled the nation on its Southeast Asian policy objectives.

Prior restraint ordinarily is barred by the First Amendment. It is an old principle of Anglo-American law that the government may not impose a prior restraint (pre-publication restraint) on the press. In *Near v. Minnesota*, the nation's highest tribunal had underlined the importance of that concept.

The Nixon Administration won the first round in Federal District Courts in New York and in Washington, D.C. Judges granted temporary restraining orders, barring the newspapers from publishing the articles. But the papers appealed to the Supreme Court.

The administration argued that the series of articles, published first in the *New York Times*, then later in the *Washington Post,* should be permanently halted because they jeopardized national security. The Supreme Court did not agree, holding that, while embarrassing and possibly even damaging to U.S. relations with its allies, they did not contain the kind of sensitive information which would threaten the nation's security.[41]

One could advance an argument that Nixon had more problems with the press than any other President in recent history. But he was not alone in his struggles with the Fourth Estate. Presidents Ford, Carter, Reagan, George Herbert Walker Bush, Clinton and George W. Bush also have had their difficulties.

Ford had a good press until he pardoned Nixon. Then the media turned on him. A graceful athlete and ardent ski enthusiast, Ford was given precisely the opposite "image" by the media. Television created an image in the public mind of the President stumbling as he got off Air Force One. Presidential pratfalls became a standing joke on "Saturday Night Live."

Carter had his "honeymoon period" with the press. But, in time, they became his adversary too. Stories about the incompetence of the "Georgia Mafia" in the White House and misbehavior by his aides appeared in the *New York Times* and *Washington Post.* Hamilton Jordan, White House Chief of Staff, was accused of snorting cocaine in New York's Studio 57, a disco bar, and of spitting Amaretto down the blouse of a young woman who rejected his sexual advances in a Washington night club. He also was accused by gossip columnist Sally Quinn of insulting the wife of the Egyptian ambassador.

All of these stories of alleged personal misconduct were bad enough. Then came the energy crisis, characterized by Carter as the most important problem Americans would face in their lifetimes. The President's inability to get a national energy policy through Congress drew fire from the media, as well as the public. Even some fellow Democrats complained that the administration did not understand how Congress worked.

The proverbial "last straw" was the seizure of Americans in the U.S. embassy in Teheran by Iranian revolutionaries. The President first exhausted every diplomatic effort to secure their release. In the spring of 1980, his patience exhausted, Carter resorted to military means. But the mission ended in catastrophic failure as American helicopters crashed in the dessert.

Secretary of State Cyrus Vance resigned because he disagreed with the military action. The President's popularity fell to the lowest figure ever recorded in the history of opinion polls. Only 18% of the American public approved of the job Carter was doing as President.

The release of the hostages became a major issue in the campaign of 1980. It did not help Carter that Walter Cronkite signed off his broadcast every night with a reminder: "This has been day number (fill in blank) of captivity for the American hostages in Iran." The number was to reach 444 before they were released.[42]

Reagan had charisma. As a professional actor, he knew how to use television effectively. But he disliked the direct confrontation of live presidential news conferences. The media grumbled when the number of press conferences diminished. Stories of ethical lapses among administration officials, followed by the Iran-Contra scandal, may have had larger results had the American public not liked the President. Reagan's popularity always remained relatively high. Pat Schroeder, an unhappy Colorado Democratic congresswoman, coined the phrase "the teflon President." Whatever anybody said in the media, nothing stuck to this President.

One of the most dramatic stories of the Reagan years occurred shortly after he assumed office. The President was shot by an emotionally disturbed, would-be assassin named John Hinckley on March 30, 1981. Rushed to George Washington Hospital, Reagan underwent surgery for removal of a bullet that had lodged within an inch of his heart. It also missed the vital aorta by one inch.

According to published reports, when he was wheeled into the operating room, the President jokingly asked his surgeon, "Are you a Democrat or a Republican?" The response was: "Mr. President, today we are all Americans." The grace and courage exhibited in those circumstances won a great deal of support for the then-new President.[43]

A common media theme during the Reagan presidency was that the people liked the President, but not his policies. Why then was he re-elected in 1984 and his Vice President George Bush chosen as his successor in 1988?

Some political scientists speculate that the American voter cares more about results than he does about ideology. In 1980, many people were more anxious to vote Carter out than to vote Reagan in, according to this theory. In both 1984 and 1988, it was hard to beat peace and prosperity, both of which the nation was enjoying under the Reagan Administration. Perceiving an economic decline in 1992, the electorate replaced Bush with Clinton.

Bush enjoyed a very good press after the Persian Gulf War. He broke all previous poll records for presidential popularity. Some 91% of the public approved of the job he was doing. Bush's future looked bright. But he was voted out of office the next year. Part of the explanation for this decline in public esteem lies in media stories about the state of the nation's economy. It was reported to be in dismal shape. Objective analysts seriously disputed this. But Bush was no "great communicator." He was ineffective on TV. He had a "preppie" image. He was an Ivy Leaguer, something of an aristocrat with whom the average citizen had trouble identifying. Clinton also had attended exclusive private schools, Georgetown, Oxford and Yale Law School, but he seemed more down-to-earth and clearly used the media more effectively than Bush.

In President Clinton's case, we are too close to the forest to see the proverbial trees. Nonetheless, many media critics believe that it had devoted too much attention to his personal life and problems and too little attention to his policy initiatives.

Although his election coverage was favorable, Clinton enjoyed only a brief "honeymoon" with the media. Some congressional Democrats thought that his health care plan was "too much, too soon." His efforts to sell it on Capitol Hill brought defeat, although his party had comfortable majorities in both House and Senate. His economic stimulus package was rejected. His first budget passed the Senate by only one vote. By July, 1993, he had the lowest approval rating of any new President in modern history.

Clinton had been in the White House only a few months when Americans began reading and viewing stories about the President and his wife being involved in financial improprieties as partners in the Whitewater Land Development Corporation. White House Aide Vince Foster's suicide drew heavy media attention. Reporters told about parties involving Hollywood stars like Sharon Stone. Hillary Clinton's investments, and old-fashioned spoils politics in the firing of members of the White House travel office came under scrutiny. Later, Clinton's alleged womanizing created headlines and the names of Gennifer Flowers, Paula Jones and Monica Lewinsky became familiar to the public.

The Clinton Administration was intensely aware of the importance of media. James Fallows, a former White House official, had written, "...When I was here, absolutely nothing was more important than figuring what the news was going to be...When you put together a press that is only interested in 'horse race' and 'inside baseball' and a White House staff that is interested only in the press, you've got the worst of both worlds."[44]

Ari Fleischer, President George W. Bush's first news secretary, published a book on his White House experiences.

If the press has a bias, Fleischer says, it is a bias in favor of conflict:[45]

"...Many Republicans, especially conservatives, believe that the press are Liberals who oppose Republicans and Republican ideas. I think there's an element of truth to that, but it is complicated, secondary and often nuanced. More important, the press's first and most pressing bias is in favor of conflict and fighting. That's especially the case for the White House press corps.

If the press finds someone fighting, they love it and they cover it. If people aren't fighting, the press are pretty good at getting them to fight. If they find a small conflict, they're skilled at making it into a larger conflict, one they can increasingly cover as the sparks fly.

If someone, anyone, from any political party, is in trouble, the press wants to know if the person is going to be fired. If not, the press wants to know why not. The political realm isn't the only place in the press where reporters love conflict; they love it anywhere they can find it. Head coaches and managers as well as athletes and, increasingly, business people, are often treated with the same conflict- driven focus..."

2. Congress

The congressional "beat" is a more difficult and less prestigious assignment for a journalist than is the White House. The very size of the institution (535 members) makes it difficult to cover. It is highly decentralized with its bicameral structure and large number of committees and subcommittees. Consequently, the media focuses its attention on the party leaders. The Speaker of the House, the majority and minority leaders of House and Senate and key committee chairs usually get the lion's share of publicity.

Local newspapers will try, if they have a Washington correspondent, to cover their local representatives and the state's two senators. But this is not always easy, particularly when they are not senior members or do not have key leadership positions in Congress. Nonetheless, stories published in their home district newspapers are of vital importance to individual members of Congress.

Congress may draw network TV cameras when it holds a sensational series of committee hearings, such as those chaired by Senators Kefauver (Organized Crime) and McCarthy (Domestic Communism) in the 1950s. The Watergate committees in the 1970s, chaired by Senator Ervin and Representative Rodino, and the Bork and Thomas Supreme Court confirmation hearings of the Judiciary Committees in the 1980s, also drew large audiences. But such hearings are the exception, not the rule.

C-Span is available today for those cable viewers who like to watch "routine" procedures of the House and Senate "live." But relatively few Americans bother to tune in.

Senator J. William Fulbright (D., AR) complained a generation ago that, "Television has done as much to expand the powers of the President as would a constitutional amendment formally abolishing the co-equality of the three branches of government."[46]

3. Courts

Of the three major organs of national government, the Federal courts have been least thoroughly covered. In part, this is because U.S. courts do not permit TV cameras in the courtroom. Consequently, they receive little coverage. Major decisions of the U.S. Supreme Court are duly reported, if not in much detail. Television viewers can hear reporters give second-hand accounts of what happened in major Federal District Court trials, such as those of the Oklahoma City bombers. But they cannot see it happen.

Federal judges, including Supreme Court justices, maintain low profiles. They almost never hold news conferences and seldom give interviews to the media. About the only exception to this rule is that justices may meet the press when they retire. Supreme Court employees are specifically forbidden from talking with reporters. Federal judges do not want to take positions which might suggest that they are less than impartial. Bob Woodward, now an editor at the *Washington Post,* complains: "The courts are a political institution and we don't cover them as such."[47]

Some attribute "judicial aloofness" to elitism. Others say it simply represents an effort on the part of judges to maintain their image. They are perceived as members of an institution resolving disputes on the basis of law, rather than politics. Although Supreme Court justices are aware of the nature and direction of public opinion, they do not follow it. Federal judges do not run for office.

Unlike Federal judges who enjoy tenure for "life or good behavior," state and local judges are usually elected. Consequently, they are not as "shy" about media contact.

Until recently, cameras also were prohibited in state and local courts. But gradually that has changed. In *Estes v. Texas* 381 U.S. 532 (1965), the U.S. Supreme Court ruled that coverage of a criminal trial denied the defendant his constitutional right to a fair trial. That decision was overruled in *Chandler v. Florida* 449 U.S. 560 (1981), enabling states to experiment with live coverage of criminal trials.

One of the most famous—some would say infamous—examples of widespread coverage of a state criminal trial was the O. J. Simpson murder case. Televised trials are gradually becoming more common in state and local courtrooms, although judges retain their discretion to keep cameras out. The cameras were excluded from the second O. J. Simpson case (civil damages trial) and it was very different from the first. In the eyes of some critics, that was "a media circus."

Since Watergate, the media has shifted its focus in covering the three branches of government. "Investigative reporting" came into vogue after Bob Woodward and Carl Bernstein of the *Washington Post* won the Pulitzer prize for their exposure of wrongdoing in high places. Old time editors shook their heads and argued that the term was redundant. "All good reporters are investigative reporters," they said.

But the Woodward-Bernstein legacy lives on. Enrollments, until the meltdown of the newspaper industry, multiplied at the nation's journalism schools. There are many more would-be Woodwards and Bernsteins than there are newsroom jobs for them. The advent of Computer-Assisted Reporting has opened the doors for sophisticated reporters and editors. They now can dig deeper into public records than ever before. Potential stories of "wrongdoing" are always on their minds.

The public appears to have a somewhat ambivalent attitude toward the media. On the one hand, no one likes a "watchdog" press that sometimes "barks" without reason. On the other hand, they understand that the media enters into the checks and balances equation. If given a choice, most Americans probably would prefer too much information, rather than not enough.

As we have seen, Congress checks the President and the President checks Congress. The Court checks both the executive and legislative branches. It is the media, however, that throws the spotlight of publicity on the activities of all public officials. Reporters understand that the public has a "right to know" about the conduct and policies of its government.

A vigilant press hopes that it serves the public interest by creating a more responsive and responsible democratic government.

That may well be precisely what Thomas Jefferson and the architects of the First Amendment had in mind.

SELECTED BIBLIOGRAPHY

Abraham, Henry J. *Justices and President: A Political History of Appointments to the Supreme Court*, 3rd ed. New York: Oxford University Press, 1992.

Altschull, J. Herbert. *Agents of Power: The Media and Public Policy*. New York: Longman, 1995.

Ansolabehere, Stephen, Roy Behr and Shanto Iyengar. *The Media Game: American Politics in the* Television Age. New York: Macmillan, 1993.

Barber, James D. *The Pulse of Politics: Electing Presidents in the Media Age*. New York: W.W. Norton & Co., 1980.

-------- *The Presidential Character*, 4th ed. Englewood Cliffs, N.J.: Prentice-Hall, 1992.

Baum, Lawrence. *The Supreme Court*. 5th ed. Washington, D.C.: Congressional Quarterly Press, 1994.

Beard, Charles. *An Economic Interpretation of the Constitution of the United States*. New York: Macmillan, 1913.

Berry, Jeffrey M. *The Interest Group Society*. 3rd ed. New York: Longman, 1997.

Beck, Paul A. *Party Politics in America*, 8th ed. New York: Free Press, 1995.

Becker, Carl. *The Declaration of Independence. A Study in the History of Political Ideas*. New York: Alfred A. Knopf, 1942.

Beer, Samuel H. *To Make a Nation: The Rediscovery of American Federalism*. Cambridge, MA.: Harvard University Press, 1993.

Blanchard, Robert O., *Congress and the News Media*. New York: Hastings House, 1974.

Blasi, Vincent. *The Burger Court: The Counter-Revolution That Wasn't*. New Haven: Yale University Press, 1983.

Bork, Robert. *The Tempting of America: The Political Seduction of the Law:* New York: Free Press, 1990.

Bowen, Catherine D. *Miracle at Philadelphia*. Boston: Atlantic-Little Brown, 1966.

Braestrup, Peter. *Big Story: How the American Press and Television Reported and Interpreted the Crisis of Tet 1968 in Vietnam and Washington*. Abridged ed. Novato, CA: Presidio, 1994.

Brezinski, Zbigniew. *Between Two Ages: America's Role in the Technetronic Era*. New York: Viking Press, 1970.

Brinkley, David. *Washington Goes to War*. New York: Knopf, 1988.

-------- *A Memoir*. New York: Knopf, 1995.

Bryce, James. *Modern Democracies*. New York: Macmillan, 1921.

Burns, James M. *Roosevelt: The Lion and the Fox*. New York: Harcourt Brace, 1956.

Cannon, Lou. *President Reagan: The Role of a Lifetime*. New York: Simon & Schuster, 1991.

Cater, Douglas. *The Fourth Branch of Government*. Boston: Houghton Mifflin, 1959.

Cigler, Allan J. and Burdett A. Loomis, eds. *Interest Group Politics*. Washington, D.C.: Congressional Quarterly Press, 1983.

Clawson, Dan, Alan Neustadt and Denise Scott. *Money Talks: Corporate PACs and Political Influence*. New York: Basic Books, 1992.

Clinton, Bill and Al Gore, *Putting People First: How We All Can Change America*. New York: Times Books, 1992.

Cohen, Richard. *Changing Course in Washington*. New York: Macmillan, 1994.

Cornwell, Elmer E., Jr. *Presidential Leadership of Public Opinion*. Bloomington: Indiana University Press, 1965.

Corwin, Edward and J.W. Peltason. *Corwin & Peltason's Understanding the Constitution,* 13th ed. Ft. Worth: Harcourt Brace, 1994.

Crabb, Cecil V. and Kevein V. Mulcahy. *Presidents and Foreign Policymaking: From FDR to Reagan*. Baton Rouge: Louisiana State University Press, 1986.

Dahl, Robert A. *Democracy and Its Critics*. New Haven, CT: Yale University Press, 1989.

-------- *Democracy, Liberty, Equality*. New York: Oxford University Press, 1987.

Davis, Richard. *The Press and American Politics*. 2nd ed. Upper Saddle River, NJ: Prentice-Hall, 1996.

-------- *Decision and Images: The Supreme Court and the Press*. Upper Saddle River, NJ: Prentice-Hall, 1996.

Delli Carpini, Michael X., and Scott Keeter. *What Americans Know About Politics and Why It Matt*ers. New Haven, CT: Yale University Press, 1996.

Dionne, E.J., Jr. *Why Americans Hate Politics*. New York: Simon & Schuster, 1991.

Drew, Elizabeth. *Showdown: The Struggle between the Gingrich Congress and the Clinton White House.* New York: Simon & Schuster, 1997.

-------- *On the Edge: The Clinton Presidency.* New York: Simon & Schuster, 1994.

Dye, Thomas R. *American Federalism: Competition Among Governments.* Lexington, MA: Lexington Books, 1990.

-------- Harmon Ziegler and S. Robert Lichter. *American Politics in the Mass Media Age, 4th ed.* Pacific Grove, CA: Brooks/Cole, 1992.

Eisenhower, Dwight D. *Mandate For Change.* Garden City, NY: Doubleday, 1963.

-------- *Waging Peace.* Garden City, NY: Doubleday and Company, 1965.

Emery, Edwin and Michael Emery. *The Press in America,* 5th ed. Englewood Cliffs, NJ: Prentice-Hall, 1984.

Exoo, Calvin F. *The Politics of the Mass Media.* Minneapolis/St. Paul: West Publishing Co., 1994.

Fisher, Louis. *The Politics of Shared Power: Congress and the Executive,* 3rd ed. Washington, D.C.: Congressional Quarterly Press, 1993.

Fitzwater, Marlin. *Call the Briefing! Reagan and Bush, Sam and Helen: A Decade with Presidents and the Press.* New York: Times Books, 1995.

Fleischer, Ari, *Taking Heat: The President, the Press and My Years in the White House.* New York: William Morrow, 2005.

Galbraith, John Kenneth. *The Anatomy of Power.* Boston: Houghton Mifflin, 1983.

-------- *American Capitalism: The Concept of Countervailing Power.* Boston: Houghton Mifflin, 1956.

Germond, Jack and Jules Witcover. *Mad as Hell: Revolt at the Ballot Box, 1992.* New York: Warner Books, 1993.

Gingrich, Newt. *Lessons Learned The Hard Way: A Personal Report.* New York: Harper Collins, 1998.

-------- and Rep. Dick Armey. *Contract With America.* New York: Times Books, 1994.

Ginsberg, Benjamin and Alan Stone. *Do Elections Matter?* 3rd ed. Armonk, NY.: M.E. Sharpe, 1996.

Goldberg, Bernard. *Bias: A CBS Insider Exposes How the Media Distort the News.* Washington, D.C.: Regnery Publishing, 2001.

--------*Arrogance: Rescuing America from the Media Elite.* New York: Warner Books, 2003.

Goldberg, Gertrude S. and Eleanor Kremen, eds. *The Feminization of Poverty: Only in America?* New York: Greenwood, 1990.

Goldman, Peter, Thomas DeFrank, Mark Miller, Andrew Murr and Tom Matthews. *Quest for the Presidency, 1992.* College Station, TX: Texas A&M Press, 1994.

Goodwin, Doris Kearns. *No Ordinary Time.* New York: Simon & Schuster, 1994.

Graber, Doris A. *Processing the News: How People Tame the Information Tide.* 2nd ed. New York: Longman, 1988.

-------- *Media Power in Politics*, 5th ed. Washington, D.C.: Congressional Quarterly Press, 2007.

-------- *Mass Media and American Politics,* 7th ed. Washington, D.C.: Congressional Quarterly Press, 2005.

Hennessy, Bernard. *Public Opinion.* Belmont, CA: Wadsworth, 1965.

Herrnson, Paul S. *Congressional Elections.* Washington, D.C.: Congressional Quarterly Press, 1995.

Hess, Stephen. *Presidents and the Presidency.* Washington, D.C.: Brookings Institution, 1996.

-------- *Live from Capitol Hill: Studies of Congress and the Media.* Washington, D.C.: Brookings *Institution, 1991.*

Hofstadter, Richard F. *The American Political Tradition.* New York: Vintage Books, 1948.

Hughes, Charles Evans. *The Supreme Court of the United States.* New York: Columbia University Press, 1928.

Johnson, Haynes. *In the Absence of Power.* New York: Viking Press, 1980.

Johnson, Lyndon B. *The Vantage Point.* New York: Holt, Rinehart and Winston, 1971.

Kennedy, John F. *Profiles in Courage,* Inaugural edition. New York: Harper, 1961.

-------- *The Burden and the Glory.* Alan Nevins, ed. New York: Harper & Row, 1964.

Kessler, Ronald. *Inside Congress.* New York: Simon & Schuster, 1997.

Key, V.O. *Politics, Parties, and Pressure Groups*, 4th ed. New York: Thomas Y. Crowell Company, 1958.

-------- *Public Opinion and American Democracy*. New York: Knopf, 1963.

Koenig, Louis W. *The Chief Executive*, 6th ed. Ft. Worth: Harcourt Brace College Publishers, 1996

Lasswell, Harold. *Politics: Who Gets What, When and How*. New York: Free Press, 1936.

Lavrakas, Paul J. and Jack K. Holley, eds. *Polling and Presidential Election Coverage*. Newberry Park, CA: Sage Publications, 1991.

Link, Arthur. *Woodrow Wilson and a Revolutionary World, 1913-1921*. Chapel Hill: University of North Carolina Press, 1982.

Lippmann, Walter. *The Public Philosophy*. New York: Harcourt Brace, 1922.

Nelson, Michael. *The Elections of 1996*. Washington, D.C.: Congressional Quarterly Press, 1997.

Neustadt, Richard E. *Presidential Power*. Rev. ed. New York: Wiley, 1980.

-------- *Presidential Power and Modern Presidents*. New York: Free Press, 1991.

Mackenzie, G. Calvin and Saranna Thornton, *Bucking the Deficit: Economic Policymaking in America*, 2nd ed. Boulder, CO: Westview Press, 1996.

Mansbridge, Jane. *Why We Lost the ERA*. Chicago: University of Chicago Press, 1986.

Maraniss, David. *First In His Class: A Biography of Bill Clinton*. New York: Simon & Schuster, 1995.

Margolis, Michael and Gary A. Mauser, *Manipulating Public Opinion*. Pacific Grove, CA: Brooks/Cole, 1989.

McCain, John, with Mark Salter. *Faith of my Fathers*. New York: Random House, 1999.

McCloskey, Robert F. *The American Supreme Court*, 4th ed., Chicago: University of Chicago Press, 2005.

McCulloch, David. *Truman*. New York: Simon & Schuster, 1992.

McGinnis, Joe. *The Selling of the President 1968*. New York: Trident Press, 1969.

Mears, Walter R. *Deadlines Past: Forty Years of Presidential Campaigning: A Reporter's Story*. Kansas City, MO: Andrews McMeel Publishing, 2003.

Mendell, David. *Obama: from promise to power.* New York: Harper Collins, 2007.

Miller, Nathan. *Star Spangled Men: America's 10 Worst Presidents.* New York: Scribner, 1998.

Mills, C. Wright. *The Power Elite.* New York: Oxford University Press, 1956.

Morris, Richard B. *Alexander Hamilton and the Founding of the Nation.* New York: The Dial Press, 1957.

Mott, Frank Luther. *American Journalism,* 1690-1940. New York: Macmillan, 1941.

Mueller, John. *Policy and Opinion in the Gulf War.* Chicago: University of Chicago Press, 1994.

Nelson, Michael, ed. *The Elections of 2008.* Washington, D.C.: CQ Press, 2010.

Obama, Barack. *The Audacity of Hope.* New York: Crown Publications, 2006.

O'Brien, David. Storm Center: *The Supreme Court in American Politics,* 4th ed. New York: Norton, 1996.

Patterson, Thomas E. *Out of Order.* New York: Knopf, 1993.

Perot, Ross. *United We Stand: How We Can Take Back Our Country.* New York: Hyperion, 1992.

Peterson, Paul. *The Price of Federalism.* Washington, D.C.: Brookings Institution, 1995.

Pfiffner, James P. *The Modern Presidency.* New York: St. Martin's Press, 1994.

Pika, Joseph A. and Richard A. Watson. *The Presidential Contest.* Washington, D.C.: Congressional Quarterly Press, 1997.

Pollard, James. *The Presidents and the Press.* New York: Macmillan, 1947.

-------- *The Presidents and the Press: Truman to Johnson.* Washington, D.C.: Public Affairs Press, 1964.

Posner, Richard A. *An Affair of State: The Investigation, Impeachment, and Trial of President Clinton.* Cambridge, MA: Harvard University Press, 1999.

Powell, Jody. *The Other Side of the Story.* New York: William Morrow & Co., 1984.

Powell, Norman. Anatomy of Public Opinion. New York: Prentice-Hall. 1951.

Reedy, George. *The Twilight of the Presidency.* New York: World Publishing Co., 1970.

Renshon, Stanley A. *High Hopes: The Clinton Presidency and the Politics of Ambition.* New York: New York University Press, 1996.

Reston, James. *The Artillery of the Press.* New York: Harper & Row, 1967.

-------- *Deadline: A Memoir.* New York: Random House, 1991.

Rhodes, John. *The Futile System.* New York: Doubleday & Company, 1976.

Roosevelt, Theodore. *An Autobiography.* New York: MacMillan, 1916.

Rossiter, Clinton. *Conservatism in America.* New York: Knopf, 1956.

Royko, Mike,. *Boss: Richard J. Daley of Chicago.* New York: Dutton, 1971.

Rubin, Bernard. *Political Television.* Belmont, CA: Wadsworth, 1967.

Russell, Bertrand. *Philosophy and Politics.* London: Cambridge University Press, 1947.

Salinger, Pierre. *With Kennedy.* Garden City, NY: Doubleday & Co., 1966.

Samuelson, Robert. *The Good Life and Its Discontents.* New York: Random House, 1995.

Schattschneider, E.E. *Party Government.* New York: Holt, 1942.

Schlesinger, Arthur M. Jr. *The Politics of Upheaval.* Boston: Houghton Mifflin, 1960.

-------- *A Thousand Days: John F. Kennedy in the White House.* Boston: Houghton Mifflin, 1965.

-------- *The Imperial Presidency.* Boston: Houghton Mifflin, 1973.

Schwartz, Bernard. *A History of the Supreme Court.* New York: Oxford University Press, 1995.

Shively, W. Phillips. *Power & Choice.*, 4th ed. New York: McGraw-Hill, 1995.

Skidmore, Max J. *American Political Thought.* New York: St. Martin's Press, 1978.

Smith, Hedrick. *The Power Game: How Washington Works.* New York: Random House, 1988.

Sobel, Lester A., ed. *Media Controversies.* New York: Facts on File, Inc., 1981.

Sorensen, Theodore C. *Decision-Making in the White House*: New York: Columbia University Press, 1963.

-------- *Kennedy.* New York: Harper & Row, 1965.

Stein, Herbert. *Presidential Economics*. Washington, D.C.: American Enterprise Institute Press, 1994.

Stein, M.L. *When Presidents Meet the Press*. New York: Julian Messner, 1969.

Swanson, David L. and Paolo Mancini, eds. *Politics, Media and Modern Democracy*. Westport, CT: Praeger, 1996.

Taft, William Howard. *Our Chief Magistrate and His Powers*. New York: Columbia University Press, 1925.

Thomas, Norman, Joseph Pika and Richard A. Watson. *The Politics of the Presidency*. 3rd ed. Washington, D.C.: Congressional Quarterly Press, 1994.

Tolchin, Susan and Martin Tolchin. *Glass Houses: Congressional Ethics and the Politics of Venom*. Boulder, CO: Westview Press, 2001.

Truman, David. *The Governmental Process*. New York: Knopf, 1951.

Truman, Harry S. *Year of Decisions*. New York: Doubleday and Company, 1955.

-------- *Years of Trial and Hope*. New York: Doubleday and Company, 1956.

Warren, Earl. *A Republic If You Can Keep It*. New York: Quadrangle Books, 1972.

Wattenberg, Martin P. *The Decline of American Political Parties, 1952-1994*. Cambridge, MA: Harvard University Press, 1996.

West, Darrell, ed. *Air Wars*, 5th ed. Washington, D.C.: CQ Press, 2010.

Westerfield, Donald L. *War Powers: The President, Congress, and the Question of War*. Westport, CT: Praaeger Publishers, 1996.

Whitney, David. *The American Presidents*. Garden City, NY: Doubleday, 1985.

White, Theodore. *The Making of the President,1960*. New York: Atheneum, 1961.

-------- *The Making of the President,1964*. New York: Atheneum, 1965.

-------- *The Making of the President,1968*. New York: Atheneum, 1969.

-------- *The Making of the President,1972*. New York: Atheneum, 1973.

-------- *Breach of Faith*. New York: Atheneum, 1975.

-------- *America in Search of Itself: The Making of the President,1956-1980*. New York: Harper & Row, 1982.

Witt, Elder. *A Different Justice: Reagan and the Supreme Court.* Washington, D.C.: Congressional Quarterly Press, 1986.

Woodward, Bob. *The Agenda: Inside the Clinton White House.* New York: Simon & Schuster, 1994.

-------- *Bush at War.* New York: Simon & Schuster, 2002.

Zimmerman, Joseph F. Contemporary American Federalism: The Growth of National Power. New York: Prager, 1992.

ENDNOTES

Chapter I

[1] David Whitney, *The American Presidents* (Garden City, NY: Doubleday, 1985), pp. 202-3.

[2] For a discussion of the role of Locke and Rousseau in the development of social contract theory, see William and Alan Ebenstein, *Great Political Thinkers* (Chicago: Holt, Rinehart and Winston, Inc., 5th ed., 1991), pp.498-99.

[3] *Ibid.*

[4] Bertrand Russell, *Philosophy and Politics* (London: Cambridge University Press, 1947).

[5] Quoted in Ebenstein and Ebenstein , *op. cit.,* pp. 654-55.

[6] Hegel's statement that, "all the worth which the human being possesses-all spiritual reality-he possesses only through the State," is contained in his *Philosophy of History.* See Ebenstein and Ebenstein, *op. cit.,* pp. 687-691.

[7] Max J. Skidmore, *American Political Thought* (New York: St. Martin's Press, 1978), pp. 12-15.

[8] Charles Adrian, *State and Local Governments* (New York: McGraw-Hill, 1960), p. 154-56.

[9] On the importance of the "environment" for governmental systems, see Daniel Wit, *Comparative Political Institutions* (New York: Henry Holt and Company, Inc. 1953), pp.17-50.

[10] One good Hitler biography is Robert Payne, *The Life and Death of Adolf Hitler* (New York: Praeger Publishers, 1973).

[11] Americans assume that the winner of an election, if the "out" party, takes over control of the government. Unfortunately, nullification of election results has been common in many other counties where the "bullet" rather than the ballot rules.

[12] Harold Lasswell, Politics: *Who Gets What, When and How* (New York: Free Press, 1936), p. 3.

[13] For more than 1000 of his "quotable quotes," see Winston Churchill, *The Wit and Wisdom of Winston Churchill* (New York: Harper Collins, 1994).

[14] H.H. Gerth and C. Wright Mills, *From Max Weber* (New York: Oxford University Press, 1958), pp. 136-144.

[15]John Kenneth Galbraith, *The Anatomy of Power* (Boston: Houghton Mifflin Company, 1983), pp. 4-5.

[16]*Ibid.*

[17]*Ibid.*

[18]Thomas R. Dye, *Power and Society* (Belmont, CA.: Wadsworth Publishing Company, 1993), p. 2.

[19]C. Wright Mills, *The Power Elite* (New York: Oxford University Press, 1956), p. 9.

[20]Quoted in Thomas D.H. Mahoney, ed., *Reflections on the Revolution in France* (Indianapolis: Bobbs-Merrill, 1955), pp. 87-8.

[21]Wit, *op. cit.,* pp. 112-122.

Chapter II

[1] Quoted in C. Herman Pritchett, *The American Constitutional System* (New York: McGraw-Hill Book Company, 1976), p. 2.

[2]For an account of Roosevelt's problems with the Hughes Court, see "Storm Over the Constitution," in Arthur M. Schlesinger, *The Politics of Upheaval* (Boston: Houghton Mifflin Company, 1960), pp. 484-496.

[3]The election of President Clinton in 1992 halted this trend, at least temporarily, although it is by no means clear that the Chief Executive gets what he expects from U.S. Supreme Court appointees.

[4]Rexford Tugwell, A *Model Constitution for a United Republic of America,* Santa Barbara, CA: Center for the Study of Democratic Institutions, 1970.

[5]Hutchins became president of the University of Chicago before he reached the age of 30. He is perhaps most widely known for his belief that undergraduate education should be based on reading the "Great Books," and that intercollegiate football contributes nothing to education. Under his administration, Chicago dropped out of the Big 10 and was replaced by Michigan State.

[6]For Senator Ervin's views on the Constitution, see Sam Ervin, *Preserving the Constitution* (Charlottesville, VA: Michie Company, 1984).

[7]Earl Warren, *A Republic If You Can Keep It* (New York: Quadrangle Books, 1972), p. 11.

[8]See *Goals For Americans,* President's Commission on National Goals (Englewood Cliffs, NJ: Prentice-Hall, 1960).

[9]Ebenstein and Ebenstein, op. cit., pp. 246-58.

[10]See "The Imperial Crisis" in James W. Davidson, William E. Gienapp, Christine Leigh Heyrman, Mark H. Lytle and Michael B. Stoff, *Nation of Nations* (New York: McGraw-Hill, Inc., 1996), pp. 121-133. Hereafter referred to as Davidson *et. al.*

[11]*Ibid.*

[12]See John Locke, *The Second Treatise of Civil Government* (New York: Irvington Press, 1979). The work was originally published in 1689.

[13]Davidson et al., *supra,* note 10, pp. 169-70.

[14]*Ibid.*

[15]Gordon S. Wood, *The Radicalism of the American Revolution* (New York: Vintage, 1993), pp. 6-7.

[16]Wilfred Binkley, *American Political Parties* (New York: Alfred A. Knopf, 1963), pp. 12-13.

[17]Alpheus T. Mason and Richard H. Leach, *In Quest of Freedom* (Englewood Cliffs, NJ: Prentice-Hall, Inc., 1959), p. 101.

[18]*Ibid.,* pp. 106-128.

[19]*Ibid.*

[20]*Ibid.,* pp. 101-103.

[21]Edwin and Michael Emery, *The Press in America,* 5th ed. (Englewood Cliffs, NJ, 1984) pp. 91-95.

[22]Quoted in Cecilia M. Keynon, *The Antifederalists* (Indianapolis, IN, Bobbs-Merrill, 1966), p. 1.

[23]Charles A. Beard, *An Economic Interpretation of the Constitution of the United States* (New York: Free Press, 1913*).*

[24]Richard B. Morris, *Alexander Hamilton and the Founding of the Nation* (New York: The Dial Press, 1957) pp. 602-608.

[25]Jane J. Mansbridge, *Why We Lost the ERA* (Chicago: University of Chicago Press, 1986).

[26]J.W. Peltason, *Understanding the Constitution,* 13th ed., (Ft. Worth: Harcourt Brace College Publishers, 1994), pp. 409-410.

[27]See Justice Byron White's dissenting opinion in *Roe v. Wade.*.

[28]James Pfiffner, *The Modern Presidency* (New York: St. Martin's Press, 1994), pp. 110-111.

[29]Reo Christenson, *Heresies, Right and Left* (New York: Harper & Row, 1973).

[30]Dye, Ziegler and Lichter, *op. cit.,* p. 95.

[31]Macaulay's quote often was cited to prove the "instinctive theory" of political party affiliation. The concept holds that voters naturally divide on the basis of their Conservative or Liberal dispositions. See Thomas B. Macaulay, Selected Writings (Chicago: University of Chicago Press, 1972).

[32]Walter Lippmann, *The Public Philosophy* (New York: New American Library, 1956).

[33]John Molloy, " The Political Philosophy of Robert A. Taft," a two-part series in *The Cincinnati Enquirer*, July 30 and August 13, 1961.

[34]Herbert Stein, *Presidential Economics: The Making of Economic Policy from Roosevelt to Clinton*, 3rd rev. ed. (Washington, D.C.: American Enterprise Institute, 1994).

[35]See David Maraniss, *First in His Class* (New York: Simon & Schuster, 1995).

Chapter III

[1]Wit, *op. cit.,* pp. 50-101.

[2]W. Phillips Shively, *Power & Choice*, 4th ed., (New York: McGraw-Hill, Inc., 1995), pp. 164-174.

[3]William H. Riker, *Federalism: Origin, Operation, Significance* (Boston: Little, Brown, 1964).

[4]Mason and Leach, *op. cit.,* pp. 490-497.

[5]301 U.S. 1 (1937).

[6]*U.S. v. Darby Lumber Co.* 312 U.S. 100 (1941).

[7]*Wickard v. Filburn* 317 U.S. 111 (1942).

[8]*U.S. v. Lopez* 514 U.S. (1995).

[9]*McCulloch v. Maryland* 4 Wheaton 316 (1819).

[10]James Bryce, *The American Commonwealth*, vol. 1, 2nd ed. (London: Macmillan, 1891).

[11]*Supra,* note 9.

[12]Nat Hentoff, *The First Freedom* (New York: Delacourte Press, 1980), pp. 79-85.

[13]See Mason and Leach, *op. cit..* p. 269.

[14]See chapter on John C. Calhoun in Richard F. Hofstadter, *The American Political Tradition* (New York: Vintage Books, 1948) pp. 68-93.

[15]*Texas v. White* 7 Wallace 700 (1869).

[16]Whitney, *The American Presidents, op. cit.,* pp. 62-76.

[17]Clark Mollenhoff, *George Romney: Mormon Politician* (New York: Meredith Press, 1968). Chapter 18 deals with the Detroit riots, pp. 273-288.

[18]On the 1963 University of Alabama integration crisis, see Arthur M. Schlesinger, *A Thousand Days* (Boston: Houghton Mifflin Company, 1965), pp. 963-977.

[19]*Luther v. Borden* 7 Howard 1 (1849).

[20]*Pacific States Telephone C. v. Oregon* 223 U.S. 118 (1912).

[21]*Sturgis v. Washington* 414 U.S. 1057 (1973).

[22]Gerald R. Ford, *A Time To Heal* (New York: Harper Row), pp. 143-46.

[23]*Branzburg v. Hayes,* 408 U.S. 665 (1972).

[24]Jerald A. Combs, *The History of American Foreign Policy,* 2nd ed., Volume 1, to 1917 (New York: McGraw-Hill Companies, Inc., 1997), pp. 40-54.

[25]Pritchett, *op. cit.,* pp. 23-28.

[26]*South Carolina v. Katzenbach* 383 U.S. 301 (1966).

[27]*Garcia v. San Antonio Metropolitan Transit Authority* 469 U.S. 528 (1985).

[28]First Inaugural Address, *New York Times,* January 21, 1981.

[29]James Bryce, *Modern Democracies* (New York: Macmillan, 1921), p. 132.

[30]In essence, Congress forced the states to raise the minimum drinking age to 21 by providing that highway funds would not be given to states which failed to do so. The theory was that teenage drivers were particularly likely to have accidents when drinking.

[31]Ontario Economic Council, *Federalism and the Canadian Economic Union* (Toronto, University of Toronto Press, 1983).

[32]Bureau of the Census, *Census of Governments 1997* (Washington, D.C. : Government Printing Office, 1998).

[33]Jurg Steiner, *European Democracies,* 3rd ed. (White Plains, N.Y.: Longman Publishers, pp. 123-129).

[34]The basis for Canadian federalism was established by the British Parliament when it passed the British North American Act in 1867, giving Canada virtually total control over its own domestic affairs.

[35]See Thomas R. Dye, *American Federalism: Competition Among Governments.* (Lexington, MA: Lexington Books, 1990).

[36]Adrian, *op. cit.,* p. 133.

[37]John Kenneth Galbraith, *American Capitalism: The Concept of Countervailing Power* (Boston: Houghton Mifflin Company, 1956).

Chapter IV

[1]Merriman Smith, *A President is Many Men* (New York: Harper & Brothers, 1948).

[2]See Robert F. Kennedy, *Thirteen Days*: A memoir of the Cuban missile crisis (New York: W.W. Norton & Company, 1969) for an inside, but obviously biased, account of the crisis.

[3]See Dwight D. Eisenhower, *Waging Peace* (Garden City, NY: Doubleday and Company, Inc., 1965), pp. 311-16.

[4]See David Brinkley, *A Memoir* (New York: Alfred A. Knopf, 1995), pp. 141-2.

[5]Newt Gingrich and Dick Armey, *Contract With America* (New York: Times Books, 1994).

[6]The case is *Raines v. Byrd* (No. 96-1671, 1997).

[7]Kennedy served only a few years in the Senate. If the U.S. had a parliamentary system like the British, his inexperience would have disqualified him from leading the nation. Lyndon Johnson, elected as majority leader by Senate Democrats, would have been chosen as the candidate because of his legislative experience.

[8]Richard E. Cohen, *Changing Course in Washington* (New York: Macmillan College Publishing Company, 1994).

[9]Harry S. Truman, *Years of Trial and Hope* (New York: Doubleday and Co., 1956), pp.164-69.

[10] Arthur Link, *Woodrow Wilson and a Revolutionary World* (Chapel Hill, NC: University of North Carolina Press, 1982).

[11] President Roosevelt's recognition of the Soviet regime was contingent on a number of conditions. See George F. Kennan, *Russia and the West Under Lenin and Stalin* (Boston: Little, Brown and Company), pp. 298-300.

[12] For the text of President Carter's statement on recognition of the People's Republic of China, see the *New York Times,* December 16, 1978, p. 8.

[13] John Spanier and Steven W. Hook, *American Foreign Policy Since World War II* (Washington, D.C.: Congressional Quarterly Press, 1998).

[14] *Ibid.,* pp. 31-2.

[15] Truman, *supra* note 10.

[16] Paul Lavrakas, *Presidential Polls and the News Media* (Boulder: Westview Press, 1995).

[17] John Spanier, *The Truman-MacArthur Controversy and the Korean War* (Cambridge, MA: Belknap Press, 1959).

[18] Robert A. Taft speech, "The Korean War and the MacArthur Dismissal," *New York Times*, April 13, 1951, p. 4.

[19] John Stoessinger, *Why Nations Go To War*, 6th ed. (New York: St. Martin's Press, 1993), pp. 80-108.

[20] *Ibid.*

[21] Lyndon Johnson, *The Vantage Point* (Holt, Rinehart and Winston, 1971), p. 435.

[22] Spanier, *op. cit.*, p. 155-59.

[23] Stoessinger, *op. cit.*, pp. 157-181.

[24] Thomas E. Cronin, *The State of the Presidency* (Boston: Little, Brown and Company, 1980), pp. 158-161.

[25] George Reedy, *The Twilight of the Presidency* (New York: World Publishing Company, 1970) pp. 14-15.

[26] For a good discussion of the split between old line and "new" Democrats, see Theodore White, *The Making of the President, 1972*, pp. 167-202.

[27] Marannis, *op. cit.,* pp. 387-94.

[28]White, *The Making of the President, 1968* (New York: Atheneum Publishers, 1969).

[29]Theodore Roosevelt, *An Autobiography* (New York: The Macmillan Company, 1916), p. 372.

[30]William Howard Taft, *Our Chief Magistrate and his Powers* (New York: Columbia University Press, 1925), pp. 139-40.

[31]Roosevelt's executive agreement with Churchill, giving Great Britain 50 U.S. destroyers in return for leases on British bases in the Caribbean was, according to critics, a violation of the Neutrality Act. See James M. Burns, *Roosevelt: The Lion and the Fox* (New York: Harcourt, Brace and Company), pp. 437-51.

[32]Harry S. Truman, *Public Papers of the Presidents of the United States* (U.S. Government Printing Office, 1949), p. 247.

[33]Arthur Larsen, Eisenhower, *The President Nobody Knew* (New York: Scribner's, 1968), p. 12.

[34]Arthur M. Schlesinger Jr., *The Imperial Presidency* (Boston: Houghton-Mifflin, 1973), p. 411.

[35]Quoted in David Brinkley, *op. cit.*, p.177.

[36]See Bob Woodward and Carl Bernstein, *All the President's Men* (New York: Simon & Schuster, 1974).

[37]Frederick Mosher, *Watergate: Implications for Responsible Government* (New York: Basic Books, 1974).

[38]Eric Goldman, *The Tragedy of Lyndon Johnson (*New York: Alfred A. Knopf, 1969*)* argues that the root of Johnson's problems was his inadequate education at Southwest Texas State Teacher's College. Goldman is a history professor at Princeton.

[39]*The Federalist Papers*, No. 70.

[40]For the role of Edith Galt Wilson during the disability crisis, see Tom Schactman, *Edith and Woodrow, a Presidential Romance* (New York: Putnam, 1981).

[41]For an assessment of Rockefeller's role in the Ford Administration, see Michael Turner, *The Vice President as Policy Maker: Rockefeller in the Ford White House* (Westport, CT: Greenwood Press, 1982).

[42]James D. Barber, *The Presidential Character*, 4th ed. (Englewood Cliffs, NJ: Prentice-Hall, 1992).

[43]Sigmund Freud and William C. Bullitt, *Thomas Woodrow Wilson: A Psychological Study* (Boston: Houghton Mifflin Company, 1966). By mutual agreement, the book was not published until the deaths of all parties involved.

[44]Nathan Miller, *Star Spangled Men: America's 10 Worst Presidents* (New York: Scribner, 1998).

[45]Arthur M. Schlesinger, "Is the Vice Presidency Necessary?" *Atlantic,* p. 37.

Chapter V

[1]J.W. Peltason, *Understanding the Constitution, op. cit.,* pp. 399-400.

[2]John F. Kennedy, *Profiles in Courage* (New York: Harper & Brothers, Inaugural edition, 1961). See chapter 6 on Senator Edmund G. Ross, who cast the decisive vote in the Johnson impeachment trial, knowing it meant political suicide ("I looked down into my open grave...").

[3]Theodore White, *Breach of Faith* (New York: Atheneum Publishers, 1975), pp. 264-68.

[4]*Nixon v. U.S.* 418 U.S. 683 (1974).

[5]White, *supra*, note 3, see appendix.

[6]*Powell v. McCormack* 395 U.S. 486 (1969).

[7]Richard E. Cohen, *Changing Course in Washington, op. cit.*, p. 68.

[8]Quoted in Charles Clapp, *The Congressman* (Garden City, NY: Doubleday, 1964), pp. 51-3.

[9]Burke was defeated in a re-election bid by the voters of his parliamentary district in Bristol, England.

[10]Ronald Kessler, *Inside Congress* (New York: Simon & Schuster Inc., 1997), p. 148.

[11]*Watkins v. U.S.* 354 U.S. 178 (1954).

[12]*McCuloch v. Maryland* 4 Wheaton 316 (1819).

[13]The item veto case of 1998, *Clinton v. City of New York,* was before the Supreme Court late in its 1998 term. The city sued to restore a provision that would have let it increase taxes on hospitals and use the money to attract Federal Medicaid payments.

[14]Louis Fisher, *The Politics of Shared Power: Congress and the Executive*, 2nd ed. (Washington: Congressional Quarterly Press, 1987), p. 30.

[15]White, *America in Search of Itself* (New York: Atheneum, 1981), pp. 125-29.

[16]Herbert Stein, *Presidential Economics, op. cit.*

[17]In May, 1997, President Clinton and Republican congressional leaders agreed on a plan to balance the budget by the year 2002.

[18]See the "one person, one vote" congressional reapportionment case, *Wesberry v. Sanders* 376 U.S. 1 (1964).

[19]Arthur M. Schlesinger, *One Thousand Days, op. cit.*, p. 723.

[20]John Rhodes, *The Futile System* (New York: Doubleday & Co., 1976).

[21]Kessler, *op. cit.*, p. 111.

[22]*Ibid.* p. 128. Only Senators Glenn and McCain were re-elected. Other senators did not survive the political fallout from the Keating Five episode. Keating went to prison.

[23]Zbigniew Brezinski, *Between Two Ages: America's Role in the Technetronic Era* (New York: Viking Press, 1970).

Chapter VI

[1] Allan G. Johnson, *Human Arrangements*, 3rd ed. (New York: Harcourt Brace Jovanovich College Publishers), pp. 34-5.

[2]*Ibid*, p.36.

[3]Jack Plano and Milton Greenberg, *The American Political Dictionary*, 10th ed. (New York: Harcourt Brace College Publishers, 1997), p. 259.

[4]Johnson, *supra*, note 1, pp. 35-37.

[5]Definitions of these concepts can be found in *Black's Law Dictionary* (St. Paul, MN: West Publishing Co., 1990), or any other legal dictionary.

[6]For an excellent account of the operation of the judicial system, see Henry J. Abraham, *The Judicial Process*, 6th ed. (New York: Oxford University Press, 1993).

[7]On the evolution of the double jeopardy clause, see J.W. Peltason, *Understanding The Constitution*, 13th ed. , *op. cit.*, 270-75.

[8]Henry Abraham: *The Judiciary: The Supreme Court in the Governmental Process*, 5th ed., (Madison, WI: Brown & Benchmark, 1994), p. 12.

[9]Davidson et al., *op. cit.*, pp. 731-2.

[10]"New Jersey Wins Ellis Island Suit," The *Washington Post*, May 26, 1998, p. 1.

[11]Bob Woodward and Scott Armstrong, *The Brethren: Inside the Supreme Court* (New York: Avon, 1996).

[12]Charles Evans Hughes. *The Supreme Court of the United States*, (New York: Columbia University Press, 1928), p. 68.

[13]John Marshall Harlan, quoted in H.L. A. Hart, *The Concept of Law* (Oxford University Press, 1961), pp. 121-22.

[14]Pritchett, *op. cit*, p. 71.

[15]J.W. Peltason, *Understanding the Constitution, supra,* note 7, pp. 28-31.

[16]1 Cranch 137 (1803).

[17]*Dred Scott v. Sanford 19 Howard 393 (1857).*

[18]343 U.S. 579 (1952).

[19]Alexis de Tocqueville, *Democracy in America* (New York: Modern Library, 1981).

[20]Near the end of his life, Marshall worried about the future of the Court in the era of Jackson and the "enormous pretensions of the Executive." See Bernard Schwartz, *A History of the Supreme Court* (New York: Oxford University Press, 1993), p 71.

[21]Lerner's criticism is that of a Liberal, angry with a Conservative Court. The same argument could have been made by a Conservative against the Warren Court a generation later.

[22]For a brief, yet detailed, account of FDR's battle with the Supreme Court, see Arthur M. Schlesinger, *The Politics of Upheaval*, pp. 468-96.

[23]347 U.S. 483 (1954).

[24]157 U.S. 429 (1895).

[25]See Richard Nixon, *RN: Memoirs of Richard Nixon* (New York: Simon & Schuster, 1990), pp.418-24.

[26]The term "borked" now is used as a verb. To Conservatives it has come to mean unfair, rough treatment by the Senate Judiciary Committee. For Bork's own account of this experience, see Robert H. Bork, *The Tempting of America: The Political Seduction of the Law* (New York: Simon & Schuster, 1990), pp. 295-355.

[27]Jane S. Elsmere, *Justice Samuel Chase* (Muncie, IN: Janevar Publishing Co., 1980).

[28]Hastings now represents the 23rd district of Florida in the 111th Congress.

[29]Class action lawsuits are those in which one or several persons may sue as members of a larger group "similarly situated." This enables persons with inadequate financial resources to make a suit financially viable. A court decision in a class action lawsuit may be more sweeping in its application than ordinarily is the case.

[30]Charles A. Leonard, *A Search for a Political Philosophy* (Port Washington, NY: Kennikat Press, 1971).

[31]Lou Cannon, *President Reagan: The Role of a Lifetime.* (New York: Simon & Schuster), pp. 804-9.

[32]*Ibid.*

[33]Davidson et al., *op. cit.,* pp. 936-37.

[34]The Senate confirmed Breyer by a vote of 87-9 and Ginsburg by a vote of 97-3.

[35]Elder Witt, *A Different Justice* (Washington: Congressional Quarterly Press), p. 26.

Chapter VII

[1] Emery and Emery, *op. cit.,* p. 125.

[2]Schlesinger, *The Politics of Upheaval, op. cit.*, pp. 626-57.

[3]Theodore White, *The Making of the President, 1964 (*New York: Atheneum, 1965), p. 331-64. Goldwater carried only his home state, Arizona, and five southern states: Alabama, Georgia, Louisiana, Mississippi and South Carolina.

[4]Samuel Gompers, *Seventy Years of Life and Labor: An Autobiography* (Ithaca, NY: Cornell University Press, 1984).

[5]See William J. Crotty, *American Parties in Decline*, 2nd ed. (Boston: Little, Brown, 1984), pp. 142-3.

[6]A good account of "spin doctors" is found in Marlin Fitzwater, *Call the Briefing: Reagan and Bush, Sam and Helen: A Decade with Presidents and the Press* (New York: Random House, 1995), Chapter 9, "Spin and Other Yarns," pp. 199-228. Fitzwater served as news secretary to both Reagan and Bush.

[7]424 U.S. 1 (1976).

[8]Quoted in Peter Woll, *Debating American Government*, 2nd ed. (Glenview, IL, Scott-Foresman, 1988), p. 125.

[9]*Vacco v. Quill* and *Washington v. Glucksberg*, No. 96-110 (1997).

[10]This is the view of his unofficial biographer, David Maraniss of the *Washington Post.*

[11]David Broder, *The Party's Over* (New York: Harper & Row, 1972).

[12]Mike Royko, *Boss: Richard J. Daley of Chicago* (New York: Dutton, 1971).

[13]The present period of American party history is called "the era of divided party government." It contrasts sharply with periods in which one of the two major parties was dominant.

[14]Joe McGinnis, *The Selling of the President, 1968* (New York: Trident Press, 1969).

[15]White, *The Making of the President 1960, op. cit.*, p. 264.

[16]As President, Truman was able to dictate the nomination of Adlai Stevenson in 1952. He failed to influence the convention in 1956 and 1960 when his choices were New York Gov. Averell Harriman and Sen. Stuart Symington of Missouri.

[17]Theodore White, *America in Search of Itself, op. cit.*, p. 401.

[18]*Ibid.*, p. 193.

[19]*Ibid.*, pp. 402-5.

[20]Richard Hofstadter, *The Age of Reform* (New York: Knopf, 1956), p. 97.

[21]E.E. Schattschneider, *Party Government* (New York: Farrar and Rinehart, 1942).

[22]Despite his paralysis and removal from the scene in 1972, Governor Wallace finished third on the final roll call vote at the Democratic National Convention. He trailed Senators George McGovern, the nominee, and Henry "Scoop" Jackson of Washington.

[23]White, *supra*, note 17, pp. 73-7.

Chapter VIII

[1] See Niccolo Machiavelli, *The Discourses of Niccolo Machiavelli* (Boston: Routledge and Paul, 1975).

[2] Jean Jacques Rousseau, *The Social Contract*, translated by G.D.H. Cole (New York: E.P. Dutton & Co., 1913), p. 89.

[3] Emery and Emery, *op. cit.*, pp. 356-58.

[4]Walter Lippmann, *Public Opinion, op. cit.*

[5] David Truman, *The Governmental Process* (New York: Alfred A. Knopf, Inc., 1951), p. 220.

[6] Bernard Hennessy, *Public Opinion* (Belmont, CA, Wadsworth Publishing Co., 1965), p. 97-8.

[7] Lindsay Rogers, *The Pollsters* (New York: Alfred A. Knopf, Inc., 1949), p. 47.

[8] For a good account of the 1992 presidential contest, see Germond, Jack and Jules Witcover, *Mad as Hell: Revolt at the Ballot Box, 1992* (New York: Warner Books, 1993).

[9] See Chapter 9, "Feeling the Draft," in Maraniss, *op. cit.*, pp. 149-166.

[10] The U.S. Supreme Court upheld movie censorship in *Mutual Film Corporation v. Ohio Industrial Commission* 236 U.S. 230 (1931). Seven states censored movies until the Court reversed its position and brought movies under the protection of the First Amendment in *Burstyn v. Wilson* 343 U.S. 495 (1952).

[11] Lippmann, *op. cit.*, pp. 18-19.

[12] Hennesy, *op. cit.*, pp. 39-42.

[13] For a classic study of Chicago politics, Royko, *Boss: Richard J. Daley of Chicago, op. cit.*

[14] If Gore was unhappy, consider the case of William Rehnquist. Some 94% of the public could not identify him as Chief Justice of the United States. See Benjamin Page and Robert Shapiro, *The Rational Public* (Chicago: University of Chicago Press, 1992).

[15] Frank Luther Mott, *American Journalism* (New York: The Macmillan Co., 1941).

[16] Quoted in Emery and Emery, *op. cit.*, p. 133.

[17] Richard Davis, *The Press and American Politics*, 2nd ed. (Upper Saddle River, NJ: 1996), pp. 28-9.

[18] Emery and Emery, *op. cit.*, pp. 140-41.

[19] *Ibid.*

[20] *Ibid.*, pp. 292-95.

[21] *Ibid.*, pp. 322.

[22] Emery and Emery, *op. cit.*, p. 356.

[23] The Federal Communications Commission has no authority to "censor" program content, although it can and has "outlawed" certain kinds of language. This has been

upheld by the U.S. Supreme Court in *FCC v. Pacifica Foundation* 438 U.S. 726 (1978). The case is commonly called the "Seven Dirty Words" case.

[24]Historically, the A.C. Neilsen ratings were the "Bible" of television. Recently, AGC Television Research has entered the field, as have other competitors.

[25]See Walter Cronkite, *A Reporter's Life* (New York: Alfred A. Knopf, 1996).

[26]Michael Parenti, *Inventing Reality: The Politics of the News Media*, 2nd ed., (New York: St. Martin's Press, 1993).

[27]Dye, Ziegler and Lichter, *op. cit.,* p. 96.

[28]"Journalism Heavy With Democrats," *The Chicago Tribune,* Nov. 18, 1992, section 1, p. 14.

[29]"Milking Cows Pays More Than Reporting," *Editor & Publisher*, April 25, 1998.

[30]Michael Moore, "How To Keep 'Em Happy in Flint," *Columbia Journalism Review,* Sep./Oct., 1985 pp. 40-43.

[31]Doris Graber, *Mass Media and American Politics, 5th ed.* (Washington, D.C.: Congressional Quarterly Press, 1997) p. 10.

[32]Richard Davis, *op. cit.,* p.21.

[33]Quoted in Reo Christenson and Robert McWilliams, editors, *Voices of the People* (New York: McGraw-Hill, 1962), p. 110.

[34]Quoted in Theodore Peterson, Jay Jensen and William L. Rivers, *The Mass Media and Modern Society* (New York: Rinehart & Winston, 1966), p. 88.

[35]Douglas Cater, *The Fourth Branch of Government* (Boston: Houghton Mifflin, 1959).

[36]David Brinkley, *Washington Goes to War* (New York: Alfred A. Knopf, 1988), p. 171.

[37]Cater, *op. cit.,* pp. 22-3.

[38]Cosby Noyes, "Will The Press Be Out To Get Nixon?" *U.S. News & World Report,* Dec. 2, 1968.

[39]Theodore C. Sorenson, *Decision-Making in the White House* (New York: Columbia University Press, 1963), pp. 54-6.

[40]Pierre Salinger, *With Kennedy* (Garden City, NY: Doubleday & Co., 1966), pp. 109-11.

[41]*New York Times-Washington Post v. U.S.* 403 U.S. 713 (1971).

[42]Jody Powell, *The Other Side of the Story* (New York: William Morrow, 1984).

[43]Cannon, *President Reagan: The Role of a Lifetime, op. cit.*

[44]James Fallows, *Breaking the News: How the Media Undermine American Democracy* (New York: Random House, 1996).

[45]Ari Fleischer, *Taking Heat: The President, the Press and My Years in the White House* (New York: Harper Collins, 2005).

[46]Robert O. Blanchard, ed., *Congress and the News Media* (New York: Hastings House, 1974), p. 105.

[47]For an interesting, if "gossipy," account of the inside workings of the U.S. Supreme Court, see Bob Woodward and Scott Armstrong, *The Brethren: Inside the Supreme Court, op. cit.*

Tavenner Publishing Company
406 Sutton Place
Anderson, South Carolina 29621
E-mail: tavpubco@charter.net

ISBN: 978-1-930208-97-1